mL £23·00

# AUTOMOTIVE MANUFACTURING
# UPDATE '81

This book is to be returned on or ┆ ┆

# SPOT ON ROBOT WELDER
## AUTOMATIC CHOICE FOR THE AUTOMOTIVE INDUSTRY.

The evolution of robot technology does not happen overnight. Five years of research went into the development of the FATA – Bisiach & Carru J80 robot spot welder – now available in the U.K. via FATA Limited, of Milton Keynes.

Advanced electromechanical technology has been applied to the new unit, specifically designed for automated welding operations. The FATA – Bisiach & Carru J80 is sturdy, mobile and versatile giving advances in speed of operation, accuracy and reductions in production costs. It is the natural choice when welding tracks need to be made in complex geometric configurations, as, for instance, in car body assembly.

Design of the robot centres around the column which has a traverse instead of rotary motion. This carries a swivelling boom with a slide carrying the tri-axial gun holder head. Control is from a specially developed system of modular design.

The J80 represents the most advanced techniques in automated welding technology... write or telephone for full details.

**FATA Limited**
Dawson Road, Bletchley, Milton Keynes MK1 1JY.
Telephone: (0908) 79611
FATA EUROPEAN GROUP S.p.A.

# CONTENTS

# AUTOMOTIVE MANUFACTURING UPDATE '81

## I Mech E CONFERENCE PUBLICATIONS 1981-13

Conference sponsored by
The Automobile Division and the
Engineering Manufacturing Industries Division of
The Institution of Mechanical Engineers
Under the patronage of Fédération Internationale des Sociétés d'Ingénieurs
des Techniques de l'Automobile (FISITA)

1-2 December 1981
Institution Headquarters
1 Birdcage Walk, Westminster, London

Published by
Mechanical Engineering Publications Limited for
The Institution of Mechanical Engineers
LONDON

First published 1981

This publication is copyright under the Berne Convention and the International Copyright Convention. Apart from any fair dealing for the purpose of private study, research, criticism or review, as permitted under the Copyright Act 1956, no part may be reproduced, stored in a retrieval system, or transmitted in any form or by any means, electronic, electrical, chemical, mechanical, photocopying, recording or otherwise, without the prior permission of the copyright owners. Inquiries should be addressed to: The Managing Editor, Mechanical Engineering Publications Limited, PO Box 24, Northgate Avenue, Bury St Edmunds, Suffolk IP32 6BW

This volume is complete in itself

There is no supplementary discussion volume

ISBN 0 85298 479 0

Printed by Waveney Print Services Ltd, Beccles, Suffolk

# VEHICLE BODY LAYOUT AND ANALYSIS

## John Fenton

Structural design and layout of vehicle bodies has recently become more significant because of weight reduction requirements for fuel saving and new safety-on-impact legislation. VEHICLE BODY LAYOUT AND ANALYSIS is a much needed review of the subject.

The work considers the preliminary concept stage of design in relation to the load envelope applying to vehicle structure, then progresses to the layout of the elements dictated by factors which fix the basic shape. Following this is an examination of thin-walled beam and plate theory, an introduction to idealization technique and a consideration of collapse behaviour under impact and fatigue loading. Two specialist chapters deal with designing for production and goods vehicle design.

The text is a mathematical introduction to the analysis of a design prior to its computer evaluation.

The book is essential reading for automotive body designers, specialist vehicle builders and engineering students at degree/HND level.

*Vehicle Body Layout and Analysis.*
ISBN 085298 445 6/234 x 156/hardcover 160 pages
UK £19.50    Overseas £27.50 (including air-speeded delivery)

I wish to order _____ copy/copies
Vehicle Body Layout and Analysis.
Remittance enclosed ☐
Please invoice me (orders over £20.00 only) ☐

Signature — — — — — — — — — — —

Name — — — — — — — — — — —

Address — — — — — — — — — — —
— — — — — — — — — — — —

ⓜⒺⓅ

ORDERS AND ENQUIRES TO SALES DEPARTMENT

## MECHANICAL ENGINEERING PUBLICATIONS LTD

PO BOX 24,   NORTHGATE AVENUE,   BURY ST. EDMUNDS   IP32 6BW

---

# robotic and monitoring systems

## ᔕᔕiᗩKY

# for flexible and automated assembly lines for the automotive industry world-wide

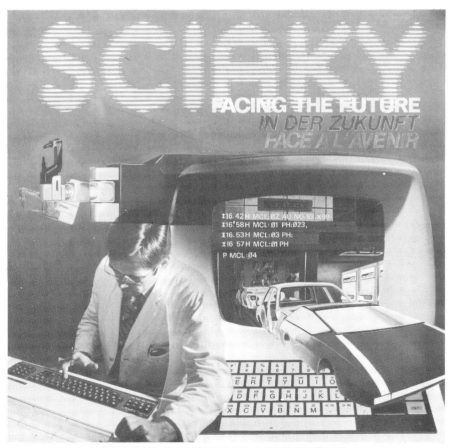

SCIAKY ELECTRIC WELDING MACHINES LTD.
212, Bedford Avenue (Trading Estate) SLOUGH BERKS SL1 4RH ENGLAND
Tel : SLOUGH 25551 - Telex : 84 72 54

# Seats, fascias, crash pads, trim panels, under-bonnet components, bumpers, soft front ends, lighting surrounds, spoilers...

## ...the list of automotive applications for polyurethanes is long and growing

Light weight, corrosion resistance, easy processing and real savings in the total energy audit are just some of the reasons why automotive manufacturers across the world are taking full advantage of this versatile family of materials. And newer developments such as cold cure flexible seating foams and tough Reinforced RIM moulding mean even greater potential for the future.

**Be sure you are up-to-date with the latest technology.**

For further information on polyurethanes, please send this coupon to:

ICI Polyurethanes
P.O. Box 2
Central Way
Feltham
Middlesex TW14 OTG

 **Polyurethanes**
*tomorrow's plastics for today*

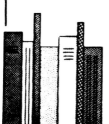

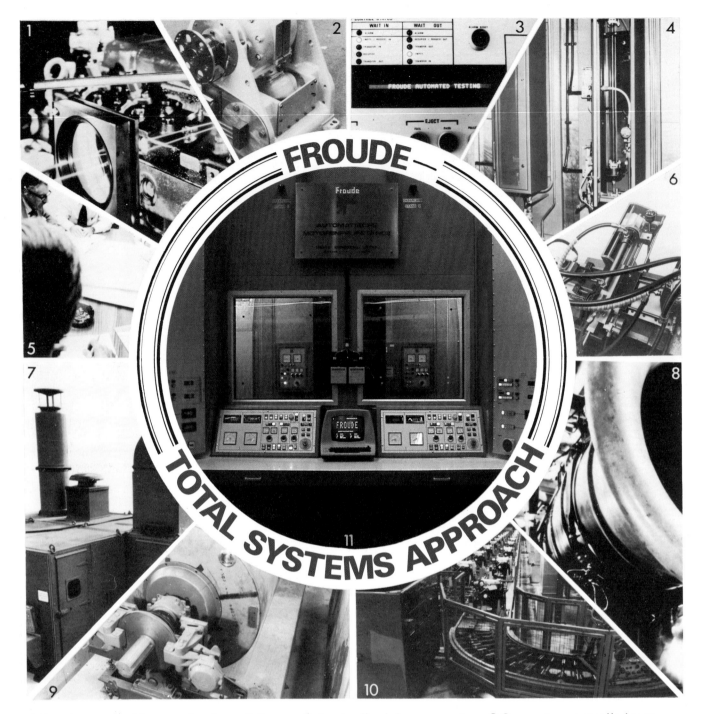

FROUDE — TOTAL SYSTEMS APPROACH

1 Development of laser technology. 2 Range of standardised dynamometers. 3 Computer controlled test plant. 4 Fuel measurement. 5 Design and product consultancy. 6 Automatic gearshift actuator.
7 Transportable test plant. 8 Aero engine test beds. 9 Vehicle test plant. 10 Engine handling systems.
11 Total engine testing systems.

Throughout the world, Froude are recognised as innovators in the field of Test Plant for Aero, Automotive, Industrial and Marine engines. With over one hundred years experience, and installations operative in more than 50

countries the evidence is undeniable. Whatever your test requirements talk to Froude NOW—and get the benefit of the Froude Total Systems Approach to the application of high technology products.

Redman Heenan Company

**Froude Engineering Limited**

1979  1981

Gregory's Bank, Worcester WR3 8AD, England. Tel: Worcester (0905) 27166 Telex: 339637 froude g

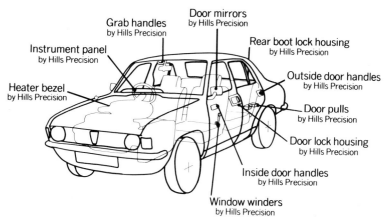
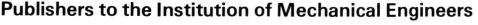

# THE INSTITUTION OF MECHANICAL ENGINEERS

## ON-LINE SEARCH SERVICE

A vast amount of information is published each year in the field of science and technology, so much that it would be impossible for any individual to keep abreast of current published literature on one or more subject.

The Library of the Institution now has access to data bases which index technical articles, journal papers, patents, conference papers, books and theses through a computer terminal housed in the Main Library.

On-line searching is the fastest and most sophisticated way of obtaining references to literature published in the technical press. The systems mainly used in the Library are 'Dialog' which is produced by Lockheed Information Systems, 'Orbit' which is produced by Systems Development Corporation and 'Dialtech' which is produced by Technology Reports Centre in Orpington. These systems have access to various data bases covering many subjects. A few of these data bases are listed below:—

| | |
|---|---|
| Compendex | Computerized Version of Engineering Index |
| ISMEC | Information Services in Mechanical Engineering |
| INSPEC | IEE Information Service — Physics, Electrical and Electronics and Computer Control |
| NTIS | National Technical Information Service |
| METADEX | American Society for Metals |
| OCEANIC ABSTRACTS | Oceanology and numerous related aspects |
| ENERGYLINE | Energy, Energy Policy etc |
| ENVIROLINE | Environmental science, eg Air Pollution |

The above mentioned are just eight of the many data bases which are available through the Institution Library via the computer terminal. Information regarding the other data bases available can be obtained from the Library along with details of costs to obtain information from each data base.

Most of the data bases used cover 1969 or 1970 to date therefore, any search of an historical nature must still be made manually; this will normally take a little longer than computer searches although the Library takes many abstracting journals covering a wide range of engineering subjects.

Enquirers are asked to give as much detail of their request as possible such as suggested keywords, price limit, time period to be covered, language restriction, etc. A form can be obtained from the Library for this purpose.

Charges for searches depend entirely on the type of search required. A guide to these costs is given below.

| | |
|---|---|
| Computer searches — minimum charge | £15.00 per search |
| Quick manual searches of 30 minutes or less | Free to members & individual members of CEI Societies |
| Manual Searches of over 30 minutes | £7.50 members & individual members of CEI Societies<br>£20.00 non-members |

CONTACT LIBRARY & INFORMATION SERVICE

1 BIRDCAGE WALK, WESTMINSTER, LONDON SW1H 9JJ TELEGRAMS: MECH LONDON SW1 TELEPHONE: 01-222 7899 TELEX 917944

# C275/81

# A comparison of US, West European, UK and Japanese Performance 1977-80

M A JACOBSON, MSc, CEng, FIMechE, FIMI, MSAE, MIProdE, MICTech
The Automobile Association, Basingstoke, Hampshire

SYNOPSIS  Many reasons have been advanced for the apparent lack of competitiveness of several West European Car Manufacturers when comparing them with those of Japan.  The underlying facts are more basic than robots replacing men, Union versus Management conflicts, low productivity, lack of investment in new plant and reluctance to adopt new processes.  Many manufacturers in Western Europe are wasteful in the use of energy at several critical stages of car production, starting with energy use in the manufacture of the primary materials, ferrous and non ferrous, plastics and tyres, proper utilisation of process heat, insulation of buildings, dispersal of facilities, leading to extra transhipment costs and holding of contingency stocks of work in progress.  Up to $\frac{1}{3}$ extra energy is needlessly spent in many plants built or refurbished in the past 2 decades - much of it being lost to atmosphere.  Over half the production cost of a modern European Motor Car is accounted for by materials and around 30% by manufacture.  With Japanese cars requiring 20% to 30% less energy during manufacture than their European counterparts, many of the old established manufacturers of cars and major components have a difficult future ahead, for the cost of energy is likely to rise year by year.  A radical re-assessment of energy utilisation during all phases of production is urgently called for.

In any review of current trends there will be no shortage of papers praising new and revolutionary concepts, more advanced technology, new materials, indicating that the future prosperity of the automotive industry on a worldwide basis, no less than in the UK, depends on introducing more advanced technology.  The author suggests that other factors ought to be considered as well - namely energy use during manufacture, plant utilisation and manning levels.

Unfortunately new plant is costly and has to be paid for either out of profits or the largesse of Government.  In other words the customer or taxpayer always pays for the next purchaser to benefit.

There is little point in modernising plants, introducing new technology, more robots and automation and not reducing manning levels at the same time.  This may be politically unacceptable but shirking the issue will not make the problems go away.  Nor should one forget that UK plants tend to sprawl, are widely dispersed and poorly insulated and tend to operate at uneconomic levels of plant utilisation.

Regrettably, many of the UK and US plants, including steel production, foundries, etc, are, by modern standards, antiquated and inefficient in terms of use of manpower and all forms of energy.  Both are prime production cost factors, which have shot up dramatically in the past decade or so and are likely to go on rising.

There is considerable scope, in UK and North American plants alike for reducing heat losses and energy consumption at many stages of production.  Without efforts in those directions, there is little hope for the automotive industries in the UK and several European countries to thrive without Government assistance or import quotas.

For the Japanese are producing comparable cars and car derivatives at significantly lower manufacturing costs.

There are a number of ways of comparing competitive makes and models.  The author has singled out 3 criteria by which to assess relative UK, West European, US and Japanese car manufacturing efficiencies:

1.  Productivity or man hours (including indirect labour) used to produce a comparable car in different countries.

2.  Labour costs.

3.  Energy utilisation.

He has based his analysis on such information as Official Statistical Data, additional confidential corroboration from leading manufacturers, employers of Labour, MITI of Japan, the Office of the Prime Minister of Japan, and statements by Senior Executives at Shareholders Meetings and to the Press, and many detailed visits to plants all over the world.

## UK vs Japanese Productivity

In 1978 some 673 000 people were directly employed in the UK car manufacture and a further 1 027 000 in indirect support as can be seen from Table Nos. 1 and 2.

Their total output was 1.22 million cars.  The grand total of 1.7 million people in the UK owing their livelihood to the private motor car amounted to about 7% of all the people in employment in 1978.  9% of all UK industrial workers owed their livelihood to domestic manufacture of cars.

There has since been a steady decline in UK output and in numbers of people directly employed in the automotive industry. But a more drastic pruning of staffing at all levels - particularly in the non-productive sectors seems unavoidable.

Staggering figures of productivity of Japanese car workers have been repeatedly quoted in support of this move. But these statistics tend to be very misleading, for they do not use the same basis of comparison.

These figures only provide a very partial answer to the question so often posed "How do the Japanese manage to produce motor vehicles with so little labour employed"? In fact they do employ a very considerable number of people, away from well known major car manufacturing plants, to support these car assembly plants.

The author's analysis of the Japanese automotive industry is based on 2 prime sources:

1. The Japanese Ministry of International Trade and Industry (MITI) 1976, 1977 and 1979 Statistics: Business in Japan, and

2. The Office of the Prime Minister (of Japan): Statistical Survey of Business Establishments' Contribution to Automotive Production. These do not however list the plastics, textile, and paper and board manufacturers', nor the public utilities, electricity, coal, oil and gas which provides the energy requirements.

No one doubts that the Japanese bring a different attitude into their every day effort at factory floor and management level alike. Such a degree of dedication and highly developed work ethics are no longer achievable in Western Europe or North America. But the Japanese are not supermen. They do not physically work any harder nor do they work at a staggering pace.

They are just more usefully employed, better trained allround, and more flexible in their approach to such tasks as doing a fair bit of maintenance on their machines and tooling to keep the work flowing smoothly and maintain a consistently good quality, rather than rely on plant maintenance men coming to their rescue. A skilled operator will have had a much longer and more thorough training than is commonly found in the UK, North America and in most West European plants, and hence can effectively be switched to do a variety of jobs without any loss of overall plant efficiency or causing inter Union squabbles.

A 25% reduction in manning levels at various manufacturing and administrative stages would be perfectly feasible at many UK plants, without affecting overall output. Fiat recently cut its labour and white collar staffing by some 25% and yet achieved about 90% of its previous output, which in 1978 was already some 65% higher on a straightforward productivity basis than its UK counterparts.

See Table No. 3.

About 60% of that labour force would be concerned with cars and car derivatives and KD parts only. This amounts to about 1.067 million people in 1976 and 1.01 million in 1978. On that basis the productivity is:

$$\frac{5.028 \text{ million cars}}{1.067 \text{ million workers}} = 4.71 \text{ cars/worker}$$

employed/annum for 1976, and

$$\frac{5.976 \text{ million cars}}{1.01 \text{ million workers}} = 5.92 \text{ cars/worker}$$

employed/annum for 1978.

These figures are, of course, very different if one were to use merely the conventional method of counting the total number of cars produced in a given year and divided them by the number of people directly employed by the car plants.

Then the productivity/man/annum would be $\frac{5.028 \text{ million}}{0.392 \text{ million}}$ or about 13 cars/man for 1976, and $\frac{5.976 \text{ million}}{0.399 \text{ million}} = 15$ cars/man for 1978.

On that basis the UK figures for 1978 would be about:

$\frac{1.222 \text{ million}}{0.205 \text{ million}}$ or about 6 cars/man/annum giving the Japanese a productivity benefit of the order of: $\frac{15}{6} = 2.5:1$

Using the analysis procedure of including all the direct support industries as well, then the 1978 productivity would be:

$\frac{1.223 \text{ million}}{0.673 \text{ million}} = 1.8$ cars/man/annum for the UK

$\frac{5.976 \text{ million}}{1.01 \text{ million}} = 5.9$ cars/man/annum for Japan

This 3.28:1 ratio is the true measure of Japanese vs UK productivity in the automotive and allied fields.

The ratio of 2.5:1, on the basis of actual output and total number of employees in the respective car manufacturing plants is bad enough, but the 3.28:1 ratio clearly demonstrates that the weakness of the UK is also in its direct support industries, including ferrous and non ferrous materials, rubber, plastics and tyre manufacture.

The author has found support for the approximation of a 3:1 ratio of productivity from confidential discussions with Senior Executives in Europe and the USA, whose business it is to keep a weather eye on competitors.

In the long run the process of reducing manning levels all round, and very drastically, may become unavoidable, particularly in the supplier sector. As long as labour rates are low by International standards, it may be possible to tolerate a degree of overmanning and the UK and Italian wages are well below the Japanese ones, but are still well above those in the emerging countries and Eastern Europe.

## Japanese versus Competitors : Production Costs
### Average wages/car worker

It has often been claimed that the relatively low production costs of Japanese versus European and US car manufacturers is due to low wages of Japanese workers. The author is not convinced of the validity of this argument, for it masks other factors, such as energy and plant utilisation.

As far back as 1976 the Japanese per capita costs for workers in the car industry were relatively high, as can be seen from Table No. 4.

According to German Statistics, in 1979 the average pay per annum, including the sizeable twice annual production bonuses, was £6,600 for car workers in Japan, and the figure for Germany was £7,950. The corresponding average wages for a UK car worker were £5,200 to £6,200, depending on the amount of overtime worked in a plant.

According to VDA - The Trade Association of Automobile Manufacturers in Germany, it cost their manufacturers in 1979 £6.25/hour to employ a worker (this includes social security and similar contributions to the Government) against Japan's £3.75 due to lower tax contributions by the employers. In fact Toyota paid its factory workers an average of just over £4 an hour in 1979, or about £8,600/annum.

It is all too easy to blame lower contributions by Japanese employers to social security and National Health Schemes, but the comparison is somewhat one-sided, for the pride of the Japanese automobile manufacturers is that they have some of the best equipped hospital and sports and social facilities to be found anywhere in the world, which are available to their workers and their families. These are funded out of company profits not via tax payments to a Government body.

It is also assumed that the Japanese work much longer hours. This is true according to the latest (1980) statistics given in a German Economic Survey. See Table No. 5.

The much lower annual hours actually worked in 1979 in the automotive industries of Europe is due in part to industrial disputes, absenteeism, and lack of sales, resulting in short time working in some plants.

The figures for South Korea, which were given to the author in 1979 on visits to Korean automotive plants, give real cause for concern. For Hyundai Motors they stood at 3350 hours/annum. Saehan, jointly owned by GM and a South Korean Finance Group claims to work 1600 hours overtime/annum/man and paid its workers $1.25/hour. Small wonder, therefore, that Opel cars produced in the modern Korean plant can be brought into world markets at well below the cost of identical cars manufactured by GM's subsidiaries in Germany and Western Europe. For the equivalent hourly rate for a German car worker was nearly 8 times as high in 1979.

The cost advantage for almost comparable productivity/man would be: £175/car produced in Korea against £865/car produced in Germany. (This includes employers contribution to Social Benefits), or a £690/car lower cost.

Other multi-nationals can obtain Japanese manufactured equivalents at around 15% to 25% below the production cost of their US or West European plants. Stiff tariff barriers - currently 0% in the USA and 11% in the EEC - and quota restrictions may hold Japanese car imports at present level but will do little to overcome the basic problems which the UK and Western Europe have still to face up to.

## Vehicle Manufacture:
### Energy Use in Japan and Comparison with GM (USA) and some UK Manufacturers

Production management in the rapidly expanding manufacture in North America and Western Europe decided that its prime objectives were increased total output, shortening of the process time, and keeping the wage content of the finished product to an acceptable minimum. Most manufacturers concerned themselves only with their own production requirements, which is made up of design, product testing, machining, metal forming, welding, assembly, painting and final inspection of their products.

Energy was plentiful and cheap and consequently the need for efficient use of it did not figure in many Board Room decisions.

Whereas energy management was of little concern to the US and European manufacturers until well after the 1973/74 Oil Crisis, the Japanese have for many decades been aware of their dependance on imported energy and hence their vulnerability. In 1979, according to the OECD, Japan imported 89% of its energy, 75% of it being Oil. The Japanese have taken more drastic steps than their competitors to reduce energy consumption during all manufacturing stages. Many of their plants are of more recent design than those to be found in the UK or USA.

Machinery employed in UK industry is, on average, more than twice as old as that in use in Japanese plants. Also, in Japan more use is made of waste heat recovery systems, the burning of solvents freed in painting processes, to assist in raising the temperature of working areas, and the purification and recycling of heated air. According to an unpublished minute of a Common Market Committee, the effect of all this, and a better assessment of electric motor drive sizes to match the actual work load, rather than an often fairly arbitrary decision to have about 10% extra capacity, has been that the energy costs of Japanese products is about 20% less than those of many of their competitors.

In Japan factories whose consumption of energy (whatever its form) exceed a stipulated amount are compelled by law to investigate what measures can be employed to reduce consumption of heat or electric power and then implement plans to reduce consumption.

The amount of energy consumed per vehicle produced has been dropping steadily from 1973 to 1978, $3.26 \times 10^6$ k cal/vehicle (13.65 GJ/vehicle) to $2.58 \times 10^6$ k cal/vehicle (10.80 GJ/vehicle), a reduction of $20\frac{1}{2}\%$. In 1973 total vehicle production in Japan was 7.08 million and 9.27 million in 1978. It is interesting to compare those figures with the corresponding ones for GM's operations in the USA and Canada which were: 250 million GJ in 1972, and 243 million GJ in 1978 with the corresponding production rates being 6.2 million vehicles in 1972, and 7.73 million in 1978.

The energy to manufacture one GM vehicle therefore works out at 40.32 GJ/ vehicle in 1972, and 31.44 GJ/vehicle in 1978, this corresponds to an energy saving of 22%, but is still well above the Japanese values.

Even allowing for the fact that both Japanese cars and trucks are much smaller and lighter than the corresponding ones produced by GM in the USA and Canada, the 1978 ratio of energy consumption during manufacture of 2.9:1 should give one cause to ponder. Allowing for the fact that the average amount of energy required to produce a vehicle is related to the weight of the finished product and that the average US built vehicle is probably 1.8 times the weight of the Japanese one, the ratio is still 1.6:1 against the US one of equal weight.

In fact the amount of energy required/vehicle produced does not rise linearly with weight, probably the relationship of extra energy to produce a heavier vehicle is nearer to 0.7 to 0.8 times extra weight, for it depends on size rather more than weight. Therefore for equally energy efficient manufacture GM (USA and Canada) would require about 1.5 times that of the Japanese to produce a vehicle. This gives the Japanese an energy efficiency bonus of 2.91 ÷ 1.5 = 1.94. In other words they use just over half the amount of energy to produce comparable size vehicles.

Part of this discrepancy is due to the Japanese automobile manufacturers relying more on outside suppliers than GM - but these are all in relatively low energy consumption activities, such as assembly of seats, small electric motors, trim, etc. Even making a very generous allowance of another $5\frac{1}{2}\%$ in favour of GM, this leaves GM, who undoubtedly are North America's most efficient giant in the automotive and allied industry field, with an excess energy consumption of around 43%. The author suggests that these figures are not a mere fluke, but at the heart of the malaise of the US car industry - and for that matter of its principal suppliers, the Iron and Steel Manufacturers.

Privately communicated information from the USA suggests that in 1979, it cost GM around $134/car just to produce it. GM paid $925 million dollars for 243 million GJ of energy required by its US and Canadian plants, which works out at $3.807/GJ or £1.73/GJ for 1978. On that basis energy consumption/car produced = 35.2 GJ. But US fuel prices (even to GM) have probably risen by about 14% from 1978 to 1979. Hence the probable energy consumption/car produced = 35.2 x 0.85 ≏ 30GJ.

For Toyota the corresponding value is around 11.5 to 12GJ.

## The UK Position

One of the UK's Vehicle Manufacturers with a similar split of car to truck to that of the Japanese Manufacturers consumed 6.05 million GJ in 1978 and produced 201 000 vehicles of a size and weight not all that dissimilar from the Japanese ones. For 1980, with rising fuel costs and a slump in demand for some UK produced cars, the values were of the order of £125 to £140/car produced, giving the Japanese a cost advantage of £100 to £115 per car produced on energy consumption during manufacture without taking wages or cost of bought-in components into account.

Of course, not all UK vehicle manufacturers are working at such a calamitous disadvantage. For comparable plants, which produced around 165 000 cars in 1978, the energy cost of production works out at around £52/car, or around 22 GJ/car, still using nearly twice as much energy/car produced. The cost advantage to the Japanese would still be of the order of £32 per car produced.

The author has been able to ascertain the breakdown of various plants and their overall energy consumption. One plant primarily concerned with car production used 4.9 million GJ in that year - but produced only 84 000 cars, which resulted in an energy cost/car of 58 GJ/car. Their production capacity is around 150 000/annum. The best energy utilisation that these plants could achieve would be of the order of 32 to 35 GJ/car, or nearly 3 times the amount of energy for a modern Japanese plant.

In monetary value this amounts to £64 to £70 per car when the plant is producing to full capacity and £116/car for the 1978 production run, for purchased energy on long contracts averaged out at £2/GJ.

The cost advantage, on energy use alone, to a Japanese competitor would therefore be of the order of at least £45/car and probably nearer £80 to £90 when the plants are not working at optimum capacity.

One must add to this the cost advantage to the Japanese of a much lower labour content per car, which is of the order of £450 to £500 when counting only direct labour employed at the giant car assembly plants, or around £1200 to £1600 when considering direct labour employed at the car assembly and all the many support industries.

Whichever way one looks at it, there remains that uncomfortable feeling that many manufacturers in the UK and Western Europe have a long way to go before they approach Japanese manufacturing effectiveness.

It has taken an extraordinary long time for Management, Trade Unions, and Politicians to realise just how wide the gulf between US, European and Japanese true manufacturing costs really is, and in many quarters it is still being questioned. The old argument of some foreigners selling their products into the US and Western Europe at dumping prices does not look so convincing any more.

Some of the more efficient East European manufacturers, while not up to Japanese productivity
are highly automated and pay is low, which gives
them real cost advantages in many markets.

## Some Avoidable on Costs

One of the hidden factors in manufacturing costs
is the extent to which "make-do-and-mend"
maintenance is employed. In many manufacturing
plants in the UK increased level of maintenance
and partial renovation in lieu of replacement
have been the preferred options. Fiscal policy
and high interest rates have discouraged investment in more modern, more robust and more produc-
tive plant and equipment. Dispersal of buildings
tends to lead to needless energy losses in the
main services, steam, heat, hot and cold water,
compressed air, as well as calling for more
expense in internal transport. All this, and
the need to have sizeable buffer stocks in storage to guard against occasional breakdowns,
disruptive industrial disputes, within a group,
or at various suppliers, or in the transport
sector, adds to the total manufacturing cost.

## Holding Buffer Stocks Costs Man Power and Energy

It is not uncommon for several UK manufacturers
to carry several weeks' supply of fairly bulky
items as a buffer in heated warehouses, whereas
Toyota in Japan and several other Japanese
automotive manufacturers rely on the Can Ban
system - or computer controlled scheduling of
quality assured parts, direct from hundreds of
its subcontract suppliers, without intermediate
inspection, binning or palletising and then
checking in and out of stores. The system
appears to work well. Some 2500 suppliers are
keyed into this system and their trucks deliver
right into the assembly halls, drawing up alongside the appropriate sections of the assembly
lines as and where their products are required.

Buffer stock holding is frequently no more than
about 3 to 4 hours supply. Of course such a
system calls for a high degree of interdependance,
control and industrial discipline. Neither the
Western Democracies nor the State run East Bloc
countries are likely to be able to enforce it.
The advantages to the major manufacturers in terms
of reduced borrowing of money, hence improved
cash flow and better return on capital invested,
are self evident. The saving in building, heating,
ventilation, lighting and people is of equal
importance. On average, the energy costs in a
modern car factory, due to heating, ventilation
alone amounts to 25% to 30% of the total energy
used. There will inevitably be occasions when a
complex system fails to perform to schedule. The
Japanese design of interlinked stamping presses,
in which die changes can be achieved within $\frac{1}{4}$
hour, instead of the European norm of $3\frac{1}{2}$ hours,
allows for a degree of flexibility of manufacture
to compensate for this, at least in part, by
changing the end product mix quickly.

The Fiat Robogate system of manufacture likewise
allows the same assembly lines to accept a much
wider range of body options, without interruption
of production, than for instance a mid to late
1960s type single product group of mechanised
welding machines will.

## Wide Dispersal of Factories Costs Energy

A factor which has often been overlooked are the
long lines of communication between major manufacturing centres, which can be found in the UK.
Shipping complete body-in-white shells from one
site to another by road transport is a major
source of needless cost of production, fuel and
manpower. Moreover, it involves the application
of a temporary protective coating, which then
has to be removed again, by application of hot
water, steam and solvent rinsing, before the
painting and assembly operations can be undertaken.

The siting of factories can have other hidden
benefits. The major Japanese car assembly and
principal component manufacturing plants are
located fairly close to the Pacific Ocean, which
gives them a fairly temperate climate all the
year round and hence, substantial saving due to
that alone of the order of 18% to 20% on energy
requirements for plant heating in the winter and
air-conditioning in the summer, when compared
with plants of roughly equal size in the Detroit
Area, and up to 15% less when compared with plants
in the UK and Germany.

In addition to this there are three factors of
some significance:

1. Modern Japanese factories tend to be more
compact, have better low grade heat recovery,
better insulation where it matters and better
re-circulation of warmed up air than in many
which the author has seen in the UK and North
America.

2. Loss of cleaned and warmed-up air through
doors and roof vents is kept to a minimum.

3. By having more continuous working - 2 shifts
instead of 1, shorter weekend shut down periods,
the building fabric stays at a more even temperature, requires less of the wasteful temperature
boosting to bring it up to acceptable working
environment level before the next shift starts
work. The heat energy input per unit produced,
which is a production cost factor, is thereby
drastically reduced.

The cumulative effect is that many Japanese
manufacturers currently use about $\frac{1}{2}$ to $\frac{2}{3}$ less
energy for the working environment sector of
car production factory complex alone than several
of their competitors in other countries. This
assumes comparable annual output per plant.

## Energy Content in Material Processing

About 75% to 82% of the weight of current motor
cars is accounted for by ferrous materials, with
steel alone representing some 60% to 70% of the
dry weight.

It is therefore relevant to look at steel manufacture in Japan and compare it with that of
other car manufacturing countries.

Japan has overtaken the USA in annual output and
ranks 2nd in the world, with the USSR in No. 1
position. It is also amongst the most energy
efficient, largely due to better plant design
and closely monitored operation.

The £10 000 million investment in energy saving equipment and production technique between 1973 and 1977 has started to pay off. Japanese steel plants today require far less energy per tonne of steel produced, i.e. only about $\frac{2}{3}$ of that required in the UK and USA.

Steel production, while not as energy intensive as aluminium production, is still calling for a great deal of energy. Any energy saving is of course reflected in the final cost of manufactured products such as vehicles. The motor industry is a major user of the dearer close tolerance special steels, from deep drawing low carbon sheet steel to high alloy ones for power units, drive lines and spring elements.

The Japanese were quick to take advantage of the continuous hot casting technique originally developed in Germany. This allows an energy saving of up to $\frac{2}{3}$ over the conventional methods, which are still the mainstay of steel production in most countries, including the UK.

The traditional method is to pour molten steel from the blast furnace into ingot moulds to freeze there into pig iron, which then has to be reheated to form slabs before these can be rolled into usable shapes, varying from formed sections to sheet steel. The number of men required to operate a large continuous casting blast furnace can be as little as 15. Backed by computers and close circuit television, they control the complete operation from charging the furnace to the stage when the steel is ready to be shaped into slabs.

In 1973 only about 20% of Japan's steel works had a continuous casting facility, by 1980 it was up to 50% and is scheduled to reach 70% by 1982. Currently it stands at 38% in West Germany, 36% in South Korea, 15.5% in the UK and only 14.2% in the US.

But continuous casting demands precise market forecasting and an assured and steady market. For this is needed when real long term adjustments are called for, including massive investment in basic industries, with shedding of labour, often without any assurance of a return on capital employed to achieve it all. Such drastic changes are not the panacea for all ills, but appear to be well suited for an Industrial Society based on the Japanese model, in which there is a high degree of concensus by Government, Banks, Industrialists and Labour in their "We-are-all-in-it-together" approach to economic and technological development.

## Steel Production : Japanese Achievements

The value of 20.35 GJ/tonne for the total energy requirement for producing bulk steel from ore, which is the best a modern integrated steel plant can hope to achieve, is in sight.

Yield ratios, tonnes of high grade sheet to tonne of hot strip fed into a cold rolling mill, of around 88% to 91% are common. For the very best European ones it can be around 94%, for less efficient plants it can drop to around 75%. It is claimed by Japanese authorities that their yield ratios are around 92% to 95%.

The total energy value $GER_m$ to produce 1 tonne of sheet steel is 40 GJ for UK, 38 GJ for US and 28.5 GJ for Japanese steel mills, as can be seen from Table Nos. 6 and 7.

## Conclusion

While no one expects that the considerable gap in manufacturing costs between essentially similar cars produced in Western Europe and the Far East will be closed within the next few years, better management of energy use during production both at the car assembly plants and at subcontractors could improve the lot of UK and Western manufacturers significantly. Since wages also play an important role, the future may well be more joint ventures of a group of competing European manufacturers investing in new plants and thereby achieving the benefits of economies of scale, by ever increasing use of robots and automation.

The days of a factory producing without people actually working in it may be some time off yet, at least as far as car assembly is concerned. But there are large sectors of the automotive industry and those who supply to it which will be able to produce efficiently and at lower costs with a fraction of its current manpower.

REFERENCES

(1) UK Central Statistical Office Abstracts, HMSO 1980.

(2) How Much Overall Energy Does The Automobile Require? Eric Hirst - Automotive Engineering, July 1972.

(3) How Much Energy Is Needed To Produce An Automobile? John G McGowan/Robert H Kirchoff, Automotive Engineering, July 1972.

(4) Energy Conservation At General Motors, Neil Dekoker, ICEUM II Conference, October 1979.

(5) Industrial Energy Conservation, 101 Ideas At Work, General Motors, USA, January 1977.

(6) D M Cowie, Bulk Steel Processes, Metals and Materials, London, March 1974.

(7) Iron and Steelmaking, State of the Art, Industrial Heating, USA, October 1979.

(8) General Motors, Public Interest Report, April 1980.

(9) M A I Jacobson, M.Sc. Thesis, University of Surrey 1980.

ACKNOWLEDGEMENT

The views expressed in the paper are those of the author and are not necessarily all held by the Committee or Directorate of The Automobile Association.

The author is therefore all the more grateful for having received permission to publish this paper, and to the University of Surrey for allowing him to use data originally submitted as part of an MSc. thesis.

## Table 1      UK employment related to motor cars — 1978 position

The author estimates are based on UK Central Statistical Office Abstract
1980 Direct Employment Data and additional confidential information
obtained from leading manufacturers and employers of labour.

DIRECT EMPLOYMENT

| | | |
|---|---|---|
| Vehicle Manufacture | 205,000 ) | |
| Electrical Machinery | | |
| Component & Parts Manufacture | 45,000 ) | |
| Material Processing & Component Manufacture | 100,000 ) | |
| Iron & Steel, Nuts & Bolts | 32,000 ) | |
| Non Ferrous Metal | 10,000 ) | |
| Chemical & Allied Industry | 23,000 ) | |
| Glass | 8,000 ) | |
| Bricks, Cement, Refractory Materials, Abrasive Material | 5,000 ) | |
| Paper & Board | 11,000 ) | Manufacture |
| Timber & Furniture (also for indirect employment sector) | 5,000) | |
| Textiles & Trim | 8,500 ) | |
| Protective Clothing & Footwear (for all workers & staff associated with motor car manufacture & servicing) | 5,000 ) | |
| Rubber & Plastics & Tyres | 55,000 ) | |
| Mechanical Engineering Handling Equipment & Erection & Contract Workers | 12,000 ) | |
| Instrument Engineering, Office Equipment, Copying Equipment & Computers | 10,000 ) | |
| Machine Tool & Allied Industry | 10,000 ) | |
| Power Industries: Coal, Gas, Oil Water & Electricity | 55,000 ) | |
| Transport & Storage, Post & Telecommunications | 78,000 ) | |

TOTAL     673,000

## Table 2    Indirect employment

| | |
|---|---:|
| Distributive Trade: Motor Repairers, Distributors Garages & Filling Stations, Auction Sales & Auto Shops | 470,000 |
| Wholesale Distribution of Fuel & Lubricants | 20,000 |
| Garage Equipment, Tools, Jigs & Fixtures | 5,000 |
| Office Machinery & Paper & Printing & Packaging Advertising | 45,000 |
| Insurance, Finance, Banking | 90,000 |
| Catering, First Aid, Security | 45,000 |
| National & Local Government, NHS, Ambulance, Fire Brigade | 100,000 |
| Motoring Press, TV, Publications & PR Personnel Printing & Publishing | 3,000 |
| Traffic Wardens, Police, Court Officials, Lawyers | 36,000 |
| Professional & Technical Services | 15,000 |
| Technical College & Universities, Research Establishments | 10,000 |
| Motoring Organisations & Breakdown Assistance | 12,000 |
| Factory Building & Repairs & General Building Work | 25,000 |
| Road Building & Maintenance & Quarrying | 105,000 |
| Iron & Steel for New Construction & Maintenance Work | 5,000 |
| Car Park Attendants & Maintenance & Cleaners + Casual Labour | 32,000 |
| Sub Total | 1,027,000 |
| Grand Total | 1,700,000 |

Indirect to Direct Labour Ratio is about 1.6:1

Table 3    Employment of people in Japan connected with the car industry

| DIRECTLY EMPLOYED (Category I) | 1976 | 1978 |
|---|---|---|
| Manufacture & Assembly of Motor Vehicles, Motor Components & Parts & Body Manufacture in Japan. | 653,000 | 665,000 |

| MATERIALS SUPPLY FIELD (Category II) | | |
|---|---|---|
| Steel Manufacturers, Non Ferrous Metal Manufacturers, Tyre Manufacturers, Glass Manufacturers, Textile & Plastics Manufacturers, Chemical and Paint Manufacturers, Timber, Paper & Board Manufacturers. | 965,000 | 865,000 |

| ENERGY SUPPLY INDUSTRY (Category III) | | |
|---|---|---|
| Electricity, Gas, Water & Coal | 40,000 | 40,000 |

| Category (IV) | | |
|---|---|---|
| Post & Telecommunications & Computer Industry | 75,000 | 75,000 |
| Machine Tools & Instrument Industry | 30,000 | 35,000 |
| | 1,778,000 | 1,680,000 |

Table 4    Based on miti data

| 1. | Daimler Benz | $19,100 or about £9,100pa |
|---|---|---|
| 2. | VW (Germany) | $16,300 "  " £7,760pa |
| 3. | GM (USA) | $17,300 "  " £8,240pa |
| 4. | Ford (USA) | $15,000 "  " £7,140pa |
| 5. | Chrysler (USA) | $14,500 "  " £6,900pa |
| 6. | Toyota (Japan) | $14,400 "  " £6,860pa |
| 7. | Nissan (Japan) | $14,300 "  " £6,810pa |
| 8. | Renault (France) | $13,600 "  " £6,480pa |
| 9. | Fiat (Italy) | $ 8,400 "  " £4,000pa |
| 10. | In the UK it stood at about | £3,800pa |

Table 5    Average hours normally worked/man in the metal working industries in 1979

| COUNTRY | HOURS/ANNUM | AVERAGE HOURS WORKED (ACTUAL) IN THE AUTOMOTIVE INDUSTRY (PRIVATELY GATHERED BY THE AUTHOR |
|---------|-------------|-------------------------------------|
| Japan | 2094 | 2200 |
| Switzerland | 2006 | - |
| UK | 1856 | 1650 |
| France | 1856 | 1850 |
| Italy | 1848 | 1500 |
| Denmark | 1844 | - |
| Sweden | 1808 | 1630 |
| Austria | 1792 | n/a |
| West Germany | 1784 | 1680 |
| Holland | 1764 | n/a |

Table 6    Weight of materials for 1978/79 built cars for same multi nationals kg

| MATERIAL | US MODEL | | EUROPEAN MODELS | | | |
| | COMPACT | % | MEDIUM SIZED | % | SMALL CAR | % |
| --- | --- | --- | --- | --- | --- | --- |
| Sheet Metal | 680 | 43.5 | 550 | 49.5 | 300 | 44.2 |
| Steel Bar, Forged, & Special | 252 | 16.1 | 227 | 20.4 | 118 | 17.4 |
| STEEL TOTAL | 932 | 59.6 | 777 | 69.9 | 318 | 61.6 |
| Cast Iron | 285 | 18.2 | 131 | 11.8 | 92 | 13.5 |
| FERROUS TOTAL | 1217 | 77.8 | 908 | 81.7 | 510 | 75.1 |
| Aluminium & Alloys | 52 | 3.3 | 15 | 1.3 | $17\frac{1}{2}$ | 2.6 |
| Glass | 50 | 3.2 | 35 | 3.1 | 28 | 4.1 |
| Rubber | 65 | 4.2 | 55 | 4.9 | 42 | 6.2 |
| Lead | 14 | 0.9 | 12 | 1.1 | $8\frac{1}{2}$ | 1.3 |
| Zinc & Zinc Alloys | 10 | 0.6 | 5 | 0.4 | $2\frac{1}{2}$ | 0.4 |
| Plastic (Excluding Paint) | 72 | 4.6 | 44 | 4.0 | 31 | 4.6 |
| Paint | 20 | 1.3 | 14 | 1.3 | 8 | 1.2 |
| Copper & Copper Alloys | 12 | 0.8 | 9 | 0.8 | $6\frac{1}{2}$ | 1.0 |
| Natural Materials (Cloth Trim, Paper, Board, etc.) | 51 | 3.3 | 15 | 1.3 | 25 | 3.7 |
| TOTAL | 1563 | | 1112 | | 679 | |

Table 7    Energy content/car due to material alone - typical 1978/79 models

|  | US COMPACT | EUROPEAN MODELS (UK) | | JAPANESE CARS | |
|---|---|---|---|---|---|
|  |  | MEDIUM SIZED | SMALL CAR | MEDIUM SIZED | SMALL CAR |
| Sheet Steel | .68 x 1.07 x 38GJ = 27.6GJ | 23.5GJ | 12.8GJ | 16.5GJ | 9.1GJ |
| Other Steel Components | .25 x 1.12 x 50GJ = 14GJ | 13.3GJ | 6.6GJ | 9.3GJ | 4.6GJ |
| TOTAL STEEL | 41.6GJ | 36.8GJ | 19.4GJ | 25.8GJ | 13.7GJ |
| Cast Iron | .285 x 1.12 x 35GJ = 11.2GJ | 5.1GJ | 3.5GJ | 4.6GJ | 3.2GJ |
| TOTAL FERROUS | 58.8GJ | 41.9GJ | 22.9GJ | 30.4GJ | 16.9GJ |
| Alluminium Alloys | .052 x 1.12 x 200GJ = 11.6GJ | 4.4GJ | 5.1GJ | 5.2GJ | 5.3GJ |
| Glass | .05 x 1.03 x 42GJ = 2.1GJ | 1.5GJ | 1.2GJ | 1.5GJ | 1.3GJ |
| Rubber | .065 x 1.03 x 140GJ = 9.4GJ | 7.9GJ | 6GJ | 7.5GJ | 6GJ |
| Lead | .014 x 1.12 x 31GJ = 0.5GJ | 0.4GJ | 0.3GJ | 0.4GJ | 0.3GJ |
| Zinc Alloys | .010 x 1.12 x 82GJ = 0.9GJ | 0.5GJ | 0.2GJ | 0.5GJ | 0.3GJ |
| Plastic (Excluding Paint) | .072 x 1.12 x 120GJ= 10GJ | 6.7GJ | 4.7GJ | 7.0GJ | 6.5GJ |
| Paint | .020 x 1.17 x 162GJ = 3.8GJ | 2.7GJ | 1.5GJ | 2.5GJ | 1.5GJ |
| Copper Alloys | .012 x 1.12 x 48GJ = 0.6GJ | 0.5GJ | 0.3GJ | 0.5GJ | 0.3GJ |
| Natural Materials Cloth Trim, Paper & Board | .051 x 1.12 x 25GJ = 1.5GJ | 1.4GJ | 0.7GJ | 0.5GJ | 0.7GJ |
| TOTAL GER$_T$ | 99.2GJ | 66.9GJ | 42.9GJ | 56.0GJ | 39.6GJ |

The GER$_T$ values assumed for each material differ from country to country and plant to plant.  The author has made an average 12% allowance for loss in weight during manufacture, due to cropping, fabrication, machining, scrappage, except for rubber and glass where he puts this at 3% and sheet steel where he puts it at 7%.

GER$_T$ = Gross Energy Requirement (Thermal)

# C276/81

# Plant floor information systems via programmable controller/computer networks

W T LESNER, Cadillac Motor Car Division, General Motors Corporation, Michigan, USA
K G HUGHES, General Motors Manufacturing Development, Michigan, USA

SYNOPSIS    Plant floor information systems are gaining popularity and importance in nearly every production environment.   Current competitive and economic considerations demand that manufacturers be more concerned with obtaining the highest levels of efficiency and quality.  In order to attain these goals, many manufacturers are implementing -- or considering implementation of -- computerized information  systems.

This paper examines the design of a plant floor information system for monitoring engine manufacturing at the Cadillac Livonia Engine Plant

INTRODUCTION

The Cadillac Livonia Engine facility is approximately 750 000 square feet in size.  500 000 square feet are part of a building addition which is currently under development.  The plant will produce major engine components (i.e., cylinder blocks, cylinder heads, crankshafts, connecting rods, pistons, manifolds, etc.).  It will also house engine final assembly and test.

In the summer of 1978, when plans were being made for the Livonia plant addition, Cadillac examined many state-of-the-art manufacturing methods.  From that analysis, a decision was made to implement a number of advanced applications, one of which is the plant floor information system described in this paper.

Although nearly all of the machining equipment in the plant has been purchased with programmable controller control, it is important to realize that the equipment is geared toward single purpose, high volume production.  This means that the information system is different than that found in many other computer aided manufacturing applications . . . where flexible numerical controlled equipment is used to produce a variety of different components.  This difference is reflected in the system's design and usage.  The design has been a joint effort between Cadillac Process Engineering, Plant Engineering, and Manufacturing, along with the Manufacturing Control Systems Group at GM Manufacturing Development.

The Cadillac system consists of a five mini-computer network which functions as two subsystems.  The Machine Monitoring and Maintenance Dispatching subsystem encompasses the monitoring, maintenance and host computers.  The remaining two computers are dedicated to the Engine Hot Test System.

The primary purposes of the Machine Monitoring and Maintenance Dispatching subsystem are collection of machine production information, machine status interrogation and efficient trades personnel utilization.  The Engine Hot Test subsystem, on the other hand, is dedicated to Hot Test process monitoring.  Although there will be communication between these two systems, this paper addresses each separately.

The following describes primary functions of each computer in the two subsystems.  Detailed information -- in terms of system components, philosophy and back-up features -- is presented in the remainder of the paper.

Monitoring computer

The monitoring computer's primary function is data acquisition from the plant floor.  The five functions described below are the heart of the plant-floor information system and will be described in greater detail in other sections of the  paper.

1.  Block line monitoring . . . the monitoring of all the machines and automatic storage units on the cylinder block line.  The line is equipped with 29 Allen-Bradley programmable controllers (PCs).  Communication with these PCs will be done with Allen-Bradley's 'Data Highway'

2.  Head line monitoring . . . the monitoring of 28 Modicon Programmable Controllers on the cylinder head line.  In this case, Modicon's Modbus will be used to communicate within the system

3.  Critical/Alarm monitoring . . . monitoring the status of critical conveyors and filtration units throughout the plant and alerting maintenance through an alarm system when they malfunction.

4.  Data entry stations . . . allow operators on the Block and Head lines to call for maintenance assistance or input non- maintenance reasons for downtime from their machine control panels.

5.  Future expansion . . . . expansion of the machine monitoring concept to encompass the whole plant is already underway.  The crankshaft line will be the first addition.

## Maintenance computer

This computer is used to support maintenance activities, as well as the unrelated function of engine component verification. Since the paper deals mainly with Machine Monitoring via programmable controllers, very little emphasis will be placed on the Maintenance Dispatching System. In fact, other than the description in this section, maintenance related details will only be discussed as they impact machine monitoring.

Cadillac Livonia has decided to implement a centralized dispatching system for all skilled trades. The centralized dispatcher will track maintenance activities via a dispatch console which consists of:

1. Critical/Alarm display . . . a color CRT which displays the status of critical/alarm points and data entry station requests for maintenance assistance.

2. Critical/Alarm printer . . . this printer goes hand in hand with the Critical/Alarm display. It is used to obtain hard copy documentation of every alarm or data entry station request.

3. Trades display . . . a color CRT which indicates the current assignments of all the skilled trades personnel.

4. Job backlog display . . . this color CRT is used to keep track of the maintenance jobs which have not yet been completed.

5. Interactive CRT . . . this black and white display, with its associated keyboard, is used by the dispatcher to communicate with the computer. All dispatcher data entries and responses are via this CRT.

6. Communications equipment . . . a standard telephone and special one-way paging system will be the primary means of contacting the tradespersons.

This computer will also perform Engine Component Verification (E.C.V.). E.C.V. has been used within the auto industry for a number of years to assure that the proper emissions-related components have been assembled to the engine.

The engine inspector uses a light pen to wand the bar code label from all emissions-related components, as well as an engine identifier. The computer correlates these, checks for proper grouping, and prints out a label which acknowledges proper assembly or highlights misassembly.

## Host computer

The purpose of this computer is to generate management reports concerning both Maintenance Dispatching and Machine Monitoring. The reporting capabilities will be discussed in later sections.

## Engine hot test computers

These two computers are used to support a comprehensive automatic Hot Test procedure. They specifically:

1. Track engines throughout the test system.
2. Communicate with the test stands via their Allen-Bradley PCs (again over the 'Data Highway').
3. Provide repair information.
4. Provide management reports.
5. Store data on individual engines for immediate access.

Further operation details will be discussed in the Engine Hot Test section of the paper.

As stated previously, these five computers constitute two functionally separate systems — machine monitoring/maintenance dispatching and engine hot test. The following section will focus on the machine monitoring function.

## MACHINE MONITORING PROGRAMMABLE CONTROLLER REQUIREMENTS

Consideration of machine monitoring systems quickly reveals the multitude of approaches that can be taken. In the past, many innovative plants installed monitoring systems that ranged in complexity from hard-wired Telecontrol to mini-computer networks. As a matter of record, a few of these systems provided expected results, some were successful in areas not originally planned for and some were relative failures.

From the initial Cadillac system planning stages, we realized that much could be learned from these earlier systems. The study revealed that many common problems resulted from the approaches taken, some of which were simply the result of then- current technology. Among these problems were the following:

1. Lack of integrity in collected data. Failures of system hardware often resulted in erroneous data for the associated shift. Unfortunately, these errors often would propogate into day, week, and month totals. This problem was responsible for the death of more systems than probably any other. In most production environments, data inaccuracies may be tolerated once, but repeated errors quickly destroy confidence and interest in a monitoring system.

2. Lack of system flexibility. Monitoring system definition involves too many variables and alternative approaches to be absolute. The initial iterations of design typically are, in fact, learning experiences for the future owner. Is it reasonable to think, then, that these changes and refinements would cease following system installation? Inflexibility to change has perhaps been the second most important factor contributing to unsuccessful systems.

3. Persistent hardware failures. Many past systems suffered from annoying and continual hardware failures. This was due, at least in some part, to the application of immature technology in the industrial environment. None the less, persistent malfunctions are devastating to the credibility, acceptance, and support of any system.

The Cadillac system was designed with these considerations in mind. Every attempt has been made to safeguard the system from these potential problems. This effort is evident in the design -- from PC data collection techniques to computer backup -- as will be seen in the following descriptions.

## Data elements collected

The Cadillac machine monitoring system is designed to help plant personnel achieve optimal piece production rates from the associated engine lines. As such, the system will serve as a tool in identification of five basic problem areas:

1. At any instant in time, which machines are not producing parts and (as much as possible) why?

2. Are any machines exhibiting degraded performance to the extent of exceeding designed cycle times?

3. Which machines suffer from -- or are trending toward -- chronic mechanical, electrical, or hydraulic problems?

4. What are the production part counts for this period, and how do they compare to standards?

5. Are there any material flow problems which are causing -- or will cause -- machines to be idle?

To provide this information the Cadillac system will collect key data elements from each monitored machine and status points from monitored automation equipment. This collection process will be executed via the programmable controllers supplied with machine tools for control, plus some additional units for automation status. In the case of machine tools, each PC will accumulate time and count information in a block of memory registers that will periodically be retrieved by the computer system. The key data elements are as follows:

1. Accumulated machine auto cycle time and occurrence count. Auto cycle time is defined as the time during which the machine is in automatic mode and has no fault conditions to prevent it from cycling.

2. Accumulated machine manual time and occurrence count. Manual time is defined as the time during which the machine is in manual (hand) mode with no fault conditions preventing it from cycling.

3. Accumulated machine fault time and occurrence count. Machine faults are defined as those fault conditions incorporated into the control logic. Examples of such conditions are emergency stop, lube fault, chip drag, probe fault, etc.

4. Accumulated machine cycle time and cycle count. Machine cycle time here represents those cycles which are considered to be normal (ref. 5 following). Each cycle includes the total piece machining time exclusive of loader or unloader waiting.

5. Accumulated machine excess cycle time and cycle count. Excess cycle time is defined as the total machine cycle time for cycles that exceed the design standard plus $x\%$.

For the Cadillac system $x$ has been initially assigned the value of 50(%). The purpose of separating 'normal' versus 'excess' cycle times is to avoid contamination of cycle time information by abnormally long cycles.

6. Accumulated machine 'waiting for cycle initiate' time and occurrence count. This waiting time is defined as those intervals in which a machine is capable of cycling (in automatic mode) but requires depression of the 'cycle start' palm buttons. This condition can occur in two situations:

   (a) the machine is in single cycle mode, or

   (b) the machine has been switched from manual or single cycle to automatic

7. Accumulated machine waiting for parts time and occurrence count. This waiting time is defined as those intervals in which a machine is clear to cycle, but cannot due to lack of material at the loader.

8. Accumulated machine waiting to unload parts time and occurrence count. This time is defined as those intervals in which a machine is clear to cycle but cannot due to material flow blockage (back-up) at the unloader.

9. Accumulated machine idle time and occurrence count. Idle time is defined as the total time in which a machine experiences one or more of the above three states -- waiting for cycle initiate, lack of material, or material unload blockage.

10. Machine part (piece) count. The total pieces produced by a machine as registered at the unloader station.

11. Machine rejected part or probe fault count. These counts, maintained for each probe station, register the number of piece faults detected.

12. Unit last cycle time. These time values are maintained for each active station (i.e., head) on a machine.

13. Tool change counters. The Cadillac plant uses two counters per machine for tool change frequency and replacement program duration. These counters are maintained by the PCs and, it may be noted, are viewable from a display panel at the machine control console.

14. Gauge classification counts. These counts correspond to the number of pieces registered in each size class. This information is used for piston and cylinder matching.

15. Torque classification counts. These counts correspond to results registered from monitored fastening (i.e., nut-runner) stations.

The above data elements are accumulated, as previously stated, into PC memory registers for subsequent retrieval by the computer system. In addition to these timers and counters, status information will be assembled into memory word 'bits' to provide current machine status summaries. For a brief illustration of this PC register utilization, consider Figure 1 and Figure 2.

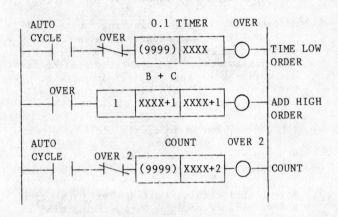

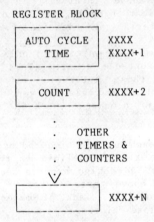

Fig 1    Accumulating PC logic

Figure 1 illustrates manipulation of the auto cycle timer and counter registers by an example PC ladder segment. Note that in this case a double precision timer is used to provide the desired range. Figure 2 illustrates a status word (register) in which bit settings reflect machine condition.

STATUS WORD

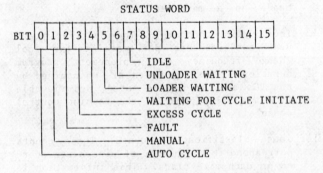

Fig 2    Example status word

Utilization of the status words in addition to accumulating timers and counters provides immediate benefits to the monitoring system. The primary advantages is that machine status information can be quickly retrieved through one or two memory words as opposed to the entire register block. Since the block is accumulative, there is no particular need to access this area frequently. A secondary benefit is simply the relative ease of status register manipulation by the computer system -- status is determined

directly from bit settings. Status determination from the accumulative register block would, on the other hand, require comparison of new to old values to recognize changes.

It should be noted at this point that the quantity of accumulative registers can become significant for a large number of monitored machines. The register count for each machine consists of a base set including machine cycle, auto, fault, etc. -- plus additional registers for unit cycle times, probe fault counts, gauge and torque classifications. If one assumes double precision registers for accumulating timers, the base set could consist of 34 registers. We could then write the following register quantity (per machine) equation:

$$N = 34 + P + L + G + T$$

where  P = probe station count
       L = number of unit last cycle times (single precision)
       G = number of gauge classifications
       T = number of torque classifications

In a hypothetical case of 100 monitored machines -- each having an average of four units, one probe, and no gauge or torque stations -- the total monitoring register count would be as follows:

$$REG = [34 + 1(P) + 4(L)] \, 100 = 3900$$

The data elements discussed previously apply to machines in the Cadillac system. Storage units and conveyors, on the other hand, are monitored in a much simpler fashion. From this equipment the monitoring system will collect only status words containing bit settings for ON/OFF and FULL/EMPTY conditions.

Data collection techniques

Using programmable controllers for machine control provides an excellent data collection vehicle for the monitoring system, a vehicle not available with relay controls. The PC, by definition programmable, can generally be 'fitted' with data collection logic to monitor any input, output, or logic coil desired. When designing the Cadillac system, however, we realized that certain guidelines (techniques) should be followed to ensure high data integrity and system manageability. These guidelines were as follows:

1. PC data collection logic should provide stand-alone accumulation for 24 hours.

2. Data collection logic should be consistent from one PC to another.

3. Data registers should form a continuous block within each PC.

4. PC logic line counts (space required) should be held to a minimum.

The first guideline is perhaps the most important, for it establishes data buffering at the PC level. As stated previously, a basic goal in the Cadillac design was to ensure data accuracy at all times. To ensure this, it is desirable to provide data buffering at lower levels of a system hierarchy, such that hardware failures at

16

© IMechE 1981  C276/81

higher levels will not result in data loss. For this purpose the data collection logic in each PC was designed to ensure 24 hour stand-alone accumulation. The primary implication of this capability was that time and count registers provide sufficient 'width' or capacity. In the case of timers, a 0.1 second time base was chosen to coincide with machine supplier cycle timing conventions. A 24 hour accumulation of time, such as 'autocycle', would then require storage of 864 000 (24 hrs. x 36 000 tenths) 1/10 second increments. For the Allen-Bradley and Modicon PCs used on the Cadillac system this storage required double precision (cascaded) registers. Counters, on the other hand, demonstrated less severe capacity requirements. As a guideline we considered that the fastest cycling machine would produce one part in 15 seconds, thus requiring a range of 5760 (24 hrs. x 240 parts per hour). For Modicon PCs this implied single precision counters, for Allen-Bradley double precision.

Consistency of logic from one PC to another was a goal to simplify system implementation and future logic maintenance. Several practices were followed to ensure this consistency. From the start of system design it was planned that timing/counting ladder logic would be identical within PCs of the same type. This commonality will generally promote troubleshooting and logic maintenance ease. Another practice was that monitoring logic would be entered into each PC at the 'end' of user memory area. This practice ensured a physical separation of control and monitoring logic lines to avoid confusion arising from interleaved logic.

The third monitoring logic guideline -- contiguous data registers to form a block -- was pursued to provide simplicity and efficiency in register acquisition by the computer system. These benefits result from a peculiarity of most PC-computer interfaces -- register acquisition requests are serviced once per scan and involve sequential memory locations. In order to minimize the number of acquisition transactions -- and thereby the software and transmission overhead -- desired registers should be 'stacked' as contiguous blocks. Multiple requests generally would require multiple PC scans, with time delays of 25-75 milliseconds per scan. One can readily see the potential for undue data acquisition delays.

The last monitoring logic guideline was that PC space requirements be held to a minimum. This goal was a function of reality as much as good design practice. At an early design stage it was recognized that some PCs would offer limited free space after the machine control logic was entered. To work within this available space, and still provide reserve for future logic modifications, the monitoring logic was optimized to reduce line count.

The above guidelines resulted in PC data accumulation techniques that ensure a high integrity, efficient, and maintainable collection process. It should be noted that Cadillac was in the favourable position of defining to machine vendors what logic would be supplied with the machine tools. The timing of machine delivery was such that this could be done, as opposed to adding monitoring logic 'in the field'. This ability can greatly simplify system implementation and should be pursued whenever possible.

## SYSTEM DATA TRANSMISSION

The design of any system involves selection of data transmission hardware that will meet both present and future requirements. In the Cadillac design, several operational requirements produced data transmission needs that were difficult or impossible to meet just a few years ago. These requirements were as follows:

1. Multi-drop (shared) PC to computer interfacing due to the large number of monitored machines.

2. High speed computer-computer links for backup capability.

3. Communications hardware that would easily support future expansion and modifications.

The following sections will discuss solutions to these requirements and the specific selections made during design -- Modicon Modbus, Allen-Bradley Data Highway, broadband coaxial cable, and high speed computer links.

### PC-Computer networks

Programmable controller computer interfaces have made possible a variety of systems, ranging from ladder logic support to process control networks. Just a few years ago the interfaces available were discrete line (one-to-one) types, where each PC was directly connected to a computer on a dedicated link. While this discrete line interfacing met the needs of many systems, it was inherently cumbersome and costly where many PCs were involved.

Production monitoring systems generally are of this type -- the Cadillac system initially will encompass 65 PCs with expansion planned to double that count. The quantity of wiring required by discrete computer-PC links and the number of computer serial channels required would be prohibitive.

The recent availability of multi-drop (shared) PC to computer networking hardware has provided an efficient communications alternative. It allows connection of multiple PCs (up to 64 in some cases) to a single serial link. This approach, as illustrated in Figure 3, places serial port and cable length requirements into a manageable range. In addition, future expansion is generally easier by only requiring extension of the nearest link.

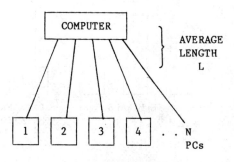

DISCRETE LINE INTERFACING
COMPUTER PORTS = N
CABLE LENGTH = N x L

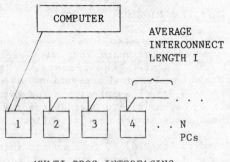

MULTI-DROP INTERFACING
COMPUTER PORTS = 1
CABLE LENGTH = L + N x I

Fig 3   PC interfacing schemes

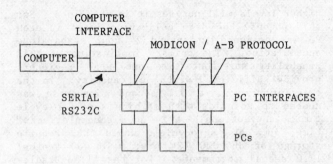

Fig 4   PC–computer interface hardware

The Cadillac system will use Modicon's Modbus and Allen-Bradley's Data Highway for these PC-computer networks.   Both products offer multi-drop capability and are supported by these manu-facturers with application software.   This soft-ware provides basic utility routines to handle I/O transactions with error detection and recovery.   Each Modbus network operates at 19.2 KBPS (1000 bits per second) and supports up to 32 PCs.   The Data Highway networks run at 57 KBPS and handles up to 64 PCs.   The Cadillac system will use one Modbus and three Data Highway networks.

Both the Allen-Bradley and Modicon networks involve multiple PC interfaces interconnected on a common cable with a computer interface for data acquisition.   A typical configuration of these networks is shown in Figure 4.

The Cadillac system makes use of this configura-tion with one major variation.   This variation is the use of broadband coaxial cable between the computer and the computer interface, as will be seen in the following.

Broadband coaxial cable

A significant characteristic of the Cadillac System is the use of broadband coaxial communi-cations.   At an early design stage it was decided to utilize broadband cable that was previously installed for a plant fire and watch system.   Broadband is high speed, multiple user and supports a wide range of information trans-mission from digital to video.

In the Cadillac system, the PC networks, comput-ers, plant floor terminals, and data entry stations are connected to the broadband cable. This interconnection is illustrated below in a simplified manner in Figure 5.

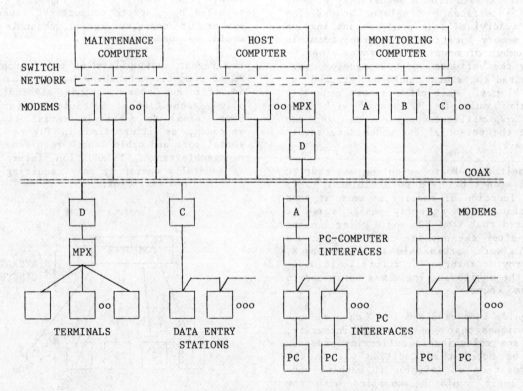

Fig 5   System communications

The boxes immediately to either side of the cable are broadband modems, some of which illustrate frequency (channel) selection by the letters A, B, C . . . . Also shown are the PC-computer network interfaces connected to the broadband via modems. The boxes labelled MPX are statistical multiplexers used for the plant floor terminal communications. These provide multiplexing of multiple terminals (up to 8) over a single serial line. The Cadillac system will initially use 21 floor terminals with a significant advantage obtained through multiplexing.

Use of the broadband system will provide Cadillac with considerable flexibility and interconnection ease, particularly in future expansions. This technology, plus multi-drop PC networking and terminal multiplexing, provide system efficiencies not possible a few years ago.

High speed computer links

An efficient method of computer backup is to interconnect the primary and secondary processors with high speed data links. These links are used for data base transaction notification and fast data file transfer for smooth control transitions. Although the broadband network is high speed on the trunk cable, the speed of most modems is restricted to 9600 BPS. This speed is not sufficient to effectively handle mass data transfers. Because of this restriction, the Cadillac system will utilize a separate network between the computers as shown in Figure 6.

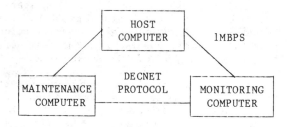

Fig 6   Computer—computer network

Due to the fact that Digital Equipment Corporation (DEC) computers are used in the system, it was decided to use a DECNET DMC11 interface network. This network is capable of running at 1 MBPS and is supported by DECNET protocol software.

The DECNET communications system will be used for time critical transmissions such as status messages and data file transfers for backup. In the Cadillac system each computer can backup another computer as per the following:

1.  The maintenance computer can backup the host or monitoring computer.

2.  The host computer can backup the maintenance or monitoring computer.

3.  The monitoring computer can provide data collection and limited report capability for two weeks in the event of maintenance and host computer failures.

It should be noted that plant floor devices are 'shared' between the computers for backup purposes. This is done by switching the subject

modems from the primary processor to the secondary when a backup transition occurs. The reverse is executed when the primary once again gains control. The Cadillac system uses multi-channel switcher networks for this modem transfer.

SYSTEM REPORT CAPABILITY

In the past, plant floor computer systems struggled with the technical aspects of monitoring . . . emphasis, many times, was put on obtaining the data, not necessarily on displaying it. The trend today, especially with the advent of PCs and more sophisticated data gathering techniques, is to concentrate on putting information into the hands of those who can really do something with it.

The Cadillac system will do this by placing 21 CRTs (4 color and 17 black and white) in the offices of supervision throughout the plant. Although there is a high speed printer available for hard copy reports, this network of CRTs is aimed at making the system as paperless as possible . . . no longer flooding supervision with reams of computer output.

One of the revolutionary ideas which is being implemented is the way which information is displayed to first line supervision. It is important, especially at that level, to present a complete, yet simple, picture of key information. In order to do this, the emerging technology of color graphics is being used.

Rather than supplying first-line supervision with reports which are hard to decypher, the Cadillac system presents supervision with a 'picture' of their line. In fact, the supervisor has the option of viewing color pictures of their whole line, of a given machine, or of individual heads on a specific machine. Color is being used to highlight key status items which require the supervisor's attention.

Under current circumstances without the computer, most supervisors spend a good portion of their time trying to determine the status of their equipment (is it running/not running? and why?). In effect, they don't have the opportunity to really supervise.

With the computer's help, however, the supervisor will be able to see the status of any part of the line on the color CRT setting on the back desk. The hope is that this type of reporting system will really change the way that supervisors run their lines.

In addition to the color graphic status reports, more detailed status and historical reports can be generated. There is enough disc storage on the system to produce historical reports, on demand, in the form of: shift or daily summaries for the past 31 days; weekly summaries for the past month; and yearly summaries.

Examples of these additional reports include:

1.  Machine Monitoring
    (a)  Specific tool change and status scheduling
    (b)  Current float levels between operations
    (c)  Machine efficiencies
    (d)  Machine idle and downtimes

(e)   Rejects
(f)   Gauge analysis

2.   Maintenance Dispatching
(a)   Response time summaries
(b)   Downtime evaluations
(c)   Accounting analysis
(d)   Attendance summaries

Along with these reports, a report and display generating package has been purchased which allows users of the system to develop their own reports (and pictures) from information in the data base, without learning a complex computer language.

ENGINE HOT TEST MONITORING

The Hot Test line is a palletized, automatic line. The engine is identified to the computer by bar code reading the engine's unit number and type. These two engine parameters are correlated to the pallet number, which becomes the key means of identification throughout the Hot Test system. The pallet number, represented by side mounted magnets, is read magnetically.

Following assembly, each engine enters one of 14 Hot Test stands controlled by Allen-Bradley PCs. The PC then retrieves from the computer the corresponding engine type. Given the type, the programmable controller can set the proper test parameters and begin the test.

When the test is completed, the PC sends test data to the computer for future reference. If an engine is sent to repair, the repair person can display the engine record and reasons for the engine's failure. Once finished, that person can enter repair information and where the engine is being sent -- either back for retest, out for further repair, or out of the system as an accepted engine.

When the engine has been accepted, either by the test stand or a repair person, it is routed to the unload station where another reader (attached to the conveyor PC) identifies the engine and verifies that it has passed all the tests.

Data collection process

Data collected from Engine Hot Test is significantly different than that collected in machine monitoring. In machine monitoring, the purpose was to act like an 'outside efficiency expert', analyzing all portions of the machining cycle, but not influencing the operation of the machine. In Engine Hot Test, the computer is an integral part of the system, and the goal is not to analyze efficiency, but to insure quality.

Each data collection source (the conveyor programmable controller, Hot Test Stand PC, and repair terminals) will be discussed briefly. The specific interaction between the PC and the computer will be covered under 'Data Collection Techniques'.

1.   The conveyor PC coordinates the initial engine identification process at the conveyor load station and the final verification at the unload station. The bar code reader is interfaced to the PC by means of a serial computer link. The magnetic readers are directly interfaced to the PC I/O (the bar code and magnetic readers are backed-up by manual keyboard entry).

When an engine is loaded onto -- or unloaded from -- the conveyor, the PC collects the proper information from the bar code reader and/or magnetic reader and passes the information to the computer. In the case of the unload station, the computer returns the status of the engine (accepted, additional repair necessary, retest, or unknown) which the PC uses to direct the load operator as to the disposition of the engine.

2.   The test stand programmable controller communicates with a variety of devices. In addition to communicating with the pallet's magnetic reader and the operator's console, the PC must also collect large amounts of test data from analog and digital I/O, as well as via a microprocessor which accumulates high speed test information.

For eight different RPM/Load combinations, the PC dynamically collects test data on items such as oil pressure, torque, exhaust pressure, vacuum, etc. and compares it to preset high and low limits. Also, certain items of data such as power contribution are broken down by cylinder.

In addition to the dynamic analog data retrieval, the PC also performs pass/fail checks on a number of items such as water cavity leaks.

At the end of the test cycle the PC, which has stored these values in its registers, transmits the test information to the computer. The PC must get a verification that the computer has received the test data before it can begin the next test.

3.   Repair area personnel can see engine test history via repair CRTs mounted on the repair stands. Only two types of data are collected from this area. The first is repair information. The operator can enter five different repair codes (selected from over 100) and comment what was done to repair the engine. The second item of data is the engine disposition -- where the engine is being sent. This item is necessary to track where engines are in the system.

Data collection techniques

There are two main distinctions between the PC/computer interaction of the Hot Test system and that of the Machine Monitoring system. The first difference is the polling technique used to obtain data from the PCs. In the case of Machine Monitoring, the computer solicits all requests for data . . . and thus has control over what (and when) data is obtained. Engine Hot Test, on the other hand, utilizes the Allen-Bradley 'Data Highway', in which the PC sends its data to the computer without any prior solicitation.

The second difference is the way that the computers are backed-up. The Machine Monitoring concept discussed previously utilizes a switching network for determining which computer polls the machines. The data obtained by the monitoring computer is then shared with the other computers over a high speed (1 MBPS) communications link.

In the Engine Hot Test system, the repair terminals are handled the same way, utilizing a switching network. The PCs, on the other hand, send messages to both computers over the 'Data Highway'. In fact, in order for the PC to begin the next test, it must have received an acknowledgement signal for both computers (when both are operational). This assures that when both computers are running, they are obtaining identical information.

When one computer fails, the other computer records all the information during that period of time. When the failed computer is functional again, the unrecorded information is transferred over the high speed link until its database is up-to-date.

## Hot test reporting

Just as in the Machine Monitoring/Maintenance Dispatching portion of the system, the Hot Test management reporting capability is considerable. Production status and historical reports, reject and repair summaries, as well as equipment and repair efficiencies, are all available on demand.

In addition, the last 20 000 individual engine records are on-line for immediate access. Information about any engine, while it is being repaired or going through final car assembly, can be obtained with a minimum of delay.

## CONCLUSION

The plant-floor information system outlined in this paper provides a good starting point for the development of a total manufacturing information system at Cadillac. Obviously, as one considers the additional applications which can be integrated into the system (such as energy control, material control, and time and attendance) it becomes evident that any information system must be built to evolve with the needs and levels of sophistication within the organization. This need for flexibility has been recognized and designed into the system wherever possible. This is evident in the use of multi-user broadband coaxial cable, the high speed inter-computer data links using DECNET, and extra capacity at each mini-computer.

Furthermore, a computer system which interfaces with plant-floor personnel should not be implemented in an isolated manner . . . it must be well planned and integrated into the overall operation of the plant. The best PC/computer interaction and information gathering techniques are useless unless the people who use the information are taken into consideration. This is especially true since computerized information systems have a tendency to generate feelings of mistrust and de-humanization. With this in mind, Cadillac has maintained plant floor supervision involvement in system design from initial stages. In addition, both management and union representatives have been informed of the design detail and project progress.

Finally, it is hoped that this paper has served, not only to highlight the technical data gathering features of the system, but that it has also accentuated the importance of transforming raw data into valuable management information.

# Modern automotive casting production

I A NOBLE CEng, MIProdE, AMIBF
George Fisher Sales Limited, London

The automotive manufacturer today requires high volumes of intricate highly cored castings. In order to be competitive these castings not only have to be at the right price, but they also need to be dimensionally accurate, metallurgically sound and should be supplied on a reliable basis.

The George Fischer organisation has been operating a number of European automotive foundries for many years and supplies most of the major European motor manufacturers. In the late 1950s these foundries were finding that there was no commercial equipment available to meet their high standards of reliability, dimensional tolerances and output requirements. It was in this period that the first 330 moulds per hour moulding plants were designed, built and installed within the Group.

## 1 Modern High Speed Automated Moulding Equipment

The principle involved for all automotive volume casting production is that of high pressure green sand moulding, i.e. a specially prepared sand and clay mixture is subjected to pressures in excess of 7 bar to achieve satisfactory mould rigidity.

## Flaskless Moulding

Recently the flaskless method of mould production has gained a great deal of popularity. This method utilises a larger cake of sand than would otherwise be necessary which gives a mould enough rigidity to be able to withstand the ferrostatic pressures of the molten metal and the forces involved in moving the mould through coring, closing, pouring and cooling operations. The system has the advantages that it is not restricted to any one depth of moulding box, and in most cases the moulding system is a cheaper system because of the lack of moulding boxes and often the lack of complicated mould conveyor. However, its dis-

advantages are that more sand may be required per mould which may increase the cost per mould. It is also necessary to review and generally re-design all running and feeding systems to adopt vertical moulding.

Flaskless moulding lines have now been developed in two different modes, vertical moulding has achieved a greater adoption because of its ease of construction and operation.

## Operation

(a) The moulding chamber which is bounded by a cope and drag pattern plate on either side is filled with sand under pressure.

(b) The sand parcel is squeezed between the two pattern plates to compact the mould.

(c) The front pattern plate is withdrawn and then lifted vertically.

(d) The mould is ejected from the moulding chamber by the rear pattern. In doing so the mould is closed with the previously made mould and the whole string of moulds is indexed.

The mould making sequence is therefore very simple and can be performed at high speeds. Equipment is not complicated and, therefore, inexpensive. Speeds of up to 700 moulds per hour have been achieved with a double strand system of vertical flaskless moulding.

The restrictions which are inherent in the system are the difficulty in placing cores, and moulding in the vertical mode involves all the metal feeding and running systems to be moulded on to the surface of the pattern, and the pattern utilisation and metal yield may thus be reduced. The changing of the patterns is not very easy and cannot be achieved within the cycle time.

Most of the shortfalls of vertical flaskless moulding systems can be overcome by horizontal moulding. However, the advantages of capital cost savings are then lost.

In a typical example of this type of machine cope and drag moulds are made in a moulding frame and cores are set. The mould is closed on accurate pins and bushes and then the complete mould is ejected from the moulding box ready for pouring and cooling.

This type of machine design is capable of making up to 280 moulds per hour with two positions for core setting in both cope and drag, pattern changing within the cycle time and a conventional horizontal metal running and feeding system is utilised.

Moulding Box Systems

Despite the recent trend towards flaskless moulding systems the majority of automotive castings are still produced on boxed moulding plants which are able to offer high production rates with good flexibility and good dimensional accuracy.

Because of the range of application of such systems, there is a wide range of machine layouts which are capable of producing up to 330 moulds per hour in moulding boxes up to 1.5 x 1.0 metres. Multi-station machines can allow several different patterns to be moulded alternately, or patterns can be changed within the cycle time. Many core setting stations can be allowed for, sufficient for setting the most complex of cores. It can be seen therefore that boxed moulding plants are the most flexible and are capable of working at the same high output rate of most flaskless machines. They are though, generally more expensive than the flaskless plants.

2   "IMPACT" Method of Mould Compaction

The heart of the moulding process is the actual sand fill and mould compaction. In order to produce a successful casting, the sand has to fill all parts of the mould and then be compacted to a uniform bulk density and mould hardness. To date there is no green sand moulding process which achieves this requirement completely and so all methods used are in fact compromises.

Jolting the mould was the original method of compaction in medium pressure moulding lines. In this principle the sand mould, mounted on a heavy steel plate, is raised a few centimetres and then dropped on to a solid base.

Several of these jolt blows are capable of compacting the sand. This method does not however achieve a very high mould compaction or hardness and is notoriously noisy. Various measures were added to the jolt to improve the mould characteristics, such as loading weights on to the back of the sand or applying a squeeze plate at the same time as the jolt. Other modifications have been made to reduce the noise level but these have only made marginal improvements.

The next development was the multi-feet-squeeze head. This is a system of multiple hydraulic rams each with a compaction foot. This system enabled the machine to apply different pressures to various parts of the mould dependent upon the depth of sand. As a result a high and more uniform mould hardness was achieved.

The next development in mould compaction was shoot squeezing. In this system the sand is pneumatically blown into the mould at great speed, thus obtaining a degree of pre-compaction. The mould is then squeezed against the shooting head and finally, the pattern is removed. This system will produce a mould almost as uniformly compacted as a jolting action used in conjunction with a multi-foot-squeeze system. Advantages are that there are many less moving parts - a sand hopper does not have to move as the mould is squeezed into the underside of the hopper grid. This allows the machine to operate much faster and with less maintenance. There is no jolting or vibration and is therefore very much quieter than other systems. However, it is difficult to obtain uniform compaction when using the flat shooting head as the squeeze plate.

The latest development in this search for improved mould compaction and uniformity is the "IMPACT" moulding process.

Figure 1

The sequence of operation of the "IMPACT" method of mould compaction.

As illustrated, the moulding box is filled with sand from a hopper, the sand hopper gates are then closed and a natural gas and air mixture is ignited. This ignition generates a shock wave which is directed at the back of the sand and generates a very effective compaction force. The resultant mould is particularly hard and is generally greater than 90 GF hardness over most parts of the mould. There is an added advantage in the permeability of the sand which increases away from the pattern plate,

© IMechE 1981  C277/81

this assists with the removal of gases from the mould during the pouring process. Conventional compacting systems require 5 to 10 times the energy to compact the same moulding box volume and the "IMPACT" system, using a primary energy source, is very much more efficient. This new compaction system can be added on to existing moulding machines, and several foundry installations are currently under construction utilising impact moulding. The moulding sequence is very much faster than previous methods and is comparatively quiet.

## Figure 2

Comparison of mould strength with other compaction processes.

By reason of its advantages in energy saving, greater casting accuracy and improved working conditions, this compaction system is likely to be the process used on high pressure green sand moulding systems of the future.

## 3   Core Making Machines

With the more complex nature of internal combustion engines, the constant call to keep casting weights down and the intricate water jackets now demanded by high performance cylinder heads, a new breed of core has been evolved.

An automotive core in particular will be almost completely surrounded by molten iron at approximately 1400 degrees C and yet should allow no metal penetration into its grain despite sections as thin as 6mm. The core should be rigid enough to support its own weight and often the weight of other cores supported only on small core vents. It should be able to contract with the casting during cooling and yet after the casting has cooled it should have completely opposite properties so as to be easily extracted from the casting. In addition, the core itself should be permeable enough to conduct away the gases evolved within itself during the pouring operation, so the requirements placed on a core are stringent indeed.

The clay bond used in green sand moulding is totally inadequate and a resin binder system is generally used. Today, the two binder systems pre-dominate generally known as "hot box" which is a heat curing process and "cold box" which is a gas curing process.

Currently most automotive foundries still utilise hot box resins which have up to 60 seconds curing time, an unpleasant working environment and

high maintenance problems associated with the gas burners and the heat affecting parts of machinery. However, the latest "Amine" cured "cold box" resins are capable of curing and purging in about 10 seconds and do not have the problems of heat at the work station. However, Amine is a toxic gas and should therefore be very closely controlled.

## Figure 3

One piece body core for a 'V8' engine block.

Cylinder blocks and heads in particular are cast as single castings, and their function depends to a large extent on the hollow shapes within them, i.e. water jackets, oil ways, inlet/outlet ports etc. It is therefore important to reproduce these shapes with the highest possible precision. These castings are heavily cored and the quality of the cores play an important part in the quality of the finished product.

## Figure 4

Complete set of cores for a cylinder head.

In order to achieve the necessary high quality cores it is evident that the core making machines must be of an equivalent high calibre design and manufacture as the precision of the cores can only be as good as the precision that the machine will allow.

The units generally used in automotive core production can be used for both hot and cold box applications. The unit includes one shooting station where the premixed resin and sand mixture is 'shot' under pressure into the core box. There are then two curing and strip stations where the core cures to such an extent that it can be removed from the moulding box. The cores are removed from the core boxes by ejector pins but are then lifted very carefully out of the stripping station. At this stage the cores are not finally cured and they must be supported very well to avoid distortion and breakage. These machines have a capacity of 100 – 180 cycles per hour depending on the curing time of the resin used. The machine illustrated will handle a core box of 1 metre x 750 so it is usual that several cores are made in each shot.

## Figure 5

A two station core shooting machine with a capacity of 135 shots per hour.

# 4  Automatic Mould Pouring Methods

The development of high speed automated
moulding plants not only requires a
supply of cores to keep up with the
moulding line, but also supplies of
molten metal.  Until the development of
modern moulding lines, metal was often
dispensed by manually operated ladles
running on monorails between the melting
units and the pouring lines.  The actual
pouring of the metal requires the
operator to constantly move the ladle
through three planes during pouring and
keep the pouring bush full of molten
metal at all times.  In early automated
foundries it was not unusual to see
queues of casters with separate ladles
striving to keep pace with the moulding
line.

Automatic pouring units have now been
developed to serve the demand of the
automated foundry.  Generally these
pouring units consist of a holding
furnace located at the moulding line.
This furnace might have a capacity of
one tonne up to 20 tonnes of liquid
metal.  The furnace will usually be
equipped with an inductor to maintain
the temperature of the metal.  It is
not practical to carry out any prime
melting or super heating in such a
furnace as the prime object is to
maintain the temperature of the metal
as steadily as possible, suitable for
pouring.  Metal is dispensed from this
furnace either by tilting, pressurising
or, more commonly, by a stopper.  The
volume of metal to be dispensed is
determined either by time, gravi-
metrically or by optical observation of
the pouring operation.

Two types of automatic pouring equipment
are now explained.

(i)  The Stopper Operated Pouring Unit

A ladle fitted with a pneumatic
stopper is located on a frame
directly over the mould track.
Liquid metal is filled into the
ladle.  A channel inductor is
fitted to the ladle which assures
constant temperatures during
pouring as well as during
interruptions in production.
Refilling of liquid metal can be
carried out without interruption
of the pouring process.

Liquid metal is metered on a time
basis through a nozzle in the
bottom of the vessel.  Flow
deflectors can be fitted to absorb
the kinetic energy of the metal.
Adaption of the flow rate to the
mould absorption is possible by the
variable remote control of the
stopper stroke.  This unit is very
suitable for medium capacity
moulding lines requiring grey cast
iron.  The capacity of these units
varies from 2.5 to 5 tonnes.

(ii) The Pressure Operated Pouring Unit

This ladle is located on a frame
at the side of the moulding track,
has a teapot spout arrangement over
the track and a pneumatically
operated stopper to actually
control the metal flow.  The metal
is enclosed in the sealed furnace
body which is fitted with a heating
inductor.  When the interior is
subject to internal pressure
applied by means of compressed air
or inert gas, the metal is forced
up the teapot spout.  Filling and
pouring can take place
simultaneously.  The iron in the
spout reservoir is maintained at a
constant level by a preset holding
pressure in the furnace body,
electrodes in the spout sense the
level of molten metal.  Pouring
takes place from a signal from the
moulding line and the furnace
pressure is automatically increased
to maintain a level of metal in the
pouring spout.

Treated spheroidal graphite iron
can be held in these holding vessels
under an inert atmosphere without
fear of "fade" of the nodularising
treatment for extended periods.
This type of pouring unit has a
large holding capacity of 7 - 14
tonnes and is particularly suitable
for high speed moulding lines.  The
advantages of these two types of
automatic pouring units are:

(a)  Holding capacity at the moulding
line evens out the irregular flow
in quantity and temperature from
the melting unit, and makes for
more consistent pouring.

(b)  The stopper pouring methods ensure
a slag free metal pour.

(c)  A consistent machine controlled
pouring will reduce overspill
and casting scrap due to
inconsistent metal pouring.
Metal yield is generally increased.

(d)  A better controlled handling of
spheroidal graphite iron.

(e)  Improvement in environmental and
working conditions.

5.  The Fettling and Cleaning of
Castings

Manual fettling of rough castings is
a tiresome unhealthy and expensive
process.  Due to the variety of shapes
and an ever-changing production
programme it is very difficult to
mechanise this process.  However, a
range of machines has been developed

which not only replace manual operations but which also perform additional tasks.

Figure 6

Automatic fettling machines.

A typical installation usually includes 3 to 6 units connected to a single electronic control and hydraulic unit.

Rough castings will always present slight variations from the original pattern shape due to temperature differences, metal shrinkage, heat treatment and pattern wear. By use of a sensitive electronic scanning system all these variables are registered and corrected in the programme. The programmes are entered on each unit by scanning the rough casting. All operations to be performed are read out on a digital screen. The whole programme is then stored on a short section of punched tape and can be entered into the memory at any time. In the meantime the other units work normally as they are independently controlled by a separate programme.

Each cycle starts by locating the workpiece in the jig or fixture. When the door is closed the following cycle can be started by push button.

1. Hydraulic clamping of the workpiece.

2. The rotary chuck plate tilts and successively brings the various surfaces to be machined in front of the tool. Scanning and correction is effected by means of short angular and rotary motions.

3. Ingates, risers and residual flash are removed by milling cutters.

4. The parting line flash is removed by nibbling. The only adjustment consists of changing the nibbling tool stroke and the contouring path when entering a new programme. The workpiece shape is scanned by the tool itself which acts as a probe constantly feeding the information back to the control circuit while the chuck plate is still moving.

5. The tilting table returns to its initial position and the workpiece is unclamped. The machine is then ready to accept a new work-piece.

   Datum face machining using bores or cast prints as reference points can be programmed on to the machine. When need be the machining allowances can also be milled away whilst still on the machine. After scalping, various porosity defects may be revealed thus saving the

final machining operation.

The advantages of an automatic fettling installation are:

1. Simplified handling of castings in the fettling area.

2. One operator can operate several machines and also inspect castings and carry out hardness tests.

3. Different programmes are easily entered.

4. Single units can handle small production runs.

5. Prolonged tool life during successive machining operations as milling does not create any surface hardening.

6. A more uniform high quality finish can be maintained.

7. Location points can be machined during fettling operations.

8. Reduction of arduous manual work.

9. Reduction of noise and dust in the fettling shop.

10. Safe operation.

Modern Shot Blast Cleaning Techniques

Fully automated moulding and casting plants require a continuous flow of material right into the fettling shop. The straight through barrel blast cleaning machine can be linked into an automatically operating production line for the desanding and decoring process. As the returns are shot blasted the slag build up in the electric melting furnaces is greatly reduced.

Figure 7

A straight through barrel type shot blast machine.

The straight through barrel blast cleaning machine mainly consists of a twin barrel positioned on an inclined rotation axis. All bearings and drives are situated outside the blasting area. The perforated wear resistant inner drum is divided into the conical blast drum and the unloading drum with a built in helical conveyor.

The blast drum and the unloading drum are built as a single unit. The whole assembly is suspended inside the outer drum by means of damping elements.

The barrel axis is inclined to keep the lower level on the conical section in horizontal plane. The drive is effected by a hydraulic motor with variable speed.

The workpieces are fed into the blast drum by means of a feeding conveyor. Pick up bars allow thorough and controlled tumbling of the casting.

One or two blast wheels are arranged so that their blast patterns cover the whole length of the blast drum. The parts which have reached the unloading drum are carried to the drum exit by means of the inner helical conveyor. They are then transported to the following work stations by conveyor. The abrasive and sand mixture falls into the outer drum and is conveyed to the separator for abrasive reconditioning.

The conical drum with its lower level in the horizontal plane prevents workpieces from rolling through the blast area. The workpiece transport is affected by the inclined rotation axis in a controlled staggered line. Frequent and thorough tumbling ensures excellent cleaning efficiency. The rotating speed of the barrel and the abrasive through-put are regulated. This leads to a constant blasting efficiency under all working conditions. The fully automatic control system increases the life time of the blast drum which can be easily serviced because of its smooth and simple surface. Because of the continuous rotation of the barrel and the helical conveyor the castings leave the machine free from abrasives. The compact design requires few safety elements. Due to the integration of the straight through barrel blast machine into a fully automatic production line, operators only come in contact with clean castings. Working places which are subject to dust, dirt and noise are eliminated.

The advantages of the straight through barrel blast cleaning machine are:

1. Reduction of production costs through integration of the shot blast process into the automatic production line.

2. Excellent wear resistance of the blast drum because of constant surface coverage.

3. Low maintenance costs due to solid design and simple surface exposed to wear.

4. Reduced transport costs due to the continuous flow of material which eliminates intermediate storage.

5. The machine can easily be integrated into existing lines by virtue of small floor area and absence of foundation pits.

6. Less operators are required in a fully automatic production line. Working places with bad environmental conditions can be eliminated.

7. The abrasive consumption is reduced to the absolute minimum by complete abrasive reclaim and a good seal on the blast drum.

## Figure 8

A ram cage blast machine for cleaning cylinder heads.

Cylinder blocks and heads require special purpose shot blast machines to ensure complete removal of complex cores and abrasives. The ram cage blast machines are designed specifically for this operation for automatic production. The workpieces are transported on a roller conveyor or slat-apron conveyor to the lifting table where they are automatically adjusted and pushed into an empty cage. The cage is designed to suit the workpiece configuration and the transport of the pieces to be blasted is effected in the cages. The cages are transferred through a sealing vestibule on to the supporting rollers with variable drive running throughout the length of the machine. The rotating cages are pushed through the blast cabinet at a specific cycle by a cylinder. The blast cabinet is equipped with several blast wheels fitted to the walls in the direction of the rotating axis. Leaving the blast cabinet, the cages are moved one after the other into the abrasive collecting vestibule where the abrasive is removed from the castings and reclaimed. In the cage unloading station the workpiece is pushed out of the cage on to a lifting table from where it is transported by an appropriate conveying system to the following operation. The empty cages are returned to the loading station. In order to operate several cage types the installation can be equipped with a cage exchange and cage store.
The operation principle of the ram cage installation is based on the continuous rotation of the workpieces around their longitudinal axis during the total cleaning process. This ensures that:

1. The abrasive angles of attack are always changing which improves the internal cleaning and the removal of fins. Therefore many subsequent fettling operations can be eliminated.

2. An excellent cleaning effect due to the continuous rotation thus preventing sand and abrasive to accumulate which absorbs the impact from the thrown abrasive.

3.  The abrasive reclaim following the
    cleaning process is effected fully
    automatically.  This is an
    important feature with regard to
    operating costs.

## SUMMARY

This brief paper has sought to
summarise some of the developments
over the last 30 years within the
automotive foundry industry.  The
developments which have been made have
not so much been made in the advancement
of technology but more so in the
application of the technology which has
been in use for many years.  However,
new generations of equipment have been
developed which makes the founding
operation more precise, less prone to
operator error, less labour intensive
and have improved the working
environment.

Sequence of function of the moulding machine

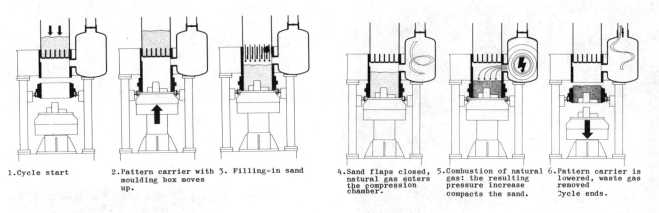

1. Cycle start

2. Pattern carrier with
   moulding box moves
   up.

3. Filling-in sand

4. Sand flaps closed,
   natural gas enters
   the compression
   chamber.

5. Combustion of natural
   gas: the resulting
   pressure increase
   compacts the sand.

6. Pattern carrier is
   lowered, waste gas
   removed
   Cycle ends.

Fig 1    The sequence of operation of the 'impact' method of
mould compaction

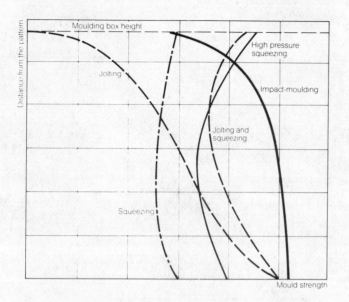

Fig 2    Comparison of mould strength with other compaction processes

Fig 3    One piece body core for a V8 engine block

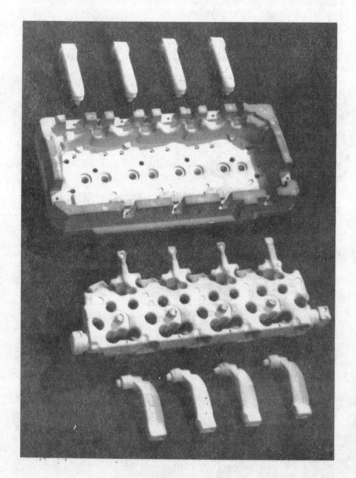

Fig 4    Complete set of cores for a cylinder head

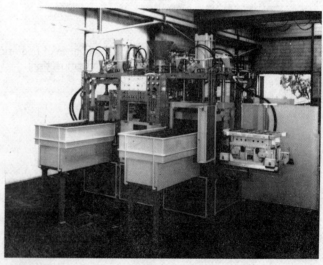

Fig 5    A two station core shooting machine with a capacity of 135 shots per hour

Fig 6    Automatic fettling machines

Fig 7    A straight through barrel type shot blast machine

Fig 8    A ram cage blast machine for cleaning cylinder heads

# C278/81

# Progress towards the introduction of HWBF hydraulic fluids

G B WOODGER, BA
BP Research Centre, Sunbury-on-Thames, Middlesex

SYNOPSIS   High Water Based Fluids, otherwise known as HWBF, are being introduced as replacements for conventional mineral oil hydraulic fluids in industrial hydraulic systems.   Hitherto such fluids have offered little more than anti-corrosion properties and fire resistance so that their usage has been largely limited to the hot metal working industry and mining.   However, with the development of new types of fluid with much improved anti-wear performance, the use of fluids in general industrial hydraulic applications, such as used in the motor industry, may be considered.   In such applications the use of HWBF in place of mineral oil should prove more economic as well as safer.

In changing from mineral oil to HWBF it is necessary to recognise the differences in fluid properties, many of which cannot be significantly changed by relatively small concentrations of chemical additives.   The main areas of performance improvement are those dependent on surface chemical effects, for example anti-corrosion and boundary lubrication.   Careful consideration of the design of the hydraulic equipment to ensure its compatibility and suitability for use with HWBF is necessary.   Equipment manufacturers are developing new generations of pumps, motors, valves etc for use with HWBF.

Systems are operating satisfactorily on HWBF where the necessary equipment conversion has been undertaken.   In the future, with purpose designed hydraulic systems, it is expected that HWBF will become established as the normal industrial hydraulic fluid for all but the most demanding of applications.

## INTRODUCTION

The earliest examples of hydraulic systems, such as simple presses and lifts, used water as the hydraulic medium to transmit force.   Such systems were designed to gain the advantage of intensifying a relatively small force to compress or raise objects.   As hydraulic systems became more widely used under extremes of working temperature and pressure, and the systems became more complex in design, the limitations of water became apparent.   Thus it could only be used over a limited temperature range, it possessed poor lubricating properties and gave rise to corrosion problems.   With the ready availability of mineral lubricating oils having particularly desirable characteristics, it was not surprising that they soon became established as the preferred fluid medium for the majority of hydraulic applications.   Water based fluids were retained for the less demanding systems where fire resistance was of major importance, e.g. in the hot metal working industry and mining. The fluids used in these systems have been little more than aqueous fluids inhibited to prevent the corrosion of ferrous metals.

Various factors are causing industry to reconsider the use of water based hydraulic fluids, now usually referred to as HWBF's or high water based fluids.   Firstly, it is recognised that the world's oil supplies are limited and new discoveries are not keeping pace with projected demand.   Political and other constraints tend to impose artificial controls on the availability of known sources of supply. The cost and availability of crude oil and the effect of this on the price of lubricating oils are becoming factors in any appraisal of long term investment.   A second factor is the increasing concern for safety in the working environment, where the inherent fire resistance of HWBF hydraulics compared with that of mineral oil is an important advantage.   The third factor is the very significant improvement in performance of the new generation of HWBF's, in particular in regard to anti-wear performance, which enables them to be considered for use in general industrial hydraulic applications, such as those typically used in the motor industry.

## Characteristics of HWBF fluids

The term HWBF is generally applied to hydraulic fluids comprising the addition of 2-10 per cent of a concentrate to water.   Typically 5 per cent of concentrate is used and the fluids are sometimes referred to as 5/95 fluids indicating the ratio of concentrate to water. When the concentrate is added to water it is required to dissolve or disperse to form a stable, homogeneous fluid medium which may take the form of a solution, colloidal solution or an emulsion; the latter may appear white and opaque, translucent, or clear and transparent depending on the droplet size of the internal phase.   The progressive development of HWBF for use in hydraulic systems has involved looking into the performance advantages of the alternative formulation approaches. A summary of the different types of fluid is given in Table 1.

The original oil based emulsifiable concentrates giving milky white emulsions were formulated to have reasonable anti-corrosion properties and hard water stability at an economic cost. More recently experience has shown that the inclusion of boundary lubricant additives can reduce wear and extend the application range of water based hydraulics. Such boundary lubricant additives react with the metal surfaces in sliding contact to form a film of low shear strength by chemical action or physical adsorption. Such films have been shown to reduce temperatures and wear rate when hydrodynamic lubricant films breakdown and metal to metal contact occurs between surface asperities (1). Formulations containing boundary lubricant additives have been shown to reduce wear in vane pumps and some successful formulations have been marketed.

Oil based emulsifiable concentrates with increased levels of surfactant and corrosion inhibitors have been developed to be stable in hard waters and to provide enhanced corrosion protection. Such formulations typically give translucent or transparent emulsions in waters of different qualities and hardness values.

Corrosion inhibited chemical solutions offer the advantage of avoiding the problems of stabilising emulsions in a range of water hardness. However, such fluids may themselves be sensitive to water quality giving rise to flocculent separation or deposits when diluted with hard water. The incorporation of boundary lubricant additives in chemical solutions incurs some difficulties as the active constituents need to be water soluble or at least water dispersible; in addition the boundary lubricant component is required to be selectively surface active where boundary lubrication conditions arise in rubbing contacts. Concentrates giving colloidal solutions in water offer the possibility of incorporating some measure of boundary lubrication performance but again such products are likely to be sensitive to water quality.

The formulation of products comprising emulsified boundary lubricant additives has extended the range of applications where HWBF hydraulic systems may be used. Formulations have been developed which in controlled testing in hydraulic pump test rigs give substantially reduced wear rates in metal to metal sliding contacts. Vane pumps and gear pumps have been employed to demonstrate such performance advantages. In addition work has been extended to factory trials.

The new generation of HWBF concentrates tend to form micro-emulsions when initially dispersed in water and the description 'micro-emulsion' has tended to be applied as a generic term. However, it could equally well be applied to other oil-based concentrates which give clear or translucent emulsions. The significant difference between the two types of product is the level of boundary lubricant performance additive. In oil-based formulations such a component may or may not be present and is in effect an optional extra whereas in the new generation of HWBF's it is the central formulation component. The importance of including such boundary lubricant additives will become evident in the discussion which follows.

Whatever form future development of HWBF hydraulic fluid takes will depend on how successfully the problems associated with each approach can be overcome. Using water as the major component will, however, dictate certain basic characteristics and it is important that industrial hydraulic equipment designers and manufacturers appreciate how the properties of HWBF differ from those of mineral oil. Many of the characteristics of water are scarcely changed by the addition of relatively small amounts of concentrate. Thus water is appreciably more dense than oil which has implications in terms of the initial start-up loading and the tendency for cavitation to occur. The thermal conductivity of water is much higher than mineral oil and its thermal capacity for a given temperature increase is more than double. Thus HWBF hydraulics will tend to run cooler and in some cases it may be possible to reduce the size of any heat exchanger fitted, provided that other temperature limiting factors are observed. The vapour pressure of water is much higher than typical mineral lubricating oils for a given temperature. This makes it necessary to limit the operating temperature of HWBF to about $50^{\circ}C$ in order to minimise cavitation and restrict evaporative loss. Water is somewhat less compressible than mineral lubricating oil which, on the one hand, will improve response in the hydraulic system, but on the other hand, will allow pressure shocks to be transmitted through the system.

The viscosity of water is less sensitive to temperature than that of mineral oil which will give more constant cycle times on production machinery and reduce warm up time on precision machine tools. The viscosity of water does not increase with pressure to the extent that occurs with mineral oil. While this means that HWBF gives less change in fluid flow characteristics with increase in pressure, it also means more significantly that HWBF has a much reduced ability to form hydrodynamic films which is a fundamental consideration in terms of the ability to lubricate loaded contacts in bearings and other areas of sliding contact (2). Whereas mineral oils may also be produced in a range of viscosities to suit particular requirements of flow, sealing or lubrication, the viscosity of water is to some extent, fixed. The viscosity of water may be increased by the addition of water soluble polymers. However, viscosity measurements, which are generally determined under low shear conditions, may be misleading as water soluble polymeric thickeners suffer permanent or temporary viscosity loss to a greater or lesser extent under high shear conditions. Thus the overall benefit of increasing the viscosity (determined under low shear conditions) will be rather less than expected in terms of the viscosity under high shear conditions in sliding contact zones.

In summary, water has a number of secondary benefits over mineral oil in terms of thermal properties and more stable viscosity but at the same time has some significant limitations; thus it has a more restricted operating temperature range, is more inclined to transmit shock and cavitate and has a much reduced ability to form

34

hydrodynamic lubricating films in loaded contacts. A summary of the differences between mineral oil and water are given in Table 2.

These comparisons of water and mineral oil refer to what may be termed bulk properties of the respective fluids. The characteristic bulk properties of water are not significantly altered by the inclusion of 5 per cent of an HWBF concentrate. However, properties dependent on surface activity, are more readily changed by the introduction of small amounts of additive concentrate.

In lubricating sliding contacts both the fluid bulk properties and surface activity are important. Wherever possible sliding contacts are designed to generate and maintain a hydrodynamic liquid film between the sliding surfaces. Where this is not possible the inclusion of boundary lubricant additives provides a major advantage as these react to form surface films which reduce wear. A detailed discussion of the mechanism is provided by Pruton et al (1).

The range of boundary lubricant additives are referred to as anti-wear or extreme pressure additives depending on the nature of their reactivity. With HWBF's it is possible to include additive components which contribute such surface reactivity. The presence of boundary lubricant additives in HWBF's is essential to compensate for the limited ability to form stable hydrodynamic lubricant films.

A second area where surface activity is important concerns corrosion protection. Water, with its ability to dissolve inorganic salts and the conductivity this affords, is particularly prone to cause corrosion of metals by galvanic action. The deposition of protective films of surface active chemicals under controlled conditions of alkalinity forms the basis of most water based anti-corrosion systems. Protection against ferrous metal corrosion is generally achieved by establishing a stable buffered level of alkalinity at pH 8.5-9.5 combined with careful selection of surface active chemicals. This system is specific to ferrous metals and is not necessarily compatible with other metals, which might be used in hydraulic systems. Certain specific inhibitors may be incorporated to protect copper, but it is not practicable to inhibit the corrosion of all metals. Thus metals which are attacked by alkalis, such as cadmium and zinc, and which cannot be readily protected by specific metal passivators should be avoided.

## Considerations in selecting and using HWBF

HWBF formulations are developed to produce stable concentrates which, on dilution with water, provide good anti-corrosion properties and anti-wear performance. Secondary factors are the ability of the concentrates to provide stable dilutions in waters of different hardness values and composition, and also the ability to resist microbial contamination. It should be noted that the quality of the dilution water is an important factor in determining the performance of HWBF's in terms of wear, corrosion and microbial resistance.

Various laboratory tests are used for screening the stability and corrosion properties of fluids. The two most important being the NCB 463/1970 specification and the 5th Luxembourg Report of the Mines Safety Commission of the Commission of European Communities. A summary of the main features of these specifications is given in Table 3. However, neither of these two sources include tests to evaluate the anti-wear performance. Since this is of major importance in converting hydraulic systems from mineral oil to HWBF, it was necessary to develop evaluation procedures to compare different fluids. A procedure has been adopted based on a Gerotor internal gear pump, Table 4. The comparative anti-wear performance of different fluids is assessed by the weight loss of the internal gear after a specified test duration. Running even small scale pump tests for evaluating fluids has been shown to offer further advantages. Thus it provides a more realistic assessment of the fluid's ability to prevent corrosion of ferrous metals, particularly cast iron, than static laboratory tests and it has also proved useful in assessing the dynamic stability of HWBF dilutions of the emulsion or micro-emulsion type.

As the development of HWBF progresses, evaluation procedures will undoubtedly be developed to assist the comparative assessment of fluids and the specification of performance levels.

Besides the more obvious requirements of stability, anti-wear and anti-corrosion performance, it is necessary to consider the compatibility of HWBF with all materials and components used in the hydraulic system. Thus items such as the hydraulic pumps, motors, seals, gaskets and hoses should be checked for compatibility. Seals, which may be satisfactory in terms of swell under static test conditions, may not prove satisfactory under dynamic conditions where the lubrication provided by HWBF dilutions is much poorer than for mineral oils. Metals used as surface treatments for ferrous metals, such as zinc and cadmium, may be attacked by alkaline HWBF's. In areas where evaporation of the water phase and condensation may occur, ferrous metals require protection. Thus hydraulic fluid reservoirs manufactured from mild steel need protection from condensation corrosion above the fluid level and on the underside of the covering lid. Conventional paints are frequently not acceptable and specially selected paints need to be used.

It is also necessary to consider the equipment required for preparing, storing and distributing the prepared dilution of HWBF concentrate in water. A static or mobile unit for preparation of the dilution in water to the required concentration is required. This may take the form of a tank with arrangements for metering in the respective components and circulating by means of a simple pump arrangement, or a venturi arrangement precalibrated to draw in the required amount of concentrate into a flow of water. Whichever method is used it is essential to ensure that a homogeneous mixture is obtained and that it is at the correct concentration.

To minimise the opportunities for microbial infection, mixing equipment should be cleaned after use. The storage of prepared HWBF dilutions in static holding tanks should be avoided as far as possible. Storage tanks should be fabricated from materials which can be readily cleaned and, if necessary, sterilised. Access for thorough cleaning should be provided. All reservoirs and tanks should be fitted with a cover or lid, preferably fixed, and fitted with a breather filter to prevent ingress of particulate or microbial contamination from the surrounding atmosphere.

HWBF hydraulic systems require sampling points to enable regular monitoring of the fluid condition in terms of stability, concentration, pH value and microbial presence.

Used or discarded HWBF dilutions need special consideration in terms of disposal. Fluids of the emulsion or micro-emulsion type need to be treated to separate off the main organic constituents as far as possible. Fluids of the synthetic aqueous solution type may sometimes be discharged in normal waste water effluent where the dilution factor is sufficient. However, major discharges of such fluids pose special problems and may require some other form of pre-treatment prior to disposal.

## Successful adoption of HWBF hydraulics

Whether the adoption of HWBF hydraulics is as a conversion of an existing system from a mineral oil hydraulic fluid or whether the system has been purpose designed to use HWBF, it is advisable for the user to confirm the selection of components and materials and recognise the characteristics of the fluid, if problems are to be avoided.

Thus the user will need to establish the necessary fluid mixing and monitoring equipment. He will need to clean and flush the system to remove manufacturing contaminants, accumulated debris and the residues of fluids previously used in the system either from in-service use or factory testing. HWBF will tend to remove and suspend some hydraulic system contaminants, and hence it is advisable to check and change filter elements following an initial flushing with the first HWBF charge. When starting up the hydraulic system and bringing the equipment into full operation, allow the pressures and flow to be brought up in stages so that trapped air is purged from the system and released in the reservoir rather than entrained in the fluid. Also check for fluid leakage at all joints and pipework connections. Leakage is more of a problem with HWBF because of its low viscosity and penetrating ability compared with typical mineral oils. Check the performance of the hydraulic equipment in terms of such criteria as cycle times, operating temperature and the fluid level in the reservoir. During the first few weeks it is advisable to check the system frequently, including the condition of the HWBF, in terms of stability, presence of contaminants and fluid strength. Samples drawn from the sampling point should always be taken with the fluid in circulation. If the suitability of any of the equipment is in doubt, it is useful to remove critical components, such as hydraulic pumps and motors, for inspection during shutdown periods to avoid unscheduled stoppages for maintenance during normal production periods.

The procedures outlined above for the selection of equipment and materials, for the hydraulic system design and for flushing, cleaning and commissioning the equipment have been used for the successful conversion of a number of hydraulic units from mineral oil hydraulic fluid to HWBF by a major European motor manufacturer. The experience gained encourages the belief that such conversions are a practicable proposition and that water based hydraulic fluids of the new generation of micro-emulsion HWBF type are suitable for use in many typical hydraulic applications used by manufacturing industry.

Cooperation between experienced equipment manufacturers, fluid suppliers and the user are essential if major problems and unnecessary expenditure are to be avoided. For the future attention is likely to be given towards minimising equipment conversion costs, improvements in hydraulic equipment performance, in particular pump and motor design, and the formulation of even better HWBF concentrates which give dilutions with greater water quality tolerance, enhanced anti-wear and anti-corrosion performance.

REFERENCES

(1)  PRUTON C.F., TURNBULL D. and DLOUHY G. Mechanism of action of organic chlorine and sulphur compounds in extreme pressure lubrication. J Inst Pet, 1946, 32, 90.

(2)  DOWSON D. and HIGGINSON G.R. Elasto-hydrodynamic lubrication. Pergamon Press, 1966.

## Table 1    Different types of HWBF hydraulic fluid

| Concentrate | In Use Dilution |
|---|---|
| 1. Oil based emulsifiable concentrates containing surfactants, corrosion inhibitors and coupling agents, with or without additional boundary lubricant additives. | Oil-in-water emulsions which appear milky white, translucent, or clear and transparent, depending on internal phase droplet size. |
| 2. Water based chemical concentrates containing corrosion inhibitors, chelating agents and water soluble dyes, with or without additional boundary lubricant additives. | Clear or colloidal solutions usually dyed a characteristic colour for identification. |
| 3. Boundary lubricant additive based emulsifiable concentrates containing surfactants and corrosion inhibitors | Emulsions of additive in water which appear clear or creamy white, depending on internal phase droplet size. |

## Table 2    Physical data on water and mineral oil

| Property | | Water | Mineral Oil* |
|---|---|---|---|
| Density at $20^{o}C$ | g/ml | 0.998 | 0.876 |
| Coefficient of Cubic Thermal Expansion    at $20^{o}C$ | $^{o}C^{-1}$ | $2.07 \times 10^{-4}$ | $9.55 \times 10^{-4}$ |
| at $40^{o}C$ | $^{o}C^{-1}$ | $3.85 \times 10^{-4}$ | - |
| Thermal Conductivity (k)    at $20^{o}C$ | $W/m^{o}C$ | 0.59 | 0.132 |
| at $40^{o}C$ | $W/m^{o}C$ | 0.62 | 0.131 |
| Specific Heat $(C_p)$    at $20^{o}C$ | $J/g^{o}C$ | 4.179 | 1.871 |
| at $40^{o}C$ | $J/g^{o}C$ | 4.175 | 1.945 |
| Compressibility (Isothermal) at $20^{o}C$ at $6.89 \times 10^{4}$ kPa | | | |
| Secant Bulk Modulus | kPa | $2.45 \times 10^{6}$ | $1.98 \times 10^{6}$ |
| Tangent Bulk Modulus | kPa | $2.68 \times 10^{6}$ | $2.24 \times 10^{6}$ |
| Secant Compressibility | $kPa^{-1}$ | $4.09 \times 10^{-7}$ | $5.05 \times 10^{-7}$ |
| Tangent Compressibility | $kPa^{-1}$ | $3.73 \times 10^{-7}$ | $4.46 \times 10^{-7}$ |
| Absolute Viscosity    at $20^{o}C$ | cP | 1.01 | 74.5 |
| at $40^{o}C$ | cP | 0.65 | 27.6 |
| at $60^{o}C$ | cP | 0.47 | 13.1 |
| Pressure-Viscosity Coefficient at $6.89 \times 10^{4}$ kPa    at $30^{o}C$ | $Pa^{-1}$ | $5.00 \times 10^{-7}$ | $2.04 \times 10^{-5}$ |
| at $75^{o}C$ | $kPa^{-1}$ | $7.85 \times 10^{-7}$ | - |
| Vapour Pressure    at $20^{o}C$ | kPa | 2.34 | $9.2 \times 10^{-8}$ |
| at $40^{o}C$ | kPa | 7.38 | $1.6 \times 10^{-6}$ |
| at $60^{o}C$ | kPa | 19.92 | $1.5 \times 10^{-5}$ |

\*   Typical HVI ISO 32 viscosity grade mineral oil

Table 3    Main requirements of NCB 463/1970 and 5th Luxembourg report

| Property | NCB 463/1970 | 5th Luxembourg Report |
|---|---|---|
| Stability of Emulsion | 5% volume in specified hard waters. 168 hrs at 70°C. No creaming >0.1 ml/100 ml | Ageing Stability. Modified ASTM D943. 200 hrs at 95°C. pH value $\geq$ 4. Stability Test. Sealed tubes stored at 20°C and 50°C for 600 hrs. $\leq$ 5 mm cream |
| Anti-Corrosion Characteristics | 2% volume in 0.05N NaCl. No rusting or pitting after 24 hrs in modified IP 135 | Steel, copper, zinc, aluminium, cadmium, brass, singly and in set pairs, part immersed for 28 days at 35°C. Limits on wt gain and loss. |
| Seal Compatibility | Standard rubber immersed 168 hrs at 70°C. Volume change 2 to 6%. | Selected rubbers immersed 21 days at 60°C. Volume -2% to +4%. Shore hardness $\pm$ 4. |
| Foaming Tendency | General statement of suitability. No specified requirement. | Air blowing through diffuser stone 25°C/50°C/25°C. 300 ml max foam. |
| Wear Test | No requirement. | No requirement for low viscosity HF-A type fluids. |

Table 4    Gerotor gear pump test

| | |
|---|---|
| Conditions: | |
| Pressure | 14 bar |
| Temperature | 50 °C |
| Pump Speed | 1450 rpm |
| Duration | 50 hours |
| Record: | |
| Weight Loss inner Gerotor element | |
| Condition of Gerotor cartridge | |
| Condition of return line filter | |

# C279/81

# Air cooled forgings

P S MONCKTON, BSc, D WHITTAKER, BMet, PhD,
P E IRVING, BSc, PhD, and K SACHS, Sc, PhD, DSc
GKN Technology Limited, Wolverhampton

SYNOPSIS   The paper discusses the background to the development of micro-alloyed forging steels, as a means of eliminating heat treatment and hence reducing the cost of forgings, albeit at some sacrifice of mechanical properties other than strength.   The rather complex interrelationships are documented, between composition, as-forged microstructure and achievable mechanical properties; particular emphasis is put on the requirement for close control over forging conditions.   Tensile strength levels up to around 1050 N/mm$^2$ can be achieved, together with fatigue strength roughly equivalent to hardened and tempered grades of similar strength level and toughness values intermediate between hardened and tempered steels and cast irons.

## 1   INTRODUCTION

In engineering, there are three methods of generating the shape that the designer has specified:

Hacking away at a solid block to carve out the finished product

Casting in a pre-shaped mould

Forming the material while it is in a plastic condition

Each of these methods has undergone profound technological changes.   As far as ferrous materials are concerned, the casting process has called in the first instance for compositions that lower the melting point and improve fluidity, and in more recent times for methods of modifying the structure to compensate for the poor mechanical properties resulting from the high carbon content required for optimum castability.   The outcome is a process that offers the greatest complexity of shape, the lowest cost, and mechanical properties that are adequate for many applications.

Forging, on the other hand, can make use of heat treatable steels which can offer the best combination of mechanical properties at the lowest cost.   Moreover, the forging process itself imposes a directionality of properties which makes forged components exceptionally tough.

Recent developments in fibre reinforced composites have led to the formal recognition of the fact that design and manufacture are inseparable, because the designer has to specify the location of the reinforcement as well as the external shape of the component.   A glance at the flow lines in two typical automotive forgings (Figure 1) shows that this has been an immanent truth all along.   Over the centuries, the blacksmith performing his functions of component designer, tooling engineer, and process metallurgist, has built up the experience which ensures that in present day

forgings the flow lines run parallel to the principal stresses and the component is not stressed severely across the flow lines.

When steel is forged and then hardened and tempered it has a fine grain size and the best combination of strength and toughness that can be obtained.   Traditionally forgings have been used for engineering components and they continue to be used where stresses are severe.

Technical progress in casting and forging has been given additional drive by parallel developments in component design and value engineering.   The improvement in mechanical properties of castings has led to a creeping transfer of manufacturing route from forging to casting, starting with the most lightly stressed components and extending progressively to a wider range of applications.   This has led to a systematic intensification of the scrutiny for each component:   What are the real stress levels imposed?   Is it possible to reduce cost by a slight reduction in the specified level of Charpy notch impact toughness without risk of failure?

When components are looked at closely in this way, it may well turn out that it is inappropriate to make a dramatic change from forging to casting, but there may still be some margin for backing off from the highest attainable mechanical properties if there are savings to be made.

One direction, which the forging industry has taken in the pursuit of savings, is the elimination of heat treatment.   The actual cost of heat treatment depends on the component and the specification.   At one extreme is the forging that is delivered with no heat treatment at all, where the saving is zero.   At the other extreme is the complex component in a plain carbon steel that has to be water quenched.   The heat treatment sequence can be very elaborate and correspondingly expensive:

Forge

Normalise

Harden

Temper (check hardness; check for cracking)

Straighten

Stress relieve (check hardness, check straightness, return distorted components to normalising)

How is it possible to dispense with heat treatment? Two technical developments have created the opportunity:

Close control of the heating, forging and cooling

The development of medium carbon micro-alloyed steel

One function of normalising is to ensure a uniformly fine grain size throughout the forging. This in turn guarantees a fine grain size in the heat treated component (and helps to reduce distortion in hardening). In forgings that are control-cooled from the press, erratic grain growth has to be prevented by control of the forging operation. In practice that calls for rigid control of heating practice and timing of heating cycles and forging rhythms.

With regard to steel development, the option of using air hardening steels - i.e. steels that transform to martensite on air cooling - has been dismissed on the grounds of cost. The structure produced in plain carbon and low alloy steels on air cooling is a mixture of pearlite and ferrite and it is this structure that is utilised. For some components its mechanical properties are adequate without modification, but the real breakthrough has been to adapt the concepts of micro-alloying originally developed for structural steel in the form of plate, pipe, sections and bars, to medium carbon steels. Precipitation of vanadium carbide in the pro-eutectoid ferrite, and in the ferrite lamellae of the pearlite, offers a further strength increment which brings forgings cooled from the press into the range of strength and fatigue resistance equivalent to hardened and tempered steel. This paper documents the mechanical properties of such forgings.

## 2    INFLUENCE OF STRUCTURE ON PROPERTIES

### 2.1.    Ferrite/Pearlite Structures

If a medium carbon forging steel is cooled in still air from the forging temperature, the microstructure produced will consist primarily of pearlite with ferrite nucleated at prior austenite grain boundaries or within the austenite grains at inclusions. A typical example of such a microstructure is given in Figure 2. For a structure of this type, strength is controlled by the microstructural parameters: volume fractions of ferrite and pearlite, ferrite grain size and pearlite interlamellar spacing. Indeed, work at GKN Group Technological Centre has verified that strength can be related to microstructure in this class of steel using the published

set of regression equations of Gladman, McIvor and Pickering (1) i.e.

Tensile Strength = (in N/mm$^2$)

$$15.44 \{ f_\alpha^{1/3} [16.0 + 74.2(\sqrt{\%Nf}) + 1.18d^{-\frac{1}{2}}] + (1-f_\alpha^{1/3}) [46.7 + 0.23So^{-\frac{1}{2}}] + 6.3(\%Si) \} \quad (1)$$

Yield Stress = (in N/mm$^2$)

$$15.44 \{ f_\alpha^{1/3} [2.3 + 3.8(\%Mn) + 1.13d^{-\frac{1}{2}}] + (1-f_\alpha^{1/3}) [11.6 + 0.25So^{-\frac{1}{2}}] + 4.1(\%Si) + 27.6 (\sqrt{\%Nf}) \} \quad (2)$$

where $f_\alpha$ = volume fraction of ferrite

d = ferrite grain size in mm

$S_o$ = interlamellar spacing of pearlite in mm

$N_f$ = "free" nitrogen content i.e. nitrogen in interstitial solid solution.

In the absence of any other strengthening mechanism, the maximum strength achievable with this type of microstructure would be derived from an almost fully pearlitic structure (say 95% pearlite or more). If a typical value for forgings produced under normal commercial forging practice of around $2.5 \times 10^{-4}$mm is assumed for $S_o$, then equation (1) indicates that the maximum achievable tensile strength would be around 750/800 N/mm$^2$ and indeed, plain carbon steels are currently utilised to produce connecting rod forgings directly from the press with tensile strengths in this range.

### 2.2    Precipitation Hardening

The maximum strength level achievable with a ferrite/pearlite microstructure, derived by air-cooling after forging, of around 750/800 N/mm$^2$ (as discussed in the previous section) would be sufficient to serve only a small portion of the market for forgings. However, the as-forged strength can be augmented by introducing a further barrier to dislocation movement in the form of a fine precipitate.

In order to produce a "precipitation hardening increment", it is necessary that the particular precipitate concerned should be capable of being taken into solution in the austenite at the soaking temperature prior to hot working and then of being precipitated out of solution in a fine form during cooling after hot working.

In the case of medium carbon steels, it is found that vanadium carbonitride is the precipitate which best satisfies these criteria. In particular, niobium carbonitride, which is often utilised in lower carbon steels, is found to have insufficient solubility at normal soaking temperatures in medium carbon steels. The use of a titanium addition could possibly be considered but this element is generally avoided in forgings which require subsequent machining.

Vanadium carbonitride precipitates in an extremely fine form, and the mode of precipitation has been observed to be "interphase" (2) i.e. precipitation occurs in row formation at the moving austenite/ferrite transformation front. Precipitation occurs both in the pro-eutectoid ferrite and the ferrite lamellae of the pearlite as indicated in Figures 3 and 4.

The magnitude of the strengthening increment is controlled by the volume fraction and mean size of the precipitates, according to the relationship derived by Gladman et al (3)

$$\Delta\sigma_y \text{(in N/mm}^2\text{)} = \frac{5.9\ \sqrt{f}}{\bar{x}}\ \ell n\ \left(\frac{\bar{x}}{2.5 \times 10^{-4}}\right) \quad (3)$$

where $\Delta\sigma_y$ is the yield strength increment,

$f$ is the volume fraction of precipitates,

$\bar{x}$ is mean planar intercept diameter in $\mu$m

$(\bar{x} = \bar{D}\sqrt{\frac{2}{3}}$ where $\bar{D}$ is the mean precipitate diameter)

For a measured (by electron microscope observations) value for $\bar{D}$ of around 5nm (50Å), the predicted increment for a vanadium addition of around 0.1 wt%, using equation (3) is close to the value of around 180 N/mm$^2$, derived by taking the difference between observed tensile or yield strengths and those calculated using equations (1) and (2), which do not allow for a precipitation increment.

A systematic study by Brandis et al (4) related the increment in 0.2% proof stress to the vanadium content "in solution" at room temperature. As in the present paper, the "increment" was determined from the difference between predictions from regression equations (1) and actual measurements. The vanadium content in solution was estimated by electrolytic extraction of carbides; the fraction that was chemically dissolved in the electrolyte was found to correlate very well with the increment in proof stress (see Figures 5 and 6). Clearly the effect is too strong to be attributed to solution hardening. Evidently the vanadium "in solution" had its origin partly in extremely fine precipitates and partly, as the German authors believe, in coherent clusters. Fig. 5 shows that the fraction of vanadium "in solution" in a steel with about 0.1% V solution treated in the range 1000 - 1200°C is in the range 50-80%, i.e. 0.05 - 0.08% V. According to Fig. 6 the proof stress increment is 26 N/mm$^2$ per 0.01% V "in solution". For a steel with a total vanadium content of 0.1% this corresponds to an increment of 130 - 208 N/mm$^2$, in good agreement with the value of 180 N/mm$^2$ found in the present work.

## 3  CONTROL OF MICROSTRUCTURE

The important microstructural parameters, which have significant influences on achievable strength levels, have been indicated in Section 2. These parameters are in turn controlled in a rather complex manner by various compositional factors and by the forging conditions, finish forging temperature and cooling rate after forging. The major interrelationships between compositional and forging conditions and resultant microstructural parameters are shown in Figure 7.

The influences of individual changes in composition or forging conditions are indicated below:

(a) A change in carbon content primarily alters the pearlite volume fraction.

(b) Altering the Mn content, because of its influence in depressing austenite → ferrite transformation temperature, affects pearlite volume fraction, interlamellar spacing, pearlite colony size and ferrite grain size.

(c) Changes in V level affect principally the precipitation increment but it should also be remembered that, as V is combining with carbon which would otherwise form cementite, the pearlite volume fraction is also affected.

(d) The finish forging temperature, i.e. the temperature at which the austenite last recrystallises during hot working, controls the austenite grain size produced. This parameter in turn influences the amount of ferrite, as this phase is primarily nucleated at austenite grain boundaries, and also the grain size of the final ferrite/pearlite microstructure. The combined effect of a lower pearlite volume fraction and a finer grain size in forgings finished at low temperatures, on resultant mechanical properties is shown schematically in Figure 8.

(e) Cooling rate after forging has a number of effects. Firstly, an acceleration in cooling rate produces an increase in pearlite content above that anticipated under equilibrium conditions. Secondly, accelerated cooling would be expected to produce a refinement in ferrite/pearlite grain size, because of a depression in transformation temperature, but this influence is apparently relatively minor within the range of experiments carried out to date.

Finally, increased cooling rate causes precipitation hardening to go through a maximum; initially a refinement in particle size causes an increase in increment but, at rapid cooling rates, some precipitation is partially suppressed and the volume fraction of precipitate reduced.

These effects of cooling rate combine to give an influence on as-forged strength as shown schematically in Figure 9.

These results are in broad agreement with those of Engineer and von den Steinen (5), whose cooling rate range from 0.033 to 0.83°C/sec places them on the steeply rising branch of the curve in Figure 9, although differences in experimental details invalidate direct quantitative comparisons.

From the above discussion, it is clear that a detailed knowledge of the influences of forging conditions and facilities to control those conditions are required for selection of the correct compositional limits, to achieve a specified range of mechanical properties in a given component.

# 4 MECHANICAL PROPERTIES ATTAINABLE

Following the early development work carried out collaboratively between European automotive manufacturers and forging companies, and in particular between Daimler Benz and Stahlwerke Südwestfalen (6), a number of compositional and property specifications for vanadium micro-alloyed steels were drawn up.

These specifications given in Table 1, are all aimed at the 800/900 N/mm$^2$ tensile strength level. In tensile strength, this approximates to the requirement of the BS970 "S" quality for hardened and tempered grades. However, if the full property requirements for the hardened and tempered qualities are examined (Table 2) it is clear that sacrifices have been made in terms of proof stress/tensile strength ratio and impact toughness.

Starting from the base of these early specifications, it is possible to increase strength to compete with BS970 "T" quality and above, by making a number of adjustments to composition and hence to resultant microstructure. These potential modifications have been investigated in a number of laboratories, including the GKN Group Technological Centre, and the general observations are discussed in the following sub-sections.

## 4.1 Increase in Pearlite Volume Fraction

The most straightforward, and cheapest, method of increasing tensile strength, in the as-forged condition, is to increase carbon content and hence pearlite content.

Table 3 presents a number of possible compositions for higher carbon grades of micro-alloyed steels. The mechanical properties quoted in the table indicate that, although tensile strength can be raised by this method, the relative influence on proof stress is low, as proof stress is less dependent on pearlite content, and hence the proof/tensile ratio is lowered further. Also, there is a substantial deterioration in impact toughness as tensile strength is increased.

## 4.2 Increase in Precipitation Hardening Increment

Increasing vanadium level provides further precipitation hardening and is clearly an alternative (though more expensive) method for increasing strength. Table 4 presents a few potential compositional ranges and indicates that the advantage of this technique is that the increments on proof and tensile strength are similar and hence the proof/tensile ratio is improved.

However, precipitation hardening is found to have similar deleterious effects on impact toughness to increasing pearlite fraction, for a given increase in tensile strength.

## 4.3 Refinement in Grain Size

The only means of improving the combination of tensile strength and impact toughness is to refine the grain size of the as-forged structure.

It has not been possible to identify a means of introducing a precipitate which will inhibit austenite recrystallisation and grain growth at hot forging temperatures. Therefore, the only means available for refining austenite grain size is the expedient of maintaining as low a finish forging temperature as possible (discussed in section 3).

However, for a given prior austenite grain size, it is possible to derive a finer ferrite/pearlite structure by making compositional adjustments, which will depress transformation temperature. This concept has led to the development by the British Steel Corporation of a range of "Vanard" grades with increased manganese levels as compared with the original specifications (compare Table 5 with Table 1).

These higher manganese grades have improved proof/tensile strength ratios and impact toughnesses compared with the previous family of lower manganese steels. Impact toughnesses are, however, still significantly inferior to the minimum requirements for the hardened and tempered grades.

However, one note of caution must be sounded. To date, these steels have been used for trials on small section forgings only (<20mm). There are some indications however that the properties attainable by this approach might be more cooling rate sensitive than for the earlier family of micro-alloyed steels. At large ruling sections, where cooling rate is slow enough to allow transformation to occur at higher temperatures, the improvements in grain size and hence in resultant strength and impact toughness may be considerably diminished.

# 5 FRACTURE TOUGHNESS

The toughness of a micro-alloyed steel, as measured by an impact energy criterion, is clearly inferior to that of a conventional hardened and tempered grade. However, in order to assess the significance of this difference in service, fracture toughness tests have been carried out and the resultant $K_{IC}$ values for a micro-alloyed steel (49 Mn VS3) and a number of hardened and tempered grades have been compared in Table 6.

Conversion of the $K_{IC}$ values to the elastic-plastic fracture parameter J allows use of the recently derived J design curve (7) to calculate crack sizes for catastrophic fracture at stresses approaching net section yield. Such calculations show (Table 6) that for 49 Mn VS3 critical defect sizes are greater than any likely forging defect. However, the higher strength micro-alloyed steels now being developed may have toughness limitations. They will have reduced toughness and will operate at higher stress levels should they, on emergency overload, be compelled to deform. Clearly, safety critical components should bend and not break under such circumstances.

For certain applications, where high rate loading occurs, impact test data may be relevant in toughness assessment as cleavage crack initiation beneath a stress concentration may be the critical event.

## 6    FATIGUE PERFORMANCE

For most automotive components, the performance criterion of major importance is the resistance to fatigue.

Fatigue data for micro-alloyed steels, as published by steelmakers, in Europe and the UK have largely been determined using load control in a rotating bend test. In essence, these results have shown that micro-alloyed steels possess similar fatigue properties to conventional hardened and tempered steels at the same tensile strength level. A typical example of the published data is shown in Fig. 10. These data, produced by Frodl et al (6), in fact indicate that the results for micro-alloyed steel are at the top end of the scatter band encountered with hardened and tempered Ck45.

Fatigue tests, carried out at the GKN laboratories on test pieces where the position of failure initiation is at a machined surface (e.g. tension compression tests on smooth fatigue test-pieces under strain control; and also compressive bend tests in load control on "one throw" sections cut from forged crankshafts) have shown that micro-alloyed steels can give comparable fatigue properties to hardened and tempered grades of the same tensile strength quality, although in most of these tests the hardened and tempered material tended to be somewhat lower in the strength band for the relevant quality. A typical example of these results is shown in Fig. 11, which refers to the tests on crankshaft throws (8).

Other rig tests, on components which are used in service in the un-machined condition, suggest that any minor differences in inherent material fatigue properties will in any case be masked by the variations introduced by the presence of defects in the as-forged surface (8).

On the subject of fatigue performance of the final component, one "hidden" benefit of micro-alloyed steels is the reduction in levels of distortion compared with hardened and tempered components and hence the reduced requirement for straightening, either by the forger or during subsequent machining operations. A detailed monitoring of distortions occurring during the machining of a particular crankshaft forging, within the GKN Group, has shown that a change in material from a hardened and tempered grade to a micro-alloyed steel can reduce the "bow" produced quite significantly.

It is established (9) that cold straightening a hardened and tempered steel can reduce the fatigue life at a given stress level by as much as 30-50%.

## 7    PRACTICAL IMPLICATIONS

Evidently the tensile strength of micro-alloyed steels is in line with hardened and tempered steels, up to the strength levels most commonly used for engineering components; work is in hand to extend the range to 1100 N/mm$^2$. The mechanical property data available up to the present are summarised in Table 6, the figures for micro-alloyed steels are based on provisional proposals for the revision of BS970. The promise of a 'V' grade is indicated, but the spaces allowed for test results are left blank. Table 6 compares the properties of micro-alloyed forging steels on the one hand and cast irons on the other.

It is clear from the Table that micro-alloyed steels are in the same category as hardened and tempered steels for strength and obviously superior to cast irons. As far as ductility and toughness are concerned they are intermediate between heat treated steels and cast iron, and the same applies with respect to cost.

A convenient way to look at the likely role of micro-alloyed steels is that they are not just half-way between conventional low alloy steels and cast iron, but an opportunity to extend the savings that have been found possible by the use of castings to components of higher strength where cast iron is unsuitable. The cost reduction is likely to be less than for cast iron but for many components it can still be substantial. In micro-alloyed steels, the strength is obtained by precipitation of vanadium carbide and this mechanism is much less sensitive to slow cooling than the transformation of austenite. As a result the high strength of micro-alloyed steels can be achieved over a very wide range of cross-sections (with some reservations). Hardened and tempered forgings of large cross-section would need low-alloy steel so that a saving of prime steel cost is added to the saving on the heat treatment operations.

In practice each component will have to be examined separately, and this applies both to cost savings and to suitability for purpose. Nevertheless a few general comments on the latter topic may be appropriate.

For automotive components the most important material property is resistance to fatigue. This cannot be readily characterised by a simple test parameter because fatigue curves are not parallel. Fatigue resistance is influenced by many extraneous factors beyond the mechanical properties of the steel. The benefits of reduced distortion and the elimination of straightening have been referred to already.

As regards the fatigue properties of the steel itself, to a crude approximation high tensile strength is accompanied by high fatigue resistance, so that the strength level of micro-alloyed steels can help identify which components are worth examining in detail. Within the framework of such an examination it will be necessary to look closely at the other mechanical properties and to decide whether the loss of ductility and toughness is tolerable in the selected application.

An important property in this context is the proof stress: the designer will be anxious to avoid a permanent "set" of the component when subjected to an unpredicted peak load. The proof ratio of steels cooled from the press is slightly lower than that of hardened and tempered steels. Of the currently available micro-alloyed grades the best proof ratios are offered by the higher manganese grades (Table 5). There are two reasons for this, both related to the action of the manganese in depressing transformation temperature:

a) the refinement in ferrite grain size and of pearlite interlamellar spacing have beneficial effects, of similar magnitude, on both proof stress and tensile strength (consider equations 1 and 2 in section 2.1 ).

b) because of this refinement in grain size, a given tensile strength level can be achieved at lower pearlite volume fractions. For the reasons discussed in Section 4.1 this leads to an appreciable improvement in proof ratio.

However, as discussed previously, the dependence on the action of manganese in depressing transformation temperature, makes the properties achievable with these steels more sensitive to variations in cooling rate.

Ductility and toughness involve more complex considerations and results of mechanical tests, even the most sophisticated ones, are not very helpful. The practical concern is to avoid fracture under extreme overload; in the case of automotive components, under conditions of abuse or accident. Two factors operate in favour of safety in motor vehicles: components are generally fairly small in section so that defect or crack propagation is not likely to proceed under plane strain conditions; and the vehicle is a complex assembly rather than a rigid structure so that shock loads are damped out.

In components where in-service load data have not been measured, meaningful predictions of the consequences of changing to a low toughness material are not possible. Use can be made of the component material proof strength, this being the maximum stress which the component could ever encounter. At the proof stress, the component should be tough enough to withstand the presence of manufacturing defects of a size defined by quality control procedures, without catastrophic fracture.

A better analysis could be performed if service load data are available, as well as a complete stress analysis of the component. In principle, at least, the probability of fracture from a given defect size can be calculated by using these data, in conjunction with fracture toughness information. However, such a quantitative approach is some way in the future, given present limitations on fracture mechanics and application of defect detection techniques.

It is clear that high toughness components will be more reliable or safer than low toughness components under variable amplitude loading. It is also clear that a move to lower toughness materials could require greater emphasis on quality control procedures, as has proved to be the case with cast irons.

Low toughness spheroidal graphite cast irons with a pearlite matrix have been used successfully in many applications and Table 1 shows that micro-alloyed steels are superior to these irons with respect to both strength and toughness.

These qualitative considerations are not rigorous enough to justify the use of micro-alloyed forging steels for any particular component, but they form the basis for selecting the most likely candidate for detailed examination. Each motor manufacturer has a well-established approval procedure, involving various test programmes, mostly culminating in vehicle tests. Unfortunately these procedures are wearisome and expensive and they will not be implemented unless there are significant potential savings and firm indications of likely success. Such pointers can be provided by life prediction procedures, based on recorded stress histories, fatigue damage prediction relating the fatigue resistance characteristics of the material to the stress cycles imposed on the component, and rig tests on components under realistic conditions.

## 8   CONCLUSIONS

Cost savings are possible for many components operating at high stresses. They can be achieved by using micro-alloyed forging quality steels cooled from the press under controlled conditions. The savings arise from the elimination of heat treatment and of subsidiary processing arising from the need to correct distortion in heat treatment. Even greater savings are possible in heavy sections used at high strength, where heat treatment calls for the use of alloy steels.

Micro-alloyed steels are available over the strength range from 850 to 1000 $N/mm^2$ and work is in progress for the development of compositions offering a tensile strength of 1100 $N/mm^2$. Fatigue resistance is broadly equivalent to hardened and tempered steels at the same strength levels.

Ductility and toughness are somewhat inferior to heat treated forgings but substantially higher than for castings that have been used successfully in similar applications at lower stress levels (e.g. crankshafts). Thus micro-alloyed forgings offer an opportunity to reduce costs in applications where the use of castings would be inappropriate.

## 9   ACKNOWLEDGEMENTS

The authors wish to thank the directors of GKN Forgings Limited and the GKN Group Technological Centre for permission to publish this paper, and many colleagues at the Centre for their contribution to the experimental work and the provision of a considerable volume of background information.

## REFERENCES

(1)   T Gladman, I.D. McIvor and F.B.Pickering; J.I.S.I., 210, December 1972, pp.916-930.

(2)   G.L.Dunlop, C.J.Carlsson and G.Frimodig; Met. Trans. A., 9A, February 1978, pp.261-266.

(3) T.Gladman, D.Dulieu and I.D.McIvor; "Micro-alloying 75", Conference Proceedings, pp.32-55.

(4) H.Brandis, E.Schmidtmann, A.v.d. Steinen and S.Engineer, Thyssen Edelst. Techn. Ber. 1978, 4 (1), pp.3-20.

(5) S.Engineer and A.v.d. Steinen; Thyssen Edelst. Techn. Ber. 1980, 6 (2), pp.85-89.

(6) D.Frodl, A.Randak and K.Vetter; Härterei-Teschnische Miteilungen, 1974, 29 (3), pp.169-175.

(7) C.E.Turner, Proc. ICF-5, Cannes 1981, 3, pp.1167-1189.

(8) P.E.Irving and R.G.Rebbeck; unpublished work at GKN Group Technological Centre.

(9) A.P.Zhigun et al; Metallovedenie i Termicheskaya Obrabotka Metallov, April 1980, No.4, pp.23-25.

Table 1    Typical compositional and mechanical property specifications, issued around 1975

| CHEMICAL COMPOSITION | | | | | | | MECHANICAL PROPERTIES | | | | | |
|---|---|---|---|---|---|---|---|---|---|---|---|---|
| C | Mn | Si | S | P | V | Total N | 0.2% Proof Stress $N/mm^2$ | UTS $N/mm^2$ | Elong % | R of A % | Hardness BHN | Impact Energy at Room temp. |
| 0.42/ 0.47 | 0.6/ 1.0 | 0.6 max | 0.045 0.065 | 0.035 max | 0.08/ 0.13 | – | 500 min | 800/ 900 | 8 min | 20 min | | 15J (DVM "U") notch |
| 0.40/ 0.46 | 1.0/ 1.2 | 0.6 max | 0.04/ 0.06 | 0.035 max | 0.08/ 0.13 | 0.03 max | 500 min | 800 min | 15 min | – | 245/ 290 | – |
| 0.44/ 0.54 | 0.6/ 1.0 | 0.15/ 0.6 | 0.045/ 0.065 | 0.035 max | 0.08/ 0.13 | – | 450 min | 780/ 900 | – | – | – | – |

Table 2    BS970 hardened and tempered qualities

| Quality | Tensile Strength | Min 0.2% Proof Stress $(N/mm^2)$ | Min Elongation (%) | Min Impact Energy at R.T. (J) |
|---|---|---|---|---|
| R | 700 - 850 | 495 | 17 | 54 |
| S | 770 - 920 | 555 | 15 | 54 |
| T | 850 - 1000 | 630 | 1_ | 54 |
| U | 920 - 1080 | 710 | 12 | 47 |

Table 3    The effect of varying carbon content on the mechanical properties of micro-alloyed steels

|  | C | Mn | Si | S | P | V | Tensile Strength $(N/mm^2)$ | 0.2% Proof Stress $(N/mm^2)$ | Min Elong. (%) | Impact Energy at RT("U" Notch) (J) |
|---|---|---|---|---|---|---|---|---|---|---|
| Increasing Carbon | 0.40/0.45 | 0.6/1.0 | 0.6 max | 0.045/0.065 | 0.035 max | 0.08/0.13 | 750/830 | 465 min | 15 | 16 |
|  | 0.45/0.50 | 0.6/1.0 | 0.6 max | 0.045/0.065 | 0.035 max | 0.08/0.13 | 780/870 | 485 min | 13 | 13 |
|  | 0.50/0.55 | 0.6/1.0 | 0.6 max | 0.045/0.065 | 0.035 max | 0.08/0.13 | 825/900 | 500 min | 12 | 12 |
|  | 0.55/0.60 | 0.6/1.0 | 0.6 max | 0.045/0.065 | 0.035 max | 0.08/0.13 | 875/950 | 525 min | 12 | 9 |

Table 4    The effect of varying vanadium content on the mechanical properties of micro-alloyed steels

|  | C | Mn | Si | P | S | V | Tensile Strength $(N/mm^2)$ | 0.2% Proof Stress $(N/mm^2)$ | Min. Elong. (%) | Impact Energy at R.T. ("U" Notch) (J) |
|---|---|---|---|---|---|---|---|---|---|---|
| Increasing Vanadium | 0.45/0.50 | 0.6/1.0 | 0.6 max | 0.035 max | 0.045/0.065 | 0.08/0.13 | 780/870 | 485 min | 13 | 13 |
|  | 0.45/0.50 | 0.6/1.0 | 0.6 max | 0.035 max | 0.045/0.065 | 0.18/0.23 | 850/950 | 570 min | 12 | 10 |
|  | 0.45/0.50 | 0.6/1.0 | 0.6 max | 0.035 max | 0.045/0.065 | 0.28/0.33 | 930/1025 | 630 min | 11 | 6 |

Table 5  Compositional and mechanical property specifications for the higher manganese 'vanard' grades

| C | Mn | Si | S | P | V | Tensile Strength $(N/mm^2)$ | 0.2% Proof Stress $(N/mm^2)$ | Min. Elong. (%) | R/A (%) | Impact Energy at R.T. (J) DVM 3mm U notch |
|---|---|---|---|---|---|---|---|---|---|---|
| 0.32/0.37 | 1.2/1.5 | 0.15/0.35 | 0.05 max | 0.035 max | 0.08/0.13 | 770/930 | 540 min | 18 | – | 20 min |
| 0.37/0.42 | 1.2/1.5 | 0.15/0.35 | 0.05 max | 0.035 max | 0.08/0.13 | 850/1000 | 600 min | 16 | – | 20 min |
| 0.42/0.47 | 1.2/1.4 | 0.15/0.35 | 0.05 max | 0.035 max | 0.10/0.15 | 930/1080 | 650 min | 12 | – | 15 min |

Table 6   Comparison of micro-alloyed steels with conventional forging quality steels and cast irons

| Material | UTS $N/mm^2$ | Proof Stress $N/mm^2$ | Eln. % | Fatigue Limit (Tension – Compression) Amplitude $N/mm^2$ | Charpy J (Room Temperature) | Fracture Toughness $K_{IC}$ $MN/m^{-3/2}$ | Critical Defect Size, a(mm) (at $\varepsilon/\varepsilon y = 1$ infinite plate) |
|---|---|---|---|---|---|---|---|
| 709M40    /V | 1098 | 1066 | | 600 | | 114 | 5.2 |
| 709M40    /U | 1042 | 922 | 12 | 550 | | 143 | 10.9 |
| 605M40 } /T<br>709M40 | 972 | 891 | 13 | 412 | | 159 | 14.5 |
| 080M40    /S | 814 | 731 | 15 | 370 | | – | |
| 105P43    /V | 1100 | | | | | | |
| U | 1000 | 600<br>625 | 10 | | 8 | | |
| T | 925 | 560<br>600 | 12 | | 8 | | |
| S | 850 | 530<br>580 | 14 | | 10 | | |
| 49Mn VS 3 | 900 | 575 | – | 310 | | 55 | 4.1 |
| SG Iron<br>(a)Pearlitic<br>(b)Ferritic | 800<br>370 | 443<br>250 | –<br>– | 253<br>200 | | 40<br>53 | 3.9<br>16.0 |

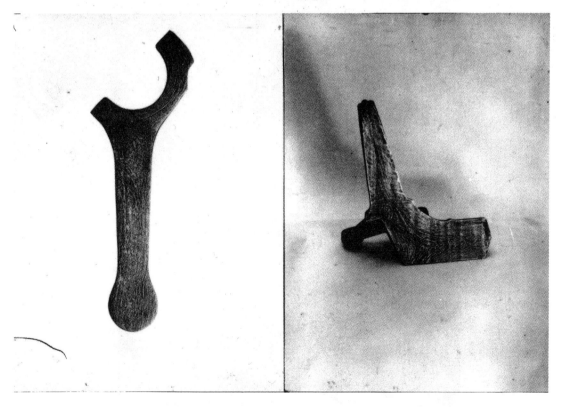

Fig 1   Typical examples of flow-lines in forgings

Fig 2   Typical as-forged microstructure of pearlite and ferrite

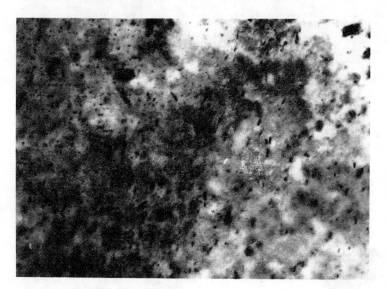

Fig 3   Transmission electron micrograph showing interphase precipitation
of vanadium carbonitride in ferrite

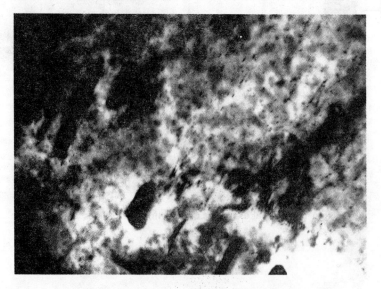

Fig 4   Transmission electron micrograph showing vanadium carbonitride
precipitation in the pearlitic ferrite

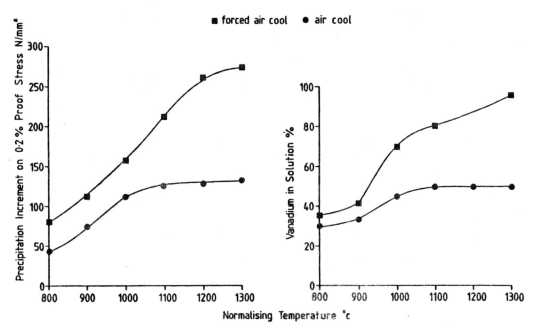

Fig 5    Effect of austenitisation temperature on 'vanadium in solution'
and on resultant precipitation hardening increment (Ref. 4)

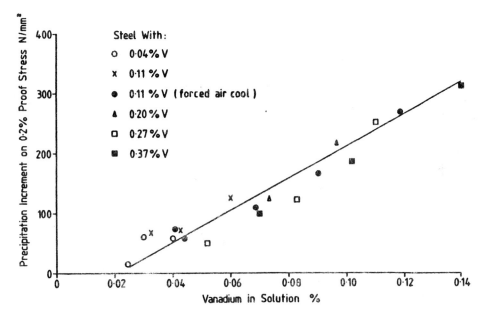

Fig 6    Relation between precipitation hardening increment and 'vanadium
in solution' (Ref. 4)



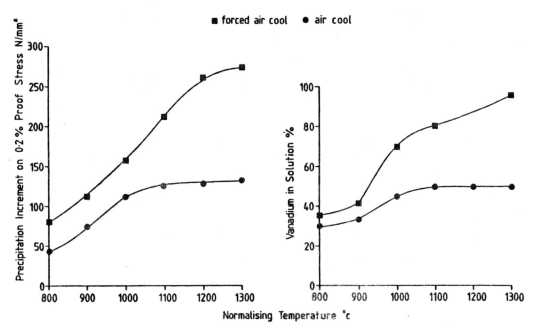

Fig 5    Effect of austenitisation temperature on 'vanadium in solution'
and on resultant precipitation hardening increment (Ref. 4)

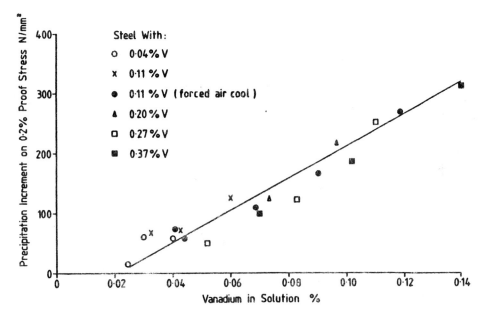

Fig 6    Relation between precipitation hardening increment and 'vanadium
in solution' (Ref. 4)

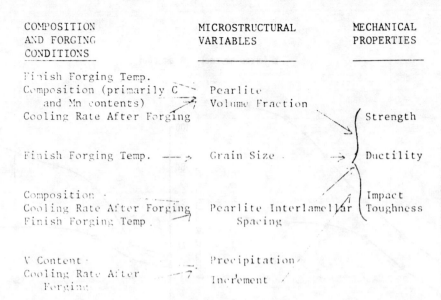

Fig 7    The interrelations between composition and forging variables,
microstructure and mechanical properties

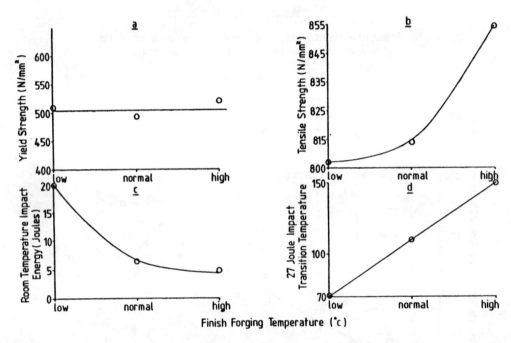

Fig 8    Influence of finish forging temperature on properties

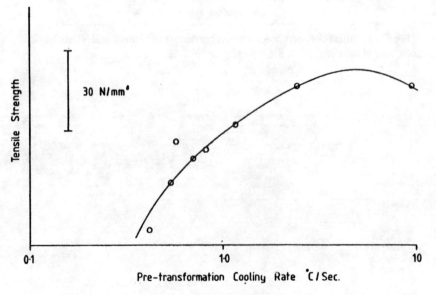

Fig 9    Effect of cooling rate on tensile strength

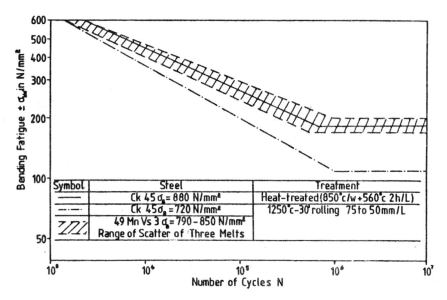

Fig 10 Published fatigue data for micro-alloyed steel (49 Mn VS 3) (Ref. 6)

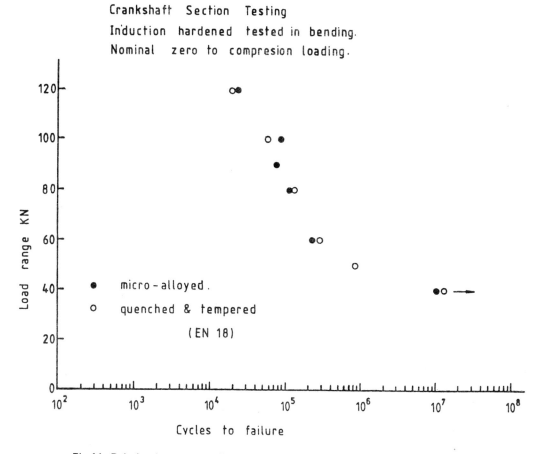

Fig 11 Relation between applied compressive load range and cycles to failure

# C280/81

# Plastics moulding operations - a review of automotive aspects

L W TURNER, BSc, FPRI, MInstP, MInstPkg
Yarsley Technical Centre Limited, Redhill, Surrey

SYNOPSIS   Plastics materials and production processes are to be reviewed hopefully to establish future demands on production.   The materials covered will be: reinforced thermoplastics and thermosets, and reinforced reactive compositions.   Consideration of processing developments will relate to both classes of materials.   The usefulness of property data - in static and dynamic situations and to ageing phenomena in moulded components is considered, including the possibilities of assessment by short-term testing of long-term behaviour.

## 1   INTRODUCTION

World-wide events of recent years have created situations in which the use of polymeric materials in car components has come under the most intense technical scrutiny.   This affects the in-house and the custom sectors of component production and the concentration of attention and effort go back to the manufacturers of polymeric materials.   Where the impetus to look closely at polymers in automobile production is at its strongest recession-hit industry might well find some inspiration and hope, but must remember that car manufacturers want economic effective performance, not plastics for their own sake. There is a considerable new challenge to the expertise inherent in the Plastics Industry and some dramatic activities have been and will continue to be seen.

One must say, and then leave the point, that there is a challenge within a challenge. However well the plastics materials and moulding technologists respond, their very response will be ongoing challenges to the metals industry who would see in any successes of the plastics industry, evidence of their own material inadequacies, in the light of the new and growing situation in car production, to meet the same challenge.

Significant features are :

(a)   the existence of vast amounts of metal handling equipment and great experience,

(b)   new plastics materials, new processing methods and equipment for their conversion are required,

(c)   customer attitudes impress elements of uncertainty upon the materials question,

(d)   disposal or reclamation problems are serious.

In this paper an up-dating review is being given with specific reference to processing technology for plastics components, but this obviously relates to materials to which first reference will be made.

## 2   AN OUTLINE OF THE SITUATION OF THE CAR IN ITS PRESENT CONTEXT   (Ref. 1 )

In summary the trend in design of cars since, say, the 60 s, has reversed; to this many factors have made contributions :

the car as a necessity rather than a status symbol

the second car wedge effect, the urban car

road traffic density, parking inadequacies in urban areas

safety in traffic, air pollution, and legislation

energy crises and the demand for less prodigal use of available resources

wider-spread production

intensive competition on world basis

materials successes in aerospace application

general advances in plastics materials and processing technology

an improving image of plastics, and changes in fashion affecting user response

In car production, the situation is being met by down-sizing, and by extensive investigation of weight saving, and wind and road resistance reduction.   In each direction polymeric materials (plastics and rubbers) are already clearly seen to have prominent parts to play.

## 3  THE 'MORES' RELATING TO PLASTICS IN CARS.

3.1 Many relevant lectures have been given and many articles have appeared in the technical press so that it is hardly necessary to cover the ground in detail here.

It is sufficient to put forward one or two diagrams, illustrating the considerable increase in the use of polymeric-based materials in car construction and the benefits which can accrue from these applications.

Two basic cautionary thoughts (already mentioned but now reiterated) should be kept in mind when the fact of large markets and the technologically exciting demands begin to fire the imagination of sectors of the plastics industry.

(a)  No car maker wishes to use plastics for plastics sake.  Meeting requirements in a cost effective manner is the decision-making aspect of what material/processes will be chosen for whatever car component.

   and

(b)  the metals industry has a long history; it is efficient with rapid processes and has much complex equipment to hand, and there is the 'fight-back factor' to bear in mind.

### 3.2     An outline of the 'mores' in specific terms

Primary     Weight reduction

            Design freedom for lower wind resistance

            Greater safety, comfort and quietness

            (None of these makes plastics components absolute musts)

Secondary   Good material supply position - low energy in production

            Rapid efficient processes - low energy demand

            High consistent quality with long-term aesthetic life

            Ease of repair and modification

            Recovery of materials

Related     Low temperature processing

            Rapid catalysation of thermosets

            Improved equipment and process control

Again in summary, technical challenges are being met as the outcome of great efforts. The world-wide inflationary situation has prepared the customer (who must always ultimately be right) to adjust his demands;

and global competition in the car industry has, at the same time, given rise to a requirement for a higher standard and new thinking on behalf of those customers. This might be summed up as the Japanese factor, i.e. a well equipped car with improved reliability without price penalties.

It is quite true to say that concentrated attention is being given to weight reductions, and any other advantages which might well result from such detailed attention in all areas of the car structure.  But the major attention, and this is a massive technology effort, is concentrated on the exterior, front and rear ends and body panels.  These are the principal topics below.

However, in view of such demonstrations of activity as recent SITEV expositions, it would be unrealistic not to refer to one or two striking recent efforts under the bonnet.

(a)   The new and much publicised Ford engine manifold

(b)   the Polimotor research 'plastics' engine

The emphasis of this paper is on materials and processing technology and it is sensible before concentrating on two specific areas to remember that, for various engineering components, a remarkable array of higher temperature injection mouldable plastics is now available.  The latest addition to mention is PEEK, poly ether ether ketone, which I.C.I. Ltd. are now producing for high temperature applications.

While it seems possible and even likely that some of these so-called 'hot' plastics will be employed under the bonnet, the trend is probably to increase employment of polyester-based DMCs, having in mind the advantages of 'granular' grades now on the market.

Cars have to have windows and glass is heavy, and it will be intriguing to see what inroads surface-treated polycarbonate (for example) could make into the glazing problems where the density and thickness of glass define a weight reduction target.  Thermal expansion coefficient difficulties and weathering resistance could override possibly any weight and safety advantages.  In contrast, there is much to be expected from treated PC for lamp 'glasses', in view of weight (less thickness, lower density) and much less tool wear during production.

Road wheels provide another target for the imagination, but the car driver is likely to be difficult to convince that any plastic containing composition would be capable of giving safe and reliable service over years of use where circumstances of steady, dynamic and impact loading and weathering combine.

## 4  BUMPERS and FRONT/REAR ENDS

Since the late 60s, aimed at meeting safety requirements and legislation, bumper development has been intensive.  While RIM technology has been generally applied, employing polyurethane formulations, other approaches, particularly injection moulding of reinforced or modified grades of commonly-used thermoplastics, have been commercially applied.  Comparisons of these approaches have been published.  There appear to be different opinions as between Europe and the U.S.A. and this is in regard to the legislation situation and to the confidence in the respective processes of conventional injection moulding and reaction injection moulding.  In these comparisons cost effectiveness is the crucial aspect.  In a mainly European context R. Murchie of Ford Motor Company has identified four main material contenders :

EPDM - modified PP - injection moulded one-piece

Modified PC injection moulded one-piece

SMC - 3 pieces, bonded together

PU as R - RIM, in one piece

After discussion of the many technical and economic factors involved, the conclusion reached is that for the early 80s the choice lies between PC and PP, but later R - RIM PU will make a strong challenge in some possible competition from nylon 66 and PC/ABS blends. Perhaps changing legislation will affect the mould-based selections and other materials, for example other polymers being converted by R - RIM processes.  It is notable that FIAT use elastomer modified polyethylene for front and rear end developments.

(Ref.2)

F. Zahn and A. Weber have also presented comparison of bumper cost analysis which, neglecting start-up time and scrap figures, point to injection moulding as being somewhat cheaper (by about 11%) than present-day RIM, while the equipment utilisation cost is rather more the other way.  If article thickness is increased PU based RIM becomes advantageous.

The immediate situation (i.e. preference for injection moulding) regarding mass production of, say, 500 000 cars per annum) is being governed by equipment availability and its readier employment, if need be, on other applications than R - RIM equipment might be at the present state of equipment development.

So far commercial RIM and R - RIM production has been based on highly developed grades of PU with glass reinforcement.  But development of materials formulations based on epoxies, nylon 6 (modified) and other candidates is intensive, and the the key will be cost effectiveness taken in the broad sense of capital outlay; materials cost and quantity availability; and process cost compounded with effectiveness in function and appearance.  The chief target must be to achieve fast cycling, which involves the ability of the resin to cure quickly (aiming at, say, 1 min. cycle time) and equipment to match.

One of the common difficulties with PU compositions is mould release.

Developments in respect of finishing are more than pertinent.  It may be possible to coat in the mould and provide improved release at the same time.  The overall press cycle would be affected (perhaps it is not too ridiculous to suggest an improvement in cycle times might be possible, even though two procedures are being integrated, by reason of quicker release).

In referring specifically to bumpers an unnecessary limitation is being made since it is practical so to design the front end to incorporate many required features in the one design and to use R. RIM PU more extensively. Wings can be made from a similar compound. Thermoplastic wings have been made by injection moulding; ABS, mod. PC, mod. PA, and thermoplastic elastomers are possibilities and the best choice will depend on many factors. (Ref.3.)  The views expressed by Mr. Murchie (Ford) with regard to bumpers as such can probably be extended to wings.  Impact resistance, recovery characteristics, damping characteristics, surface damage resistance are probably the most significant mechanical factors to be looked at in making an 'effectivity' decision;  and cycle time (notoriously sensitive to the necessary thickness to meet needs) governs the production cost.  At present FIAT concentrate on self-coloured mouldings with further finishing for rear and front end, but expect to have to tackle finishing for more aesthetic results (Ref.4.)

## 5  BODY PANELS

Of all aspects of plastics applications in cars aimed at weight reduction the most intensively studied and widely publicised is that of body panels where the lighter plastics components would be expected to perform as well or better than the long-used steel shells.  Design and production studies of SMC for such components has been dominant with particular emphasis recently being given to the design of the resin material for rapid curing, press construction for precise and controllable closing of the presses;  and the process technology and control.  Major car producing companies, especially those in the U.S.A., but elsewhere too, have instituted greater or lesser programmes on moulding equipment, improvement of component and mould design and the processing operations.  The major SMC suppliers have followed co-related courses aimed at improved resin formulations and reinforcements.  SMC materials with somewhat greater toughness have been developed, and some consideration has been given to hybridisation of reinforcing fibres (carbon being added to glass).  Lesser attention has been given to the use of woven materials, though attention has been drawn to the possibilities of creating tougher structures by using, for example, chemically modified PET fabric in mixed patterns.

Before these intensive efforts, which began in 1979 to explore SMC processing technology for body panels, such large area mouldings suffered from relatively poor surfaces, sink marks and tended to warp. Handling damage was serious and output rates then possible were inadequate in comparison with metal techniques. The American technical and trade press has amply publicised the great efforts that have been made by glass and resin manufacturers in their respective areas and by the car giants of Detroit particularly in process improvements. The combined outcome is a great step forward in SMC processing. Work in other parts of the world, while having much less written about it has been significant without being so dramatically concentrated. Other approaches to the plastics body panel have also received rewarding attention.

Other techniques for combining resin and reinforcement have been receiving attention such as development towards pulforming and pulmoulding; expansion of filament winding capabilities; better resin transfer moulding and vacuum injection moulding; in mould surfacing and decoration.

Particularly in Europe, the possibilities of injection moulding have not been forgotten because of the availability of large-size moulding capacity and the advanced state of process control. Taking the processing technology as more or less existing, the development has chiefly been directed to materials suitable for body panel applications by General Electric Plastics Europe, who demonstrated at SITEV their development of a new range of polycarbonates by the use of one grade CL 100 for car panels. The particular modification (combining a crystallising polyester with polycarbonate) produces an impact-resistant grade which is capable of crystallising to a degree and thereby developing greater stiffness and much greater resistance to environmental stress cracking while maintaining excellent toughness. Weight saving advantage accrues against SMC. Comparative stiffness data are not given in the publicity literature so far seen, but the view is expressed by the material manufacturers that this new material development will be part of advanced European car technology which they compare, with apparent good reason, with advances anywhere else.

To summarise the present position in weight saving, and in related energy saving, the present reduced demand for cars and the marketing in all major car producing areas of considerable numbers of smaller Japanese (with a high level of customer appeal) there is apparent some slowing down in implementation of new plastics technologies. This is especially so for body panels, and the main thrust in the early 1980s cars would seem to be related to down-sizing and designing for reduced drag, licensing of particular models and the beginnings of the 'world' car concept. As part of the down-sizing trend the fight-back factor is prominent, being directed by the metals industries at weight saving by improvements to steel, use of superior galvanising,

greater use of aluminium (especially under the bonnet) and growing attention to magnesium. In some instances these developments are being based on metal/plastics combinations e.g. polypropylene/metal laminates, Al-plastics foam - Al panels and adhesive bonding amongst new assembly techniques.

Where the application of plastics materials and technology will continue to show to great advantage will be in smaller components. A few have been referred to, but there are many more which could be listed, as is obvious from the exhibits shown at the 1981 SITEV.

One might expect that the most dramatic inroads of plastics materials will not be seen in the early 80s models, but in the next round of models, say 1985 onwards, as the full effects of the technological studies of recent years bear fruit. An expectable situation might be outlined as :

1. Bumpers and front ends by R-RIM techniques, since lighter, cheaper moulds favour styling modifications as against thermoplastic injection.

2. Body panels by thermoplastics injection (with finish and colour 'built-in'). Chief advantages over fibre reinforced thermosetting materials lie in scrap handling; equipment and technology all available.

3. Steady development of smaller applications using an increasing range of thermoplastics, some thermosets and elastomers as materials improvement continues along many lines.

6  DATA AND DESIGN

Attention is now given to the kinds of mechanical property data that are obtainable directly or established as estimates from limited results, and which can be used for design purposes or as giving guidance in 'trouble-shooting' situations. By way of illustration, and choosing the more significant situations, the cases of matrix reinforcement with long-fibres uniaxially disposed (i.e. the continuous case) and the case of short-fibre reinforcement (the discontinuous fibre case) are compared.

Continuous fibre reinforcement - aligned in the direction of stress.                      (Ref. 5)

The material is orthotropic, being stronger when loaded along the fibres, and stiffer when bent across them, than otherwise. The frequent effect of fibre reinforcement is not to improve the impact resistance, however. The actual failure event under impact blows will depend upon the effects of directional influences; in direction of blow; details of support of the component; and in the case of functional mouldings (as opposed to simplified test-pieces intended for materials evaluation), inherent shape features.

Since glass fibre is at present (and likely so to remain) the commonest reinforcing filament, and this would be depictable as brittle, the effect of ductile filaments will not be referred to at this point.

Young's Modulus, Tensile Strength and Impact Resistance are the most often determined data and the most significant items in applicational terms. When both matrix and filament are behaving elastically under applied load it can be shown experimentally that the law of mixtures, based on their volume fractions, is applicable and $E_c = E_f V_f + E_m V_m$ where suffixes represent composite, filament and matrix successively.

For the case where the matrix behaves in a plastic manner

$$E_c = E_i V_f + \frac{(d\sigma_m)}{(dE_m)_c} V_m$$

Since $\dfrac{d\sigma_m}{dE_m}$ is usually small, this can be

reduced simply to $E_c = E_f V_f$ (effectively a simple cross-section reduction formula)

For example, in uniaxial GRP the ratio of moduli would be around 20, so that, at 10% glass fibre loading by volume fraction, 69% of the load is carried by the glass reinforcement.

With regard to the Tensile Strength, if $V_f$ is greater than a minimum value and filaments break first, then failure of the matrix, thus put under load, must follow.

## Discontinuous filaments - of equal length and uniform diameter.           (Ref. 6)

In this case there is a critical length of filament. It is useful to derive experiment-ally values for $\beta$, the ratio between the continuous and discontinuous data values, for constructions which otherwise correspond. The critical fibre length value for the dis-continuous reinforcement is that at which for an applied stress level (acting along the length of the fibre surface and increasing toward the middle point) the stress at the centre of the filament length reaches the fibre breaking load.

### Table   1.

Typical critical length and $\beta$ values at 23°C.

| Matrix | Fibre dia. | Critical lengths (mms) | Efficiency $\beta$ |
|--------|-----------|------------------------|--------------------|
| PA6    | 5 - 7     | 6.28 - 0.6             | 0.55               |
| PP     | 7         | 3.1                    | 0.50               |
| Mod.PP | -         | 0.9                    | 0.51               |
| PMMA   | 7         | 0.8                    | 0.63               |
| POM    | 7         | -                      | 0.61               |
| SAN    | 7         | -                      | 0.65 - 0.72        |

The efficiency factor demonstrates the extent to which the weaker matrix carries some of the stress in transmission of the load to the reinforcement when this is discontinuous, and the matrix being weaker than the fibre the result will be a 'de-rating' of continuous filament properties.

It will be realised that it has been assumed that the glass filament reinforcement has time-independent properties, so that $E_c$ and $T_c$ do not reduce with time under load as is the case for the matrix, which itself will exhibit viscoelastic properties.

Not all stresses applied to uniaxial composites in service in sheet form will be directed along the lines of the fibres, and stress-direction effects are highly significant, commonly reducing the maximum tensile data by at least 50%. In the case of random GRP a quite different situation pertains. For injection-moulded components made from DMC or from fibre-reinforced thermoplastics many factors have to be taken into account when establishing suitable data for design purposes. Firstly (and principally relating to the material) allowance for time and temperature effects is essential; and secondly (and principally governed by component shape) there will be thickness effects upon flow pattern. Apart from thickness effects on flow, there will exist rather complex fibre orientation and skin effects, and allowance will be necessary for weld lines of different kinds (e.g. butt and side-side). The lack of all-embracing mechanical data is quickly apparent and to provide comprehensive data to cover a wide range of materials would be a formidable task. An important method of making design assess-ments is to employ further 'de-rating' factors in order to enable due allowance to be made for the various circumstances which reduce the applicability of the data obtained for long-fibre uniaxial orientation, or data for dis-continuous uniaxial fibre distribution.

By way of illustration reference can be made to g.f. reinforced polypropylene injection mouldings. Such an example will be particularly pointed in view of the increasing tendency to make large area components by injection moulding of g.f. reinforced thermoplastics.

(Ref.7 and 8)

Such experimentally determined de-rating factors for g.f. PP cannot be taken as directly applicable to other materials, and further tabulations of de-rating factors for other materials would be necessary. The levels of the various factors serve, however, as a clear warning that a whole set of circumstances have to be taken into account if reliable applica-tions are to be achieved.

TABLE 2

Typical 'de-rating' factors for GFPP
(0.25 glass by weight)

(Based on data given by R.C.Stevenson)
(Ref.6.)

| Geo-metry | Direct-ion | Thick-ness mm | Test Mode | 'De-rating' factor |
|---|---|---|---|---|
| End-gated test bar | Flow direct-ion | 3 | Ten-sion | 1 |
| | | 6 | " | 0.85 |
| | | 12 | " | 0.45 |
| End-gated plate | Flow direct-ion | 3 | Ten-sion | 0.9 |
| | Across flow | 3 | " | 0.6 |
| Centre-gated plaque | Radial | 3 | Ten-sion | 0.55 |
| | Tangent | 3 | " | 0.8 |
| Butt weld | Across weld | 3 | Ten-sion | 0.6 |
| Side-side weld | Across weld | 3 | Ten-sion | 0.5 |

Further, it has to be borne in mind that data for, say, stiffness (normally given as single values) has a statistical distribution of test results relevant to it. This is not pursued here but reference to, say, Jayatilaka (Ref.9) is worth making. So far static behaviour only has been examined (stiffness and strength) apart from some passing reference to impact resistance. The use of instrumented falling-weight impact machines can be valuable in making empirical evaluations of complex components or for systematic studies of test-pieces for materials evaluation. There is specific value in such test-pieces being sub-components in type rather than tensile strength and impact bars as in conventional materials testing to specification.

But cars are intended to be dynamic, not static, and to be capable of continuous running for longish periods so that fatigue behaviour could often be more significant than either impact behaviour or static-loading tensile strength. The magnitude of deflections in dynamic situations relates to stiffness of which static tests give good indications. Fatigue life data (as depicted by the customary S-N diagrams) are important. It can be imagined that some conflict could exist as between energy absorbence (in the interest of freedom from noise) and excellent fatigue life (where low absorbence is beneficial).

A comparison of cfrp and gfrp fatigue behaviour by means of Goodman diagram(s) (Ref.10) illustrates the great fatigue-resisting possibilities of carbon fibre reinforcement and supports any ideas relating to development of hybrid composite panels etc. or, more specifically, local use of, say, pultruded cf. profiles in panels and bumper designs, also aid in coping with anti-intrusion requirements for side panels and end-on impacts respectively.

There may have been attempts made to employ a de-rating factor approach, via (as step 1) an efficiency factor (as $\beta$) comparison of continuous and discontinuous composite behaviour in fatigue situations, but it is not known if this step has been envisaged and extended down (as was indicated above for static situations) to the variability in properties in injection-moulded discontinuous-filament laminates.

Impact resistance is highly significant and an approach to real mouldings as opposed to test-pieces using ductility factors for specific materials allied to 'de-rating' for size, shape and flow features has been published (Ref.11).

Another data area, again long-term and difficult experimentally to evaluate for this reason, is that of environmental and weathering effects, i.e. due to erosion, dirt accumulation, road dirt impact, moisture, U.V. and ambient temperature as these affect panels. Usually it is the coating system which bears the brunt of exposure to such conditions and it might be added that experience is often as valuable as short-term test data.

REFERENCES

(1) D. Charlesworth, Materials in Engineering 2, 1981, 149.

(2) F. Zahn & A. Weber, Kunststoffe 70 (1980) 467

(3) R. Murchie   The Plastics & Rubber Institute Conference 1980 - 'Plastics on the Road' and Plastics & Rubber Weekly, 1980 8th August, Page 8.

(4) C. Noris   Plast. & R. Proc. & Applic. 1(2) (1981) 95.

(5) F. Ramsteiner & R. Theysohn   Composites 1979 (April) 111

(6) F. Ramsteiner   Composites 1981 (Jan.) 65.

(7) R.C. Stephenson   Plastics & Rubber Materials & Applications 4, (1979) 45.

REFERENCES (contd.)


(8)   P. Gutteridge & S. Turner  The Plastics
                        & Rubber Institute
                        Conference
                        Plastics on the Road 1980.

(9)   A de S Jayatilaka  F.M. of Brittle
                        Materials, Applied Science
                        Publishers, London, 1979.

(10)  R.W. Hertzberg & T.A. Manson  Fatigue
                        of Engineering Plastics,
                        Academic Press, London,
                        1980.

(11)  D.R. Moore, C.J. Hooley & M. Whale
                        Plast. & R. Processing
                        and Applications 1(2)
                        (1981) 121.


SELECTED BIBLIOGRAPHY

Reaction Injection Moulding
                        W.E. Becker (Ed.)
                        Van Nostrand, London, 1979

The Plastics & Rubber Institute Conference
                        'RIM - what's in it for me'·
                        1981

The Plastics & Rubber Institute Conference
                        'Plastics on the road'
                        1980

Modern Plastics    May July 1980,
                        Feb. Mar. April 1981 issues

Plastics World     July, Nov. Dec. 1980,
                        Feb. 1981 issues

Plastics Engineering, Mr. Nov. Dec. 1980

Plastics Technology   Mar. 1981

K. Radermacher Kunststoffe 70 (1980) 443

N. Jaeschke & D. Shultze  Kunststoffe 71
                        (1981) 155

Materials Engineering  Sep. 1980

G.E. Plastics Europe 'Euroscene' May 1981
                        issue for SITEV

H. Kulkarni & P. Beardmore   Composites
                        1980 (Oct.) 225

R.W. Hertzberg & T.A. Manson   Fatigue  of
                        Engineering Plastics,
                        Academic Press,
                        London, 1980.

# C281/81

# The use of High Water Based Fluids 'HWBF' in machine tool hydraulic systems - circuit component

A R DAVIES, BSc, CEng, MIMechE
Vickers Fluid Power, Swindon, Wiltshire

SYNOPSIS    In parallel with the development of high water based fluids the manufacturers of hydraulic components and system designers have been evaluating the capability of their equipment with these fluids.  This has led to the current availability of a comprehensive range of components and system design know-how.  The problems which confront the pump/valve designer are discussed as are the details of a power unit designed specifically for use on HWBF.

## INTRODUCTION

The overall concept of designing hydraulic systems for operation on water is not new. The majority of early systems designed in the last century used water as the hydraulic medium. In more recent years the inherent fire resistant property of water has led to a considerable expansion in the use of soluble oil emulsions in coal mining and high fire risk areas of metal production.  The general requirement for these industries has been and still is essentially hydraulic components capable of operation at pressures up to 170 bar, using a specified fluid and able to survive the severe environment typical of mines and steel works.  The emulsion fluid used in mining conforms to a specification which prescribes the anti-corrosion capability together with a number of chemical effects.  However, it does not truly describe a high performance fluid for use in a complex hydraulic circuit.  The resultant equipment is somewhat specialised and typified as being aluminium free, heavy duty and in comparison with machine tool hydraulics, costly.

The components generally used in machine tool hydraulic systems are the results of many years development by the industry and are tailored to meet user specifications and in many cases ISO standards for international interchangeability. The operating pressures are generally low; over 80% of systems currently in use operate at pressures less than 70 bar.

During the last five years the growing awareness by the large machine tool users, in particular the automotive industry, of the potential economic and environmental advantages of systems using a hydraulic fluid containing up to 95% water has resulted in considerable development and test activity with hydraulic elements.

It should be acknowledged at this stage that the automotive manufacturing industry has itself been instrumental in carrying out very extensive testing on both equipment and fluids which has greatly reduced the time scale for the successful introduction into use of such equipment.  A large proportion of this work has been carried out in the USA and the automobile industry in that country has been successfully applying high water content fluid technology in manufacturing plants for over three years.

## The designers problems

The characteristics of these high water containing fluids, now commonly referred to as high water based fluids (HWBF), which confront the component designer with potential problems can be listed as follows:

(a)   Low viscosity

(b)   Cavitation tendency

(c)   Boundary wear protection limitations

(d)   Corrosion of ferrous and non-ferrous metals

(e)   Life reduction effects on rolling contact bearings

When considering these properties in more detail it should be remembered that there are some advantageous properties of HWBF compared with mineral oil; e.g. much higher specific heat.

(a)   The viscosity of a typical HWBF is essentially that of water; Fig.1 shows the temperature viscosity relationship for a typical HWBF together with a typical 46 grade hydraulic mineral based oil.  In theory therefore leakages subject to visco effects such as in laminar flow will be increased relative to mineral oil as a direct viscosity function.  In practice it is often found that leakages are not increased in such a gross manner due, it is thought, to the highly adhesive thin film of grease-like compound formed on the surfaces by the HWBF constituents. The result is that the clearances are effectively reduced by this surface build up in predominantly laminar flow conditions.

Some attention has been given to introducing thickeners to HWBFs usually similar to those used in water glycol fluids.  If these have acceptable shear stability then positive improvements in leakage rates are clearly possible.  A spin-off advantage is that glycol additives give a wider temperature range and overcomes problems due to freezing.

(b)   Any liquid will tend to cavitate when the local pressure of the fluid falls below the vapour pressure. Material damage takes place when the vapour pockets formed are re-absorbed, a process which takes place quite violently and is often accompanied by a characteristic noise. Areas of local depression in a fluid can also result in air release which, whilst not as damaging as true cavitation, can reduce volumetric efficiency and adversely affect control performance.

The high vapour pressure of water compared with mineral hydraulic oil promotes circuit and component problems with HWBFs. The inlet passages in pumps are particularly prone to cavitation and it is for this reason combined with the relatively high density of water that a positive pressure is desirable at pump inlets when operating on HWBF. Special port timing in positive displacement pumps can be beneficial and this is described later.

Flow erosion is a particular form of cavitation erosion caused, it is believed, by local turbulence in thin fluid films such as exists for example between cylindrical spools and housing bores. The damage caused by flow erosion can be quite severe and result in a considerable volumetric loss. Fig. 2 shows a control spool which was badly eroded after only a few hundred hours operation at 140 bar with an HWBF. Evidence does suggest that flow erosion is influenced considerably by fluid formulation and studies are currently in progress aimed at establishing an acceptable test method for evaluation of such a fluid property.

(c) The lubricity defined as boundary wear protection afforded by an HWBF is totally dependent upon the fluid concentrate formulation. Much has been achieved by the oil and chemical industries in achieving anti-wear packages, however it must be appreciated that comparability with even a very low viscosity modern mineral oil based hydraulic fluid has yet to be achieved. One problem which is shared by the component manufacturer and user is that an acceptable standard test method to assess fluid anti-wear properties has yet to be developed.

(d) Corrosion, particularly with ferrous metals was always considered to be a potential problem from the point of view of the component and systems designer. In practice so long as the fluid is maintained at the correct concentration ratio and water within the specified hardness is used in the mix, then ferrous corrosion has not been a major problem. The volume above the liquid level is naturally water saturated vapour and unless precautions are taken rust can then be a problem. It is often found that the slightly sticky or greasy deposits formed on components by the fluid act as a barrier for attack. The particular problem relating to fluid reservoirs is discussed later.

(e) A collated study (1) has shown that the fatigue life of ball bearings operating in a water containing fluid is drastically lower than when operated in a mineral oil. In the case of H.F.A. category fluids (the ISO designation covering HWBFs) the $L_{10}$ fatigue life of a ball bearing is approximately one twentieth of the theoretical life using mineral oil at a c/p of 6. The referenced work concludes that the life reduction ratio is itself a function of the operating c/p ratio.

## Component development status

In looking at a typical hydraulic system the heart of such a system is generally the pump. Initial testing with small piston pumps, generally of the axial piston type, showed these to be basically suitable for HWBF use at pressures to 70 bar, with generally some detail design attention.

To overcome the life limiting feature of ball and roller bearings some manufacturers have fitted pre-greased sealed bearings which can be effective so long as ingress of the HWBF into the bearing is totally prevented. In practice this does imply that care should be taken in preventing high pressures in the pump case. Another approach has been to replace such bearings with plain journals lined with a suitable plastic.

Volumetric efficiencies of over 90% at 70 bar are typical with no change in fixed clearances.

Cavitation and flow erosion are perhaps two of the most common causes of performance decay with piston pumps. Fig.3 illustrates the effect of flow erosion on the port plate of such a pump after 2000 hours operation at the somewhat higher pressure of 140 bar.

Improvements in the performance and noise levels of piston pumps can be achieved by optimisation of the port timing. Kelsey et al (2) have reported on effects of fluid viscosity on such an optimisation and clearly illustrate that further improvements are possible on current units when used on HWBF type fluids.

Vane type pumps have been very popular with machine tool hydraulic designers over many years, as they have been shown to give reliable quiet operation. The adaptability of the basic vane pump in both the fixed and variable displacement types to operate on HWBF has been the subject of considerable development over the last few years.

The main area of concern has been the boundary lubrication requirements of a vane tip. Improved metallurgy such as the use of high grade tool steels for both the cam ring and vanes coupled with optimising the geometry of the vane tip has resulted in much improved lives. A reduction in the vane tip loads has been achieved on at least one design of variable delivery pump by the use of two vanes in one slot with a pressure feed to the area enclosed by the vane tips. With such an arrangement the vane loads are partially hydrostatically balanced, hence reducing the reliance on boundary wear requirements from the fluid.

In order to achieve acceptable volumetric efficiencies the control of rotor side clearance is most important. The use of pressure loaded port plates offers an obvious advantage and such designs give volumetric efficiencies comparable with piston pumps.

Some gear type pumps (both of the external

spur gear and internal gear design) have been successfully operated on HWBF. Higher pressures have been demonstrated by multi-staging of the internal gear unit with very promising results.

The requirement for acceptability of pumps for machine tool use has been specified by one major automotive manufacturer as being a minimum life of 10 000 hours at 70 bar using an 'approved' HWBF. This would appear to be a very reasonable specification, however, it should be noted that, in practice, a large proportion of systems operate at pressures considerably lower than 70 bar, hence considerably longer lives can be expected. The service life of a pump, and in fact most components of a system, will be influenced greatly by fluid control criteria such as cleanliness and temperature.

In looking at the performance of valves in HWBF systems they can be divided into two basic categories. The first are selector valves, often operated by electrical means and the second are pressure and flow control valves that continuously modulate the system parameters.

Of these the selector valves present the least problem and in practice the commonly used 3 or 4 way valves have been found to give long troublefree lives so long as the increased internal leakage is accepted. One important proviso when using solenoid operated valves is that the sealed pressureproof tube design is used in order to avoid possible leakage of the HWBF into the electrical connections. Valves using either spool seals or poppet seals are available to perform selector operations which exhibit very low internal leakage, however, in practice these are only used on higher pressure systems when the extra cost can be justified.

Valves which meter fluid flow must be considered very carefully. The problem area is naturally cavitation and flow erosion due to the inevitable high localised fluid viscosities. The problem increases with pressure and special purpose valves are usually recommended for pressures much above 70 bar.

It is very difficult to generalise on the total suitability of established relief and reducing valves as even the fluid formulation effects the operational lives. It is increasingly the case that even valves with cast iron seats are now proving to give adequate reliability at machine tool pressures.

Flow control valves including feed valves, have also proved to be less of a problem than was feared. Early recommendations for HWBF systems in fact specifically excluded their use in feed applications.

The results of considerable laboratory and in-plant operation has clearly established that this class of valve can be reliably used; erosion can, however, be a problem at very low flow settings.

In converting hydraulic power to perform mechanical functions the hydraulic cylinder is by far the most commonly used component. Few, if any, problems are encountered with the conventional cylinder although with some HWBFs the use

of viton type of rubber seals is advisable. Hydraulic motors can present problems and only a select few motors have been cleared for long term use on HWBFs.

The major problem with such motors is most likely the reliance on boundary lubrication under static or very low speed conditions which cannot be always met by an HWBF. The relatively high internal leakages associated with fixed clearances in such motors must also present a problem particularly during the critical almost static situation.

The ancillary equipment required for HWBF hydraulic systems differs little from established oil hydraulic practice. Care should be taken in the selection of filters as not all elements are compatible with HWBF. Most HWBFs exhibit good paint stripping capability which creates problems with components such as fluid reservoirs. Approved paints, of the epoxy type, do exist but the author personally believes that the use or part use of stainless steel reservoirs is a desirable design feature. The major area of concern is the condensation on the under side of the tank top which, with inadequate protection, will form rust and contaminate the system. The use of a stainless steel tank top offers an obvious trouble-free solution. Fibre glass or similar materials for fluid reservoirs are currently under evaluation and may well be an ideal solution so long as standardisation of tank sizes is established in order to justify the high tooling costs.

System design considerations

An example of a hydraulic power unit designed for use with HWBF and incorporating most of the points mentioned is shown in the photo in Fig.4.

The unit incorporates a twin-vane type of pressure compensated vane pump which draws fluid from a side positioned stainless steel reservoir via a suction strainer. Pressurised fluid is supplied to the machine tool by way of selector valves positioned on a strip manifold located on the top of the tank. The common return to the reservoir is fitted with a low pressure positively sealed check valve to prevent the machine circuit draining during a shut-down period. In line with modern thinking the unit has a filtered-fill arrangement - access to the reservoir is by way of a quick release connector and the 10 micron return line filter. This unit has been in service for over 12 months in an automotive plant in the UK and operates at approximately 40 bar. It is perhaps interesting to note that due to the considerably higher specified heat of a HWBF the capacity of the reservoir is approximately half that of the original oil system and normal operational fluid temperature has not exceeded 35°C.

The conversion of existing hydraulic systems does naturally present a few problems. Generally pump exchange for an HWBF approved version is possible with no pipework modification, however, the majority of existing oil hydraulic installations have the pump mounted on top of the oil reservoir and hence have a negative inlet pressure. As previously mentioned it is desirable to have a flooded and slightly positive inlet pressure at the pump for maximum life but if a small reduction in life can be tolerated a number of pumps have been tested under such conditions for periods up to 10 000 hours with acceptable results.

The pressure compensated vane pump with which the author's firm is involved has been used successfully for over 2½ years in a number of USA automotive plants and approximately 30% of all applications have been tank top mounted retrofits. Attention to the valves and ancillary circuit components must of course be undertaken viz; filters, valve solenoids, materials, etc.

Fluid suppliers naturally specify fairly close tolerance on the water/concentrate ratio of HWBFs and this does tend to lead to inconvenience in maintenance engineering.

A fixed ratio automatic mixer unit is a logical acquisition and such units have been in coal mining service for a number of years. To take advantage of the reduced storage requirements a conveniently located automatic mixing tank can be supplied for system 'top-up' purposes. This does, however, lead to an interesting concept which can be considered with HWBF systems due to the relatively low pipework pressure drop criteria inherent with such a low viscosity fluid. If a relatively large mixing tank is provided the concept of centralising a group of pumps adjacent to the reservoir and feeding a number of machine tools with fluid from this area can be considered. Return lines to the reservoir could, dependent upon layout, be linked to a common pipe and filtration would also be centralised at the reservoir. All valves would be located on the machine tools with which they are associated. This concept is naturally rather similar to a complete ring main but does not require individual flow control valves at each station with their associated power loss. It does however share with the ring main design the not minor advantages of centralised fluid control and centralised pump maintenance. Added reliability could also be achieved by the use of a single standby pump which would take over the duty of any other pump in the group which required maintenance attention.

## Conclusion

This paper has not attempted to debate the case for using HWBFs in machine tools - it is the users who are now issuing specifications calling for equipment suitable for use on such fluids for all new machines. The hydraulic component manufacturing industry and system designers have, by working closely with the fluid suppliers and user industry, generated a comprehensive range of equipment and system know-how to enable such specifications to be met with the minimum of cost penalty.

REFERENCES

(1) KENNY, P. and MARCH, C.N. 'The Fatigue Life of Ball Bearings when used with Fire-Resistant Hydraulic Fluids' Performance testing of Hydraulic Fluids PP495-519 (Heyden and Son, London 1979 on behalf of the Institute of Petroleum)

(2) KELSEY, J., TAYLOR, R. and FOSTER, K. 'Fluid Properties; The effect of the Fluid being Pumped on the Noise Emitted by an Axial Piston Pump.' Seminar on Quieter Hydraulics. Institute of Mechanical Engineers October 1980.

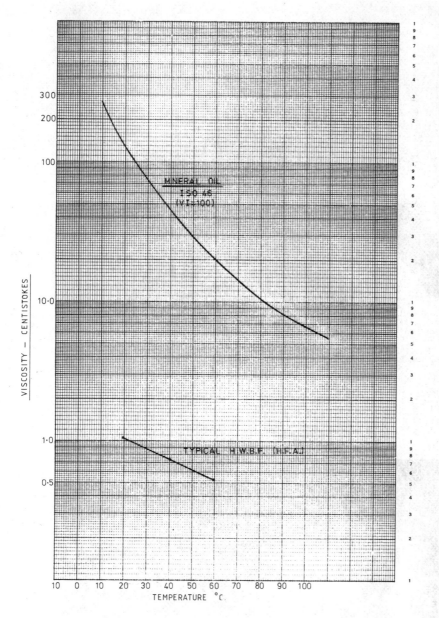

Fig 1    Viscosity comparison

Fig 2    Flow eroded spool valve

Fig 3    Flow erosion on piston pump port plate

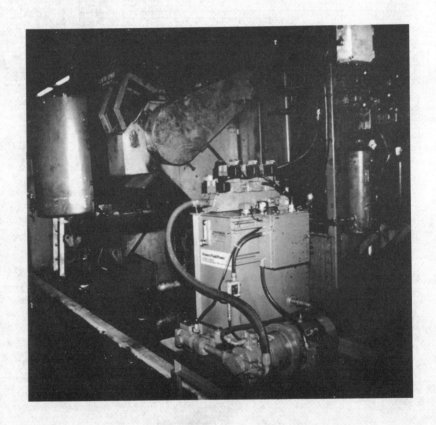

Fig 4    Installation of an HWBF hydraulic power unit

# C282/81

# Recent developments in welding processes suitable for use in vehicle manufacture

K I JOHNSON, BSc, PhD, FWeldI
E D NICHOLAS, MIM, MWeldI CEng
The Welding Institute, Abington, Cambridge

SYNOPSIS    There have been a number of welding process and equipment developments in recent years which are particularly suitable for use in automobile manufacture.  These include innovations in the friction welding technique, the development of magnetically impelled arc butt (MIAB) welding and availability of high power lasers.

Friction welding has been widely adopted throughout the world.  The automotive industry realised very quickly the technological, economic and production benefits that this solid phase welding process had to offer.  Some of the current and potential applications of conventional friction welding are reviewed and the potential of the more recently developed radial, orbital, linear reciprocating, angular reciprocating and synchronised friction welding techniques described. The materials (metals, plastics etc) and part shapes (round, square, hexagonal) for which the process is suitable are also highlighted.

MIAB welding is becoming increasingly attractive for the butt welding of hollow sections and suitable applications are described.  The process is very fast and rotational symmetry is not required.  Until recently it was only suitable for components of wall thickness of less than ~ 4mm, but the process has recently been successfully applied to tubes of wall thicknesses up to 10mm.  Potential applications are described.

High power $CO_2$ lasers are capable of welding steel at very high speeds with minimum distortion. Commercially available equipment are reviewed, and potential applications outlined.

## INTRODUCTION

1.    A number of new welding techniques have been developed in the last 10 - 15 years which are particularly suitable for use in the vehicle manufacturing industries.  These techniques have been developed for use in production because they allow faster welding schedules, are more reliable than previously used methods and/or allow greater design flexibility with regard to weldable joint configurations and material combinations. Developments in the semi-automated forge butt welding techniques and high energy density processes particularly apply to the vehicle manufacturing industries since these processes are well suited to mass production use in that they are rapid and involve minimum operator skill.

2.    This paper describes some of the recent innovations in the friction and MIAB (magnetically impelled arc butt) and laser welding processes.

## FRICTION WELDING

3.    When two or three or more parts are subjected to relative motion while in contact under an applied pressure, thermal energy is developed to permit a solid phase weld to be made when the heat cycle is terminated.  The simplest and most commonly used method for friction welding is shown in Fig. 1.  The major welding parameters to be considered are relative surface velocity, applied pressure for friction heating, forge consolidation, and heating duration.  For the conventional rotation process typical variables are:  peripheral velocity 2m/sec, friction pressure and forge pressure of 45 to $90N/mm^2$ respectively.  The nature of heat generation together with material displacement provide ideal conditions for joining a very wide range of similar and dissimilar material combinations (ref. 1).  For example steels and aluminium alloys to themselves present little problem, while certain combinations of these metals can also be successfully bonded.  Also non-metals such as a wide variety of plastics can equally be joined with ease.  By careful selection of welding conditions joints of excellent metallurgical, and mechanical properties can be achieved matching those of the parent materials involved.

4.    Friction welding equipment is now highly developed to meet the production engineers desires of reliability, high productivity and quality reproducibility while needing only semi-skilled operators to 'mind' and 'feed' the machines. Today, machines are available from commercial suppliers (ref. 2) to accommodate a size range from 1mm to 150mm diameter in solid bar form or tubular sections of nominally equivalent cross sectional area.  such machines can be purchased to include automatic load of parts and means of removing the collar by either shearing or turning methods.

5.    Remembering that Quality Assurance of welded assemblies is of paramount importance, equipment manufacturers (refs. 3, 4 and 5) and Research Institutes (refs. 6 and 7) alike have developed 'in-process' monitoring systems based on detailed sensing of the major welding variables such as rotation speed, welding pressure and axial metal displacement, whilst work is actively progressing at the Welding Institute to both understand and devise ultrasonic methods for Non Destructive Evaluation of solid phase welds.

6.    A simple way to portray the rapid developments in friction welding since the late 50's and its future potential in the automotive industry is to refer to Table 1 which classifies friction welding processes, then examine each of the motions now available.

## Rotational Motion

7.    This is the most common of the motions adopted in industry today for both the continuous drive and Stored Energy (Inertia) process variants. The parts to be welded are generally round and of bar/bar, tube/tube or bar/plate forms. Examples of each of these geometric arrangements being joined at present under high volume production conditions are: bimetal exhaust valves, heavy and light duty rear axle casings and beams, drive shafts, and gear clusters respectively. Where necessary double ended machines to make two welds simultaneously are used to boost production output.

8.    The relatively new development of radial friction welding (refs. 8 and 9) also deserves mention. By using radial compression or expansion, rings can be attached onto solid or tubular assemblies, and into parts with complete or partial bores respectively. Simple schematics Fig. 2, serve to demonstrate this welding method. Equally both deformation modes can be used to join tubular parts.

## Linear Oscillation

9.    The process using this motion is commonly referred to as Vibration Welding (ref. 10). The heat needed to produce a bond is generated by pressing the parts together while one is moved at $\sim$ 100Hz through a small relative displacement in the plane of the joint. It is thought that at present this method is only being used for the welding of plastics. Plastic parts as long as 560mm and as wide as 305mm are apparently being welded on standard equipment. In certain instances total weld areas have exceeded 6500mm$^2$. The technique is quoted as being particularly useful for crystalline resins such as acetal copolymers, polyamides, thermoplastic polyesters, polythene and polymides, thermoplastics polyester, ploythenes and polypropylene.

## Angular Oscillation

10.    This method is another example of vibration welding but with the motion occurring through an arc. The frequency of oscillation was again $\sim$ 100Hz. This motion may prove to be superior to conventional rotation for many applications under consideration since it allows accurate angular alignment of parts after welding.

## Orbital Motion

11.    References to this motion for friction welding indicate that the method can be used to bond plastics and metals (refs. 11 and 12). However, because of the engineering difficulties associated with this motion its exploitation has been restricted. At present welding by this motion is carried out by: a) rotating both parts to be joined in the same direction and at the same speed, b) displacing one part off axis by $\sim$ 3mm then applying the friction load, c) after sufficient heat generation the displaced part is returned to the machine centre axis and the forge pressure applied, d) the welded assembly is finally arrested.

## Applications

12.    When reviewing applications associated with rotary motion then there are many areas being exploited in the automobile industry today. Examples of these have been mentioned earlier. However, with the continuing need to conserve fuel the weight of vehicles assumes considerable importance. Clearly in this respect changes will be introduced to replace solid parts with tubular sections and make use of lighter materials.

13.    One potential application in particular that is at present being examined is a drive shaft. In this respect the replacement of steel by an aluminium alloy in its construction is under review. Unfortunately friction welding of thin wall ($\sim$ 1.5mm) alloy tubulars is not as straightforward as it would first appear. Limited experience with the continuous drive variant would indicate that the rotational speed needs to be increased with greater emphasis given to improved braking efficiency, machine alignment and stability, and reduced spindle inertia. Also since the internal flash collar cannot be removed care must be taken to select welding conditions to give a generous radius between the flash and bore to improve fatigue performance.

14.    Speculating as to potential applications for the radial welding method, collars to shafts, sleeves in bores and piston fabrication as revealed in Fig. 3 are worthy of consideration. For the latter, wear grooves can be attached by compressive deformation while expansion of less thermally erodable materials could be introduced at the combustion bowl location. Expansion could also be used to weld in gudgeon pin bearings.

15.    Turning to the linear oscillation motion typical applications cited as occurring in the automotive industry are tail lamp assemblies and emissions control canisters. The latter show weight savings of 0.7kg each over metal canisters and over 3 million of these are quoted to have been made in the USA up to 1978.

16.    The literature suggests that the welding of large complex parts such as car body panels, doors, and bumpers may be feasible, exploitation of Angular oscillating motion in production was reported a few years ago for the fabrication of plastic thermostat control housings, Fig. 4.

 C282/81

17. From the aforegoing, the use of both angular and linear motion is essentially confined to joining of plastics. Clearly it is easier than joining metals because of the lower thermal conductivity and strength associated with plastics, thereby making it easier to establish a bonding interface at relatively low power. For either of these motions to be applied to metal parts a research and development programme will be necessary to determine the relationship between amplitude of vibration, frequency and welding force in order that process parameters could be specified to assist design of a dedicated machine.

18. With reference to the last motion considered, namely that of orbital, it is unfortunate that its use has not been further exploited since the motion has many favourable attributes. The first that was recognised was its capability to join non-round parts together to provide correct alignment after welding, Fig. 5, which of course is not easily achieved with rotational motion. However, it is of interest to note that the Japanese (ref. 2) have developed what they call a synchronised friction welder to twist parts into the correct alignment after heat generation. The second important feature is that the surface velocity is constant across the rubbing faces, (Note: - a velocity gradient from maximum at the outside to zero at the centre is observed for rotation). This will allow many individual assemblies (such as exhaust valves), or many parts to one part, Fig. 6 to be made in one welding sequence. Quite clearly this aspect of the motion could lead to greater productivity and fabrication of complex assemblies. Uniform surface velocity may also be advantageous when joining more of the difficult bimetal combinations such as titanium to steel, aluminium alloys to steel etc. since the interfacial temperatures will be lower and uniform. This aspect of the motion requires further investigation to realise its full potential.

MAGNETICALLY IMPELLED ARC BUTT (MIAB) WELDING

19. MIAB welding is a forge butt welding technique in which heat is generated prior to forging by the rapid movement of an arc (at 300 - 1000Hz) over the ends of the weldments by a magnetic field. The arc is drawn between the adjacent ends of the two weldments and is rotated around the weld line by the force, F, resulting from the interaction of the arc current, I, and the magnetic field, B, Fig. 7a. One method for generating the radial magnetic field, B at the weld line during MIAB welding is that shown in Fig. 7b. Two solenoids of opposed polarity are arranged as shown, and the radial component at the solenoid ends gives the required field. Clamps to hold the tubes and apply the forging forces are also shown. A more compact arrangement is shown in Fig. 7c in which a number of individual solenoids are arranged radially around the weld line. This permits the welding of components with flanges close to the weld line.

20. The MIAB welding technique should be con-sidered for those applications which are currently suitable for welding by resistance butt, flash, or friction. All of these processes are suited to the mass production industries in that the operator has only to load the components in the machine and activate it. Thereafter the machine automatically goes through the welding cycle. All these processes give solid phase welds. The welding cycle consists of a heating stage, followed by a forge to consolidate the weld. The major differences between the processes and the welds formed are in the techniques used to heat the components. Thus heat is generated by electrical resistance during resistance butt, by resistance and arc during flash, mechanically during friction, and by arc during MIAB.

21. Apart from the width of the HAZ, which can be modified by the use of 'hard' and 'soft' welding conditions, i.e. short time, high power, or long time, low power, conditions respectively, weld structures obtained by using these techniques are similar. Friction welds, however, give a different flash profile as a result of the severe working which occurs at the weld inter-face.

22. The major advantages claimed for MIAB welding over the alternative forge butt welding processes are that: very short welding schedules can be employed for thin wall components, the process is relatively clean, and it can be used to weld closed sections of various shapes (square, oval etc).

23. A working MIAB machine was established in Leipzig in 1973 (ref. 16) having the arrangement shown in Fig. 7b. This machine was suitable for welding low carbon and low alloy steel tubes of diameter 17 - 90mm and of wall thickness 1.5 - 5mm. Machine development was also pursued in West Germany and a range of machines is now available with maximum upset forces ranging from 3 - 40kN (ref. 14) suitable for welding tubes of diameters up to 200mm. The maximum weldable wall thickness, however, remains at 4 or 5mm because of uneven heating due to the preference of the arc to rotate around the outer edge of the tube.

24. A detailed evaluation of the performance of a MIAB welding machine was recently conducted when welding 50mm diameter x 3mm wall mild steel tubing (ref. 7). It was established that the technique could indeed make welds which satisfy normal requirements for high quality applications and that there was sufficient tolerance to the major welding parameters to enable the maintenance of weld quality under shopfloor conditions (see Fig. 8). Good quality MIAB welds were obtained which were solid phase, with a light etching band at the weld line consisting primarily of ferrite. The HAZ was parallel to the weld line, the width being dependent on the welding conditions employed. Welds could be made at a 6 second schedule in air where a variation of $\pm$ 10% in welding current, $\sim$ $\pm$ 30% in forge force (see Fig. 9) or $\sim$ $\pm$ 25% in duration could be tolerated and the bend test criterion still be met. The initial welding gap could be increased from 1.5 to

2.0mm with no effect on weld quality and
an end squareness mismatch of up to 1.0mm
could be tolerated.  Alternatively a 2 second
schedule could be employed giving similar
but slightly inferior weld quality, but $CO_2$
gas shielding was necessary to achieve this.

25.   MIAB machines have been used to butt weld
mild steel shock absorber tubing (ref. 18)
(25mm diameter, 1mm wall) at a rate of 600/
hour (0.5sec weld duration).  The alternative
flash and friction welding techniques required
5sec/weld and 50% higher forging forces.
Perhaps the most interesting recent application,
however, is that reported by the Ford Motor
Company (ref. 19).  MIAB welding is used to
weld two flanges to a car axle assembly (60mm
diameter tube, 3mm wall).  The process was
chosen instead of friction welding because
of the need for alignment between the two end
forgings, and flash welding was not favoured
because of doubts on weld reliability and
difficulties encountered in ensuring final
length tolerances.  MIG welding was also
considered but was much slower and adequate
fitup was difficult to ensure.  This
component is now welded in production on an
automatic double ended MIAB machine at a
production rate of 1000/day (two shifts).
The arcing duration is 2.5sec (approx. 25%
of that needed for flash and friction
welding) and the total loss of length is
only 3mm/weld (approx. 30% of that needed
for flash or friction).  Extensive qualif-
ication trials have proved the reliability
of the technique for this application.
10% of a total production run of 7500 axles
were destructively tested and all passed the
mechanical requirements for this weld.
Quality is maintained by periodic batch
destructive testing and by automatically
monitoring various parameters during
the welding cycle and de-activating the
machine when these are outside prescribed
limits.

26.   As mentioned above, a major current
restriction to the MIAB technique is that
it is currently only suitable for thin wall
steel components (up to 4 or 5mm).  This
limitation on wall thickness mainly arises
from the finite arc width causing uneven
interfacial heating with thicker wall
components.  This problem is currently
under investigation at the Welding Institute*,
since a practical solution would make the MIAB
welding of heavier wall tubing (as used,
for example, in truck and lorry axles)
attractive to industry.  Even arc heating
can be achieved by mechanically orbiting
one tube about the other at a low frequency+
($\sim$ 1Hz).  If the axis is displaced by a
distance equal to the tube wall thickness,
the arc follows a path from the inside edge
to the outside edge of each tube as a result
of the arc bridging the shortest distance
between the tube faces.  Orbiting one
tube about the other creates a large number of

---

* Project funded by Blacks Equipment and the UK
  Department of Industry.

+ Patent applied for.

arc paths over both tube faces giving smooth
evenly heated faces, as shown in Fig. 10a.
Alternatively the arc can be electro-
magnetically moved over the tube end.  When
such tubes are forged, welds of good quality
can be achieved, Fig. 10b.

## LASER WELDING

27.   Both the electron beam and laser welding
processes are suited to the mass production
industries since they allow the rapid
welding of complex shaped components.  Both
techniques give narrow deep fusion welds
formed by the impingement of a high energy
electron beam or light (laser) beam on to
the workpiece, see Fig. 11.  Electron beam
welding has been available since the 1950's
and is currently capable of welding up to 250mm
thick steel in one pass (75mm/min) whilst
the capacity of high power laser welding
equipment, (up to 10kW) has been increased
during the 1970's to a current level of
up to 12mm steel (25mm/min).  Whilst both
techniques are suitable for mass production
use, the laser has the advantage over electron
beam in that welding can be performed in any
desired atmosphere.  The technique does not
suffer therefore the constraint of electron
beam where welding is normally performed
in a vacuum chamber and the laser is more
suitable for continuous flow production use.

28.   The continuous $CO_2$ laser consists of
an optical cavity between two mirrors and
the lasing medium is a gas (a mixture of
helium, nitrogen and carbon dioxide) which
is excited by the passage of a high voltage
electrical discharge.  The excited molecules
produce photons of 10.6$\mu$m wavelength by
vibration-rotation transitions.  Cooling of the
gas is essential as the electrical discharge
produces heat and the efficiency of the lasing
action falls as the gas temperature increases
above 200$^{\circ}$C (ref. 20).

29.   In low power lasers (< 1kW) cooling can
be achieved by convection in the gas in the
discharge tubes and by conduction across the
tube walls.  To prevent the build-up of gas
decomposition products the gas mixture is
extracted from one end of the discharge tube
and new gas fed in at the other, this slow
gas flow also contributing to the cooling.  At
powers of 1kW and above forced cooling of the
gas is required.  The gas mixture is circulated
rapidly from the lasing region to heat
exchangers and back to the lasing region.

30.   Both transverse flow and axial flow
lasers are available at powers above 1kW.
In the transverse flow laser (Fig. 12a) the
gas crosses the optical cavity at right
angles to the optical axis.  This has the
advantage that the dwell time of the gas in the
laser cavity is short and the gas velocity
need not be high, but the energy distribution
in the output beam is not ideal for welding.
On the other hand, in the fast axial flow
laser (Fig. 12b) the gas travels along the
optical axis, which gives an energy distribution
closer to the ideal for welding, but
necessitates very high gas velocities to keep
the dwell time short.

31.    As the 10.6μm wavelength laser light produced by the $CO_2$ laser is in the far infra-red portion of the spectrum, the beam is manipulated by copper mirrors, which may be gold plated, and is focused with zinc selenide or potassium chloride lenses.

32.    The penetration achieved during laser welding depends on the power, focusing, and mode structure of the laser beam and the travel speed of the workpiece relative to the beam. Increasing the travel speed causes a decrease in weld depth but the weld depth cannot be increased indefinitely by using slow travel speeds because as the speed is decreased the interaction of the beam with the plasma becomes more severe. This lessens the penetration and produces a conduction limited zone near the metal surface. The capability of various commercially available high power laser systems when welding steel are shown in Fig. 13. It is clear from this that these high power lasers are capable of welding at speeds which compete with the established resistance welding techniques used in the vehicle industries. Thus, 1mm steel can be welded at speeds of up to 8m/min and 3mm steel at 6m/min using appropriate equipments. For this reason a number of pilot trials have been performed on timing gear covers, laminations of starter motor armatures, various configurations of gears and other transmission parts, collapsible steering column jackets, petrol tanks and wheels (refs. 22 and 23). Fig. 14 shows examples of such welded components. Although none of these applications are currently in industrial production it is clear that there is great potential for laser equipments in the market. The success achieved, however, will be dependent on the jigging and work handling systems devised since good workpiece fitup is critical.

## REFERENCES

(1) WANG K K. Friction Welding. WRC Bulletin (204), April 1975, pp21.

(2) The Welding Institute, Exploiting friction welding in production, Information Package Series, 1979, pp41 - 58.

(3) Electrostatic, Control unit for friction welding monitor. Publicity Information Literature.

(4) KUKA, Friction welding monitor 'controller'. Publicity Information Literature.

(5) Thompson Friction Welding. Digital friction welding monitor. Publicity Information Literature.

(6) ELLIS C R E and NICHOLAS E D. A quality monitor for friction welding. Advances in Welding Processes Conference, Harrogate, May 1974, paper 39, pp14 - 20.

(7) DREWS P et al. Development and application of a computer control system for friction welding. IIW Document No. III-581-78, June 1977.

(8) NICHOLAS E D. Friction welding when applied to hollow sections. Second International Conference on Pipewelding, London 1977, paper 8, pp279 - 283.

(9) Welding Institute, Friction welding methods and apparatus, British Patent 1,505,832, 30 March 1978.

(10) ANON. Vibration welding (of plastics) permits novel designs, Design Engineering January 1978, pp47 - 48.

(11) SEARLE J. Friction welding non-circular components using orbital motion. Welding and Metal Fabrication, August 1971.

(12) ASTROP A. Friction welding lines up more jobs. Machinery and Production Engineering May 1979, pp41 - 43.

(13) SCHLEBECK E. Welding with a magnetically moved arc (MBL welding): a new means of rationalism. Welding Institute Conference - Advances in Welding Processes, Harrogate, May 1978, 249 - 56.

(14) GANOWSKI F J. The magnet arc welding process, Welding and Metal Fabrication, 42 (6), 1974, 206 - 13.

(15) Pressure butt welding machine MBL-S6.3. Technical Information Leaflet, LEW Henningsdorf, German Democratic Republic.

(16) TORNOV H. The MBL-S6.3 pressure butt welding machine. Schweisstechnik (Berlin) 24 (4), 1974, 156 - 7.

(17) JOHNSON K I. The MIAB welding of steel tubes and its reliability. Welding Institute Pipewelding Conference, London 1979.

(18) Rotating arc speed tube welding. Iron Age Metalworking International, 12 March 1974, 31 - 32.

(19) HAGAN D and RILEY N. An industrial application of MIAB welding of tubes: a rear axle cross tube assembly. Welding Institute Pipewelding Conference, London 1979.

(20) CHARSCHAN S S et al. Guide for material processing by laser. Laser Institute of America, 1977.

(21) EBOO M, STEEN W M and CLARKE J. Arc augmented laser welding. Advances in Welding Processes, Conference Proceedings, Welding Institute, Harrogate, May 1978, 257 - 265.

(22) DESFORGES C D. Current and future applications of laser to materials processing technology. Paper 3 in Laser Processing of Engineering Materials, Symposium Proceedings, Institute of Physics, London 1977.

(23) Avco Everett Research Laboratory Incorporated, Trade Literature.

Table 1    Classification of friction welding processes

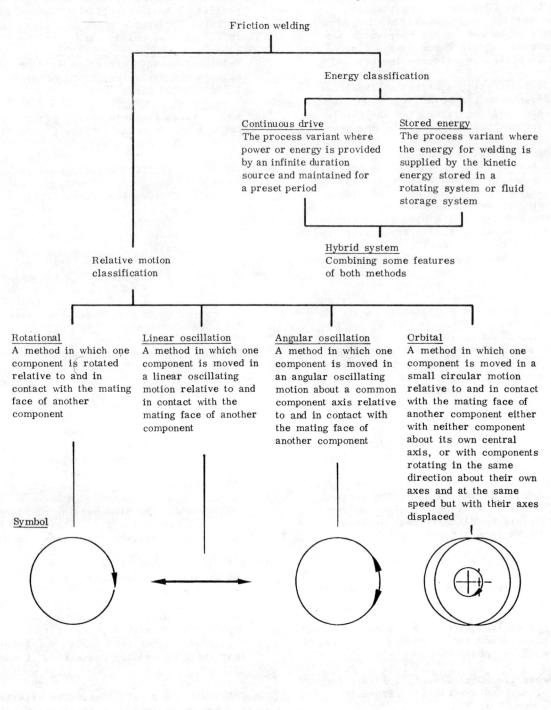

Friction welding

Energy classification

Continuous drive
The process variant where
power or energy is provided
by an infinite duration
source and maintained for
a preset period

Stored energy
The process variant where
the energy for welding is
supplied by the kinetic
energy stored in a
rotating system or fluid
storage system

Hybrid system
Combining some features
of both methods

Relative motion
classification

Rotational
A method in which one
component is rotated
relative to and in
contact with the mating
face of another
component

Linear oscillation
A method in which one
component is moved in
a linear oscillating
motion relative to and
in contact with the
mating face of another
component

Angular oscillation
A method in which one
component is moved in
an angular oscillating
motion about a common
component axis relative
to and in contact with
the mating face of
another component

Orbital
A method in which one
component is moved in a
small circular motion
relative to and in contact
with the mating face of
another component either
with neither component
about its own central
axis, or with components
rotating in the same
direction about their own
axes and at the same
speed but with their axes
displaced

Symbol

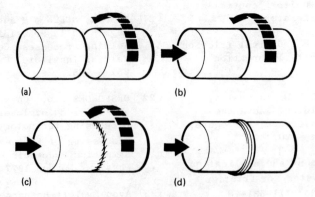

(a)                    (b)

(c)                    (d)

Fig 1    Simplest method of friction welding: (a) rotary member spun;
(b) advanced into contact under load; (c) contact pressure
maintained; (d) rotation stopped (switching off motor, or fly
wheel coming to rest), pressure maintained to produce weld

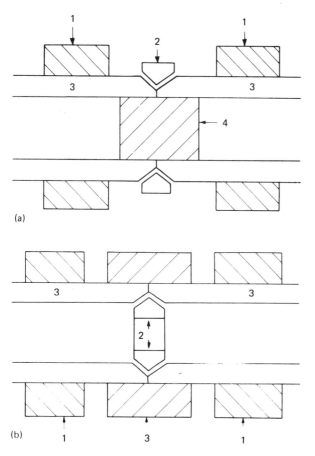

(a)

(b)

Fig 2 Radial friction welding technique using: (a) compression; (b) expansion, 1 clamps, 2 ring rotated and compressed/ expanded, 3 pipe, 4 backing plug/sleeve

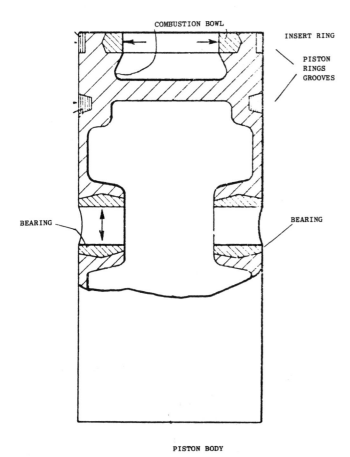

COMBUSTION BOWL

INSERT RING

PISTON RINGS GROOVES

BEARING

BEARING

PISTON BODY

Fig 3 Potential application for radial friction welding

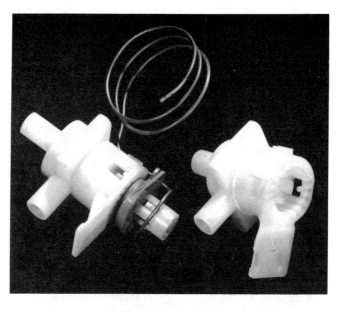

Fig 4 Thermostat housings fabricated by angular reciprocating friction welding

(a)

(b)

Fig 5 Non round steel bar friction welded using orbital motion: (a) as welded; (b) bend tested

Fig 6 Multiple joint in clear perspex produced using orbital friction welding

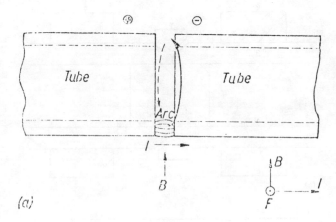

(a)

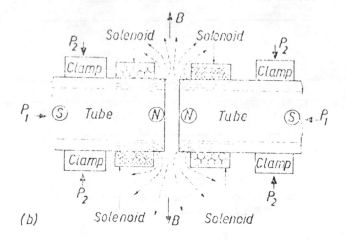

(b)

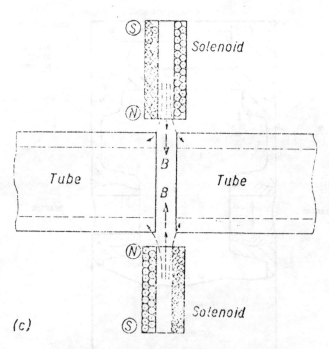

(c)

Fig 7 Arrangements used for MIAB welding: (a) general direction of current, 1, and applied magnetic field, B, indicated, with direction of resultant force, F, on arc; (b) opposed solenoid, as used in ref 1: $P_1$ forging force, $P_2$ clamping force, B radial magnetic field; (c) compact solenoid, as used in ref 2. Individual solenoids, connected in series, arranged radially around weld line

(a)

0        10 mm  20        30        40        50

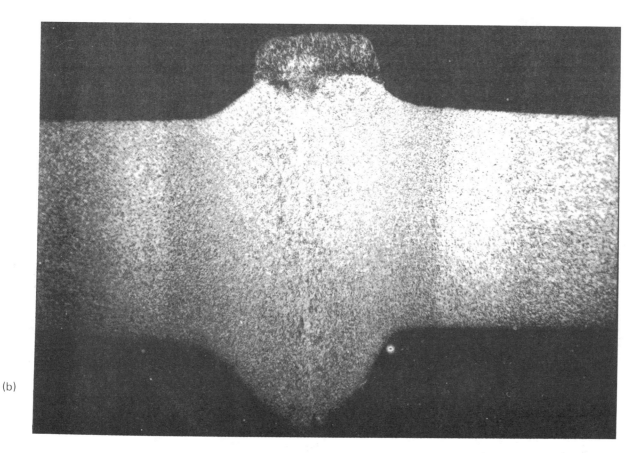

(b)

Fig 8    Good quality MIAB welded mild steel tube, 51 mm OD x 3 mm wall,
(a) half section showing bore; (b) metallurgical section

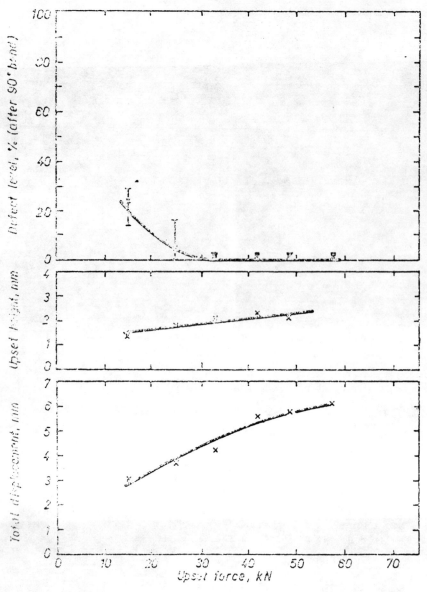

Fig 9   Effect of forge force on defect level (after 90° bend test), upset height,
and total displacement.  Current: stage 1,  296A. Duration: 6.1 s.
Current: stage 2, 1430 peak.  Duration: 0.2 s. Welded in air

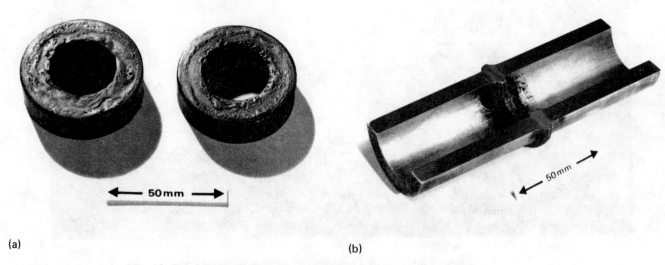

(a)

(b)

Fig 10  The achievement of (a) even arc heating of 12 mm tube ends;
(b) good MIAB weld quality in 10 mm wall tubing by mechanically
orbiting one tube axis relative to the other

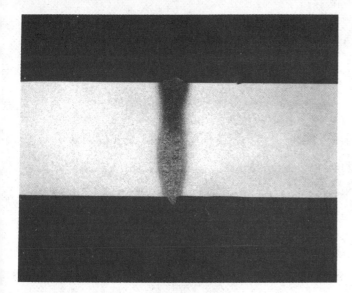

Fig 11 Deep penetration high power laser weld in 9.5 mm thick mild steel, 6 kW, 1.2 m/min

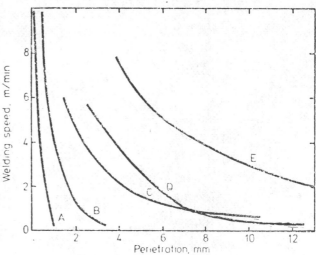

Fig 13 Performances of several $CO_2$ lasers when welding steel (after ref 9 and 10); A 375 W slow axial flow; B 1.5 kW fast axial flow; C 7 kW transverse flow; D 6 kW fast axial flow; E 12 kW transverse flow

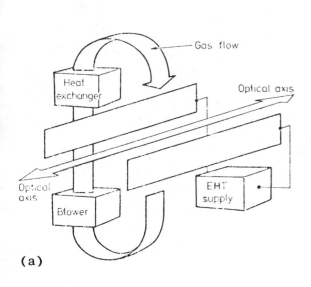

**(a)**

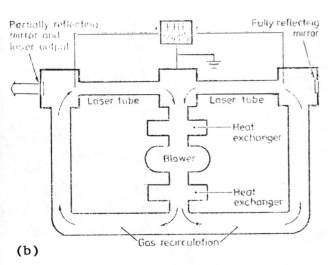

**(b)**

Fig 12 Principle of operation of (a) transverse flow $CO_2$ laser; (b) fast axial flow laser

(a)

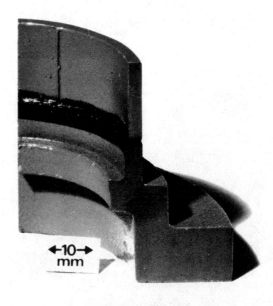

(b)

Fig 14 Examples of laser welded vehicle components: (a) synchromesh gear mm steel, 2 kW ~ 15 s; (b) axle/stub assembly mm steel, 5 kW, 4 s

# C283/81

# Development of an on-line transfer line monitoring system

O B YEOH, MSc,
BL Technology Limited, Materials and Manufacturing Technology, Birmingham

SYNOPSIS    The timely acquisition and analysis of relevant and accurate data is essential for the efficient operation of any complex manufacturing system.  The time aspect of information is particularly important in automotive manufacturing due to the high rate of production output.  These considerations have resulted in the development and implementation of an on-line real-time Transfer Line Monitoring System at BL's Longbridge plant.  The low-cost microprocessor-based system is linked on-line to a transfer line to provide instant reports on the output, inter-operational stock, status, reasons for stoppages and line performance.  This paper discusses the ideas behind the project and provides an account of the achievements made.

## NOTATION

$b(i,j)$  Accumulated time when signal $j$ of machine $i$ is currently on logic level 0.

$B$  Current Stop Time Matrix, $B = \sum\sum b(i,j)$.

$c(i,j)$  Number of occurrences when signal $j$ of machine $i$ is on logic level 0.

$C$  Stop Count Matrix, $C = \sum_{1}^{n}\sum_{1}^{13} c(i,j)$

$d$  Day number.

$d_1$  Lunch duration.

$d_s$  Shift duration.

$m(i)$  Machine $i$ in transfer line.

$n$  Number of machines in transfer line.

$p(i)$  Production output of machine $i$.

$p(0)$  Number of workpieces input into transfer line.

$p(n+1)$  Number of workpieces despatched from the transfer line.

$p_{ef}(i)$  Forecast end-of-shift production output of machine $i$.

$r_p(i)$  Accumulated time when signal $j$ of machine $i$ is on logic level 1.

$r(i,j)$  Accumulated time when signal $j$ of machine $i$ is on logic level 1.

$R$  Run Time Matrix, $R = \sum_{1}^{n}\sum_{1}^{13} r(i,j)$

$s$  Shift number

$s_t$  Total stock level in the transfer line.

$s_c(i)$  Stock level in buffer $i$ at current point in shift.

$s_e(i)$  Stock level in buffer $i$ at end of shift.

$s_s(i)$  Stock level in buffer $i$ at start of shift.

$t_e$  Elapsed time since start of shift.

$t_s$  Shift start time

$t_f$  Shift finish time

$t_1$  Time left before end of shift.

$u(i,j)$  Percentage of elapsed time when signal $j$ of machine $i$ is on logic level 1, $u(i,j) = (r(i,j)/t_e) \times 100\%$

$U$  Utilisation Matrix, $U = \sum_{1}^{n}\sum_{1}^{13} u(i,j)$

## INTRODUCTION

Automotive manufacturers today face a multitude of problems.  Of these problems, which may be economic, social, legal or technological, the need to improve cost competitiveness is a major issue. Automotive component manufacturing requires massive investment in expensive and complex plant and machinery. In order to attain minimum manufacturing cost, it is essential that all available manufacturing resources (men, machines, tools, energy and materials) be utilised as much as possible in the production of components of the highest quality whilst maintaining optimum work-in-progress inventory.

The timely acquisition, analysis and communicating of relevant and accurate data is vital to the efficient operation of the automotive manufacturing organisation.  This aspect of information is particularly important in automotive manufacturing because of the high rates of production output.  The recent availability of low-cost microprocessor technology, coupled with associated electronics and software, has made it economically and technically feasible to provide most automotive component manufacturing organisations with means to acquire essential production and quality data in real time and communicate the necessary information to the appropriate managers and supervisors.  The result will be improved line management effectiveness arising out of the ability to take decisions based on up-to-date facts. As a consequence, the manufacturing system will become more efficient in terms of productivity as well as quality. The application of on-line real-time monitoring will provide the means and impetus for the optimisation of automotive manufacturing systems.

In early 1980, the decision was taken for BL Technology Limited to develop low-cost technology for the on-line real-time monitoring of automotive component manufacturing systems. The microprocessor-based system which has been evolved is linked on-line to the transfer machines to provide instant reports on output, inter-operational stock, machine status, causes of stoppages and the performance of the transfer line.

## MANUFACTURING PROBLEMS ASSOCIATED WITH TRANSFER LINES

Hatvany (1) has defined a <u>manufacturing system</u> as "an integrated material and data processing system". The material processing aspect involves the physical manufacturing processes, the machine tools and the devices for workpiece handling as well as people. The data processing aspect includes the machine control software and line management information.

The materials processing aspect of transfer lines has many problems relating to the selection of efficient processes, line layouts, improved tooling, machine tool accuracy and facility reliability. These problems have long been the concern of production engineers in the automotive industry. In contrast, the data processing aspect has been largely neglected until recent years. In the past, conventional transfer lines have suffered from poor reliability in electromechanical controls, difficult fault diagnosis in the event of breakdowns, low machine uptime caused by machines being 'starved' or 'blocked' and difficult line supervision due to the lack of detailed information on the output, status and performance of the line.

In the last decade, hard-wired electromechanical controls increasingly are being replaced by more reliable solid state programmable logic controllers. These programmable logic controllers, some of which are microprocessor-based, enable control sequences to be written in 'software'. Spin-offs arising from using such software-based control systems include automatic fault diagnosis, limited local production monitoring and data communication link-ups with other programmable controllers or computers. However, programmable logic controllers are quite expensive: the retrofitting on existing transfer lines can cost several hundred thousand pounds and can tie up the machines for lengthy periods of time. Fortunately, most new transfer machines are now supplied with programmable controllers.

Transfer line losses due to 'starvation' or 'blockage', which may cost up to 25% of line running time, can be minimised by the optimisation of buffer stocks. This can be achieved through either computer simulation using sampled historical data or the use of 'real time' data for 'dynamic' and adaptive optimisation under changing practical constraints. Computer simulation using historical data has been developed by Kay (2), Roggenbuck (3), Hanifin et al (4) and Biles et al (5). Real time and dynamic optimisation of existing transfer lines requires on-line real time monitoring.

## INFORMATION REQUIREMENTS

The importance of information is illustrated aptly by G.M. Ferrero who is quoted by Olivia-Lopez (6) as having written, "Knowledge of facts is the blood of an organisation, and the communications channels are its arteries and veins". In order to be effective and efficient, line managers or supervisors need reliable information on factors such as targeted and actual output levels, dynamic buffer stocks, machine stoppages and malfunctions, work standard, labour productivity, tooling usage, and line scrap rates. For instance, the reporting of a machine stoppage as soon as it occurs can save vital minutes in total downtime, and the availability of the line inter-operational stock figures can allow the line supervisor to act quickly either to redeploy machine operators or labourers or to direct maintenance effort to repair machines with the worst consequential ('knock-on') effects. In the longer term, analysis of the causes of machine downtime will enable line management to direct effective action against the most offending causes.

Fundamentally, any manufacturing information system will need to have the following sub-systems:
(1)  the acquisition of data (from source)
(2)  the transmission of data
(3)  the filtering out of irrelevant data ('noise')
(4)  the interpretation and analysis of the relevant data
(5)  the presentation of the analysed information
(6)  the communication of the relevant reports to the right person(s)
(7)  the storage of important data/ information for future reference and subsequent analysis.

Furthermore, the information requirements of a manufacturing system can be examined under following factors:

(1) 'newness' and 'timeliness' - the
    smallest allowable time unit.
(2) accuracy - the degree of 'noise'
    immunity.
(3) amount of detail required.
(4) relevance and value of the data/
    information.
(5) sampling rates - for data
    acquisition or report interrogation.
(6) interpretation of data/information.
(7) type and degree of analysis.
(8) format and presentation.

STATE-OF-THE-ART

In the last decade, there has been a
rapid advance in the large scale
integration of electronic circuits
which has resulted in the tumbling
prices of micro-miniaturised 'chips'.
The economics of microelectronics has
been orchestrated so that lower costs
generate more applications, which, in
turn, enable the costs to be reduced
further through increasing economies of
scale.

Microelectronics has already found wide
applications in the automotive industry
(7); yet, these applications appear to
be merely the 'tip of the iceberg'. For
instance, programmable microprocessor-
based systems can be applied to virtually
every machine tool, press tool, robot,
conveyor, process plant, and inspection/
testing machine in the automotive
factory. In fact, microelectronics can
be adapted to most control and/or
monitoring applications.

One of the most important uses of
microelectronics is in its contribution
to the relatively new information
technology (8). Scarrott (9) has
described the evolution of the new
discipline of information engineering
from communication theory and the
concept of a 'bit' as a quantitative
measure of information. The information
engineer will be concerned with the
collection, manipulation, communication
and use of information.

Production monitoring has now been
applied in many manufacturing plants. In
1963, Thomas (10) described an electromechanical system based on punched
cards which was complicated and slow.
Throughout the late 1960s and the 1970s
a number of applications of minicomputer-
based systems for monitoring production
status and performance have been
reported, for example, by Johnson (11),
Cornelius (12), Aronson (13), Campbell
(14) and Chambers (15). Automotive
manufacturers in the USA, Japan and
Germany have been using shop-floor
computers for many years. Entrekin (16)
reports in 1970 on four minicomputer
applications, in the USA, on monitoring
automotive transfer lines for
efficiencies, downtime, cycle time and
parts counts. The application of on-
line computer monitoring on a cylinder
block machining transfer line in West
Germany (17) has resulted in the

achievement of up to 85% machine
utilisation because it unveiled vital
information which led to improvements
in organisational and operational
control.

Fukuma et al (18) have developed a
minicomputer-based system in Japan for
monitoring a 50-machine line which
produces automotive rear axle shafts.
The integrated system incorporates
sequential control, production monitoring,
hazard monitoring (for emergencies),
quality monitoring (of workpiece accuracy)
and automatic tool adjustments. Bozich
(19) has reported on on-line condition
monitoring of rotating machinery to
assist maintenance planning. Jones (20)
has described the use of factory data
highways and microprocessor-based
'intelligent' data collection units.
Meleka (7) has described the widespread
use of programmable controllers for
fault diagnostics, in addition to the
normal sequential control of machines.
Finally, Crumpton and Yeoh (21) have
introduced the concept of 'total factory
monitoring' which is the integration of
all these monitoring technologies
covering production monitoring, quality
monitoring, condition monitoring and
fault diagnostics.

THE 'O' SERIES BLOCK LINE

The 'O' Series Engine Block machining
transfer line (see Figure 1) is 500
metres long and has a maximum output
rate of 120 pieces per hour. (The
practical achieveable output rate is 80
pieces per hour, taking into account
losses due to tool change, breakdowns,
and other contingencies). It consists
of 18 synchronous transfer machines, 2
washing machines, 2 leak testing
machines, one dunk test machine, 4 manual
bearing cap assembly stations, one
automatic nut runner, 2 fine boring
machines, 2 honing machines, 2 cylinder
bore inspection and grading machines,
and conveyors in an asynchronous line.

Pre-set tooling is used on the transfer
line, with tool setting being carried
out in a setters' pen, and tools on the
line being changed by operators.
Cutting tools are classified into 6 tool
groups, named alphabetically from A to
F, with A representing the tools with a
400-component life, B representing a
800-component life and so on. Counters
in the machine control panels count the
number of components machined and 15
components before each combination of
tool change groups is due, an indication
lamp at the machine is switched on to
indicate the tool groups requiring
changes. At the same time, the same
combination of lights also come on at
the display panel in the control room-
cum-foremen's office. When the tool
change is actually due, the machine is
automatically stopped and the necessary
tool change is carried out before the
machine is manually re-started again. In

order to eliminate waiting for tools, a spare set of tools is always available on tool blocks at each machine; this set is replenished after each tool change.

The transfer line provides in-line storage for a limited number of work-pieces between each machine. This in-line buffer stock is supplemented by a stock of partly-processed workpieces which are stacked on floor storage areas beside each machine. In the event of a machine 'starvage' or 'blockage' due to the stoppage of other machines in the line, the workpieces are manually on-loaded or off-loaded, using the floor buffer stock, in order to keep that machine (and also upstream or downstream machines) in production. Maintenance resources are shared with other lines in that factory.

When the transfer line was installed, a display panel was also provided (see Figure 2) consisting of 295 lamps which light up to indicate the following information on each of the 18 transfer machines:

(1)  Tool change required for group indicated.
(2)  Tool change completed.
(3)  Tool broken or adjustment.
(4)  Machine in production.
(5)  Machine in setting mode.
(6)  Machine in automatic cycle mode.
(7)  Unloading conveyor empty - i.e. machine 'starved'.
(8)  Loading conveyor full - i.e. machine 'blocked'.
(9)  Lubrication required.

Although the display panel provides valuable data on the production status on the line, it does not enable the information to be analysed in any form nor stored for subsequent retrieval. Moreover, in order to use the display panel properly, the line foreman needed to watch the 295 indicator lamps almost all the time. It was an obvious solution to use a low-cost microcomputer to monitor, analyse and provide reports on the valuable production information. The '0' Series Block transfer line was an excellent candidate for the development and the pilot scheme implementation of transfer line monitoring.

TRANSFER LINE MONITORING

The project was aimed at developing the technology and methodology for the successful implementation of low-cost, microprocessor-based transfer line monitoring systems. The first application on the '0' Series Engine Block transfer line was a pilot scheme to demonstrate the economic and technical feasibility of on-line real time transfer line monitoring. The technologies required included sensors for data acquisition, interfaces, data transmission

techniques and software. A modular approach was adopted for the software to allow flexibility and adaptability for future monitoring applications. The initial design objectives were:

low cost
expandability
effective analysis and presentation of information.
accuracy of information
ergonomic man-machine interfaces
simple system operation
relevance of information presented
satisfaction of user requirements
system maintainability

The low cost criterion was satisfied by the use of standard 'off-the-shelf' hardware units. Wide applicability and expandability were accommodated in the modular design of the software. The maintainability of the system was enhanced by the provision of "engineers reports". The accuracy, relevance, ergonomics and effectiveness of the information presented by the system were important considerations throughout the applications software development phase. Close collaboration with the users of the system was maintained to evolve software which suited practical requirements in the most effective way. Wide use was made of pictures and graphs to enhance the impact of the reports displayed on screen or printed out. The simplicity of operation was necessary to enable the system to be easily operated by any line foreman. Finally, the principles of 'Management by Objectives' and 'Management by Exception' were harmonised in the design of the system reports.

PROJECT METHODOLOGY

The project was carried out in the following sequence: feasibility study, finance approval, system design and functional specification, system selection, system engineering, software development, system testing, documentation installation and commissioning. The feasibility study identified the outline system requirements as well as the necessary information for obtaining finance approval. After the functional specification was determined, proposals were invited from a number of systems suppliers. In the system selection phase, it was decided that all the hardware would be outsourced but the bulk of the software would be developed in-house so that it can be controlled more closely to meet all the local user requirements. Moreover, in-house software development reduces the dependance the company would have other-wise on suppliers for the many software modifications and enhancements which would be required subsequently. In order to reduce lead time, the modular software was split for parallel development by two engineers, system testing was completed during commissioning and the documentation was written in parallel with the installation and commissioning phases.

Throughout the project, the approach adopted has been to evolve a workable and practical system gradually, starting with the gentle introduction of new technology through education and involvement of the potential users. Full participation of everyone concerned was obtained through a series of formal and informal meetings. It is very important to obtain maximum commitment and interest by the users because the success of the system depends ultimately on this.

SYSTEM DESIGN AND EQUIPMENT (Hardware) SELECTION

Phase 1 of the project involved the application of production monitoring on the 18 transfer machines on the 'O' Series Block transfer line which already had been linked via multi-core cables to the display panel in the control room. Phase 2 will cover the rest of the line at a later stage, and will include quality monitoring. The signals monitored in Phase 1 are:

(1) component count
(2) machine awaiting maintenance
(3) machine under repair by maintenance
(4) machine under setting mode
(5) machine under off-standard/unplanned tool change.
(6) machine stopped, waiting for components (blocked or starved)
(7) tool broken or out of adjustment
(8) planned tool changes in the groups A to F

The transfer line monitoring system hardware is divided into four main segments: (1) data acquisition interfaces (2) data scanning and concentration devices, (3) data analysis and storage devices and (4) output devices. Figure 1 illustrates the configuration of the system.

The data acquisition interfaces are wired up to 178 different data points with different voltages such as 18 VAC or 24 VDC. All input channels are optically isolated. The data scanning device is a multiplexer capable of scanning all the inputs once a second. The data concentration device (called the MBX) is a twin-Z80 microprocessor unit with adequate random-access memory (RAM) to hold all the accumulated input data. The MBX holds its control and data manipulation programs on programmable read only memory (PROM). It formats and transmits the accumulated data, at predetermined frequencies, down a 20mA current loop, twisted pair wire line to the data analysis microcomputer. The MBX also holds data files such as shift patterns, input data formats and an automatic calendar and clock. Furthermore, the MBX has a Centronics-type parallel printer interface which

enables it to be connected to the printer so that the formatted, accumulated data can be printed out if required, by-passing the data analysis microcomputer. Another report which can be printed out from the MBX is the Engineers' Report which shows the status of each input signal at one second intervals - this is very useful for system diagnostic purposes. The multiplexer and the MBX were supplied by Dextralog Limited.

The data analysis microcomputer used is a standard CBM 3032 desktop microcomputer which uses a 6502 microprocessor central processing unit (cpu) and had 13K bytes of read only memory (ROM) and 32K bytes of RAM. This microcomputer performs all the communication with the MBX via a twisted pair of wires, linked to a 20mA serial interface which, in turn, is connected to the microcomputer through the IEEE-488 bus. The data transfer along this communications link is carried out at a speed of 4800 baud. The data is formatted in serial ASCII with 7 data bits, 2 stop bits and even parity. The microcomputer also performs all the analysis of the data and formats the information into reports for output via the output devices. The data storage device used is a CBM 3040 dual floppy disk drive which is linked to the microcomputer via the IEEE-488 bus. The CBM 3040 provides a total on-line storage capacity of 340K bytes on both floppy disks. All the applications programs and permanent data files are stored on one floppy disk. The second disk drive is used to obtain a duplicate copy of that floppy disk for back-up. The data analysis microcomputer also contains an integral video screen - this is the main device used for the output (display) of reports in real time. There is also an 80-column printer which is linked to the microcomputer via the IEEE-488 bus for report printouts. This 120 character per second printer has a 3K byte data buffer to enable it to run almost in parallel with the other devices. It also has an inter-changeable Centronics-type parallel interface which enables it to be linked directly to the MBX, by-passing the microcomputer.

APPLICATIONS SOFTWARE DESIGN AND DEVELOPMENT.

The in-house software development included the software specification, the sub-division of programs for parallel program development and testing, program coding and assembly, testing of sub-program modules, program linking, program testing, system testing and validation, software implementation and continual software enhancement. Most of the programs were written in interpreted BASIC, but the time-critical parts were written in 6502 assembler which were assembled into machine code for normal operation.

The software sub-system was designed to be as ergonomic and user-friendly as possible. This includes the use of prompt messages during batch mode data entry or manipulation, the provision of an audible bell to signify the time-out and return from the serial input scanning mode, and extensive use of graphical presentation of reports. The software was also designed to enable the CBM microcomputer to be software-disconnected at any time and re-connected later without any loss of vital data. This means that instant system recovery can be achieved by hardware substitution in the event of a failure in the hardware devices. It also means that the microcomputer system can temporarily be diverted to other processing tasks such as batch-mode tool cost calculation.

The software sub-system is divided into the batch mode and the real time mode. The batch mode enables the batch entry of the current date and time at system start-up and updates of data files such as shift times, production targets and capacities and inter-operational stocks. The real time mode involves the monitoring, real time analysis and the report generation functions.

The serial input scanning and data analysis functions, which have the highest real time priority, take 28 seconds. This means that in every 2 minute interval the microcomputer is available for 77% of its time for report enquiries. Screen-based report generation requires a maximum of 5 seconds of cpu time, whilst the real time report output on the printer uses 2 seconds of cpu time. Figure 3 is a flow chart showing the operation of software sub-system.

DATA FILES

The system data files are stored in random access memory (RAM) for use in the real time mode, and on floppy disk for permanent reference as well as for further analysis in the batch mode. The main RAM data files are structured in two-dimensional matrices, where the rows are machine numbers and the columns are signal numbers:

R, the accumulated run time matrix,
C, the stop count matrix,
B, the current stop time matrix, and
U, the utilisation matrix.

The floppy disk data files are all stored on one 170K byte single sided, single density $5\frac{1}{4}$-inch mini floppy disk. All these files are sequential files with variable length records. They include:

| ELOG | the event log-file which is updated every 10 minutes in real time. |
| SSUMd-s | the shift summary files, one for each shift up to 21 shifts, where d = day of the week (1 to 7) and s = the shift number (1, 2 or 3). |
| STOCKFL | the inter-operational stock file. |
| WEEKw | the weekly summary file, one for each week, w,(w 52). |
| CURRENTWK | the current week file (week-to-date). |
| SHIFTFL | the shift pattern (times file. |
| SCRAPFL | the line scrap file. |
| TITLES | the title strings file used in report headings. |
| LINEDATA | the file containing constant line data. |
| SHIFTARGET | the shift targets (standards) file. |

ALGORITHMS

The current inter-operational stock, $s_c(i)$, at buffer i is calculated from the current production output(i) and the inter-operational stock at the start of shift, $s_s(i)$:

$$s_c(i) = s_s(i) + p(i-1) - p(i)$$

and the total stock in the transfer line, $s_t$ is calculated in the following way:

$$s_t = \sum_{i=1}^{n} s_c(i)$$

where n is the total number of machines in the transfer line.

Signal number 1 (i.e. j = 1) is used to identify whether a machine is in production or if it is stopped. Machine i is in production if the current stop signal, $b(i,1) = 0$ and the machine is identified as stopped if $b(i,1) > 0$.

Signal number 6 is the 'waiting component' signal. Machine i is identified as 'blocked' waiting component if:

$$b(i,6) > 0 \quad \text{and} \quad b(i+1,1) > 0$$

and the machine is 'starved' if:

$$b(i,6) > 0 \quad \text{and} \quad b(i-1,1) > 0$$

The forecast end-of-shift production output, $P_{ef}(i)$, of machine is calculated using the average production rate, $r_p(i)$, during the shift time elapsed and the time left before the end of the shift $t_1$:

$$P_{ef}(i) = t_1 \times r(i)$$

Since the output rate:

$$r_p(i) = p(i)/t_e$$

where p(i) is the production output of machine i, and $t_e$ is the time elapsed since the start of the shift, and all production output must be integer values,

$$P_{ef}(i) = int(t_1 \times p(i)/t_e)$$

## APPLICATIONS PROGRAMS

The main applications program is BLMS2.0, the block line monitoring system program, which is 13K bytes long and contains over 20 BASIC sub-routines. BLMS2.0 handles all the system start-up operations, the management of the real time monitoring as well as the formatting and presentation of the screen-based and printout reports (see Figure 3). This is complemented by MCP5, the machine code program which performs the serial input scan, RAM matrix data file initialization and updating, partial analysis of the data, all the code conversions (e.g. Hexadecimal to Decimal) and the periodic dump to disk file, ELOG. In practice, the microcomputer operation alternates between BLMS2.0 and MCP5 in a manner transparent to the user. The other supplementary programs include:

FLPROG          which is a general purpose file maintenance program for all the floppy disk-based-data files,

EOSREP          the end-of-shift reports program which is automatically chained in at the monitoring system close down, at the end of shift, to provide detailed printout reports in the batch mode, and

HELP            which provides helpful information on system parameters, operating procedure and precautions in the batch mode.

## SYSTEM OUTPUT REPORTS

The transfer line monitoring system provides 12 different reports in the real time mode and 6 reports in the batch mode at the end of the shift. The real time reports are:

(1)  Line Mimic Diagram
(2)  Machine Status Report (One per machine)
(3)  Line Status Report
(4)  Inter-operational Stock Report
(5)  Tool Changes Report
(6)  Week-to-Date Summary Report
(7)  Line Utilisation Report.
(8)  Production Output Distribution (bar chart)
(9)  End-of-Shift Production Forecast (bar chart)
(10) Stock Distribution (bar chart)
(11) Engineers' Report

(12) Shift Summary Printout Report.

Only the Line Mimic Diagram (see Figure 4) is automatically displayed on the screen; all the other reports are displayed only when the appropriate key on the microcomputer is depressed. At the end of every 2 minutes, the system automatically reverts to the Line Mimic Diagram on which flashing blocks indicate machines which are stopped currently. Figure 5 illustrates the Machine Status Report.

The end-of-shift batch mode reports (see Figure 6 for some examples) are:

(1)  Production Output Report (bar chart)
(2)  Downtime % Report (bar chart)
(3)  Shift Tooling Report
(4)  Line % Lost Time Report
(5)  Line Utilisation Report (bar chart)
(6)  Inter-operational Stock Report (bar chart).

## SOME PRACTICAL PROBLEMS

A number of practical problems were encountered in the course of the project: some of these required engineered solutions. Signal data accuracy and reliability was maintained by the use of opto-isolated inputs, stabilised power supplies, software filters and error-self-checking routines in the software. Data security and integrity was improved by the use of battery-backed RAM storage in the MBX, the use of password entry to the MBX files and restricted access to microcomputer data files. Human errors in hardware design, assembly and installation were gradually eliminated through system testing and post-installation commissioning. Human errors in software were overcome by thorough software testing prior to implementation supplemented by software commissioning after implementation. Human errors in the operation of the system were prevented by the use of software checks and prompts as well as through gradual on-the-job user training. Many potential problems were solved quickly through close liaison between the project team and the system users. Furthermore, a comprehensive manual was provided for future user reference.

## CONCLUSIONS

It is believed that the evolutionary approach which was adopted and the search for cost-effective information are important consideration for a project of this type.

## ACKNOWLEDGEMENTS

The author wishes to thank Mr. F.A. Wilcock and Mr. S.R.D. Tea of BL Technology Limited for their advice and assistance in the project, the line management and staff of Austin Morris Limited for their interested co-operation and Dr. T.J. Grayson of Birmingham University for his guidance during the writing of the PhD thesis of which this project was an important part. The project and the PhD thesis were financed by B.L. Technology Limited.

REFERENCES

(1) HATVANY, J., The Distribution of Functions in Manufacturing Systems. Advances in Computer-Aided Manufacture, ed. D. McPherson, North-Holland Pub. Co., 1977, p. 22-30.

(2) KAY, E., Buffer Stocks in Automatic Transfer Lines. Int. J. Prod. Res., 1972 10(2), p. 155-165.

(3) ROGGENBUCK, R.A., Computer Simulation of Transfer Lines. SME Technical Paper MR75-172, 1975.

(4) HANIFIN, L.E., LIBERTY, S.G. AND TARAMAN, K., Improved Transfer Line Efficiency Utilizing Systems Simulation. SME Technical Paper MR75-169, 1975.

(5) BILES, W.E., GUILD, R.D. AND ENSCORE, E.E., Modelling and Analysis of Automatic Transfer Lines in Manufacturing. Prod. AIIE Spring Conf, May 1980.

(6) OLIVIA-LOPEZ, E., Integrated Manufacturing Systems. unpublished M.Sc. dissertation, University of Birmingham, 1975.

(7) MELEKA, J., The Application of Microelectronics to Automation and Control of Metro Production. Electronics & Power, Jan. 1981, p. 42-47.

(8) LEAVITT, H.J. AND WHISLER, T.L., Management in the 1980s. Readings in Production and Operations Management, ed. E.S. Buffa. John Wiley & Sons, 1966.

(9) SCARROTT, G.G., Role of Information in Human Affairs. Electronics & Power, Nov/Dec 1979. p. 804-809.

(10) THOMAS, P.J., A Factory Data Collection System. Trans. Soc. of Inst. Tech., Mar 1963. p. 12-26.

(11) JOHNSON, N.E., Real-Time Data Collection Systems. J. Of Systems Managment, Sep 1969, p. 26-29.

(12) CORNELIUS, V., The Application of a Data Collection System in Machine Shops and Assembly Shops. Proc. Industrial Application of Small Computers Conf. Birniehill Inst, Oct 1970, p. 1-14.

(13) ARONSON, R.L. In-plant Sensors Help Schedule Work and Watch Costs in Brass Rod Mill. Control Engineering, Jul. 1970. p. 40-43.

(14) CAMPBELL, G.J., Tapping your Plant's Hidden Capacity. Industry Week 18, Nov. 1974. p. 52-54.

(15) CHAMBERS, P., The Potential of Microtechnology in Industry. Proc. Inst. Conf. New Frontiers in PLC Data Logging and Microprocessors, London 1978.

(16) ENTREKIN, D.A., Computer Control - Why, How?. American Machinist, Mar 1970.

(17) ANON., Cutting the Downtime on Production Lines. Automotive Industries May 1978, p. 12-18.

(18) FUKUMA, N., NAKAO, H. AND SATA, T., Development of an Information Processing System in Manufacturing, Manufacturing Systems: Proc. C.I.R.P. Seminar, 1976, 1, p. 63-80.

(19) BOZICH, J., Computer-Managed Monitoring of Plant Machinery. Part 1. Noise Control, Mar 1978. p. 99-101.

(20) JONES, G., Real-time, Distributed, Shop Floor Data Collection, Proc. Seminar on Minis and Micros in Manufacturing. I.Prod.E., Nov 1980.

(21) CRUMPTON, P.A. AND YEOH, O.B., Total Factory Monitoring, Infotech State-of-the-Art Report on Factory Automation. 1980, 8 (6), p. 81-97.

(22) WEISE, D., Production Data Recording and Processing System Uses Circular Charts. Ind. & Prod. Eng., 1978, 2, 137-142.

(23) HITOMI, K., Manufacturing Systems Engineering, Taylor & Francis, 1978.

(24) CHANDLER, C.H., Monitor Downtime to Boost Productivity. Ind. Enging. Jun 1977. p. 36-39.

(25) FENTON, G.G., Shop Reporting and Incentive Pay. American Machinist, Apr 1979. p. 141-145.

(26) WILLIAMS, J.L., The Future of Data Logging, Proc. Int. Conf. New Frontiers in PLC Data Logging and Microprocessors, London, 1978.

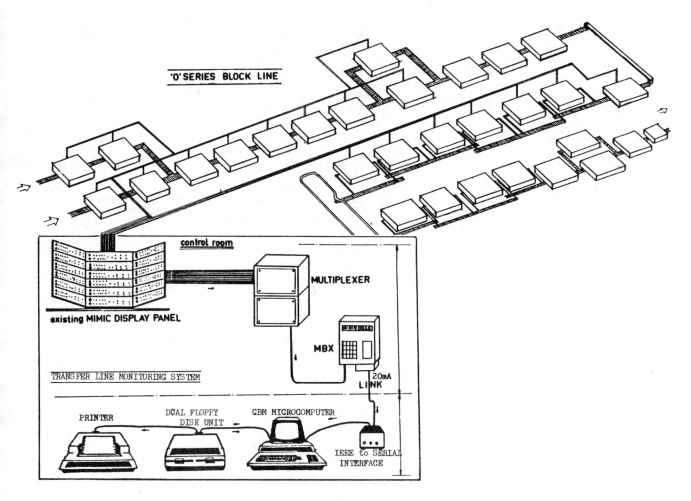

'O' SERIES BLOCK LINE

control room

MULTIPLEXER

existing MIMIC DISPLAY PANEL

MBX

TRANSFER LINE MONITORING SYSTEM

20mA LINK

PRINTER

DUAL FLOPPY DISK UNIT

CBM MICROCOMPUTER

IEEE to SERIAL INTERFACE

Fig 1    Illustration of the 'O' series block line and the transfer line monitoring system (implemented at Austin Morris, Longbridge)

Fig 2    Photograph of the display panel in the 'O' series block line control room

C283/81    ©IMechE 1981

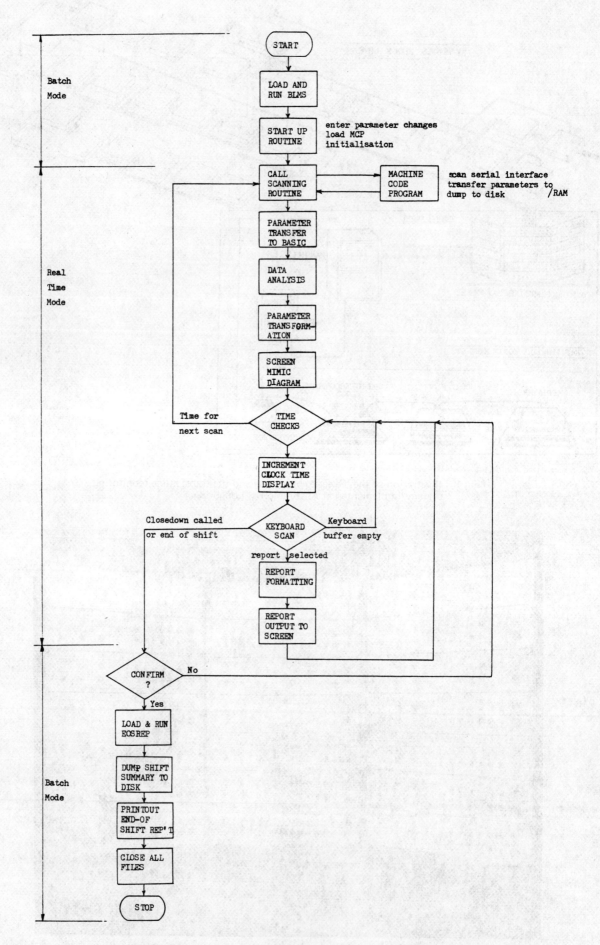

Fig 3 Flow chart showing the operation of the transfer line monitoring system

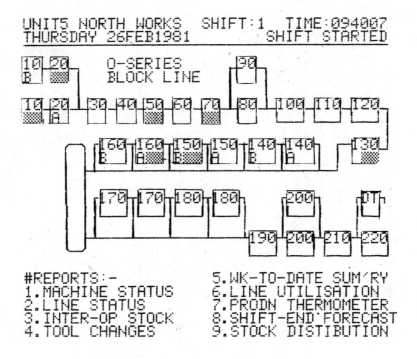

```
UNIT5 NORTH WORKS    SHIFT:1   TIME:094007
THURSDAY 26FEB1981              SHIFT STARTED
```

```
#REPORTS:-                  5.WK-TO-DATE SUM'RY
1.MACHINE STATUS           6.LINE UTILISATION
2.LINE STATUS              7.PRODN THERMOMETER
3.INTER-OP STOCK           8.SHIFT-END'FORECAST
4.TOOL CHANGES             9.STOCK DISTIBUTION
```

Fig 4    Screen-based line mimic diagram

```
UNIT5 NORTH WORKS    SHIFT:1   TIME:094212
O-SERIES BLOCK LINE MONITORING SYSTEM
THURSDAY 26FEB1981

MACHINE STATUS REPORT:M/C.35884 OPN130

SHIFT OUTPUT 220    STOP MINS NOW 1
OUTPUT RATE 56/HR   CUMLTV MIN.LOST 74
M/C UTILSATION 68%  AVG CYCL MINS .72

%TIME LOST DUE TO FOLLOWING REASONS:-

 TA TB TC TD TE TF OT BT WC AM MT SE %

 0  6  8  6  7  0  0  5  6  6  5  6

%TIME BLOCKED= 0
%TIME STARVED= 0

ELAPSED TIME  233  MINS
```

Fig 5    Screen-based machine status report

O-SERIES BLOCK LINE MONITORING SYSTEM

END OF SHIFT SUMMARY.                    9TH APRIL 1981

@1 PRODUCTION OUTPUT

| OPN | 0 | 200 | 400 | 600 |
|-----|---|-----|-----|-----|
| 10A | 0 | | | |
| 10B | 70 | | | |
| 20A | 148 | | | |
| 20B | 224 | | | |
| 30 | 322 | | | |
| 40 | 410 | | | |
| 50 | 473 | | | |
| 60 | 438 | | | |
| 70 | 14 | | | |
| 80 | 90 | | | |
| 90 | 414 | | | |
| 130 | 326 | | | |
| 140A | 205 | | | |
| 140B | 208 | | | |
| 150A | 210 | | | |
| 150B | 192 | | | |
| 160A | 187 | | | |
| 160B | 183 | | | |

@2 DOWNTIME %

| OPN | 0 | 50 | 100 |
|-----|---|-----|-----|
| 10A | 100 | | |
| 10B | 86 | | |
| 20A | 100 | | |
| 20B | 89 | | |
| 30 | 64 | | |
| 40 | 57 | | |
| 50 | 51 | | |
| 60 | 78 | | |
| 70 | 90 | | |
| 80 | 14 | | |
| 90 | 45 | | |
| 130 | 51 | | |
| 140A | 52 | | |
| 140B | 51 | | |
| 150A | 48 | | |
| 150B | 53 | | |
| 160A | 61 | | |
| 160B | 63 | | |

O-SERIES BLOCK LINE MONITORING SYSTEM

END OF SHIFT SUMMARY.

@3 TOOLING REPORT(TOT.MIN/SETUPS)

| OPN | PLANNED TOOL CHANGE GROUP | | | | | | OFF STD. TOOL/CH. | BROKEN TOOL | ALL TOOLING |
|-----|---|---|---|---|---|---|---|---|---|
| | A | B | C | D | E | F | | | |
| 10A | 0 0 | 0 0 | 10 1 | 0 0 | 0 0 | 0 0 | 11 4 | 0 0 | 21 5 |
| 10B | 0 0 | 0 0 | 20 1 | 20 1 | 0 0 | 0 0 | 7 4 | 0 0 | 47 6 |
| 20A | 0 0 | 0 0 | 0 0 | 0 0 | 0 0 | 0 0 | 17 2 | 0 0 | 17 2 |
| 20B | 0 0 | 0 0 | 0 0 | 0 0 | 0 0 | 0 0 | 18 4 | 0 0 | 18 4 |
| 30 | 14 1 | 0 0 | 0 0 | 0 0 | 0 0 | 0 0 | 6 1 | 0 0 | 20 2 |
| 40 | 0 0 | 75 1 | 75 1 | 0 0 | 0 0 | 0 0 | 80 4 | 0 0 | 230 6 |
| 50 | 11 1 | 0 2 | 0 2 | 0 2 | 0 2 | 0 0 | 25 | 45 | |
| 60 | 0 0 | 0 0 | 0 | 0 | | | | | |
| 70 | | | | 0 | | | | | |

O-SERIES BLOCK LINE MONITORING SYSTEM

END OF SHIFT SUMMARY.

@5 LINE UTILISATION

| CATEGORY | AV% | MINS | STOPS |
|----------|-----|------|-------|
| MAINTENANCE | 1 | 0 | 0 |
| OFF/STD T/C. | 9 | 213 | 60 |
| SETTING. | 24 | 879 | 119 |
| BLKD/STVD. | 36 | 611 | 906 |
| BROKEN TOOL. | 8 | 82 | 16 |
| T/CH.(F) | 3 | 0 | 0 |
| T/CH.(E) | 4 | 0 | 3 |
| T/CH.(D) | 5 | 20 | 4 |
| T/CH.(C) | 2 | 125 | 7 |
| T/CH.(B) | 2 | 75 | 4 |
| T/CH.(A) | 0 | 60 | 4 |

7TH APRIL 1981    UNITS NORTH WORKS SHIFT:1    TIME:10:50

O-SERIES BLOCK LINE MONITORING SYSTEM

END OF SHIFT SUMMARY.

@6 INTER OPERATIONAL STOCKS

| OPN | STARTING STOCK | PRODN. | CLOSING STOCK |
|-----|----------------|--------|---------------|
| 10 | 20 | 52 | 20 |
| 20 | 136 | 46 | 142 |
| 30 | 34 | 3 | 77 |
| 40 | 31 | 0 | 34 |
| 50 | 223 | 0 | 223 |
| 60 | 24 | 0 | 24 |
| 70 | 122 | 0 | 122 |
| 80 | 80 | 0 | 80 |
| 130 | 480 | 264 | 216 |
| 140 | 250 | 492 | 22 |
| 150 | 32 | 510 | 14 |
| 160 | 11 | 471 | 50 |
| 170 | 0 | 0 | 0 |
| 180 | 0 | 0 | 0 |

Fig 6    Examples of four end-of-shift reports printed out

# The exciting challenge of sheet moulding compounds (SMC) to the engineer of the 80s

M J SEAMARK
Bifort Engineering Limited, Blackpool

## INTRODUCTION

The Glass Reinforced Plastics (GRP) industry can be conveniently divided into three segments according to the moulding method used: hand lay-up for low volume production; cold press moulding and resin injection for medium volume production; and hot press moulding of sheet moulding compound (SMC) for high volume production.

In the past twenty years GRP has become the accepted material of construction for many low volume cars such as Lotus, Reliant and Mattra Simca Bagheera, and indeed the General Motors Chevrolet Corvette all GRP bodied car celebrated its Silver Jubilee back in 1978. Most truck manufacturers in Western Europe and the United States use GRP for many parts of their cabs.

In recent years, as volumes have increased, the labour intensive hand lay-up techniques using polyester resins and glass fibre reinforcement have proved totally inadequate and SMC has become the widely used material, becoming virtually traditional for many applications. The Corvette has been converted in recent years from wet lay-up hot press to SMC to provide a superior surface finish dramatically reducing finishing costs. The ERF 'B' Series cab has been clad totally in SMC onto a steel safety cage for over six years and leads the world in this concept of cab construction. Other US truck manufacturers look likely to follow ERF's lead. "All plastic cars" comprising a high proportion of SMC are to be introduced during the 80's and electric cars are also being designed with SMC moulding in mind.

SO WHAT ARE SMC's? They are thermosetting, crosslinked, dimensionally stable materials and unlike thermoplastic materials do not soften under the influence of heat and are therefore not recycleable.

Developed in the early 1960's, in both the UK and West Germany, they are now being used in virtually all industries including electrical, lighting, building, energy supply, telecommunications, chemical plant, water storage, business and domestic appliances. However, automotive is still one of the largest single outlets for SMC worldwide, and they offer outstanding properties to the automotive engineer for a wide variety of parts from large complete body parts to tailgates, roofs, bonnet and hoods, radiator supports etc.

This paper is intended to outline what SMC is, its manufacture, moulding and properties, tooling and component design. In addition a main emphasis of the paper is intended to highlight the many current applications in all aspects of the Automotive Industry, ranging from car wheels to complete truck cabs. SMC is without doubt the most exciting material for the future for structural body parts both for trucks and cars, and their low energy conversion costs compared with steel makes SMC an even more challenging prospect.

## 2 SMC- THE MATERIAL, ITS MANUFACTURE, MOULDING AND PROPERTIES

### 2.1 What is SMC?

Sheet Moulding Compound is a combination of glass fibre reinforcements dispersed in thermosetting resin paste. The resin paste uses an unsaturated polyester resin system as the base. A number of other materials are incorporated to provide desirable processing and moulding characteristics and optimum physical and mechanical properties. Glass fibre reinforcements improve the performance of polyester by upgrading mechanical strength, impact resistance, stiffness and dimensional stability.

### ADVANTAGES OF THERMOSETTING POLYESTER RESINS

Thermosetting polyester resins which are universally used in SMC production offer many advantages:

1. Ease of handling

2. Rapid cure

3. Good balance of mechanical, electrical and chemical properties

4. Good dimensional stability

5. Easily modified for special characteristics

6. Low cost

Variations can be made in the composition of the base polyester to yield resin pastes with a wide range of properties during and after polymerization.

Through careful selection and control of the ingredients, the polyester resin producer can synthesize a suitable material for specific end-use applications.

SMC's are complex engineering plastic materials, containing in addition to glass, resin and fillers, the main constituents, catalysts (for curing), thermoplastic additives (to control shrinkage), pigments, thickeners, internal release agents and flame retardents. It can, therefore, be appreciated the development chemist can build into SMC a wide range of specific properties, an inherent feature in their technology.

So, in addition to Automotive grades with good impact properties toughness and excellent paintability, there are electrical, flexible, low density and furniture grades, as well as reduced fire hazard and chemical resistant grades, high glass content for structural load bearing components, and taint free grades for foodstuffs.

## 2.2 How is it Manufactured?

Early machines manufactured SMC from a chopped strand glass mat, but in recent years the more standard and economical approach has been to manufacture from continuous strand glass fibre roving. The glass fibre is chopped to the desired length, usually 25-50 mm and randomly deposited onto a coat of polyester resin-filler paste travelling on a sheet of polyethylene film. After fibre deposition is complete, a second sheet of polyethylene film carrying resin paste joins the first sheet forming a continuous sandwich of glass and resin. This is compacted and rolled under controlled tension into standard package-size rolls at the wind-up station of the machine.

SMC is normally allowed to mature at a controlled temperature of 25-30° C for 2 to 7 days depending on the resin formulation. Maturation for most SMC formulations require approximately 3 days, the SMC can then be removed from the maturation room and is ready for use.

Machine widths can vary from 0.6 - 1.8 metres and are capable of producing up to 3-4 tonnes per hour depending on the weight per unit area. Normal nominal weight is 3.5 - 4.5 kg per metre square.

## 2.3 Moulding SMC

SMC's cure under heat (130-160° C) and pressure (3.5-10 MPa). In addition it is essential to carefully control and monitor all the moulding conditions to ensure part reproduceability, hence the following detail is recorded on initial tool trials and closely adhered to:

Charge weight and pattern

Tool temperatures, punch and die

Moulding pressure

Closure speed

Cycle time

Moulded 'on' or 'off' stops

Press identification

Opening speed

Ejector force

## 2.4 Properties of SMC and Cost Competitiveness

Properties of SMC are usually quoted on a supplier's moulded test plaque and these do not necessarily relate to the properties of a moulded part, since charge shape and press conditions can influence final properties. Generally however properties of the moulded part, depending on complexity, should not be less than 80% of the values of the moulded test plaque. Table 1 gives details of a typical specification for SMC.

Table 1 Typical Specification for minimal shrinkage grade of SMC 25% glass content agreed with an automotive company

|  | UNITS | TEST METHOD | MINIMUM MEAN VALUES |
|---|---|---|---|
| Tensile strength | MPa | ISO 3268 | 60 |
| Flexural strength | MPa | ISO R178 | 150 |
| Flexural modulus | GPa | ISO R178 | 9.0 |
| Impact strength Charpy unnotched | KJ/m$^2$ | ISO R179 | 60 |
| Oxygen index | % | ASTM D2863 | 24 |
| Glass content | % | ISO/R 1172 | 20 |

On moulded test plaques

Table 2 gives a cost comparison of SMC against body steel and aluminium, and two thermoplastics, increasingly referred to in technical articles on the use of plastics in automobiles, Reinforced Reaction Injection Moulded Polyurethane (RRIM) and polycarbonate (PC).

Table 2 Cost Comparison

| Property | Material | | | | |
|---|---|---|---|---|---|
|  | Body Steel | Alum-inium | P U RRIM | SMC | PC |
| Density (g/cc) | 7.8 | 2.8 | 1.2 | 1.8 | 1.2 |
| E Modulus (GPa) | 207 | 69 | 1.0 | 12.5 | 2.15 |
| Cost/Tonne £ | 254 | 1412 | 1200 | 1000 | 1800 |
| Thickness mm | 0.8 | 1.2 | 3.0 | 2.0 | 3.0 |
| Weight (Kg/m$^2$) | 6.2 | 3.4 | 3.6 | 3.6 | 3.6 |
| Cost (£/m$^2$) | 2.10 | 6.01 | 4.32 | 3.60 | 6.50 |

## 2.5 Glass Fibre Reinforcement - its effect on mechanical properties

One of the major factors affecting the strength of a finished SMC part is the amount of glass fibre used. Scientists in the glass fibre industry have now succeeded in increasing the 20 to 35 per cent glass loadings common in sheet moulding compounds to as much as 65 per cent, thereby dramatically increasing the mechanical properties of the compound.

The orientation of the fibres is another major factor affecting part strength. Randomly dispersed glass fibre gives strengths in all directions and this strength increases only in direct proportion to the amount of glass used. Reinforcements applied in a single direction give greater strength in that direction, but little strength perpendicular to it. A combination of the two, however, allows a design engineer to tailor performance to the application.

Hence we can have an SMC in which continuous lengths of glass fibre roving are laid on top of the random fibres, with a little tension to ensure high and uniform load transmittal. In this SMC the small addition of continuous rovings produces an impressive increase in strength. With a content of 22 per cent by weight of random chopped strand and 8 per cent by weight of continuous rovings, for example, flexural strength increases by 50 per cent and impact strength by 85 per cent when compared with the standard SMC with the same total glass content. A commercial example of the use of this approach is the Renault 5 SMC bumper which contains 37% random glass fibre content to meet the European impact of 5 km/h without damage, and incorporating a relatively small additional of unidirectional glass fibre enables the same bumper to meet the increased US requirement of 8 km/h without damage.

References 1 and 2 cover detail design properties of SMC.

3   TOOLING FOR SMC

Choice of tool steel.

The choice of tool steel for a particular application is dependent on a number of factors.

1.   The total number of parts required

2.   The type of SMC to be used

3.   The budget for the project

Tools cut from high quality pre-toughened nickel steel, with a surface finish of 600-1000 grit will be suitable for 250 000 parts plus.

Tools cut from cast steel with a surface finish of 350 grit will be suitable for 100 000 - 150 000 parts.

Tools cut from cast steel with a surface finish of 250 grit will be suitable for 20 000 - 50 000 mouldings.

Cast alloys, such as Kirksite or Meehanite, although often used for extended runs, are best suited for prototype work or short runs up to about 1000 parts.

SMC is capable of reproducing fine detail and will faithfully reproduce the mould surface in every moulding. The mould should, therefore,

have the best possible finish, commensurate with the economics of the particular component. Where practical, moulds should be chrome or nickel-plated to give optimum release and maximum tool life. It is important to remember that chrome/nickel-plating does not improve the surface finish of the mould. A suitable system of ejection is often necessary to ensure ease of part removal.

The use of heated tools, either by employing electric, cartridge or oil heating, will enable close control of the tool surface temperature to be maintained, essential where optimum surface finish to a moulded part is required.

It is also important when using high quality tools, to ensure adequate pressures are available to mould an acceptable part. Inadequate tonnage presses can produce poor quality parts from good quality tooling. Presses up to 3-4 000 tonnes capacity are now being installed to ensure the standard of finish demanded can be maintained on much larger components.

4   DESIGNING FOR SMC

In the past some engineers have taken a part in steel and produced the same part in SMC. Such an approach can cause serious problems, since there are basic guidelines to follow when designing a part in SMC which also gives to designers greater flexibility and freedom in styling.

SMC offers the following 10 key basics:

MODERATE TOOLING COSTS

TEMPERATURE RESISTANCE

SELF COLOUR OR PAINTING

HIGH ELECTRICAL INSULATION

MECHANICAL STRENGTH

DESIGN FLEXIBILITY

DIMENSIONAL STABILITY

RIGIDITY

GOOD SURFACE FINISH

CORROSION RESISTANCE

The most important feature when designing for SMC is parts consolidation, that is incorporating a number of existing parts, say in steel, into a single moulding in SMC. Still probably the best example of this approach is the typical US car front end illustrated in Figure 1, previously comprising 16 individual steel parts, it is moulded in one piece in SMC, thus greatly reducing assembly costs.

4.1 Size

The size of the mouldings made from SMC will be limited only by the size of press in terms of both tonnage and platen area. At Bifort Engineering our largest press is one of 3 000 tonnes capacity with a platen area of 3.0 x 2.7 metres and 2.2 metres daylight.

## 4.2 Draft Angles

Minimum draft angles recommended are:

| | |
|---|---|
| Up to 200 mm | $1\frac{1}{2}^{\circ}$ |
| up to 200-500 mm | $2^{\circ}$ |
| over 500 mm | $2-3^{\circ}$ |

When a grained or textured tool surface is to be used 1 additional degree per 0.03 mm of grain depth should be used.

## 4.3 Wall Thickness

The wall thickness of a part will be dictated by performance requirements. The strength of SMC is known, and by using the following safety factors part thicknesses can be determined.

| NATURE OF LOADING | MINIMUM SAFETY FACTOR |
|---|---|
| Static short term loads | 2 |
| Static long term loads | 4 |
| Variable or changing loads | 4 |
| Repeated loads | 6 |
| Fatigue or loads reversal | 6 |
| Impact loads | 10 |

The minimum recommended wall thickness is 1 mm and 25 mm the maximum. Parts can be moulded with wall thicknesses greater than 25 mm. We have moulded parts up to 62 mm thickness, but the cure time is extended.

## 4.4 Corner Radii

A minimum internal radium of 1.5 mm is recommended for corners, and where possible constant wall thickness should be maintained on corners. The use of well rounded corners ensures the prevention of potential areas of stress.

## 4.5 Holes

Holes can be moulded into components made from SMC, however their placement in the part is all important. Holes should be at least three times their own diameter from any edge or from any other hole in the part. Through holes can create flow lines and fibre orientation, these should be avoided where possible. The use of blind holes ensures the continuous flow of SMC and gives random fibre distribution, so preventing the formation of potential weak areas. Holes can be moulded into the part both parallel or perpendicular to the ram action.

## 4.6 Bosses

Bosses can be moulded into parts made from SMC as anchorage sites for inserts or studs. Where possible the wall thickness of the boss should be the same as the wall thickness of the part or not more than twice the diameter of the hole. Single bosses situated on a flat area of a part should have built-in fins both for support and to ensure good material flow. Two or more bosses, adjacent to one another, should be linked, improving strength and ensuring good material flow.

## 4.7 Inserts

Inserts are commonly used in parts made from SMC. The inserts can be moulded in place which can take up valuable press time, or be driven in as a subsequent operation. Moulded in inserts rely on the effective flow of SMC around the inserts to attain sufficiently high pull strengths.

Driven in type inserts require high shear threads to achieve a suitable key.

The push-in type, simply having knurled edges, are locked in place by an inner brass slug driven to the bottom of the hole, or when the screw is applied the insert is expanded and grips the bore of the hole. This second type is used for straight-through holes.

## 4.8 Ribs

Ribs have three basic functions:

1. To bring strength and rigidity to the part without excessive increases in part thickness

2. To control warpage

3. To facilitate material flow

Rib design will be determined by the function the part has to perform and the grade of SMC used in its manufacture. In order to satisfy the three basic functions of a rib, it should have a lead-in radius of 3 mm, and $1-3^{\circ}$ taper on each side and be at least 2 mm thick. Where perfectly flat, paintability surfaces are required a lead-in radius of 0.1 - 0.3 mm is necessary. Where possible rib width should be the same as part thickness, to avoid excessive disturbance during material flow. If extra-wide ribs are required they should be hollow or cored.

## 4.9 Undercuts

These should be avoided if possible as split moulds required to produce undercuts can be expensive, production rate slower and components more costly. Undercuts may not be possible even when a split mould is used.

## 5 IMPACT PERFORMANCE

The energy absorbing properties of GRP are outstanding, but unlike steel it does not yield and give permanent deformation, but fractures at the point of ultimate strength. The safety aspects of the performance of a GRP car or truck can best be summed up by an extract from an article on the subject appearing in The Times as long ago as July 1972, yet equally as relevent today.

"A glass-fibre reinforced plastic car body strewn over the road in pieces hardly inspires confidence. But not long ago the driver of a mid-engined Lotus Europa, which hit a lorry at 45 mph, walked away from the scene unhurt although the front of the car was smashed to fragments.

In that case the cockpit was reasonably intact, whereas the lives of three lorry drivers in a multiple pile-up on the M1 at the end of last year are said to have been saved by the complete disintegration of their glass-fibre reinforced plastic cabs.

They got out of the wreckage while other drivers in steel cabs died from their injuries or in the fire after the collision."

## 6   THE APPLICATIONS

### 6.1   Cars in the United States

Still the largest single application for SMC is the grille opening panel or front end which in 1980 was used on 65% of all US cars, typical parts weighing between 4.6 and 5.9 kg. And the largest single use application is the Chevrolet Corvette, illustrated in Figure 2, it has been a test bed for future materials technology and has made extensive use of GRP for over 28 years.  Recently many body panels have been converted to compression moulding with SMC, the latest a bumper face bar and support system based on high glass content SMC gives a 61% weight saving over steel.  (Reference 4).

An ever increasing number of tailgates in double skin SMC are now in production, and Ford's testing on the latest development is extremely enlightening - the SMC tailgate withstanding 311 joules impact tests and also the impact of a 211 kg barrel dropped on its edge from a height of six inches.  A Chevrolet tailgate in production is illustrated in Figure 3.  Skirts for rear wheel openings, hood louvres, spoilers, head lamp and tail lamp housings, are all common components in SMC.

Seat Shells is an area studied by Ford in prototype development work and a high glass content containing SMC at 65% glass fibre, often referred to as HSMC, was found to be feasible from a design and performance standpoint, it was indistinguishable from a steel seat in ride evaluations and has little or no permanent set from continuous use.  It can be designed to offer a cost saving versus aluminium.  This was the award winning paper at the Society of the Plastics Industry Conference in 1980. (Reference 5)

Ford have also done prototype development work on a 3 piece Radiator Grille Support, again based on HSMC (65%).  Conclusions were: "Engineering feasibility has been established for an HSMC Radiator Support.  The primary objective to proceed with a production programme is to achieve weight savings.  This part would represent the first multipiece bonded high strength SMC component for a structural application on a Ford car." (Reference 6)

A 4 piece SMC hood for The Jeep weighs a total of 36 lbs. and assembled measures 1.9 m long x 1.5 m wide x 0.77 m high and is moulded by

General Tire and Rubber Reinforced Plastics Company for the American Motor Corps - Jeep.

Two recent major developments for SMC, both involving Owens-Corning Fiberglas in the United States, have been a hood for the Chevrolet Citation and front and rear double skin doors for the Peugeot 305.  Using prototype hoods and finite element analysis the feasibility of a one piece hood was demonstrated, preliminary testing indicating that satisfactory performance was achievable when compared to the existing steel design. A production tool has now been made for this component and SMC mouldings have confirmed the initial development work. (References 7 and 8)

The prototype SMC doors used 13 fewer components than the production steel door. It showed that the design parameters of the door could be met with SMC, including a proportion of unidirectional glass reinforcement for additional stiffness in the door frame and giving a 37% weight saving compared to the steel production door. (Reference 9)

The Budd Company Technical Centre have done a study of a GRP body for an electric car and designed to be compatible with the SMC moulding process.  (Reference 10)

### 6.2   Cars in Western Europe

Due to totally different car design concepts in Western Europe, front ends are not a feature, hence the largest single outlet currently is bumpers with Renault leading the field, having pioneered the use of SMC in the early 70's on their R5, and having since extended its use to several other models including the Renault 14, Renault 18 Turbo and the Fuego.

The Porsche 924 has an SMC bumper, permitting the moulding to be painted in body colour down conventional paint stoving ovens, not possible with most thermoplastics.  Both Mercedes Benz on the 280S model and Peugot on the 505 have introduced SMC bumpers. (Peugot 505 Reference 11 and Figure 4)

In the UK Rover have chosen SMC for their restyled bumper to be introduced in 1981 and again the ability to withstand low speed impact without damage and capability of painting at high temperature were crucial to the decision.

Saab on their 900 model have used SMC for their heater housing, giving dimensional stability over a wide operating temperature range ($-40^0$ to $20^0$ C).

Ford  introduced an SMC "C" Pillar Grille on their Cortina (Taunus in West Germany) some 5 years ago, this model was restyled in 1979 the single grille being replaced by two SMC grilles to provide an additional styling feature.  With volumes of 8000 mouldings per day this was an outstanding success story for SMC, since the mouldings had originally been designed for an injection moulded thermoplastic and found to be totally unsuited to the demands of the application. Similar SMC components have been used by Ford on their Granada models with equal success. This case study is covered in Reference 12.

British Leyland use SMC for the Sherpa Van Front Grille, the Allegro Door Sill, and the Rover Parcel Shelf - a low density grade SG-1.30.

The Lancia Delta - 1980 European Car of the Year uses SMC for the front and rear fascia panels to enable painting to body colour. Porsche, Fiat and Renault all use SMC for hard tops for certain sports cars.

Also Mercedes Benz, on their recently introduced van, have chosen SMC in preference to thermoplastics, for the bumpers, offering the most cost effective answer to stiffness to weight ratio compared with steel and to eliminate corrosion.

## 6.3 Trucks in the US

GRP is a traditional building material for truck parts such as hoods and fenders in the US, the volume determining the processing technique employed. In order to amortize the higher tooling costs for SMC, volumes in excess of 3-4000 per year are generally necessary. International Harvester, General Motors, Mack and Ford all use SMC. In addition both General Motors and Mack have recently introduced all SMC doors on their trucks, reducing weight and eliminating corrosion. The GM door incorporates an outstanding example of self coloured, textured interior door trim in SMC with four "moulded in" colours.

In the future it is possible Cabs could be clad exclusively in SMC. There are indications that development work is ongoing in this direction by at least two companies.

Grilles, rear fenders, engine covers, head-lamp surrounds, roof assemblies, tailgates are other components moulded in SMC.

## 6.4 Trucks in Western Europe

The UK has pioneered the use of exclusive cladding of a truck cab with SMC, when way back in 1974 ERF introduced its new 'B' Series Cab with 26 SMC Panels fixed to a steel safety cage, to meet the proposed EEC frontal impact legislation. (Reference 13 and Figure 5)
However, ERF first used SMC on doors and grilles on an earlier model cab in 1972, gaining valuable experience on its material benefits.

Volvo were first to introduce an SMC hood on to a truck on their N Series in 1973 featuring a 45 kg two piece bonded hood, it gave a weight saving over steel of 45% and a 50% saving in tooling costs over steel. Saab Scania has recently introduced an SMC hood comprising seven individual mouldings, again it was cost effective over steel and

overcomes corrosion. (Figure 6)

Leyland, Ford, Talbot Dodge and Vauxhall have all used SMC to some extent for a variety of exterior and interior parts. The introduction of self coloured SMC for interior fascia panels for the Leyland G Cab introduced in 1979 and Talbot Dodge Commando 100 Series and 50 Series cab in the same year was a breakthrough in SMC technology. (Reference 14 and Figure 7) Both companies chose SMC in preference to thermoplastics for greater dimensional stability over a wide operating temperature range, with temperatures recorded under the windscreen up to 130° C in certain Middle East countries where trucks are exported.

Mercedes Benz and Ford use SMC engine covers, and the Mercedes Unimog 150/425 has a one piece SMC bonnet. A four piece SMC instrument fascia is also featured on a Mercedes truck.

Regrettably, an unfortunate experience with SMC on the Leyland Marathon has resulted in no SMC exterior panels on the recently introduced T45 Road train. The problems lay entirely with the moulder, now no longer trading, for refusing to co-operate with either Leyland or material suppliers in the industry to resolve the problems. THIS EXPERIENCE SERVED TO HIGHLIGHT THE VITAL IMPORTANCE OF TOTAL CO-OPERATION FROM THE OUTSET OF A NEW DEVELOPMENT, BETWEEN THE MATERIAL SUPPLIER, THE MOULDER, THE TOOLMAKER AND THE CUSTOMER. That message cannot be put across too strongly.

## 7 TRACTORS

SMC is finding increasing use in tractor parts for complete cab roofs, bonnets, side panels, bonnet extentions and instrument panels. The need is for a material which has excellent mechanical properties for a robust service life, dimensional stability over a wide temperature range, excellent weathering, good paintability, and SMC was the obvious choice. J I Case in the US use 24 kg of SMC on their bonnet and side panels, and David Brown Tractors in the UK have recently started to use SMC on their bonnets. (Figure 8) In West Germany Mercedes Benz and Deutz use SMC extensively on their tractors and Ford in the US and W Europe use a double skin SMC roof for their "top of the range" air conditioned cab.

## CONCLUSIONS

The extent to which GRP has become an accepted material of construction for cars and trucks augurs well for the future, especially with increasing emphasis being placed on energy conservation where it scores heavily over metals. It is encouraging to our industry that an ever-increasing number of engineers are at last beginning to appreciate just what this group of materials can offer, and SMC is now being increasingly specified on drawings where even a few years ago it would not have been considered. It has been a slow process of education, but that effort is now being rewarded.

Compression moulding with SMC gives the designer and engineer a material which can be virtually tailored to suit specific applications, with the additional strategic use of glass reinforcement. So where reduced weight, parts consolidation with reduced assembly costs, dimensional and heat stability are key requirements, SMC offers the most exciting and challenging material for the engineers of the 80s.

REFERENCES

(1) "Design Data Fibreglass Composites" Published by Fibreglass Limited, St Helens, Lancashire, England

(2) "The Mechanical Properties of an SMC - R50 Composite" Published by Owens-Corning Fibreglas Corporation, Toledo, Ohio, USA

(3) J Best "Reinforced Plastics to minimize energy consumption over life cycle of an Automobile" Proceedings of the 36th Annual Conference Reinforced Plastics/Composites Inst., SPI, Section 21-A

(4) J A Delmastro, J W Schejbal and D Landwehr "Development of a Fiber Reinforced Plastic Bumper Structure" Proceedings of the 35th Annual Conference Reinforced Plastics/ Composites Inst., SPR, Section 18-C

(5) Michael H Stefani "Structural Plastic Split Bench Seat for Passenger Car Applications" Proceedings of the 35th Annual Conference Reinforced Plastics/Composites Inst., SPI, Section 13-E

(6) Richard T Dickason "HSMC Radiator Support" Proceedings of the 35th Annual Conference Reinforced Plastics/Composites Inst., SPI, Section 13-A

(7) W E Bettac and E Gray, Jr "Squeeze Moulding Technique as a means of simulating SMC moulded part performance" Proceedings of the 36th Annual Conference Reinforced Plastics/Composites Inst., SPI, Section 21-D

(8) I J Bence, R C Bloom and E Gray, Jr "Design, Finite Modeling and Structural Performance of a one-piece SMC auto hood" Proceedings of 36th Annual Conference Reinforced Plastics/Composites Inst., SPI, Section 21-E

(9) J Gerard, J Keown and B Loyat "Designing and Prototyping a European Automotive SMC Door" Proceedings of the 36th Annual Conference Reinforced Plastics/Composites Inst., SPI, Section 21-G

(10) G P McCafferty "Plastic Carbody for an Electrical Vehicle Application" Society of Automotive Engineers, Inc. Passenger Car Meeting June 1979 Dearborn Paper 790702

(11) R W Leibold "High Strength Bumpers for Cars in Series Production with SMC-C" Proceedings of the 36th Annual Conference Reinforced Plastics/Composites Inst., SPI, Section 11-B

(12) Polyester Compounds Group "Quality Polyester Compounds for High Production Components" British Plastics Federation Reinforced Plastics Congress 1978. Paper 32 Page 211-215

(13) M J Seamark "Facelifting the World's First all SMC Clad Truck Cab after 5 years' production - A unique case study" Proceedings of the 36th Annual Conference Reinforced Plastics/Composites Inst., SPI, Section 11-C

(14) M J Seamark "Self Coloured SMC used to facelift the Interior of Truck Cabs - Two Cast Studies" Proceedings of 35th Annual Conference Reinforced Plastics/ Composites Inst., SPI, Section 8-A

Fig 1    General Motors Buick Regal grille, opening panel in SMC

Fig 2    General Motors Corvette car

Fig 3    General Motors Chevrolet tailgate

Fig 4    Mercedes Benz 280S bumper

Fig 5    ERF 'B' series all SMC clad truck cab on a steel safety cage

Fig 6    Saab Scania hood

Fig 7    Leyland vehicles Super G cab interior fascia mouldings in self-coloured unpainted SMC

Fig 8    David Brown tractors bonnet nose upper and lower and instrument fascia

# C285/81

# Investing for a successful future - engine manufacturing at Land Rover

C M BURNHAM, BSc, CEng, MIProdE
Ingersoll Engineers, Rugby, Warwickshire
C J EMERY, CEng, MIProdE
Plant and Production Engineering, Land Rover Limited, Solihull

SYNOPSIS   The environment in the Automotive Industry is changing.  Business decisions are influenced by efforts to get ahead of the Japanese as well as the escalating cost of fuel.  Investments and productivity improvements are being planned and implemented at a time when manufacturing technology is advancing rapidly.  The facilities built this decade reflect the rate of change.  Whether they are the last of an old generation or the first of the new one is a matter of fine judgement especially when projects are being completed with aggressive time and cost targets, and quality must not be compromised.

This paper concentrates on how the business needs of Land Rover have been satisfied by reasoned application of production engineering and project management disciplines to provide a facility which will remain advanced into the 1990s.

## INTRODUCTION

Many parts of British Manufacturing Industry have been experiencing difficulty in maintaining profits and market share.  The situation has been aggravated by high interest rates and high exchange rates.  These factors are not primary causes, but they have highlighted some of the worst effects of a gradual decline in both product and cost competitiveness in our industry.

Nowhere have the problems been more pronounced than in the automotive and related industries. British Industry is not alone in this - sectors of the American and European Industries have been suffering as well.  The common factors, apart from the effects of ever increasing oil prices, are the inroads being made by the Japanese and the increasing trend towards some level of local manufacture in many markets.

We don't want to dwell on these factors, but rather to record them as a backcloth to this paper 'Investing for a Successful Future'.

Ultimately we all know that manufacturing companies will only be consistently successful when they market products of the right quality at a price people want to pay.  Mass production tends to be interpreted as conformity, but in most instances the market demands a level of variety - perhaps less from some fleet users than the private buyer or some State-financed organisations.

It is against this background that efforts are being made to improve the productivity of existing facilities and to invest in the manufacturing plants of the future.

For the last few months BL Cars have rightly been in the news as a result of the successful launch of the 'Robot-built' Mini Metro.

Considerable progress has taken place elsewhere in BL.  For instance, Land Rover have been undertaking major investments, part of which has been spent on transforming the North Works plant at Solihull into a modern and sophisticated engine plant which is as advanced as any in the world today.  It produces both petrol and diesel varieties of the 5 bearing 2.25 litre engine.

## 1   FACILITY OUTLINE

The total facility comprises:

- machine shop for major components (cylinder block and bearing caps, cylinder head, crankshaft, connecting rods)

- automated stores (raw material, finished machined and bought out finished parts)

- engine assembly lines

- engine test

- engine handling system

- support services and amenities.

The complete engine plant occupies some 40 500m² divided about equally between major component machining and stores, assembly and test.  The total capital investment for new engine facilities, including building refurbishment, was £66.5 million - £10.4 million inside the target budget.

This saving was achieved, not because the original estimates were padded, but by careful technical/economic evaluation at the specification/order stage and tight management of the various sub-contracts.  This saving was in addition to earlier investment reduction during conceptual planning and project approval stages.

Each element of the facility has its own local control with appropriate sideways and upwards communication. There is a wide use of micro-electronic technology with around 70 mini-computers and microprocessors in and associated with the plant. This subject, together with a more comprehensive discussion of the systems aspect is dealt with in another paper.

The first completed engines came off the production equipment on 1 July 1980 - the date set as sacrosanct from the start of the project - 24 months after the engineering concept for the new facility was agreed between senior management and the project team.

The manufacturing facility of the 1980s and 1990s has to meet a number of potentially conflicting objectives:

provide rapid response to often fast changing or fluctuating market requirements

ensure a high level of built-in product quality with rapid feed back of reliable information

give a high rate-of-return on investment from high productivity resulting in low unit cost

be sociologically and environmentally acceptable.

Achieving the correct balance between these required concise attention from the early conceptual stages. This was particularly the case as the new plant was being introduced to replace facilities which had existed for many years, and the new operational control systems had to interface with established company-wide systems, since, in addition to the 'new' plant, substantial expansion in capacity was required at other existing manufacturing locations to support the increased assembly volumes.

It was concluded early in the project that to provide the most responsive and cost effective facility there needed to be close integration of all manufacturing and support activities, and particularly of the stores, assembly and test facilities. This integration was achieved by the use of the most appropriate engineering, linked and controlled by computer systems to improve the quality and flow of operational control information (Fig. 1 refers).

Before discussing this in more detail, it is worth recording the specific parameters within which the new facility was developed.

## 2 PLANNING OBJECTIVES

The planning objectives set for the Joint Project Management Team were:

Introduce product improvements to meet future legislation and remain technically competitive.

Expand capacity to maintain Land Rover's position as a major 4 x 4 manufacturer.

Introduce improved manufacturing methods and facilities based on state-of-the-art technology which would give increased efficiency in the plant and quality in the product.

Contain investment within strictly controlled limits whilst not sacrificing product quality or manufacturing flexibility.

Ensure the space, lighting and working environment meet the highest standards.

Have the right production facility available to meet the Job 1 date of 1 July 1980 and subsequent rate-of-climb requirements.

In seeking to achieve these objectives the project team took particular care to reflect on the changing environment in the Automotive Industry and specifically the influences of rapidly advancing technology and the efforts to get ahead of the Japanese (the 'AJ' syndrome). We will return to this subject later after a brief description of the facility and the rationale behind it.

It is worth mentioning first that various planning exercises were undertaken at an early stage to consider alternative production capacities and investment levels, the best use of the sites available, the need for continuity both of production and skills, and long term job security in the context of alternative manning levels and the future trends in working hours.

## 3 FACILITY DESCRIPTION

### 3.1 Machine Shop

Due to changes in noise emission legislation, Land Rover needed to introduce a new engine, and in order to do so quickly decided upon a minimum change engine. Product Engineering, therefore, re-designed the bottom end of the engine to give a 5 bearing configuration in place of the existing 3 bearing, stiffened the cylinder block and took the opportunity of improving the rear engine oil seal by means of a new flywheel housing.

The facilities producing the major components for the 3 bearing engine were old (some almost 30 years) and their capacity was a limiting factor on total engine output. To provide continuity of production and improve productivity, quality and the environment, new facilities have been introduced into Solihull for cylinder blocks, crankshafts, cylinder heads and connecting rods.

Cylinder Blocks  The new cylinder blocks for the 5 bearing engines are produced on eighteen fully automatic transfer machines with two washing machines to ensure cleanliness standards are maintained prior to assembly of bearing caps and cup plugs. Components are conveyed between machine tools by substantial power and free conveyor systems which also provide adequate intersection buffering. All machine tools are controlled by programmable logic control systems with diagnostic plug-in capability. The majority of machining operations are performed dry and efficient dust extraction and air cleaners have been installed to keep the area free from cast iron dust. The final operation is to inspect and grade cylinder bores to ensure they are all within a maximum shape deviation of 0.0125mm (0.0005") and to inspect all other salient features of the cylinder block.

The new line is capable of producing 2500 cylinder blocks based on a normal two shift system.

Crankshafts   The new crankshaft for the 5 bearing engine is cast iron with journal and pin fillet radii undercut and rolled to give sufficient strength for the diesel engine application. It is produced on 20 individual machine tools and two washing machines. Again the machines are linked with power and free conveyors, and P.L.C. systems are used for machine control and fault diagnosis.

The installed capacity of the crankshaft line is 1800 per week, but the layout has been planned with spaces for additional machines to meet future capacity increases. All crankshafts are automatically balanced before despatching to assembly.

Connecting Rods and Cylinder Head   These components are essentially carry-over components from the 3 bearing engine and a similar philosophy has been used for the new machining lines to give increased capacity and improved productivity. Petrol and diesel heads are produced, with minimal changeover, through the same line containing 26 machine tools and washing machines linked by conveyors. Connecting rods are transported in baskets, to prevent damage, on manual roller conveyor between the 16 machine tools.

General   The programme logic controls have been installed to give rapid local access via VDUs with the ability to expand later to integrate with the management reporting system.

Particular emphasis has been paid to supporting these high investment facilities with good tool control and planned maintenance systems to ensure a high level of operating efficiency.

All the machine tools and equipment have been installed on specially constructed foundations as the original floor was built for lighter applications.

Additional plant has been installed at other Land Rover Plants to meet the revised Production requirements.

## 3.2 Automated Stores

The new engine component Stores is a fully computerised facility capable of handling all incoming material and finished components. In determining the most appropriate configuration and control, more basic and stand-up floor and narrow aisle facilities were considered. These were rejected primarily on the basis of space requirements, high manning levels and poor operating environment.

The automated store overcomes these problems and in addition provides for highly flexible operation with excellent stock control, security and quality procedures for all production material. (A schematic view of the Store is shown in Fig. 2).

The store has a capacity of 3960 pallets representing 10 days' average component stock, including allowances to match the particular market demand requirements often found in this sector of the automotive business. There are six aisles for pallet storage and one aisle for small parts containers. Each aisle has its own computer controlled stacker crane, although the one for small parts is operated with a man aboard. The store accommodates 90% of existing pallet variety used in-house and by external vendors. This results in only around 2% repalletisation and has been achieved by using one common hole size and slave pallets. The configuration of the store allows any future increase in capacity requirements to be achieved by the gradual introduction of a rationalised pallet policy.

The store gives speedy access for the intake – up to 50 vehicle deliveries per day – and issue of materials, whilst at the same time maintaining accurate stock records. The ability to identify the parts in stock and their quantity ensures engines can be assembled on a planned production schedule to match the vehicle build programmes. In addition the automated store accommodates raw material to support the four dedicated machining lines located in the plant.

The development and implementation of the advanced computer systems were controlled by the project's joint management team, though the detail software writing was undertaken by an external software house.

At the specification (user and functional) stage, great care was taken to identify not only the existing systems interfaces, and operational control requirements of the store and the rest of the plant, but also the method of operation in the event of failures, and how the facility was to be commissioned.

The approach adopted in introducing sophisticated computer technology to the shop floor has resulted in, for example, a store that can still operate to support production even if the computers go down; the dispersal of individual components in more than one aisle; multiple routing through the conveyor system; the ability to isolate faults at an elemental level; significantly less commissioning problems and delays than are often encountered.

The store provides the maximum security for the parts and instant access to accurate stock records for both quality and quantity to support the assembly activities.

## 3.3 Engine Assembly

Engine Assembly is linked to the component inventory records via a 'Can Build' programme which is run daily to identify the following 24 hour build requirements. The daily programmes multiplied by a list of parts for each type of engine to be built ensure all components needed are available and reserved for committed build. In the event stock shortages are identified, revised programmes are generated to avoid building incomplete engines. Components are issued from the stores in priority sequence and delivered to their assembly locations in pallets or smaller worktins by tow train or local fork lift truck.

Track associated storage is configured on a '2 bin' or '2 hour' principle to maintain parts availability at a controlled level. Light pens are used throughout the assembly area to record the need to replenish supplies, and appropriate inputs by this means can be used by management to set overriding priorities for the stores.

The assembly area layout is heavily influenced by the need to manage variety and achieve a short main build time by maximising the level of sub-assembly. The emphasis in the assembly area is on building quality into the engines. To this end parts are delivered to designated locations at lineside or in sub-assembly areas via appropriate washing facilities, and with correct materials handling and protection to avoid damage.

Control over assembly and sub-assembly quality is aided by the use of advanced torque control tooling and leak check equipment so finding problems early, avoiding adding value to incorrect assemblies, and allowing the operators to identify with the quality.

The main assembly area has three primary 'tracks'. The first is a 150m Pedestal Slat type, which allows all round accessibility and provides rigidity for multi-tool applications. This selection was agreed with the assembly operators and shop management as the most effective for the production requirements. All engines, diesel and petrol, are built down this track to a closed condition to ensure the important internals of the engine are kept clean. The second and third tracks, both 30m long - one dedicated to petrol and one to diesel engines, but with the ability to double up if required - are on an overhead conveyor which ultimately transports the engine through to the test facility and finishing areas.

This final configuration for the assembly area was determined after considering many options including non-synchronous systems. It provides for good control in a relatively high variety environment, efficient utilisation of labour, flexibility to meet fluctuating build mix demands (petrol/diesel and KD/built-up), and is integrated with other manufacturing activities to enhance the level of built-in quality.

### 3.4 Engine Handling

The engine handling system is the central element in the integration of assembly and test. It is an advanced overhead powered monorail system using quiet, motorised trolleys to transport engines through the facility under full computer control - from the end of first stage assembly to final wax protection ahead of despatch.

The monorail is more than one kilometre in length and there are 200 trolleys, each equipped with its own twin lift hoist to provide maximum operating flexibility, high stability, and limit the investment in expensive drop sections. Extensive use is made of side transfer sections to maintain system efficiency by limiting the level of interference during off-line activities. Achieving less than 1% loss of efficiency required careful simulation during the planning and design stages.

All trolleys are tracked and routed through the facility with the computer control maintaining on-line records of:

    engine type, location and status
    performance data
    maintenance and downtime records.

Management information on current status is available through standard visual display units, and colourgraphic display units provide a working route map of the whole handling system to provide rapid communication of problems and enable swift corrective action to be taken.

In the event of computer failure the handling system can be operated in a semi-automatic mode by introducing a limited number of operators at strategic decision points. The local zone control logic allows production to continue.

The powered trolley type engine handling system gives a high level of operational flexibility and management control, it also contributes significantly to achieving a low overall manufacturing lead time. It was selected after considering a multiplicity of alternatives for the different manufacturing activities - assembly, rig, test cell loading, de-rig, rectification and final dress. It has the considerable advantage of solving the operational needs with a single integrated system and is an important element in maintaining a high level of utilisation for the various operations. (Fig. 3 shows the handling system/test shop interface).

### 3.5 Engine Test

Engines are routed from assembly through a buffer store, which has capacity for approximately 100 engines, to the pre-test rig area, where they are prepared for test by loading into common 'cradles' to minimise the in-cell time. Other features which also help to achieve this include a high degree of common service interfaces, hot oil fill, and of course the high level of built-in assembly quality.

The cells, 20 production, 4 audit and extended test, are capable of accepting either petrol or diesel engines at random. Engines and cradles are delivered by the engine handling system to the load/unload station above each cell via side transfers which move the engine off line. The engine is lowered through a hatch in the cell roof onto the test bed. The final docking, initiated by the operator, is made under powered control through a match plate to connect water, fuel, power and exhaust.

All engines are taken through a full, automatically sequenced test cycle which allows for operator intervention to perform the limited number of manual tasks and adjustments. The automated control checks the engines performance consistently against established parameters. The engine test operators are provided with the facts on visual display units so that any required adjustments can be made to meet the specification.

The hierarchical computer system has one microprocessor per two production beds (one to one for audit beds) providing control and data collection.

The management computer communicates to test bed level information regarding the engine to be tested, it also provides statistical analysis, engine report print-outs and management information.

The engine test services are integrated with the test bed system via barometric pressure and air and water temperature. An annunciation panel continuously monitors the pressure and temperature of engine and dynamometer (which is of the eddy current variety) cooling water together with oil and air flow rates. A level of energy recovery is achieved using heat exchangers and hot wells.

The test facility incorporates the most modern technology available for the production testing of engines. In addition the audit test facilities meet the stringent requirements of such bodies as the Ministry of Defence. As importantly, they incorporate advanced diagnostic capabilities which not only improve the flow and quality of information now, but are an investment in the future in a rapidly changing technological world. They will assist in making further improvements to product performance and could ultimately lead to a substantial change in the hot test activity as it is today - changes which the facility can respond to.

## 3.6 Engine Finishing

After test, engines are routed to the de-rig area where those for K.D. Assembly overseas are drained of oil and have internal inhibitor applied. All good engines are routed on to final dress, where there is a very wide range of work content dependent upon whether the engines are destined to be assembled directly into vehicles or for the K.D. market.

Any engines requiring rectification are sent to the rectification area where they join up with instructions routed between the test and handling computer systems. Engines destined for vehicles are finally removed from the powered monorail system ahead of the final waxing operation before being despatched.

## 3.7 Some Questions to Answer

When a facility such as the one we have described is being created there are certain aspects which always come under close scrutiny.

Why have an automated component store when the Japanese work on the 'Kanban' system?

A substantial proportion of Land Rover's market is contract orientated with associated high level of special to customer requirements. In this situation it makes sense to hold inventory where the added value is least and maintain the emphasis on reducing manufacturing lead time.

However, component supply and control will improve in the future and the available storage capacity created is planned to be used to support other activities on the Solihull site. Already components for the adjacent axle assembly area are passing through this facility - aiding control and freeing up valuable floor space for further improvements to the manufacturing areas.

Why isn't the engine assembly more automated?

Essentially the answer is that it wasn't economic at the production volumes anticipated. The emphasis has been to make the components right and build quality into the engine. Keeping the investment low and the facility simple has helped to achieve this. Sophistication has been put into the supply and control of materials to the line and transportation of the engine through the finishing areas.

Why have a major fixed investment in engine test?

No manufacturer is near to not testing this class of engine. Test cycles are falling but it is unlikely testing will ever be entirely eliminated. The test shop at Solihull has a highly automated test cycle and advanced diagnostic capability. Both of these will help in even greater productivity from the existing cells and ultimately additional capacity for future generations of engine.

Of course with hindsight there are things we could have done differently:

Some parts of the facility are rather more complicated than they need be (e.g. Stores conveyor, rig/de-rig area).

The final commissioning programme for certain areas was made overly difficult by responding absolutely to the production rate of climb requirements (e.g. Engine test).

The software 'Engineering' was simplified by preventing piecemeal enhancement; it could have been made even simpler by eliminating more 'nice to have' features.

Perhaps too many management decisions had to be forced by time constraints.

To have done them differently would either have involved changing history or getting an imbalance between the constraint of time, cost and quality.

## 4 HOW WAS IT ALL ACHIEVED?

We don't want to turn this part of the paper into an abbreviated management text book. In any case we don't know all the answers and there **is** no simple formula which, when applied, automatically ensures the balance between quality, time, and cost is maintained. What we will do is list a few of the things which, from our experience, have proved to be important and are often difficult to achieve. Most of these were used in creating the plant we have described - some better than others.

## 4.1 Management Philosophy

Identify, agree and communicate key objectives. (Making sure everyone understands and avoiding changing them are quite different matters!).

Set and achieve aggressive targets, recognising the need for realism.

Help everyone understand the importance of identifying the real problems before attempting to find solutions.

Avoid letting short term expedient action compromise long term objectives.

Recognise that management decisions are often heavily on the critical path.

Prevent people from putting up smoke screens to protect parochial interests.

## 4.2 Engineering (Facility and Systems)

Establish a well thought through conceptual manufacturing approach and facility/systems outline for the total plant. Obtain agreement and commitment to it at all levels of the organisation.

Define data input and information output requirements on a minimum 'need to have' rather than a maximum 'like to have' basis, but plan the 'system' to allow for expansion.

Determine the right level of integration within each element and between elements of the plant. Concentrate on improving the quality, throughput and efficiency of production and avoid over-emphasis on the niceties of the facilities and systems engineering.

Use dynamic simulation techniques to test engineering solutions as early as possible.

Make sure economic evaluations reflect all the benefits of the engineering in addition to the direct labour savings, and including:

    reduced inventory and work-in-progress levels
    improved operational control
    improved quality
    better working environment (high labour efficiency)
    reduced lead times
    lower building costs.

Take account of the rapid rate of advancement in technology to avoid over-investment in facilities which do not add value.

Recognise there are limitations to the rate at which new technology can be absorbed by people who have to use it and plan accordingly. Avoid introducing too many sequential or concurrent learning curves – custom and practice become established very quickly.

## 4.3 Project Control & Project Management

Ensure both tender specifications and contract extent of supply identify fully, not only the functional and performance requirements, but also the obligations of all parties and the method of control through to a commissioned facility and beyond to the end of the warranty period (and after!).

Assume all people/companies will be less than adequate at project management and be prepared to take the necessary corrective action. Insist on detailed programmes and continually look for ways of improving them.

Determine the details, sequence and nature of inspection/commissioning/acceptance – off- and on-site – so that any problems are isolated at the elemental level. This is particularly important where there are multiple levels from basic mechanical and electrical through to hierarchical computer systems.

Simulate the computer software before interfacing with the physical equipment.

## 4.4 Operations Management

Become knowledgeable about, and involved in, the planning at an early stage.

Establish participation and training programmes as soon as the facilities engineering is sufficiently firm.

Identify new skills requirements and plan recruitment in advance of the facilities programme.

Organise participation in commissioning programmes for maintenance people as well as operations.

There are many, many more items which could be added, but these are some of the most important practical considerations in achieving a successful project completion and sound operating facility.

## CONCLUSION

In this paper we have described what we believe is an 'Investment for a Successful Future' – the business requirement was clear, the planning objectives concisely stated and a responsive plant is operating to help Land Rover maintain its position as a major manufacturer of four wheel drive vehicles.

Overall it was highly successful from a 'Project' viewpoint and the indications are that it will continue to be from an operational one.

FOOTNOTE (An acknowledgement)

The Land Rover engine plant at North Works, Solihull, was planned and implemented by a Joint Project Team comprising:

    Land Rover Production & Plant Engineering
    Land Rover Plant Management
    BL Systems Limited
    BL Construction Projects Limited
    Ingersoll Engineering Projects Limited.

# MANAGEMENT INFORMATION & CONTROL

## COMPUTER CONCEPTS

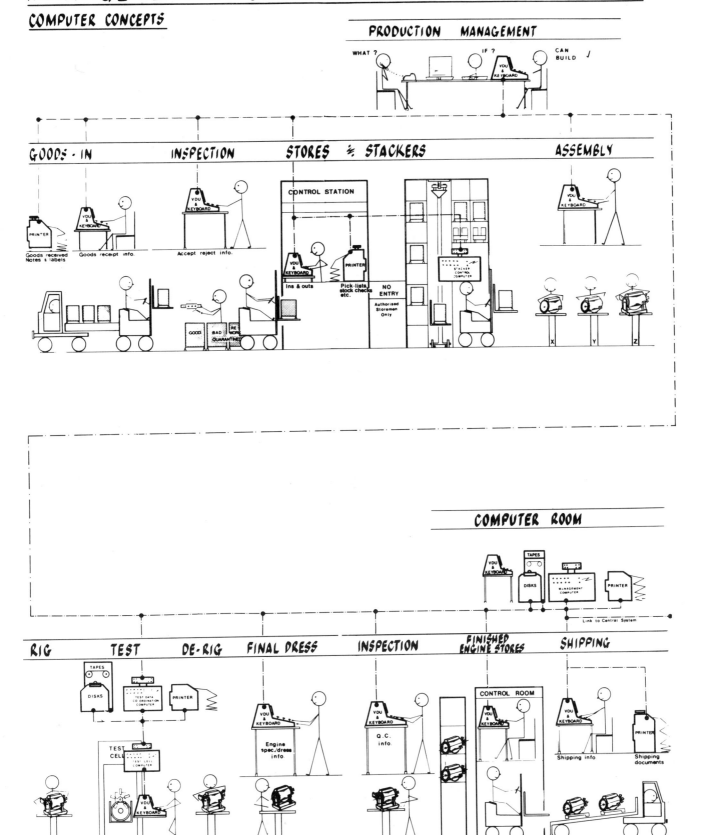

Fig 1    Facility/system integration and hierarchy

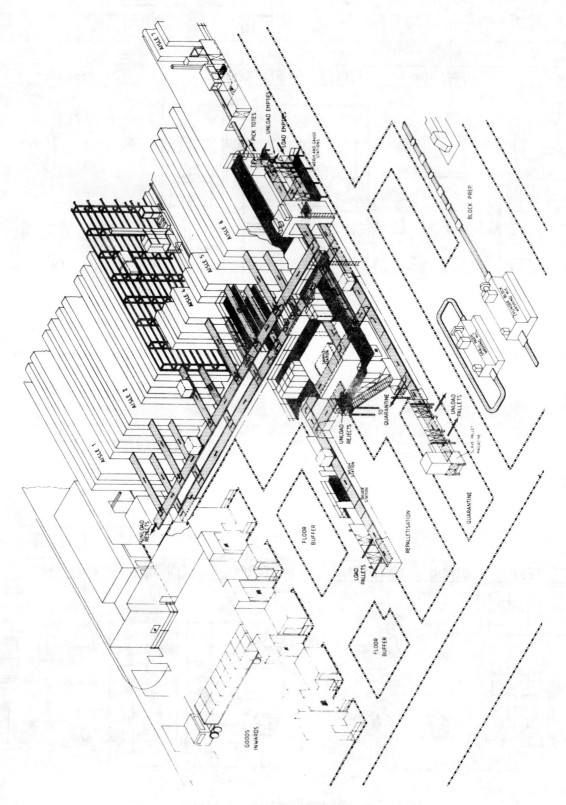

Fig 2    Goods inwards/stores/assembly interfaces

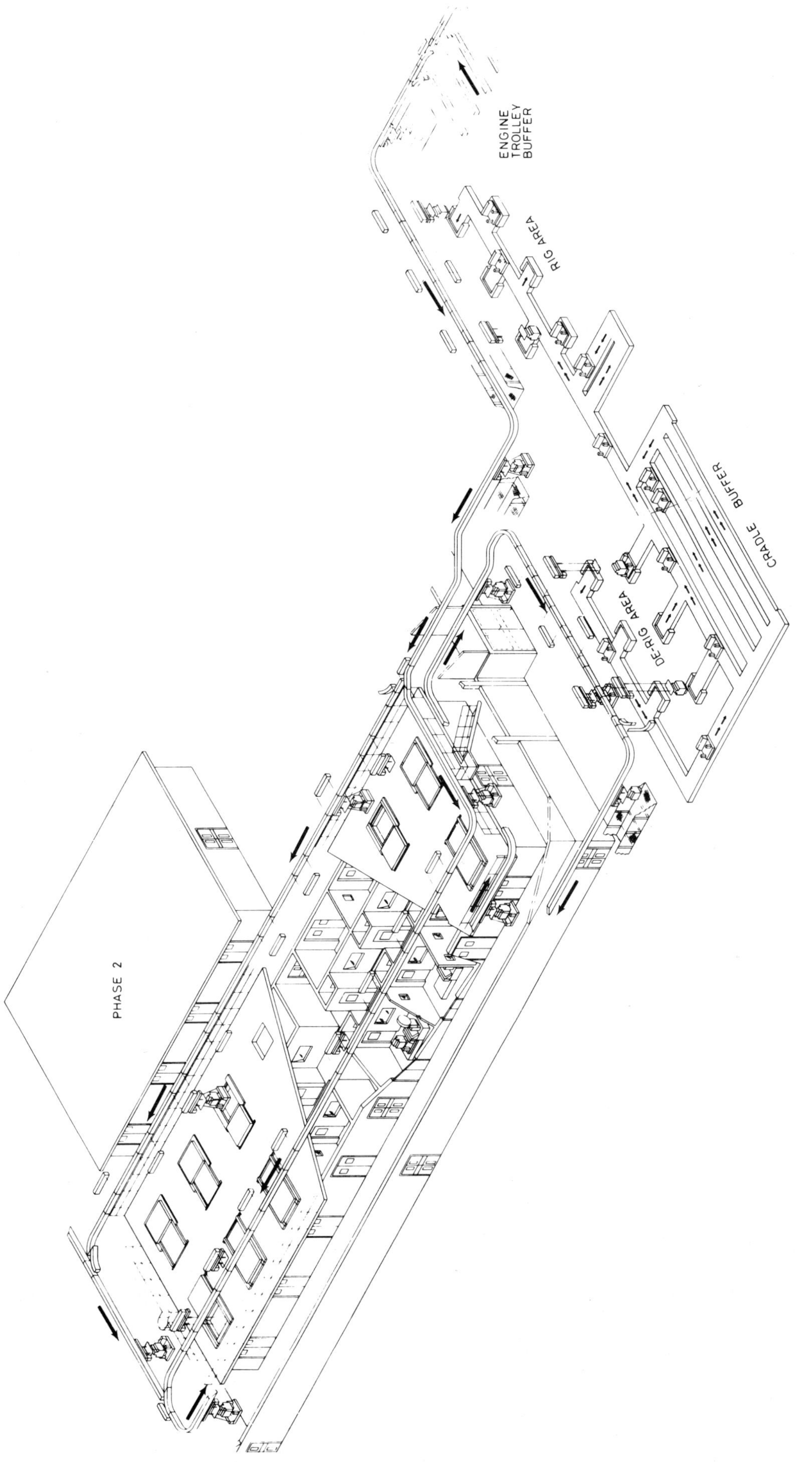

PHASE 2

ENGINE TROLLEY BUFFER

RIG AREA

CRADLE BUFFER

DE-RIG AREA

Fig 3    Handling system and test shop

# C286/81

# An integrated computer aided engineering system for prototypes and tooling of automotive parts

H R O HUMPHREYS, MSc, CEng, MRAeS, MBIM, MIProdE
Delta Computer Aided Engineering Limited, Birmingham

## Introduction

Increasing emphasis is now being placed on the benefits of an integrated system with the basic information generated at the draughting stage being held on the computer and manipulated to produce cost estimates, drawings, production control information, machine control and certification of quality. The integration of these functions, together with the integration of component production, prototype manufacture and toolmaking, can result in reduction of both lead times and cost of production. The application of CAD/CAM within Delta is of general interest because Delta's companies (average size 300-400 employees) are in many ways typical of mechanical engineering companies and the specification of the computer aided design and manufacturing system which Delta has introduced, would be applicable to many small to medium sized engineering companies.

## Description of the DELTACAM System

The DELTACAM system developed by Delta is based on four programs to produce an integrated design, draughting and machining package. It provides a low cost system for 2D draughting and machining with the capability of designing 3D shapes and generating NC tapes for complex 3D surface machining. 2D draughting is performed using a distributed intelligence interactive draughting package (DIAD) developed by the Computer Aided Design Centre (CADC) at Cambridge. CADC software is also used for 2D machining (GNC) and for 3D design and machining (POLYSURF).

In addition, DELTACAM includes the DUCT program developed by the Wolfson Cambridge Industrial Unit. This 3D design and machining program is comparatively easy to use and has many useful features such as a volume calculation to assist with optimising design. The relationship of these programs is shown diagrammatically in Fig. 1.

The DELTACAM system contains a number of programs which can access 2D profiles, known as Kcurves. These can be created either by the draughting system (DIAD) or by two alternative geometry processors, one using the Kcurve language and the other using APT syntax. The 2D profiles can subsequently be used as a basis for work surfaces in GNC, or as patch boundaries (often representing cross-sections) in the 3D modules (POLYSURF and DUCT).

If small batches of complex parts are to be machined economically, the programming method must be very efficient. Using DELTACAM, with its interactive graphics programs, provides a method by which a computer controlled system can compete with the traditional methods of manufacture not only in reducing lead times but also in cost.

The program is available to other companies outside the Delta Group either as a bureau service, or as an in-house system. A bureau service is attractive to the smaller manufacturing unit and to the average toolmaking operation. It also allows the larger company to gain first hand experience before committing itself to a full system. A major requirement of Delta's CAE system was that the capital requirement at each company should be minimised without compromising the functionality and performance of the system installed.

Another important requirement was that the CAE system must have good facilities for the definition, manipulation and manufacture of non-analytic 3D surfaces and these are commonly present on automotive components. The modelling of the complex assembly of non analytic surfaces found in castings and mouldings is a particularly testing application for CAD/CAM. The goal is the preparation of a unique unambiguous shape description by the designer. Instead of using the traditional patternmaker and copymill, the engineer has a repeatable stable model, which can be analysed more accurately and machined more efficiently, using numerical control.

## The DIAD Draughting Program

DIAD has many features of the more expensive draughting systems and is available as a single workstation. Each workstation is a self contained unit for the production of the drawing and would be equivalent to the drawing board. A telephone link to a host computer is available for storage of drawings and permits access to a large data base. The 2D profiles generated by DIAD may be used as input to the GNC programs for machining. The profiles can also be input to the 3D surface description and design programs for modelling and subsequent machining of 3D shapes. The host computer is available on a bureau basis thus providing the smaller company with the facilities of a fully integrated CAD/CAM system at a lower cost.

Like many computer aided draughting systems, the productivity improvements in creating a completely original drawing are likely to be between 1 to 1 and say 3 to 1. This will obviously vary depending, for instance, on the number of repeating features. In many cases, drawings are more likely to be modifications of existing drawings or use features from previous drawings. In performing these typical tasks, very large productivity improvements could result, especially if a comprehensive data base has been established, but one should not under-estimate the time required to establish such a data base. An example of a DIAD drawing is shown (Fig. 2).

Input to a DIAD workstation is made using a keyboard, function buttons, and a graphics tablet with electronic pen (Fig. 3). A total of 384 words can be entered by function buttons and generally it is not necessary to use the keyboard. An electronic pen and tablet is used to control a cursor on a screen, the pen is used to construct lines, identify features, and for dimensioning, windowing etc. The pen can also be used to identify key words which for convenience are marked on the tablet and are required with this mode of operation. The system uses a Tektronix storage tube because with the fast screen repainting times obtained from DIAD's dedicated computer, the greater definition of a storage tube outweighs the advantages of the refresh screen. A refresh screen could be retrofitted when development results in improved definition at an acceptable cost.

## Graphical Numerical Control - GNC

The geometry developed by DIAD is used at the next stage for controlling the path of the cutter. The GNC system caters for the preparation of NC tapes for a wide range of NC machines with 2D capabilities. The system uses low cost

graphics terminals to allow the part-programmer to prove-out his machining sequences away from the machine tool. The essence of the system is that the component, and any fixtures can be displayed on the screen in working situations. The part-programmer can use the cursor to position the cutting tool during fresh air or roughing moves, thereby eliminating the need for elaborate cutting sequence definitions. The machining sequence can be checked visually and modified until the part-programmer is satisfied with his machining program.

One important GNC feature is the macro facility which allows the part-programmer to define repetitive shapes (e.g. Fig. 4) and machining operations using general parameters. The specific parameters can be defined with simple input statements when the macro is called within the part program. This is particularly useful where, for example, machining of a die pocket must be done in several stages of depth.

GNC contains machining modules for turning, milling, drilling, wire spark erosion machining, flame cutting and nibbling. It also has facilities for shape nesting, plotting and curve fitting.

A simple example of a milling sequence to rough out and finish a profile is shown in Fig. 5. GNC automatically generates two permanent data files on exit. The first of these is an up-dated source file containing a complete record of the job to date, including geometry definition and machining commands. This file can subsequently be re-run as required. The second file is a standard format CLDATA file which can be postprocessed automatically for the desired machine tool to produce the operator listing and paper tape.

## 3D Surface Programs

The DIAD and GNC draughting and machining programs are limited to 2D profiles. Much of our work requires the use of DUCT and/or POLYSURF to design and machine 3D surfaces. The use of these programs will be described using practical examples.

## Production of Tooling for Car Body Panels

Input to the programmer can be computerised design data, a drawing, or a model which can be digitised on a 3D measuring machine.

The first example is a plastic panel fitting behind the rear window Fig. 6. The required mesh of points was digitised from a model to generate a

POLYSURF mathematical model based on polynomial surface patches. POLYSURF creates a mesh of patches, by splining through the measured points or nodes. A span between two nodes can be constrained to be an approximation to a circular or elliptical arc. Once the surface has been modelled as a POLYSURF it can be manipulated e.g. the scale changed. In this instance the surface was offset to allow for panel thickness and also mirrored, the tapes were then produced to machine a punch and die set.

The user of POLYSURF can define a variety of simpler surfaces. These include planes, cylinders, cones, spheres and tabulated cylinders. POLYSURF has comprehensive facilities for the drawing and machining of surfaces including their intersections.

A second more complex example was a plastic panel forming part of the gull wing door on a sports car, Fig. 7. In this instance the information was obtained from a drawing. Once the shape had been formed as a number of intersecting polysurfaces, the shape had to be correctly orientated for ease of moulding and extraction of the mould from the plastic mould tool.

POLYSURF has a very useful regional milling facility and a tool path can be produced automatically in response to a command to clear the region by moving along the intersection between the part surface and a series of equally spaced parallel sectioning planes. This method of machining has the advantage that, if the section planes are chosen to be one of the principal planes of the NC machine, NC tape lengths can be reduced since most movements will be two axis, not three.

POLYSURF generates a standard CLDATA output file for post processing for the required NC machine.

## Use of the DUCT Program for Engine Design

The DUCT program is used to define a wide variety of shapes it has been found to be particularly suitable for the design of engine inlet and exhaust ports. It has been used by B.L. to design an engine cylinder head in conjunction with Delta CAE Ltd. and patternmaker, G.Perry & Sons Ltd. This work has been described in detail in a paper presented to the Automobile Division in March 1981 (Ref.1).

The British Leyland designer was using the DUCT program on the Delta computer linked to an inexpensive design terminal at Longbridge (cost about £3500). Delta was then responsible for producing the machine control tapes and for cutting the flow box model. The same data could then be manipulated

using a shrinkage factor to produce a sand core box in cast iron.

Once the basic inlet and exhaust port shapes were designed, the DUCT surfaces were then offset to model the water jacket sand cores. By this method the designer is able to control precisely the thickness of the port walls and thus optimise the design for minimum metal and maximum water, (Fig. 8).

One advantage of both POLYSURF and DUCT is the unique definition. The designer no longer relies on the patternmaker's interpretation. Also of importance is the ability of the designer to have control over and retain details of any modifications.

Castings with doubly curved surfaces are often most easily defined on a drawing by three orthogonal views together with a number of sections. The DUCT system of surface representation developed by the Wolfson Cambridge Industrial Unit is based on planar cross-sections, positioned in true cartesian space by means of a fully three dimensional space curve, known as a spine. Cross-sections are defined orthogonal to the spine curve (Fig. 9).

The creation of the mathematical surface model using DUCT is done with the aid of a graphics terminal. The system has powerful facilities for the interactive design of cross-sections and spine curves should this be required. Both the original design cross-sections and interpolated cross-sections can be modified interactively. DUCT also automatically calculates the cross-sectional and surface area, together with the volume of the component. This can be valuable for determining the material contained within a casting or moulding. It can also be used to optimise a design to conform to a volume constraint or, in the case of a turbine scroll, for example, to ensure a uniform decrease in the cross sectional area along the length of the passageway (Fig. 10). Another important feature of DUCT is the facility for finding complex die split lines. It also has an automatic blending facility to smoothly join two intersecting surfaces.

DUCT has facilities for machining the surface and producing NC tapes. It includes an automatic roughing strategy which allows the removal of the bulk of the material from a die cavity with a large milling cutter before proceeding with finish machining.

## Integration of activities on different Sites

While in many cases we still have to extract geometric data from existing drawings and models, we are now entering the era when information from design to manufacture is controlled by computer and can be transferred from site to site. In the case of the B.L. engine, we have design on one site, computing and machine programming on another site, with machining possible on a third site, with three different companies involved.

One of our bureau customers is machining prototype combustion chambers with the computing and some programming assistance done remotely. Some of the work overload was transferred at hours' notice to a different NC milling machine operated by another company. Another bureau user is engaged in the production of brass stamping dies for synchromesh rings, Fig. 3. The company has recruited and trained a programmer, its present work load is insufficient to justify its own NC milling machine so the machining is done remotely at another unit with data transferred by telephone line.

Delta CAE Ltd. is currently machining tyre moulds from design data and cutter information supplied by a tyre company. This information is processed by Delta to suit a particular machine tool.

The practice of manufacturing information being transferred by telephone must be adopted universally by both prime-contractor and sub-contractor if the maximum benefits are to be obtained from an integrated computer aided engineering system.

## Delta's approach to introducing CAE

Experience has shown that for small companies who require access to advanced 3D surface programs, the specialised bureau provides a cost effective solution, by this method the capital expenditure required by each company is kept to a minimum. To support its bureau activity, Delta CAE has established a production service unit and a sub-contract machine shop and toolroom.

The introduction of CAD/CAM to smaller companies is relatively painless using a step by step approach. Interested companies can examine the applicability of CAD/CAM techniques to their own problems by subcontracting some initial work to Delta CAE. The company can also second their own staff to Delta CAE for a period prior to taking a decision on whether to introduce CAD/CAM to their own company. Shop stewards and shop floor personnel are encouraged to visit Delta CAE to become familiar with the technology.

Two Prime 550 time-sharing mini-computers are being used exclusively for CAE. This system acts as a host both to the draughting system workstations and to the graphics terminals located in customer companies, (Fig. 11). Delta CAE's workshop facilities include CNC equipment for milling, turning, wire erosion machines, and a computer linked inspection machine.

CAD/CAM work is normally performed using graphics terminals running at 1200 baud. This speed of transmission is acceptable since the user is generally performing major tasks in the manipulation of 3D surfaces or the preparation of cutter paths. A dumb graphics terminal operating at 1200 baud would not be attractive for computer aided draughting, where the user is making a large number of edits on geometry and text, hence the reason for using the DIAD system to gain independence from line speed constraints and from the variable response times of the host.

## Conclusion

The system described provides the designer with absolute control of shape both for engine and body design. It assists in producing prototypes quickly and the subsequent development of tooling for mass production with a high level of confidence that the mass produced product will be identical to the finally approved prototype. This should assist innovation and provide the designer with the tools required to optimize parameters to improve airflow and reduce weight of both engine and bodywork. The results should help to reduce both manufacturing cost and fuel consumption.

## Acknowledgement

The support of the Department of Industry in the development of DELTACAM is gratefully acknowledged.

## References

Welbourn D.B. and Cox G.M.A. 'Patterns and Moulds for the Automotive Industry', Institute of Mech. Eng. Proceedings, 1981, Vol. 195, No. 10.

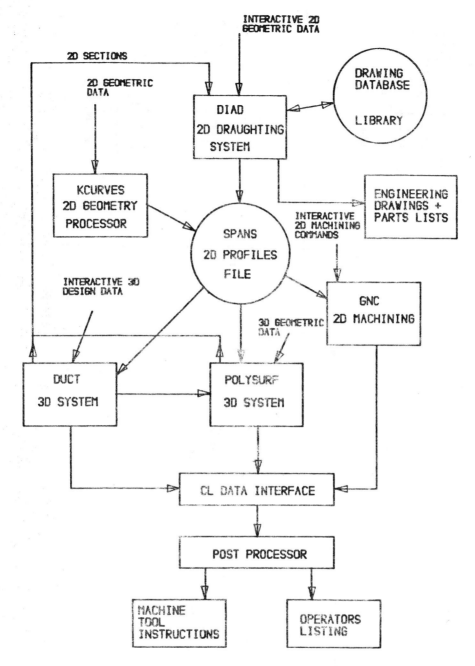

Fig 1    Relationship of programs used within Deltacam

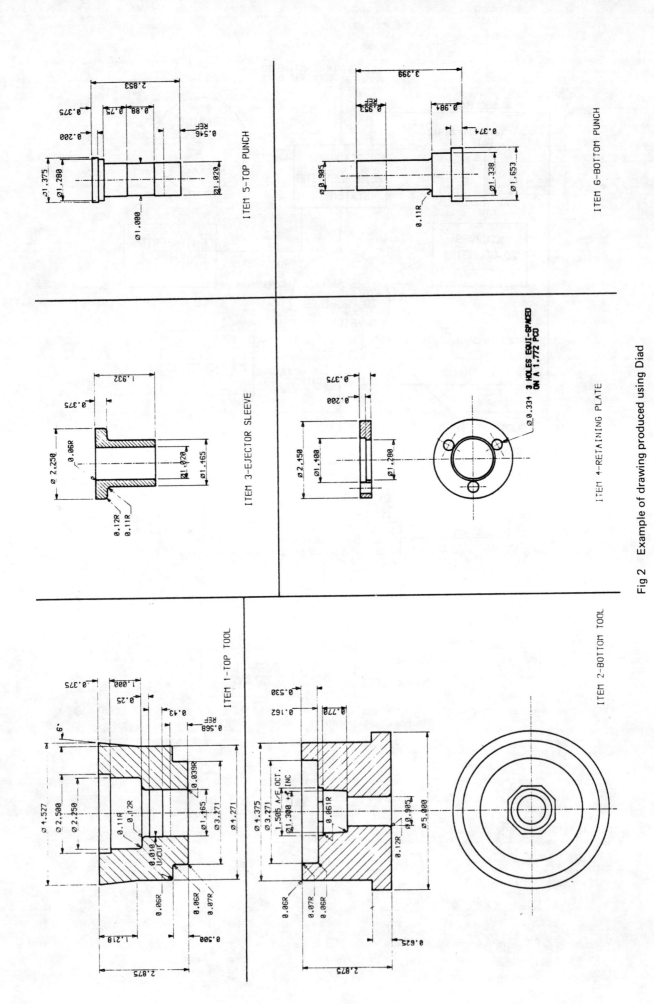

Fig 2    Example of drawing produced using Diad

116

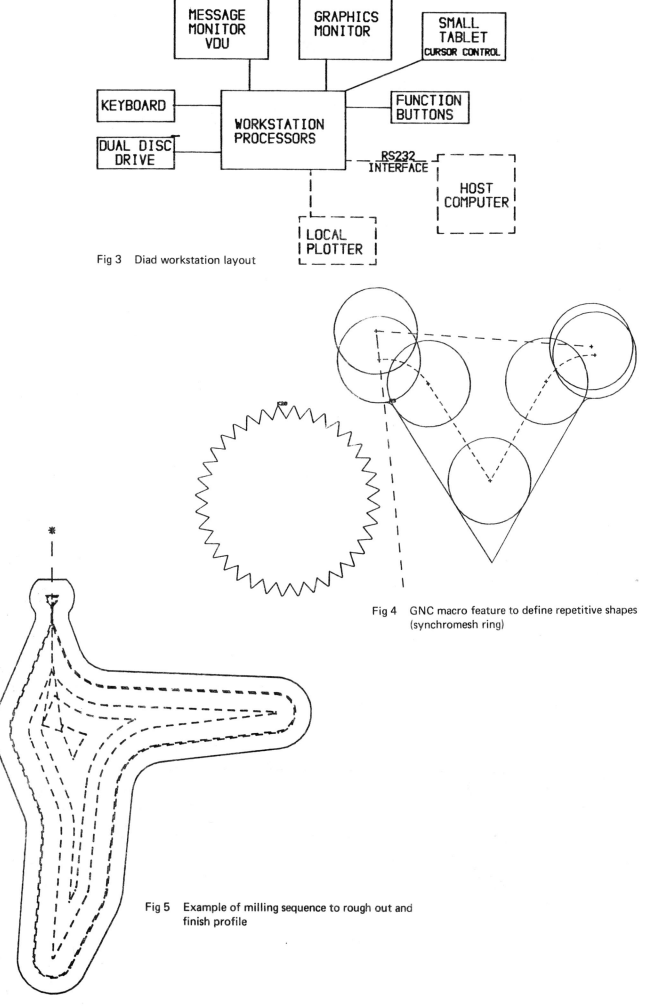

Fig 3    Diad workstation layout

Fig 4    GNC macro feature to define repetitive shapes
(synchromesh ring)

Fig 5    Example of milling sequence to rough out and
finish profile

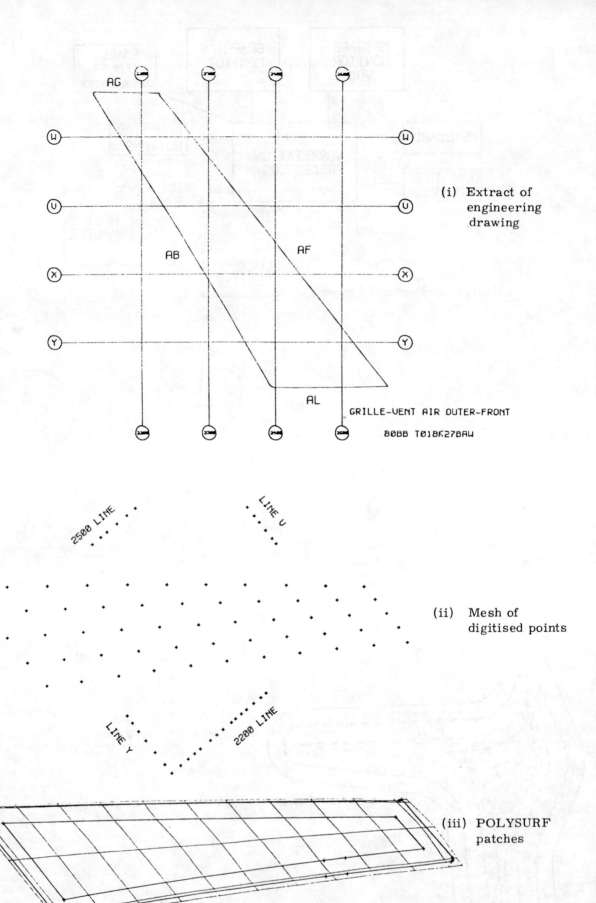

(i) Extract of engineering drawing

GRILLE-VENT AIR OUTER-FRONT

80BB T018K27BAW

(ii) Mesh of digitised points

(iii) POLYSURF patches

Fig 6   Plastic panel — Polysurf

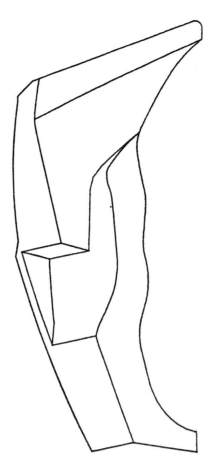

Fig 7    Gull wing door panel — Polysurf

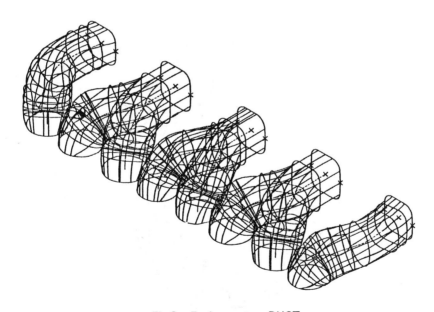

Fig 8    Engine ports — DUCT

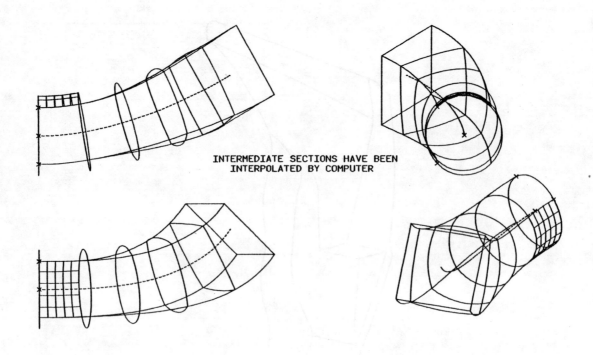

INTERMEDIATE SECTIONS HAVE BEEN
INTERPOLATED BY COMPUTER

A3   25.00   MM = 1.000
THIRD ANGLE   AND ISOMETRIC VIEW

Fig 9   Cross sections — Orthogonal to spine — DUCT

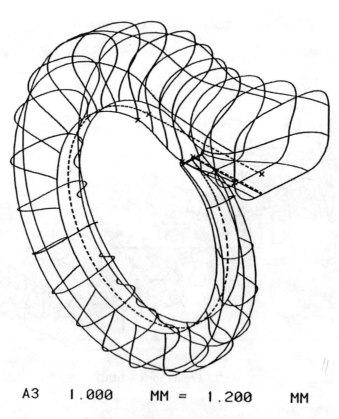

A3   1.000   MM = 1.200   MM

Fig 10  Turbine scroll — DUCT

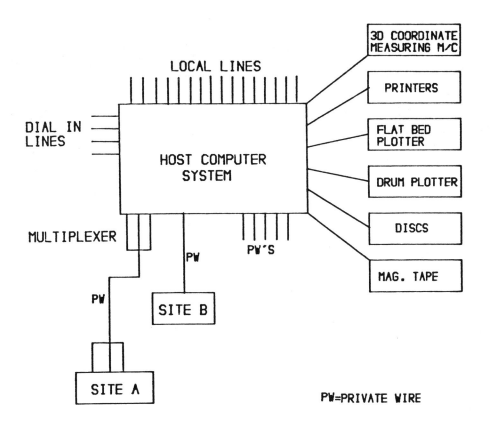

LOCAL LINES

DIAL IN
LINES

HOST COMPUTER
SYSTEM

3D COORDINATE
MEASURING M/C

PRINTERS

FLAT BED
PLOTTER

DRUM PLOTTER

DISCS

MAG. TAPE

MULTIPLEXER

PW

PW'S

PW

SITE B

PW

SITE A

PW=PRIVATE WIRE

TERMINALS ARE:-

    DIAD WORKSTATIONS FOR DRAUGHTING

    STORAGE OR RASTER GRAPHICS TERMINALS FOR CAD/CAM

    PRINTERS + PAPERTAPE PREPARATION EQUIPMENT

Fig 11  Schematic diagram of system

# Resistance spot welding of high strength steels

T B JONES, BSc and N T WILLIAMS, BSc, PhD, CEng, MIM, FWeldI
British Steel Corporation, Welsh Laboratory, Port Talbot

SYNOPSIS  The resistance spot welding characteristics of a range of high strength steels have been investigated and a number of factors have to be considered for optimum results.  They are:

(i)   The selection of welding conditions, particularly the choice between simple or complex welding schedules for a specific sheet thickness or steel strength.  In this context weldability lobes are presented for various types of solution hardened, precipitation hardened and dual phase steels.

(ii)  The static and dynamic properties of spot welds depend on the mechanical properties of the base steel.  The relevance of these to various applications are discussed for both single and multi-weld arrays.

(iii) Shop floor testing criteria, in particular  the mode of fracture obtained on peel testing, need to be reviewed and possibly revised to allow for different material characteristics and fracture mode.  It is concluded that this latter is related to the type of welding schedule used, the dimensions of the weld nugget and the testing method.

## 1  INTRODUCTION

There is a trend towards the use of high strength steels in the automotive industry and, to be acceptable for vehicle construction, high strength steels must be compatible with mass production fabricating techniques, in particular high speed welding techniques. Unlike most fabricating industries, fusion welding plays a relatively minor role in high volume applications.  Resistance welding dominates the fabrication of an autobody as well as the structural members, there being 3000–5000 spot welds in the body and frame components of a typical automobile.

A number of factors have to be considered when evaluating the weldability of such steels for automotive applications.

### 1.1  Suitable welding conditions compatible with existing equipment.

Due to the high capital investment of tooling costs associated with multi-spot welding equipment and component transfer lines, the introduction of any new material which would make existing tooling obsolete must realise sufficient cost benefits to offset any additional expenditure on new equipment.  Any material with welding characteristics requiring excessively long weld times, special control functions, high electrical power demands or frequent electrode maintenance, can often be limited in application if high volume production rates are mandatory.

### 1.2  Adequate mechanical properties

Since one aim of using high strength steels is to replace unalloyed steel of greater thickness, it is essential that the mechanical properties of spot welds should at least equal those of welds in the steel being replaced.  Higher strength levels are generally required compared to lower carbon steels so that the full benefit of high strength steels can be exploited by allowing higher design stresses.  In addition, the load bearing capabilities of automotive structures are sometimes determined by the fatigue strengths of welds and, in the event of a crash situation, by the ability of the welds to withstand impact loading.

### 1.3  Ability to be tested on the shop floor

The routine shop floor testing of spot welds is normally carried out by means of chisel or peel testing.  Acceptance criteria have been and still are based on a minimum weld size or the occurrence of plug rather than an interface weld failure.  The latter can be attributed to one of two reasons: firstly, stuck or extremely small welds and secondly, failure in a full size weld along the original weld interface. Close examination of an interface failure can determine which of these two mechanisms applies in any particular instance.  Thus, an interface failure of a full weld nugget is generally crystalline in appearance whereas failure of a stuck weld tends to be fibrous (Figs. 1(a) and 1(b)).  Difficulties can arise on the shop floor in differentiating easily between the two types of interface failure and it has been common practice to reject all interface failures irrespective of the fundamental correctness of such a decision. In the case of high strength steels, the various fracture types must be identified since the type of fracture obtained depends on steel type and strength, sheet thickness, weld size and testing technique.

## 2  WELDABILITY OF TYPICAL HIGH STRENGTH STEELS

In practice, confusion can arise with high strength steels in selecting welding conditions due to the variety of steel types which are available. While any particular steel type may be welded, it is often found that the same welding conditions may not be suitable for other steel types. High strength steels can obtain their strength by a variety of means. This can involve controlled processing to give fine grain structures e.g. low slab reheating temperatures, controlled rolling, and/or controlled cooling techniques, selective annealing cycles or, alloying by, for example, phosphorus and/or silicon to give solid solution hardening or by niobium, titanium or vanadium to give precipitation hardening. In addition, dual phase steels have been developed which, as a result of alloying and heat treatment yield a structure consisting of a mixture of 'soft' ferrite and 'hard' martensite or lower bainite. Such a structure confers better ductility at a given tensile strength level compared with other types of high strength steels.

### 2.1  Solution Hardening Steels

Weldability lobes for a phosphorised steel of 0.060% carbon are illustrated in Fig. 2. These lobes possess sufficient width to ensure few problems in a production situation. The available current range is significantly improved by using a larger electrode force compared with unalloyed low carbon steel. For a sheet thickness of 0.67mm, increasing the electrode force from 1.0kN to 1.5kN is sufficient to ensure adequate weld quality. The available current range decreases with increasing C+P level, see Fig. 3, this being attributed to the fact that splash or overheating occurs at a lower current value. In general, the current levels necessary to produce a certain weld size can be up to 15% less for phosphorised steels compared to unalloyed low carbon steel.

Typical strength levels for a range of phosphorised steels are summarised in Table 1, from which it may be seen that breaking load in tensile-shear increases with C+P level and the carbon equivalent whereas these factors have little effect on the cross-tension strength. The failure mode in cross-tension is generally of the partial plug-interface type, the plug component varying between 55-95% depending on the C+P level. Similar weld strengths but with plug failures were obtained in a silicon-phosphorus steel.

This latter steel, when tested in tensile-shear, exhibited a failure mode which was generally of the double plug type. It was difficult to establish any firm trends from the tensile-shear impact, or energy absorbed values during tensile-shear or cross-tension testing but, failure mode was of the double plug type. Fatigue results obtained in the push-pull mode, with a load ratio R = 0.1, are shown in Fig. 4. These results are similar to those obtained for unalloyed low carbon steels. Considerable improvements in fatigue life can be obtained by increasing the weld size or the number of spot welds see Fig.5.

The theoretical fatigue strength of a linear weld array can be obtained by a simple multiplication of the fatigue strength of a single spot weld by the number of welds. However, lower strengths than predicted are generally obtained in practice. From Table 2, it can be seen that the % reduction in fatigue strength at a given number of cycles at high loads increases as the number of welds in the array increases up to an array comprising 7 welds. It would appear that the amount of reduction remains constant with larger weld arrays and at low loads. With a 3 weld array, the % reduction in fatigue strength is greater at the lower loads, although this trend is not significant with weld arrays containing more than 3 welds. The lower fatigue properties of multi weld arrays is due to unequal loading of each spot weld in the weld array during testing. It is considered that weld design, pitch and number have to be carefully examined, if benefits are to be derived from the higher basic fatigue properties of a high strength steel.

In almost all instances, failure during fatigue testing occurs in the heat-affected zone of a spot weld, crack initiation taking place at the inner surface between the sheets and propagating through the sheet thickness to the outer surface of the sheet. Interface failures are only obtained with small or sub-standard weld sizes e.g. $3\sqrt{t}$ welds where t = sheet thickness in mm. In a weld array, failure occurs exclusively at the outer welds of the array.

Partial plug failures are the most common type of failure observed with phosphorised steels when peel testing welds of diameter $5\sqrt{t}$ and the plug component can vary between 80-90% of the total weld area.

The occurrence of plug type failures is influenced by weld size, and typical results obtained on peel testing a carbon-phosphorus steel of thickness 0.67mm (Fig. 6) have shown that 100% plug failures are always obtained with a weld size greater than $7.5\sqrt{t}$. Failure mode is also influenced by the electrode tip diameter. For example, as the electrode tip diameter increases, the larger is the weld size necessary to give a 100% plug failure. Typical results obtained when welding a steel of thickness 1.0mm are given in Table 3. With electrode tip sizes up to 6mm diameter, it is necessary to grow the weld size to a value larger than the electrode tip size to guarantee 100% plug failure. With larger electrode tip diameters, plug failure is obtained at weld sizes less than the electrode tip size.

## 2.2 Precipitation Hardening Steels

Typical weldability lobes for a number of steels precipitation hardened with titanium in sheets of gauges between 1.0 and 4.0mm are illustrated in Fig.7. It can be seen that, increasing sheet thickness results in a significant increase in the available current range to give a weld size $>4\sqrt{t}$, Table 4. The selection of niobium or titanium as the hardening alloy does not influence the available current range to any great extent but, there is a marked shift in the weldability lobes. In general, niobium treated steels require a lower current to produce a given weld size compared with a titanium treated steel, this effect being greater as the steel thickness increases, Fig. 8. Similarly, lower welding currents are necessary with both titanium and niobium treated steels compared with unalloyed low carbon steels. The base strength of the steel does not influence the welding parameters necessary to give a certain weld size, though higher electrode forces are necessary with high strength steels compared with unalloyed low carbon steels.

Typical spot weld mechanical properties for a range of high strength steels and sheet thicknesses are summarised in Table 5. It can be seen that the tensile-shear strength is more dependent on sheet thickness than base steel strength. In addition, other trends obtained indicate that:

(a) The tensile-shear strengths of welds in high strength steels are higher than those for unalloyed low carbon steel and increase with steel strength.

(b) Cross-tension strengths are similar or slightly lower than those obtained for the same thickness of unalloyed low carbon steel.

(c) Ductility ratios in the range 0.2-0.6 are obtained for high strength steels compared to 0.4-0.9 for unalloyed low carbon steel.

Plug failures are generally obtained on peel testing welds made in sheet thicknesses up to 1.6mm using single impulse weld schedules on steels of yield strength levels up to 400 N/mm$^2$. However, partial plug failures were observed with a 1.0mm steel having a yield strength 530 N/mm$^2$ even at weld sizes $>5\sqrt{t}$.

For sheet thicknesses >1.6mm either a multiple impulse welding schedule or a post-heat pulse must be incorporated into the welding schedule in order to ensure plug failure on peel testing on a number of steel types.

These results are summarised in Table 6 from which the following conclusions can be drawn:

(a) With single impulse welding schedules:

(i) The thicker the steel, the greater is the weld size necessary to give plug failure.

(ii) With thin steels partial plug failures are only obtained at the very high strength levels (YS~550 N/mm$^2$).

(b) With post heat schedules:

(i) At sheet thicknesses up to 2.0mm, post heating decreases the weld size at which plug failure is obtained.

(ii) On the basis of the available experimental data, it would appear that at sheet thicknesses greater than 2.0mm, the thicker the steel the less effective post-heating becomes in giving plug failures at the higher yield strength levels. However further work using a number of other post-heat schedules need to be investigated.

Multiple impulse schedules used in the present investigation consisted of a 5 cycles on: 2 cycles off current programme. Increasing the number of pulses with this programme results in plug failures being obtained at a smaller weld size and at a lower weld current level, some typical results obtained with a 3.1mm thick titanium steel being summarised in Table 7.

Improvements obtained using a single impulse followed by a post-heat pulse depends on the level of current in, and the duration of, the post-heat pulse. Typical results obtained with a 2.1mm thick niobium steel are summarised in Table 8.

No difficulties are experienced in welding precipitation hardening steels to each other or to an unalloyed low carbon steel of similar or dissimilar thickness. Current levels necessary to give acceptable weld quality are those used for welding the high strength steel to itself.

## 2.3 Dual Phase Steels

A 1.0mm thick cold rolled and 4.0mm thick hot rolled silicon/molybdenum dual phase steel have been studied and weldability lobes for the latter steel are shown in Fig. 9.

As with other steel types, increasing sheet thickness results in a significant increase in the available current range, typical weld mechanical properties for both steels are shown in Table 5. Ductility ratios of 0.48 and 0.98 reflect the higher tensile-shear strengths of dual phase steels as compared to unalloyed low carbon steels. Plug and interface failure are noted with the 1.0 and 4.0mm thick steels respectively in tensile-shear, cross-tension and peel tests. However using multiple impulse welding schedules comprising of 0.34s on; 0.02s off results in plug failures with the thicker steel.

# 3 DISCUSSION

As initially pointed out, the following have to be considered when welding high strength steels:

(a) The choice of welding conditions.

(b) The need to develop adequate mechanical properties in the weld.

(c) Capability of assessing weld quality using conventional shop floor testing techniques.

## 3.1 Welding Parameters

In general it may be summarised that for cold reduced high strength steels, the weld times required are the same or only slightly longer than those for unalloyed low carbon steels. Similarly, welding currents are of the same level but in some instances can be lower due to the higher resistivity of high strength steels. However, this can often be offset by the decrease in contact resistance arising from the necessity to use higher electrode forces with these steels due to their higher basic strength, and the need to take into account the increased springback which can occur.

Longer weld times may be necessary with hot rolled high strength steels compared to unalloyed low carbon steels, this being due to the need for using pulse or post-heat welding schedules to ensure plug type failures. However, it should be emphasised that such welding schedules are frequently used for hot rolled unalloyed steels and should therefore not present problems in terms of equipment availability.

## 3.2 Mechanical Properties of Welds

Adequate properties must be capable of being obtained in spot welds of high strength steels under both static and dynamic modes of testing. It may be summarised that, the maximum tensile-shear strength of high strength steel spot welds is proportional to the thickness and yield strength of the base steel and is not much influenced by chemical composition. Improvements of between 1.3 to 2.0 times the strength of unalloyed low carbon steels are generally obtained. In contrast, the cross-tension strength does not necessarily increase with increase in base steel strength and in some instances may even be slightly inferior when compared with unalloyed low carbon steel of the same thickness.

With regard to dynamic properties, the impact properties of high strength steels are slightly inferior to those of unalloyed low carbon steel and fracture mode depends on the steel type and thickness. Double plug failures are most frequently noted with impact tensile-shear tests whereas in the cross-tension impact test, failure is generally of the plug type. Double plug failures are generally noted at larger thicknesses for dynamic as compared with static tensile-shear testing up to thicknesses of 1.3mm. A mixture of interface and plug/partial plug failures would be expected at greater thicknesses, although in practice interface failures become more prevalent as the thickness and strength increases.

The shape of fatigue curves for spot welds is similar to the regular S-N curves for unwelded materials but lower fatigue ratios (i.e. the ratio of the fatigue strength at $10^7$ cycles to the static shear strength of the weld) are exhibited. Compared with spot welds in low carbon steels, spot welds in high strength steels tend to have slightly higher fatigue strengths at the higher stress - low cycle conditions although these differences are negligible at or greater than $10^5$ cycles. It may be concluded that the fatigue strength of welds in high strength steels is no better than that observed in unalloyed low carbon steels. This is to be expected since the properties of resistance welds are similar for all steels for a particular joint configuration since crack propagation occurs in the heat affected zone and is independent of the heat-affected zone structure. Also, there is no need to initiate a crack in a resistance spot weld since this is already present in the joint geometry.

## 3.3 Hardening Behaviour

HAZ/weld hardnesses in the range 307-409HV were noted with a range of phosphorised steels of composition up to 0.093% Carbon and 0.48% Manganese of thickness $\sim$ 0.7mm. While these hardness levels are considerably higher than those generally considered acceptable for unalloyed low carbon steel, the predominant mode of failure in welds of diameter $5\sqrt{t}$ is 80-90% partial plug failure with occasional 100% plug failure. Increasing the hold time from 0.1 to 0.6s does not markedly influence the maximum hardness values measured in sheet of thickness 0.7mm but for thicker phosphorised steels ($\sim$1.0mm), a lower cooling rate is obtained for a given heat input which results in a lower maximum weld hardness.

Maximum weld/HAZ hardness values of 233-418 HV were noted with a range of niobium and titanium treated high strength steels of thickness. 1.0-4.0mm (see Table 9). A gradual decrease in weld hardness being observed with increasing thickness. This can be attributed to two major factors; either the slower cooling rate associated with thicker strip, or the use of a more complex welding schedule thereby giving a higher heat input. For steels of thickness 3.0-4.0mm, hardness values lower than those of the parent material are occasionally observed in the heat-affected zone.

The significance of high hardness values in resistance spot welds is not fully understood. For example, for unalloyed low carbon steels, it is considered that the maximum hardness should be below 300Hv if interface failure is to be avoided. However, results obtained by the authors on both phosphorised steels and precipitation hardening steels containing either niobium or titanium indicate that, plug type failures can be obtained with a maximum weld hardness well in excess of 300Hv. In these instances, it is not possible to accept or reject spot welds on criteria normally acceptable for unalloyed low carbon steels and therefore other criteria must be considered in the final analysis.

## 3.4 Shop Floor Testing Criteria

A number of different fracture types have been observed when testing resistance spot welds in both unalloyed and high strength steels. The type of fracture obtained depends to a large extent on the:

(a) Type of test used

(b) Weld size relative to the sheet thickness

(c) Steel strength.

The failure mode in spot welds is predominantly governed by two factors viz:

(a) Geometric factor     i.e.

The ratio of sheet thickness to weld size and also the sheet width, i.e. the degree of constraint imposed on the weld.

(b) Metallurgical factor     i.e.

The relative strengths of the weld, heat-affected zone and base steel.

Increasing the parent metal strength, and hence the rigidity of the test piece, increases the tendency for either partial plug or interface failure in both cross-tension and tensile-shear testing. Consequently, with high strength steels, the incidence of interface failure can be high. It is difficult, because of the complexity of the stress system developed around a spot weld under service conditions, to relate mathematically weld size, base metal strength, weld metal strength, and metal thickness to failure mode. Whether plug or interface failure occurs depends upon the relative stress levels at the weld interface and the heat-affected zone. These two stress levels have recently been calculated using the von Mises Distortion Energy criterion and the equivalent stresses compared with the stress required for failure at each location in order to give a prediction of failure type. This analysis indicated that to avoid interface failure and ensure plug failures, then

$$\frac{d}{t} > \left( \frac{1.5 \ Sy_{PM} \ W}{Sy_{WM} t} \right)^{\frac{1}{2}} \ \ldots\ldots\ldots (1)$$

where $Sy_{PM}$ = yield strength of parent material

      $Sy_{WM}$ = yield strength of weld metal

      $d$ = weld diameter

      $t$ = sheet thickness

      $W$ = specimen width

Such factors as chemical composition, grain size and microstructure must play an important part since they can influence the terms $Sy_{PM}$ and $Sy_{WM}$ in the above equation. Microstructure is also important because a soft ductile structure at the root of the notch marking the intersection of the two sheets assists the avoidance of interface failures i.e. if the notch ends in a tough ductile structure, then plug failure results whereas if the notch is sharp or ends in a low toughness region, interface failure occurs.

The influence of chemical composition on the mode of fracture can be explained in terms of its effect on the basic strength of the sheet and thereby on the conditions prevailing at the base of the notch.

Consequently in order to ensure plug failure in high strength steels, it is necessary to use different criteria than those normally employed for unalloyed low carbon steels.

Certain practical expediences can be taken to ensure plug failure on testing. For example, increasing weld size above the generally specified size of $5 \sqrt{t}$ can result in a change from interface or partial plug to full plug failure. Plug failures can also be ensured by incorporating either a post-heat cycle into the weld schedule or by using multiple pulse schedules. The effectiveness of such schedules depend on sheet thickness, steel composition and heat-affected zone strength since, the main role of such schedules is to modify the metallurgical structure at the base of the natural notch of a spot weld. To ensure a full plug failure, it is essential that a ductile structure is formed in this zone. It is considered, for example, that the ability to soften slightly a narrow region in the heat affected zone of precipitation hardening or dual phase steels accounts for a greater ability to pull plug type failures in these steels compared with solution hardening type steels. In the latter steel type heat-affected zone softening is most unlikely to occur.

Further factors which must be considered are the importance of the degree of triaxiality at the notch which depends on the notch acuity, and whether the initial stress concentration is due to a blunt notch or a sharp crack which can change the fracture mode. If the notch is blunt then failure occurs by pulling a plug whereas in the case of a sharp notch, the likelihood of interface failure is increased.

Such factors as the degree of misfit between the sheets being welded and the weld nugget dimensions relative to electrode tip diameter govern the sheet angle at the notch, and it has also been shown that if the weld diameter is much smaller than the electrode tip diameter, a sharp notch can result causing interfacial failure. As the weld diameter approaches and exceeds that of the electrode tip, a blunt notch is formed and plug failures predominate. It has also been observed that the larger the electrode tip size, the larger is the weld size necessary to change from interface to plug failure. Conversely, as the electrode tip size becomes smaller, plug failures can be induced at smaller weld sizes even when using electrode tip sizes less than that calculated from the 5√t criterion.

It may be summarised therefore, that in unalloyed low carbon steels and high strength steels, the likelihood of interface failure can be determined by practical as well as basic metallurgical factors. In terms of the latter, it is concluded that the incidence of interface failures increases with sheet thickness and steel strength as indicated in Fig.10.

## CONCLUSIONS

High strength steels can be readily resistance spot welded provided proper attention is given to determining suitable welding conditions.

Considerable improvements in weld strength can be obtained with high strength steels under tensile-shear loading conditions compared to unalloyed low carbon steel. Weld strength in tensile shear is proportional to the tensile strength of the parent material. Similar results to those obtained with unalloyed carbon steel are observed under cross-tension, impact and fatigue loading conditions. However increasing the weld size can lead to a marked improvement in fatigue properties.

Full plug failures can be obtained when testing spot welds in high strength steels and their occurence depends on such factors as sheet thickness, steel strength, weld size and electrode size.

## ACKNOWLEDGEMENT

The fatigue data referred to in this paper represented results obtained from work carried out under the aegis of the European Coal and Steel Community to whom thanks are extended for permission to publish.

### Table 1 Mechanical properties of phosphorised steels

| % C | C+P | CE** | Tensile-Shear (kN) Breaking load | Failure Mode | Cross-Tension (kN) Breaking load | Failure Mode | Ductility Ratio | Energy Absorbed at Maximum Load (Joules) Tensile Shear | Cross Tension | Impact Tensile Shear - Joules)* |
|---|---|---|---|---|---|---|---|---|---|---|
| 0.034 | 0.109 | 0.097 | 3.89 | DP/PP/P | 1.96 | 90% PP | 0.50 | 6.0 | 11.3 | 17.2 |
| 0.044 | 0.119 | 0.108 | 3.91 | DP/PP/P | 1.69 | 95% PP | 0.43 | 6.0 | 8.9 | 16.1 |
| 0.040 | 0.120 | 0.103 | 3.87 | P | 2.16 | P/PP | 0.56 | 9.6 | 16.5 | 12.4 |
| 0.047 | 0.148 | 0.097 | 4.57 | DP | 2.29 | 95% PP | 0.50 | 11.2 | 23.0 | 16.5 |
| 0.064 | 0.157 | 0.117 | 4.52 | DP | 1.90 | 70% PP | 0.42 | 0.6 | 8.6 | 13.8 |
| 0.065 | 0.185 | 0.145 | 4.49 | P | 2.02 | P | 0.44 | 15.3 | 15.3 | 9.0 |
| 0.089 | 0.219 | 0.147 | 4.90 | DP | 1.44 | 70% DP/PP | 0.29 | 11.2 | 11.2 | 22.4 |
| 0.093 | 0.223 | 0.151 | 4.70 | DP | 1.76 | 55% DP/PP | 0.37 | 19.3 | 10.3 | 15.6 |

DP = Double plug failure

PP = Partial plug/interface failure

P = Plug failure

\* All double plug failures

\*\* CE = %C + $\frac{\%Mn}{6}$

### Table 2 Ratio of actual fatigue strength/theoretical fatigue strength for multi spot welded arrays

| No. of Welds | 1 | 3 | | | 5 | | | 7 | | | 9 | | |
|---|---|---|---|---|---|---|---|---|---|---|---|---|---|
| No.of cycles | Actual Strength (kN) | Strength (kN) Theoretical | Actual | Ratio* K | Strength (kN) Theoretical | Actual | Ratio K | Strength (kN) Theoretical | Actual | Ratio K | Strength (kN) Theoretical | Actual | Ratio K |
| $10^5$ | 2.2 | 6.6 | 5.5 | 0.83 | 11.0 | 8.1 | 0.74 | 15.4 | 9.6 | 0.62 | 19.8 | 13.0 | 0.65 |
| $10^6$ | 1.4 | 4.2 | 3.0 | 0.71 | 7.0 | 5.3 | 0.76 | 9.8 | 6.6 | 0.67 | 12.6 | 9.2 | 0.73 |
| $10^7$ | 1.2 | 3.6 | 2.2 | 0.61 | 6.0 | 5.2 | 0.70 | 8.4 | 4.8 | 0.57 | 10.8 | 7.0 | 0.64 |

\* Ratio K = $\frac{\text{Actual Strength}}{\text{Theoretical Stength}}$

Table 3    Influence of electrode tip size on weld size required for plug failure for 1mm phosphorised steel (C + P = 0.14%)

| Electrode Tip Size (mm) | Weld Size for Plug Failure (mm) |
|---|---|
| 5 | 5.3 |
| 6 | 6.1 |
| 7 | 6.9 |
| 8 | 7.6 |

Table 4    Influence of sheet thickness on available current range for various high strength steels

| Steel Type Strengthening Element | Thickness (mm) | Yield Strength $N/mm^2$ | Current Range (mm) |
|---|---|---|---|
| Titanium | 0.95 | 530 | 1.95 |
| Niobium | 1.60 | 350 | 3.40 |
| Niobium | 2.60 | 350 | 3.50 |
| Titanium | 3.06 | 490 | 3.00 |
| Titanium | 3.12 | 450 | 3.60 |
| Titanium | 4.00 | 430 | 4.00 |

Table 5    Mechanical properties of a range of high strength steels of various thicknesses

| Steel Type Strengthening Element | Thickness (mm) | Yield Strength $N/mm^2$ | Tensile Shear Strength (kN) | Cross Tension Strength (kN) | Ductility Ratio |
|---|---|---|---|---|---|
| (a) Precipitation Hardening Type | | | | | |
| Titanium | 0.95 | 530 | 8.23 | 2.13 | 0.26 |
| Niobium | 1.60 | 350 | 17.50 | 6.42 | 0.37 |
| Niobium | 2.14 | 400 | 24.22 | 7.41 | 0.31 |
| Niobium | 2.60 | 350 | 35.50 | 6.75 | 0.19 |
| Titanium | 3.06 | 490 | 47.50 | 25.00 | 0.53 |
| Titanium | 3.12 | 450 | 51.00 | 20.00 | 0.40 |
| Titanium | 4.00 | 430 | 85.50 | 41.00 | 0.48 |
| (b) Dual Phase Type | | | | | |
| Mn-Si-Mo-Cr | 1.00 | 350 | 10.40 | 5.00 | 0.48 |
| Mn-Si-Mo-Cr | 4.00 | 450 | 41.00 | 40.00 | 0.98 |

**Table 6  Fracture characteristics of spot welds in precipitation hardening steels of various strengths and thickness**

| Yield Strength ($N/mm^2$) | Thickness (mm) | Welding Schedule * | Fracture Characteristics | | |
|---|---|---|---|---|---|
| | | | Weld Size of 5 $\sqrt{t}$ ** | Weld Size of 7 $\sqrt{t}$ | Weld Size to give plug |
| 300 | 1.2 | S | P | – | – |
| | 2.0 | S | I | – | 6 $\sqrt{t}$ |
| | | PH | P | – | – |
| 350 | 1.6 | S | P | – | – |
| | 2.6 | S | I | – | 6 $\sqrt{t}$ |
| | | PH | 90% PP | – | – |
| 450 | 2.0 | S | I | P | 7 $\sqrt{t}$ |
| | | PH | I | – | 6 $\sqrt{t}$ |
| | 4.0 | MP | P | – | – |
| 500 | 3.0 | S | I | I | – |
| | | PH | I | I | – |
| | | MP | P | – | – |
| 550 | 1.0 | S | 90% PP | – | – |
| | 2.1 | S | I | – | 5.5 $\sqrt{t}$ |

*    S    =    Single pulse

     PH    =    Single pulse + post-heat pulse

     MP    =    Multiple pulses

**    P    =    Plug failure

     PP    =    Partial plug failure

     I    =    Interface failure

Table 7   Influence of number of pulses (5 on 2 off) on minimum weld size to give plug failure in a 3.1 mm
titanium treated steel

| No. of Pulses | Welding Current (kA) | Weld Size to give* Plug Failure | |
|---|---|---|---|
| | | (mm) | (f)$\sqrt{t}$ |
| 5 | 18.5 | 9.7 | 5.5 |
| 7 | 15.5 | 9.3 | 5.3 |
| 9 | 14.5 | 9.0 | 5.1 |

\*   Nominal $5\sqrt{t}$   =   8.83mm

Table 8   The influence of post heat time on the weld size and fracture mode of spot welds in a 2.1 mm
niobium treated steel

| Weld Current (kA) | Post Heat time(s) | Post Heat current(kA) | Weld Size (mm) | Mode of Failure |
|---|---|---|---|---|
| 11 | 0 | 8 | 8.4 | Face |
| 11 | 0.2 | 8 | 8.6 | 80% Plug |
| 11 | 0.4 | 8 | 9.8 | 70% Plug |

(a)                                                      (b)

Fig 1    Appearance of typical interface type failures: (a) Crystalline
         appearance of a strong weld;  (b) Fibrous appearance of a
         stuck weld

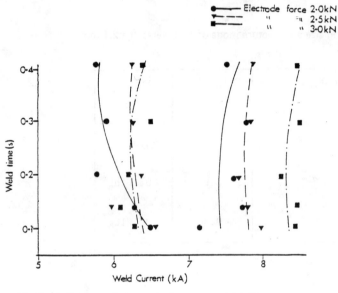 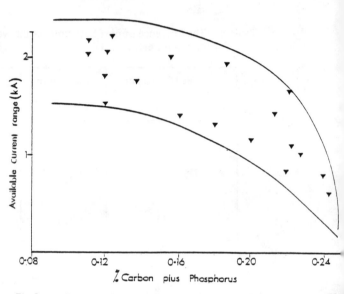

Fig 2    Influence of electrode force on weldability lobe carbon-         Fig 3    Influence of C + P level on available welding current range
         phosphorus steel

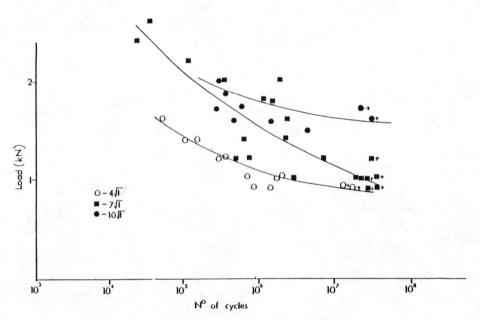

Fig 4    L/N curve for 4√t, 7√t, 10 √t welds carbon-phosphorus steel

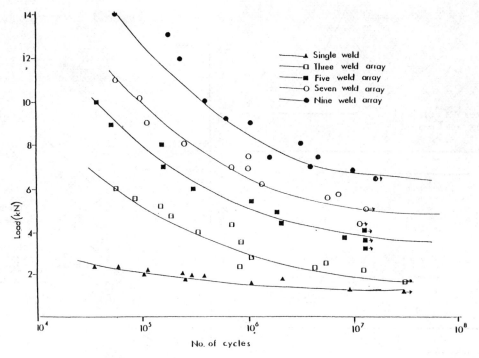

Fig 5    L/N curve for multi spot welded linear arrays of 5√t diameter welds for a 0.7 mm phosphorised steel

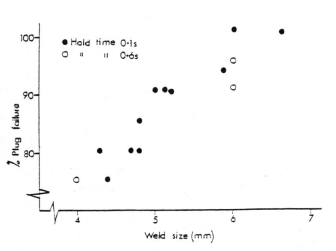

Fig 6    Relationship between weld size and degree of plug failure during fracture for a phosphorised steel

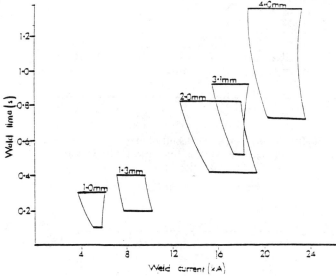

Fig 7    Influence of steel thickness on weldability lobes for titanium steels:

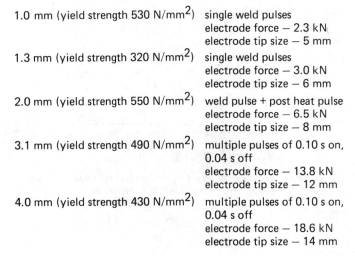

1.0 mm (yield strength 530 N/mm$^2$)    single weld pulses
electrode force — 2.3 kN
electrode tip size — 5 mm

1.3 mm (yield strength 320 N/mm$^2$)    single weld pulses
electrode force — 3.0 kN
electrode tip size — 6 mm

2.0 mm (yield strength 550 N/mm$^2$)    weld pulse + post heat pulse
electrode force — 6.5 kN
electrode tip size — 8 mm

3.1 mm (yield strength 490 N/mm$^2$)    multiple pulses of 0.10 s on,
0.04 s off
electrode force — 13.8 kN
electrode tip size — 12 mm

4.0 mm (yield strength 430 N/mm$^2$)    multiple pulses of 0.10 s on,
0.04 s off
electrode force — 18.6 kN
electrode tip size — 14 mm

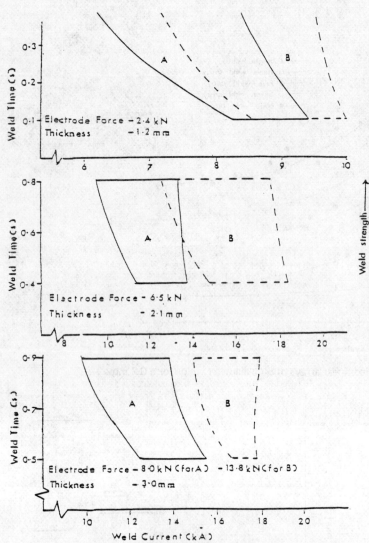

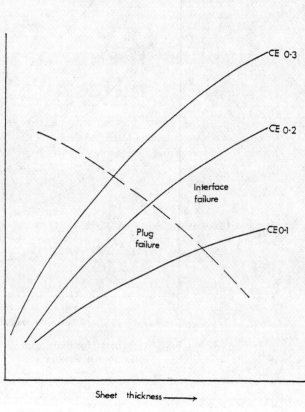

Fig 10 Relationship between carbon equivalent, sheet thickness, weld strength and failure mode

Fig 8 Comparison of weldability lobes for niobium and titanium strengthened steel of thickness 1.2 to 3.0 mm:
A = niobium; B = titanium

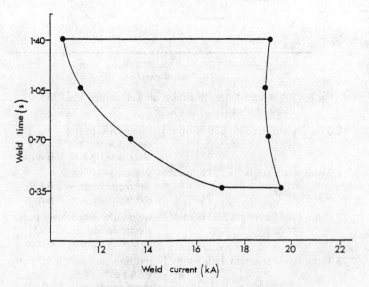

Fig 9 Weldability lobe for a 4 mm hot rolled dual phase steel containing molybdenum/silicon

134

# C288/81

# Advances in automatic quality control for the flexible manufacture of vehicle components

P A McKEOWN, MSc, CEng, MIMechE, FIProdE, FIQA
Cranfield Unit for Precision Engineering, Cranfield, Bedford

SYNOPSIS   The sequence of actions for effective control of quality are analogous to a closed-loop error feedback system.   Maximum efficiency of quality control occurs at the highest speed of response and closest point of application to manufacture.

The rapid development and application of "in-process" and also "immediate post-process" techniques of control are a result, and increasing time and effort are being devoted to the "automation" of quality control in this way.   Important technological developments, such as the C.W. gas laser, refined optical grating transducer technology (coupled with high precision/response closed loop servo systems) and microcomputer technology will be related to their applications in flow and large batch production systems for I.C. engine components.

Applications discussed include Automatic Cylinder Bore Inspection by laser scanner, providing automatic optical detection of single and cluster surface defects, as well as boring and honing pattern. Another application concerns complex profile, high precision components such as camshafts, the accuracy of which is critically important to power, fuel economy and exhaust emissions control. Both the CNC manufacture and the comprehensive quality analysis of camshafts will be described. The latter in particular leads to rapid error analysis in terms of lift, lift slope, and follower velocity and acceleration errors.   Higher quality and efficiency of manufacturing result, with improved production rates, reduced lead times for changeover, and immediate compatibility with CAD of cam forms.

## 1    Improving Industrial Competitiveness

Any company aiming to improve its competitiveness and profitability in national and international markets can make a three-pronged attack, namely:

Improving real productivity

Planning and achieving successful innovation of products and services

and

Improving the quality of its products and services

This glimpse of the obvious is nothing less than the formula for wealth and creation, for halting economic decline and achieving economic growth.

## 2    Product Quality

Successful product innovation is inextricably bound up with the company function of quality assurance.   Indeed it is the quality of a product that more than any other factor will determine its success in the market.

QUALITY is FITNESS FOR PURPOSE

WITH VALUE FOR MONEY

Successful companies educate their staff to understand that

"We exist to provide quality satisfactions at a profit"

Only against this overall objective can the company command markets in the future by which to make profits and thus continue to exist. In other words, existing and future products must exhibit total fitness for purpose and provide value for money.

## 3    Quality Costs

A detailed knowledge of the COSTS of Quality (including quality failures) is essential if a manufacturer is to succeed in implementing and operating an efficient quality control programme.   Many manufacturers, and certainly the larger ones in the automotive industry, have developed systems for determining their quality costs, usually under the four well known prime categories of:

prevention

appraisal

internal failure

and     external failure

The importance of detailed knowledge of quality costs is:

(i)    The sheer magnitude of the costs of quality under the above headings can motivate top management to invest the necessary funds for formal programmes of efficiency/quality improvement in each area.

(ii)   The breakdown of total quality costs into

not only the above prime categories, but also into products, departments, and the prime causes of poor quality, enables management to set priorities in any such improvement programme.

(iii) The progress of an improvement programme and a criterion for measuring future performance in quality is, of course, best achieved through a continuous assessment of quality costs.

In planning reductions in quality costs, i.e. through improved quality assurance programmes, the criteria for acceptance and implementation by top management are going to be primarily financial. The quality specialists in industry will gain acceptance by top management of their proposals only if they show a *direct relationship to improved profitability of operation.*

## 4    Inspection

There are still far too many companies who are preoccupied with inspection of the type that the Bell Company was determined to eradicate when in 1920 it first introduced what has developed into the quality control of today. Inspection of the type which means "sorting good from bad after manufacture" should be regarded as an indictable offence against society. This form of inspection is still widely practised and many other companies that have introduced departments of "quality control" have merely changed the departmental label from "inspection".

Inspection is, of course, still a necessary function. *Inspection is an important sub-function of quality control.* Inspection involves either measurement or subjective assessment, an analysis of the result and then a decision. To increase the efficiency of dimensional inspection it is necessary to:

increase the speed of measurement

increase the speed of recording results

and then    increase the ease and speed of analysing the results so that the resulting decision and necessary corrective control action can be implemented with minimum delay.

(With closer tolerances more and more necessary to improve performance, wear-life and reliability, there is an increasing demand to increase the resolution, repeatability and accuracy of measurement).

## 5    Control of Quality

*The sequence of actions to control quality can be likened to a closed-loop error-feedback servo-system.* Maximum efficiency of the control of quality can be achieved when the speed of response of this servo is at its highest. In other words, the closer the control loop is applied to the point of manufacture the greater the efficiency. This alone accounts for the rapidly increasing development and application of "IN-PROCESS CONTROL' and also 'IMMEDIATE POST-PROCESS CONTROL' techniques and systems. We

are now seeing in modern manufacturing industry more effort, time and cost than ever before devoted to the automatic control of quality. Increasingly, quality control of an automated nature is being planned into the manufacturing processes at the earliest possible stage of planning against the financial criteria already listed.

In flow or large-batch production of complex components, where inspection is to be used in inter-operational mode, production line balance can only be ensured by equal operating speed of the inspection system. *When in-process or immediate post-process* control can be installed, line balancing is more readily achieved. Thus, in-line inspection and quality control must be part of the production planning function.

*Automatic control of machines and processes produces highly repeatable results; the reducing of randomness to insignificance enables any remaining systematic error to be readily corrected virtually to zero value.*

In the last decade the most important technological developments for improving the efficiency of industrial in-line metrology equipment for the control of quality include:

the c.w. gas laser

refined optical grating transducer technology (and high precision/response closed loop servo-systems based on these)

and    the microcomputer.

Four applications of these developments to the manufacture and quality control of internal combustion engine components will be described.

## 6    Automatic Cylinder Bore Inspection

For many years the overall inspection of engine cylinder bores has been a manual/visual process, usually combined with a manually operated sizing and grading operation with appropriate marking/recording of this grading. The technology has existed for some time to build, install, and profit from, automatic cylinder bore gauging equipment with the ability to inspect up to 94 dimensions at rates in the order of 35 blocks per hour of 4, 6, and 8 cylinder engine blocks. This equipment will measure, record and accept/reject on measurements of diameter, taper and ovality. However, the problem of *assessment of the cylinder bore surface* (and a similar problem exists for cylinder liners) has necessitated the retention of manual/visual, labour-intensive inspection techniques. Several viewing inspectors are required to service one production line, especially as the increasing speed of engine production lines is being uprated to better than 2 per minute. The equipment illustrated in Fig. 1 has been developed to provide for the *automatic optical detection of single and cluster surface defects* (porosities, blow holes and imperfect machining), including for example the retention of boring marks and inadequate depth of cross-hatch honing (see Fig. 2). Thus the complete function of viewing inspection, gauging, recording, and thence accept/reject, is mechanised. The system can be configured to process one engine block every 23 seconds. The vital part of this optical surface inspection system is an HeNe laser rotating scanning head which uniquely combines two techniques.

(a) flying spot scanner

and (b) diffraction pattern analysis

The laser head causes a spot of light to helically scan the entire surface of the cylinder bore or liner. The design enables the photoelectric/electronic control which can be preset to suitable threshold values, to measure:

Single defects for

maximum permissible width of defect,

and maximum permissible length of defect

Cluster defects for

maximum width of cluster

maximum length of cluster,

and maximum number of defects in the defined or chosen area of scan.

Thus, this laser optical sensor system generates information on properties of the surface of the bore which have not been readily available before the development of this type of equipment. The measurement of these properties and their possible relation to cylinder wear/oil consumption, etc. offers the eventual possibility of the manufacture of an improved engine product. However, the system is intended primarily as a direct, faster, and more discriminating replacement for the labour-intensive QC methods used by the industry at the present time. To sum up, this development enables:

exact surface integrity parameters to be prescribed for acceptance and rejection

the operating speed of the machine is many times faster than a human inspector and automatic production line balancing can be more readily assured.

operator fatigue and any of the human ills which can cause variation in the judgment performance of an inspector, are eliminated.

Calculations show that in general, engine block manufacturing lines producing at about 60 blocks per hour or more can justify this equipment on immediate quality cost criteria alone, without recourse to the more philosophical argument of potentially improved product in the future.

7    Quality Control in Manufacturing Camshafts

Camshafts are components of complex profile, the accuracy of which is critically important to engine performance both in power production and exhaust pollution control. This is particularly true for diesel engines, the world production of which is currently increasing at over 10% per annum. Camshafts for both fuel injection and exhaust valve gear are medium-to-large batch produced, the cam lobe profile

being ground as a final operation on grinding machines which currently incorporate master cams for copying purposes. Most engine manufacturers multi-source their supply of camshafts not only from their own factories but also from one or more specialist camshaft sub-contract manufacturers.

Efficient inspection (against the criteria set out in Section 4 above) has been a major problem to most manufacturers. Using traditional manually operated inspection equipment (based on optical dividing head etc.) a 13 lobed camshaft will take approximately 5 hours to comprehensively measure, record and analyse the result of measurement on which QC corrective action can be taken. (To make a "master campack" for a traditional copying type camshaft grinding machine will take much longer. The lead time for a replacement campack is often 3 to 4 months).

Optical grating systems (these days commercially available with 0.1 $\mu$m linear and 0.1 arc sec. angular resolution, if required) have been integrated into CNC camshaft measuring machines which will comprehensively inspect a 13 lobed camshaft in 10 minutes, giving print-out and graph plot errors (see Fig. 3) for

(i)   Cam follower lift values as measured

(ii)   Errors in lift errors

(iii)   Slope of lift error curve

(iv)   Follower velocity error

(v)   Follower acceleration error

(Automatic correction for camshaft bend in the as measured state is also made possible by the mini-computer of the machine).

8    High Precision CNC Grinding of Camshafts

Camshafts are produced conventionally by the grinding process which uses a master cam and follower to generate the rise and fall profile of the cam under manufacture. The master campack in this following type machine has to be produced by a method which normally imposes a long lead time. Assuming that the master campack can be produced accurately enough, the subsequent cam manufacturing process by this method is still subject to errors caused by:

diminishing grinding wheel size of the machining process (wear and wheel dressing)

Varying surface speed at the point of contact between grinding wheel and work-piece causing variations in the grinding process (as Fig. 4 shows, this speed variation with constant rotational speed of the camshaft can give rise to a 300 to 1 change of surface speed).

The effects of wear on the master cam caused by the follower.

Following errors associated with the master campack and the following mechanism.

Furthermore, CAD techniques used in the design of the cam for optimum performance when in the engine cannot be directly applied to control of the manufacturing process.

A new CNC high precision camshaft grinding machine has recently been developed in the United Kingdom as a result of collaborative design and development by the author's industrial unit and a leading UK machine tool manufacturer. In this machine, the master campack is replaced by polar co-ordinate values which are held in the core store of the computer control system. During grinding, the workpiece is held between centres, the machine workhead contains a direct drive permanent magnet dc torque motor tacho generator and an angular optical rotary grating transducer. This provides '$\theta$' information (typically 0.1 degree bit size is found to be adequate), to which is slaved the grinding wheel infeed servo control system also based on a linear optical grating displacement transducer and a high torque permanent magnet dc torque motor driving through a recirculating ballscrew. The whole carriage is mounted on hydrostatic guideways to give high stiffness, low friction and high damping. The high velocity and position loop bandwidths of the rotary and linear infeed servos enable:

the rotational speed of the camshaft to be varied in accordance with cam profile so that the surface speed of the grinding wheel over the profile is virtually constant (this enables a high production through-put to be achieved with optimised surface finish/integrity)

a high profile also to be achieved (well within 5 micrometers).

With the rapid set-up and changeover provided by the CNC system, the new CNC camshaft grinding machine is particularly suited to the manufacture of model cams, master campacks for copying type, long series production machines, experimental camshafts and short run manufacture, especially where high precision profile and size is important.

## 9 CNC Adaptive Quality Control for the Grinding of Cams

The maximum efficiency of quality control is achieved by building the quality servo loop into the production process and this has been achieved in a new CNC grinding machine for ring cams. The system incorporates an in-process measuring system for adaptive control of profile and size of the ring cams. Again, high resolution optical grating transducers are used and the design philosophy of this CNC adaptive control system is shown in Fig. 5. During grinding the 'R' and '$\theta$' information on actual workpiece profile is derived respectively from the linear grating transducer attached directly to the cam follower 180° disposed to the grinding wheel and from the optical rotary grating transducer in the workhead. At each angle of '$\theta$' typically at 0.1 degree bit size, the value of the actual radius 'R' is compared with the required radius and a new value of grinding wheel position is calculated in order to remove the required amount at the next pass of the grinding wheel. Thus the grinding wheel is instructed to remove metal in predetermined

steps at approximately 180° after measurement until the correct size and profile are achieved. The time required to measure process and control motions is 800 μs for each discrete angular position of 0.1 degrees. Therefore, the reliability and response of the total system has to be very high. The total system has velocity bandwidth in the order of 800 Hz and position bandwidth of over 80 Hz. This machine, with its in-process size and profile control is what might be called an "ideal manufacturing system" in that, through its CNC system it effectively achieves *zero defect production of these complex internal cam shapes* which demand manufacturing tolerances in the order of ± 2 μm. The CNC quality adaptive control system represents a major development in automatic quality control of an important automotive component coupled with higher overall production rates - in that the subsequent inspection process normally associated with copy type grinding is effectively eliminated. To summarise, the advantages of this development are:

higher quality and efficiency of manufacture through automatic quality control, producing virtual elimination of scrap and rework.

high production rates with greatly reduced lead times for changeover to manufacture of different cams (the greater flexibility/ efficiency in batch production endowed by NC)

Immediate compatibility with CAD of the cams.

## 10 Conclusion

Three new quality control machine systems have been developed through the determination of some leading automotive component manufacturers to incorporate improved quality control systems into planned new flow line and batch manufacturing systems. With the increasing reliability of electronic control systems the traditional reluctance of the automotive industry to incorporate such systems into component and sub-assembly manufacturing processes will be progressively overcome. The quality cost benefits derived from automatic in-process and immediate post-process techniques of control will help to speed up the introduction of these advanced technologies.

REFERENCES

(1) P.A. McKeown, P. Cooke, W.P.N. Bailey, "The Application of Optics to the Quality Control of Automotive Components" Society of Photo-optical Instrumentation Engineers, Seminar on Quality Control, San Diego, May 1975.

(2) P.A. McKeown, J. Dinsdale, and J. Loxham, "The Design and Development of a High Precision Computer Controlled Cam Grinding Machine", CIRP Annals, Vol. 23/1974, pp.115/116

(3) Frank M. Gryna, "User Quality Costs v Manufacturer Quality Costs", the 20th EOQC Conference, Copenhagen, June 1976, Vol.B,p 11.

(4) A.G. MacGregor, "The Cost of Quality as Seen by an International Company", Conference Proceedings of "Quality - Foundation of an Industrial Economy", the Institute of Quality Assurance, October 1979.

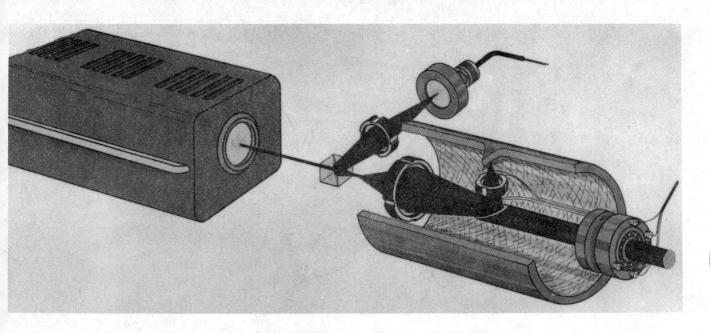

Fig 1    Principle of automatic cylinder bore surface quality inspection system

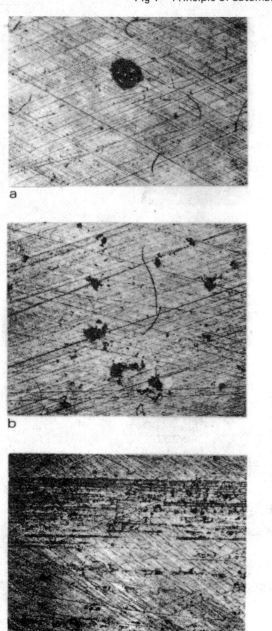

Fig 2    Examples of typical cylinder bore defects

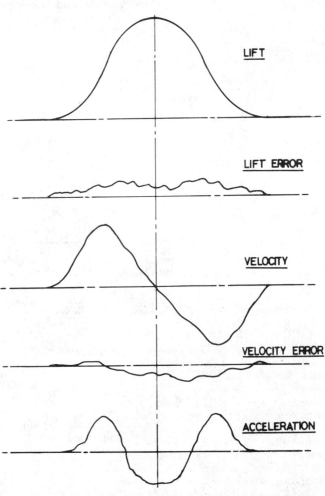

Fig 3    Graph plots of outputs of the Horstmann-Cranfield high speed
CNC camshaft measuring machine

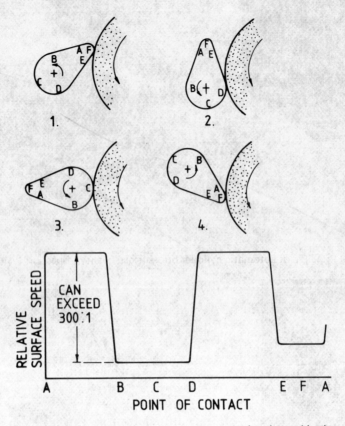

Fig 4    Surface speed variation at constant rotational speed in the grinding of cams

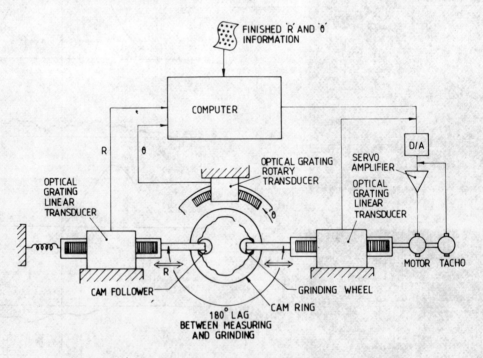

Fig 5    CNC adaptive quality control cam grinding machine system philosophy

# C289/81

# New technology sheet steels for the automotive industry

N A WATKINS, BSc
British Steel Corporation, Newport, Gwent

SYNOPSIS  Steel sheet or strip currently comprises up to 50% of vehicle curb weight on cars and light commercial vehicles and between 20 and 50% on trucks.  This paper summarises the most recent developments in sheet steel product technology and describes a number of areas of application where benefits are being realised.

The steel industry is responding to ever increasing demands by the vehicle designer for cost effective weight reduction, damage resistance, safety and durability, by rapidly developing and bringing on to the market new technology steels such as high strength and coated steels.  A summary is given of the philosophy behind these developments.  Examples are discussed on the ways in which higher strength steels, in particular new formable grades, are being used to improve structural performance and achieve vehicle weight reduction.  The range covered is comprehensive, from truck chassis members at thicknesses of 8mm down to car body panels at 0.7mm.

The drive towards improved vehicle durability has resulted in the increased application of late of pre-coated steels on vehicles to achieve inbuilt corrosion protection.  Again a number of examples are discussed together with the potential for marrying up the advantages of both high strength and coated steels.

Some views are expressed as to the direction sheet steel products will develop beyond the 1980's including the potential for steel/plastic laminates.

## INTRODUCTION

Most indications suggest that sheet steel will remain the major building block for autobody construction throughout the 1980's. Alternative materials such as aluminium and plastics will undoubtedly play significant roles but their adoption in mass produced vehicles will probably be evolutionary rather than revolutionary.

There are a number of reasons why this is indicated:

Availability: it is highly likely that steel will remain in plentiful supply throughout the 80's and at relatively stable prices. The steel industry worldwide is currently in a state of over capacity. As third world manufacturing markets grow so too will basic steelmaking capacity. Developed countries will concentrate increasingly on producing and supplying higher technology steels.

Energy: the 1970's saw the awakening of the developed world to the serious consequences of energy price rises. Steelmaking remains a relatively low energy consuming process particularly when compared with alternative autobody materials (see Table 1). This position is being improved even more by new production techniques such as continuous casting.

| | Energy to produce 1 kg (kWh) | Approximate equivalent to 1 kg steel sheet for autobody applications (kWh) |
|---|---|---|
| autobody steel sheet | 9.3 - 10.4 | 9.3 - 10.4 |
| polyester SMC (+30% glass) | 22 | 19.8 |
| polypropylene (+30% glass) | 25 | 13.6 |
| polycarbonate (+40% glass) | 42 | 25.6 |
| nylon (+33% glass) | 62 | 37 |
| aluminium sheet | 60 - 70 | 30 - 35 |

Table 1  Energy required to produce various autobody materials (data for steel and aluminium are based on BSC estimates. Data for plastic based on published data by ICI (ref. 1).

Secondary energy savings in fuel consumption can be achieved by using materials of lower density than steel but these must be presented in a cost effective manner to the consumer. It is questionable for instance whether a new car buyer will regard as a priority, net energy/cost savings which can only be realised after 40 000 miles of motoring.

Technical Performance: It is fairly certain, given enough research time and effort, that many of the manufacturing problems associated with steel alternatives will be solved for volume vehicle production. There remain, however, a number of fundamental issues in terms of performance which may or may not present insurmountable barriers at any rate throughout the 80's. Perhaps the most important of these is safety. Sheet steel has the ability to absorb energy under crash conditions without catastrophic failure, particularly important in monocoque body construction.

Steel Developments: Sheet steel is not a static material. Continuing developments in steel technology are giving rise to an ever increasing range of high performance products available to the automobile designer. It is the purpose of this paper to summarise these developments.

## High Performance Sheet Steels

Quite obviously there are an ever increasing number of constraints being placed on the vehicle designer and manufacturer. Perhaps these may be summed up most simply as the need to make a vehicle which is competitive and capable of meeting all relevant legislation.

In so far as this affects the body structure, this generally means high performance, controlled costs and the achievement of a style with structural integrity.

The British steel industry is now continually engaged in close co-operation with the British motor industry in rapidly bringing new steels through from the research and development stage to full production in order to contribute towards meeting these objectives.

New high strength steels and corrosion resistant zinc coated steels are two sheet steel developments which have resulted from this work. High strength steels are a tool the designer now has at his disposal to help achieve weight reductions on bodywork. Zinc coated steels have been developed with new coating specifications to improve resistance to bodywork corrosion.

## High Strength Steels

Traditionally low carbon sheet steel hot or cold rolled, has offered an excellent general purpose combination of strength and formability for vehicle body panel and light chassis manufacture. More recently these advantages have been realised on heavy (ie. truck) chassis where, up to 8mm thick, sheet steel is now cold formed into sidemembers.

There are, however, many areas on a vehicle which can benefit from a higher strength steel. The elastic modulus of steel cannot be raised but higher yield and tensile strengths enable sheet gauges to be minimised against strength related structural criteria. In areas where strength rather than stiffness is the controlling criterion, the benefits materialise as a reduction in sheet thickness and hence weight from that had the component been made in mild steel.

It is unfortunate, however, that the general rule applies that as the strength of a steel is increased its overall forming ability is decreased. The recent history of high strength sheet steels has been one of trying to minimise this fall off in formability with increasing strength. There are a number of parameters by which formability is assessed. Each parameter will have a ranking order of performance for different types of high strength steel.

There are a variety of methods by which higher strength sheet steels can be produced.

Cold Rolling: This is only applicable to the thinner gauges ie., those that would normally be produced as cold rolled gauges rather than hot rolled. Cold rolling strengthens a steel when prior to annealing, it is said to be full hard. By only partially annealing, strength is retained but at the expense of ductility.

Carbon Manganese Steels: Strengthening is achieved by increasing levels of carbon and manganese. Again this produces a steel of relatively poor formability.

Micro Alloyed Steels: Also referred to as high strength low alloy steels, this method utilises small additions of alloying elements such as vanadium, titanium or niobium (columbium) and the mechanism of precipitation hardening to give extra strength. These steels have been produced for a number of years, but have only recently been refined to a level suitable for major usage in the automotive industry. HSLA's can be considered the first of the formable high strength sheet steels. These steels are readily available in hot and cold rolled gauges from the British steel industry.

Rephosphorised Steel: Also referred to as phosphorised, strictly speaking this is another HSLA steel which uses micro additions of phosphorous. However, the strengthening mechanism is one of solution hardening which for a given strength level will give a more formable steel than the V Ti or Nb grades. Developed within the past 2-3 years, this grade is now finding wide application in cold rolled gauges on some of the more difficult autobody pressings and is commercially available from the British steel industry.

Dual Phase Steels: These are the most recent development in the field of high strength sheet steels. These are again strictly speaking, HSLA steels utilising a variety of different alloying systems including manganese, chromium, molydenum and other elements. However, these steels require an extremely close control of heat processing either during the hot rolling stage or during subsequent annealing. Basically this results in a microstructure of martensite islands dispersed in a ferrite matrix. The strength of the steel will depend on the volume fraction of martensite which can be adjusted to give low initial yield strengths some even comparable with mild steel. The peculiarity of dual phase steels is that they then exhibit rapid strain hardening under the press often together with bake hardening during paint stoving, giving a finished component of intrinsically higher yield strength whilst having utilised a large range of improved formability. Dual phase steels also exhibit higher tensile strengths than would normally be associated with low initial yield strengths.

## Application of High Strength Steels

The full potential of high strength sheet steels in the automotive industry has still to be established. Initial applications have been in areas of vehicle construction which place a major emphasis on strength requirements and minimal emphasis on forming. Truck chassis members in the UK for example, are now almost universally made in hot rolled HSLA steels ranging from 3mm on cross members up to 8mm thick on side members with significant gauge/weight reductions as a result.

Moving on to lighter chassis work on light trucks, vans and car subframes, manufacturers are currently evaluating hot rolled gauges of HSLA in the range 1.6 to 5mm and have in many cases specified these materials for new models.

Bodywork on cars and truck cabs presents a greater problem to the design engineer. Here structural engineering parameters are less easily defined, although the immediate benefits of high strength steels to improve dent resistance have been recognised.

In spite of the advances in such engineering tools as finite element analysis, manufacturers are still faced with having to build numbers of prototype vehicles to check out strength related applications. So far, a number of advances have been made and several European manufacturers are planning to use rephosphorised and HSLA steels on new models to achieve weight reductions. Designers have tended to err on the side of caution, and reductions in bodyweight are still below 10%. However, once further experience is gained and applications proved, weight savings of up to 20% over mild steel are predicted.

Further engineering know how is still required to fully utilise the sophisticated properties of dual phase in vehicle design. Much information is currently published on the use of dual phase in Japanese car models (two of the most recent papers are given in references 2 and 3). Information varies greatly as to how much is used and what weight savings are being achieved.

In Europe, steelmaker and motor manufacturer are proceeding hand in hand to evaluate the potential of these materials. It is foreseen that 1983 will represent the earliest date after which dual phase will be included in vehicle product plans.

With the advent of higher strength steels, the designer now has at his disposal a continually developing range of steels with minimum yield strengths from mild steel c. 180 N/mm$^2$ to 450 N/mm$^2$ and above. With these he can seek to optimise the material for any component in terms of structural performance, gauge/weight and cost.

Applicability will be controlled by ability to make the part, the important formability parameters being determined by component shape.

Each of the new formable high strength has something to offer in this respect. It is not true to say for example, that dual phase steels are the most formable high strength steels. For a given initial yield strength level they will be superior to HSLA and rephosphorised in stretching. In drawing, for a given strength level, dual phase will be approximately equivalent to HSLA and inferior to rephosphorised.

Ideally each component would have an optimum steel in terms of performance and cost effectiveness. Practically, however, this would present major difficulties to both steel producer and motor manufacturer. Closer co-operation is required in the UK to arrive at a practical number of mutually identifiable grades.

## Zinc Coated Steels for Corrosion Protection

Vehicle body corrosion remains a problem which can be most effectively tackled at the design stage. Corrosion is basically of two types.

### 1. Internal (Structural) Corrosion

Ingress of moisture, road debris and de-icing salts into box sections causes internal corrosion. The result is demonstrated quite often by deterioration on the bottoms of doors, sills etc. The process is quite often aggravated by poor design and lack of adequate ventilation and drainage. Areas where motor manufacturers' protective systems do not penetrate or are inadequate are particularly prone to internal corrosion.

Although the corrosion of internal surfaces is not always evident, sometimes throughout the vehicle life, its effects are insidious since the structural integrity of the vehicle may be undermined, often unsuspected by the owner or operator.

### 2. External Corrosion

This can occur either as a result of damage to the paint film e.g. by stone pecking or by inherent defects in the paint/pretreatment. External corrosion usually results in cosmetic corrosion initially although metal penetration and structural damage can subsequently occur, undermining the integrity of the vehicle.

Both types of corrosion may be attributable to a number of factors:

(i)     inefficient cleaning processes
(ii)    poor phosphating
(iii)   inferior paint coverage and adhesion

(iii) is generally due to a combination of (i) and (ii) and can be due to an excessively dirty or rusty surface and/or poor access to the hollow section.

Poor design can also result in inadequate washing of the section between the cleaning, phosphating and painting sequences. Residual phosphates in particular are difficult to remove and can cause corrosion. Disruptions and delays in the pretreatment sequence can adversely affect the painting process owing to the formation of a coarse or too heavy phosphate coating.

Performance can be improved against these factors by:

(i)     good design
(ii)    correct processing
(iii)   application of post build protective systems e.g. underseal.

The adoption of electrophoretic painting notably

cathodic, is also giving rise to improved performance.

There are a variety of methods which have been developed for precoating steel with zinc.

## Electrozinc (EZ)

Zinc is electrolytically applied to one or both surfaces of the strip by continuous immersion through an electric cell with pure zinc as one series of electrodes, the steel strip forming the other electrode. These steels are available from the British steel industry.

## Hot Dip Galvanised (HDG)

Zinc is applied to both surfaces of the steel strip by continuous immersion through a bath of molten zinc. Available in the UK as a two sided product although techniques have been developed abroad to produce one sided coatings. The full benefits of one sided HDG are still being evaluated in the UK.

## Iron Zinc Alloy Coating (IZ)

Manufactured by subsequent passing of HDG strip though an annealing furnace to achieve an alloying at the steel/zinc interface. This process gives rise to a very smooth surface for improved painting and also has improved welding performance over ordinary HDG. Also available from the British steel industry.

## Zincrometal

Zincrometal is a two part organic coated steel the top coat of which is zinc enriched. In the UK the British Steel Corporation holds a licence to produce Zincrometal but has so far seen most of the advantages for the British motor industry contained in EZ and IZ.

Protection afforded by the electrozinc and hot dipped zinc products is sacrificial. Mechanically damaged coatings in manufacture or subsequent vehicle use will protect the steel substrate owing to the preferential dissolving of zinc under corrosive conditions. This also applies to exposed steel at cut edges.

Zinc coated steels offer the designer the facility to build in corrosion protection prior to vehicle assembly and processing. The range of products available allows suitable coating thicknesses to be selected for areas of different corrosion risk.

## Application of Zinc Coated Steels

A number of joint exercises have been carried out in the past two years between the British steel industry and motor industry to improve corrosion packages on both new and existing vehicles.

Leyland Vehicles have incorporated one sided and two sided elctrozinc on a number of body panels on their new C40 truck cab system currently being used on Roadtrain, Constructor and Cruiser trucks. These include door outer and inner panels, floor panels and cab back panels.

Seddon Atkinson are now specifying door outers and inners and floor panels in electrozinc on their new range of truck cabs.

Vauxhall Motors are using both electrozinc and IZ coatings throughout the whole front end of their new CF van.

Within the car sector a number of manufacturers are now evaluating zinc coated steels on their vehicles.

It is the author's belief that as the trend towards thinner steel gauges continues, particularly with the advent of high strength steels, the demand for zinc coated steels to improve corrosion performance will increase.

## Future Developments in Sheet Steels

The need to develop high strength steels with improved formability will remain throughout the 1980's. Gauge reduction on all components will, however, be eventually limited by stiffness requirements.

Recently, development work has taken place (ref. 4) to devise materials which offer even greater potential for weight reduction yet retain the excellent strength and surface characteristics of sheet steel. One such development has been the investigation of a steel/plastic/steel sandwich produced by continuous lamination.

Typically, a sandwich of 0.5mm polypropylene between two skins of 0.2mm steel can offer the same stiffness as a homogeneous steel at half the weight.

Clearly much has yet to be done to establish manufacturing, structural and processing viability of such a material and initial investigations are already under way in the British steel industry.

Finally, with regard to corrosion resistant steels, further progress is being made to reduce required zinc coating thicknesses to a minimum for a given corrosion performance. One of the techniques being developed to achieve this is the doping of the coating with heavy metal elements. The British steel industry is well advanced on this development.

REFERENCES

(1) BARRIE I.T., SMART J.M. and WYCHERLEY G.: Cars, Plastics and Energy, SITEV - 80 Symposium, May 19, 1980.

(2) TAKAHASHI I., KATO T., HASHIMOTO H., SHINOZAKI M. and IRIE T.: Properties of Hot Rolled High Strength Steel Sheets for Automotive Use - Kawasaki Steel Technical Report No. 2, March 1981.

(3) IRIE T., SATOH S., HASHIGUCHI K., TAKAHASHI I and HASHIMOTO O.: Characteristics of Formable Cold Rolled High Strength Steel Sheets for Automotive Use - Kawasaki Steel Technical Report No. 2 March 1981.

(4) DICELLO J.A.: Steel - Polypropylene - Steel Laminate - A New Weight Reduction Material, SAE Paper 800078, February 1980.

# Developments in polyurethanes for the automotive industry

D N LAWSON, MA, PhD, DIC
Imperial Chemical Industries PCL, Manchester

## INTRODUCTION

It is clear that there will be an increasing usage of plastic materials in the automotive industry in the future, which will come about both by direct substitution of existing parts and by re-designing to take advantage of the properties and processing possibilities offered by plastic materials. The use of plastics will come about for a number of reasons:

a) Energy conservation during manufacture

Plastics are frequently less energy intensive to produce (even allowing for the energy cost of the raw materials) than traditional materials.

b) Energy conservation in use

The lower weight of plastic parts, and the ease with which aerodynamically efficient shapes can be produced will help to reduce fuel consumption during the life of the vehicle.

c) Long life/corrosion resistance.

The resistance of plastic materials to most of the corrosive agents that afflict cars is a major advantage, as is the deflectibility of most plastic body parts which allow them to suffer minor impacts without damage. This aspect is most noticable in the US 'soft front end' concept where the ability to recover from deformation of the soft front end is an essential part.

d) Comfort and aesthetics.

Polyurethanes are the most versatile of the plastics materials of interest to the automotive manufacturer. Their use ranges from seating to gaskets and to body panels. This versatility can be understood more easily if we consider the chemistry of the polyurethane production reactions.

Polyurethanes are produced by the reaction of two chemical components, a polyol and an isocyanate:

$$HO-R-OH \ + \ OCN-R^1NCO \longrightarrow \ -R-OCONHR^1-OCONHR-$$
$$\text{polyol} \qquad \text{isocyanate} \qquad \qquad \text{urethane}$$

Water reacts with an isocyanate to produce carbon dioxide:

$$R^1NCO + H_2O \longrightarrow RNH_2 + CO_2$$

A combination of these two reactions and/or the addition of external blowing agents to the reaction mix produces varying degrees of blowing i.e. various foam densities. The polyol and isocyanate molecules have at least two reactive groups per molecule. Alterations in the chain length between the reactive groups can alter the flexibility of the polyurethane structure: increasing the number of reactive groups per molecule can increase the cross linking in the molecule. giving increased rigidity. It is this structure and density adjustment that enables polyurethanes to fulfil so many diverse roles in the automotive sector.

In this paper we briefly illustrate several novel application of polyurethanes in the automotive area

## MOULDED DOOR PANEL PRODUCTION

High density foam laminated to fabric or PVC offers significant end-use advantages in comfort and design for shaped door and roof panels. The foam, of density in the range 100-200 kg/m$^3$, not only is self-supporting but offers sound and shock absorption too. The foam, faced with a suitable fabric, gives the car interior a 'luxury' feel. However, the production of these parts has been either difficult, or expensive, or both, making these products only suitable for the more expensive car. There are two alternative methods of manufacture. One involves the injection of liquid polyurethane chemicals into a cavity in a high pressure press, with the fabric facings also held in the press. A barrier film may be necessary to prevent the liquid PU chemicals penetrating and spoiling the facing fabric. In the other method, preformed slabs of foam can be heated, covered in fabric and then pressed to shape. Both of these processes have disadvantages, such as the high cost of press and interlayers and the high incidence of surface imperfection via the injection process, and the high cost of heating preformed foam in the second.

The development of a process which combines the simplicity of the pressing process with the economic advantages of using liquid chemicals and making the foam in-situ mean that laminated foam liners can now be seriously considered for the mass produced car.

The parts are produced in two stages: in the first a flat slab of uncured foam is produced; just after the end of rise of the foam, but before it has set, the foam slab is transferred to a press and moulded to shape. Decorative fabric facings can be incorporated at the second stage without fear of strike through (or at the first stage if they are non-permeable).

A sheet of polythene (or the non-permeable facing sheet) is held in the base of a shaped flat tray mould at 40°C by vacuum, and the preblended components of the polyurethane chemical mix are dispersed onto it through a traversing mixing head from a conventional dispensing machine. The mould lid is closed and the chemicals react and foam. Just after the end of rise, but before the foam has cured, the foam is transferred to a shaped mould, covered with fabric (if necessary) and pressed to its final thickness. The decorative fabric is attached to the mould lid and is integrally bonded to the foam. For deep profiles, a stretch fabric is recommended.

The process can be readily automated, and the total cycle time is of the order of 150 seconds:

| | |
|---|---|
| Foaming | 60 seconds |
| Transfer | 30 seconds |
| Press | 60 seconds |

Different chemical formulations can be produced to suit particular end property (density, hardness, etc) requirements.

Many different products have been made by this process, in at least prototype form, and they are shown in Table 1. Each product has been successfully fitted to a vehicle, and met the relevant automotive specification.

TABLE 1

PROTOTYPE PARTS PRODUCED BY THE PRESSFOAM
PROCESS

| Product | Car Model | Facing |
|---|---|---|
| Door Panel | Fiat Ritmo | Cloth & PVC |
| Door Panel | Innocenti A112 | Cloth,Carpet PVC flocking |
| Door Panel | Fiat 132 | Cloth PVC |
| Door Panel | Citroen CX | Cloth |
| Rear & Front Posts | Fiat 132 | PVC |
| Rear & Front Posts | Lancia Delta | PVC |
| Door Panel Insert | Lancia Delta | Cloth |
| Wheel Arch | Fiat 127 | Cloth,Carpet |

CRASH PADS

Soft feel crash pads normally consist of composites of a rigid former (polypropylene, metal, fibre board etc), on one side; a plastic film such as ABS or PVC on the other, and a filling of low density semi-rigid foam. The plastic film is usually pre-vacuum formed, placed into an open mould, the liquid chemicals dispensed onto it and the mould closed with the rigid former pre-attached to the lid. However, this technique leads to variability in the positioning of the liquid chemicals. Increasingly, high pressure chemical injection into a closed mould is used. This, in turn, can cause problems because the mouldings are usually

complex with sharp corners, sudden thickness changes, and obstacles to flow. Rejects arise in this technique from three main causes:

1  Folds and creases in the plastic skin
2  Air pockets trapped in the foam
3  Blisters caused by localised excessive foam pressure

These rejects are expensive, as the rigid former and plastic skin may also be lost. Faults in the plastic skin must be minimised by technique; and air traps can be reduced by paying particular attention to the mould position, and filling and venting points. Blisters can be eliminated by extending the demould time, although this is economically undesirable in production. In addition, significant improvements can be made by increasing the flow characteristics of the foam. This is not merely a case of lowering the viscosity of the initial liquid components, although that is also beneficial, but of ensuring a very slow build up of viscosity in the reacting mix without extending the total reaction time.

This property enables the foaming mix to flow freely into the areas of different thickness, even at the end of the foaming reaction, so that pressure is equalised throughout the moulding, and post moulding blisters are avoided. Air pockets have more time to escape through the vents, even with complex mould shapes. Such systems have recently been developed and the ease of flow of these systems leads to lower in-mould pressure (high pressures were previously needed to insure complete mould filling). This leads in turn to shorter demould times, (down to as little as 2 minutes). The better pressure equilibration in the mould leads to significantly (10-20%) lower overall foam density, with consequential weight, cost, and energy savings.

The major improvement to the formulation has been on the polyol side, but additional benefits can be obtained from the isocyanate by tailoring the functionality (i.e. the number of reactive groups per molecule) to the particular polyol formulation. However, this tends to lead to a more expensive isocyanate.

INTEGRAL SKIN FOAM FOR STEERING WHEELS

Integral skin polyurethane foam steering wheels are soft, warm and resilient and have much customer appeal. They are normally produced by a similar technique to that for crash pads, except of course there is no outer skin as the polyurethane forms its own skin during the reaction. The foam is injected into the narrow cavity between the metal former and the metal mould surface. The moulds are complex and varied but all demand that the foaming system has flow fronts which meet and weld together. Any moulding faults result in rejection of the complete wheel, as it is very difficult to recover the metal insert from the well adhered foam, and this is very costly. Faults are usually caused by the non-welding of the flow fronts (possibly 3 or 4 of them).

The problem can be minimised by improving the flow of the system, so that the flow fronts meet well before the end of reaction, and hence merge into each other. This is not merely dependent upon the flow of the mix but also of the state of cure of the surface of the flow fronts. A crucial factor here has been found to be the level of iron contained in the isocyanate. Iron acts as a catalyst for the polyurethane cure reaction and controlled low levels are essential for good flow and good welding of flow fronts. Levels of 10 ppm or less are beneficial for this application and can easily be distinguished in practice from iron levels of 20 ppm in the isocyanate. The level must be strictly controlled, to eliminate product variation and this low level must be coupled with the requisite isocyanate functionality to give the needed processing and foam properties, particularly abrasion resistance.

Coloured steering wheels offer advantages to the automotive designer. Previously these have been produced by painting the finished steering wheel or by the use of special in-mould coating techniques. Neither of these is very attractive in production. Before painting the wheel must be thoroughly cleansed and dried while in-mould coating needs the mould to be sprayed with release agent and then paint which must be cured before the mould can be filled. In the latter case it is, of course, not possible to rectify minor surface defects before painting. Self-pigmented integral skin foam would appear to be the most attractive route. The early disadvantage of self-pigmented systems (being able to produce only one colour per production run) has now been overcome using one of the various schemes available from suppliers of urethane mixing and metering equipment. It is now possible to inject colour masterbatch directly into the mixing head of the urethane mixing equipment, and more frequent colour changes are now practical.

Self pigmented integral skin polyurethane foams can be produced with excellent resistance to UV if the system is based on specialised aliphatic isocyanates, but doubts have been raised about the storage stability of blends based on aliphatic isocyanates; and about the thermal stability of the resulting mouldings. Normal integral skin foams are based on aromatic isocyanates: such systems are cheaper and more readily available. Light stable mouldings have recently been produced based on aromatic isocyanates, by the addition of specific UV stabilisers to the polyol blend. Further improvements can also be obtained by using lower functionality isocyanates.

Non stabilised foam gives a rating of 2/3 on the gray scale after 480 standard fade hours exposure to the xenon lamp. Stabilised foams give a rating of 3/4 and to almost 5 (i.e. no visible degradation) by the use of purer isocyanate.

The effect is one of yellowing of the base polyurethane polymers, when the results are compared on the blue wool scale we get (after 480 hours exposure to the xenon lamp):

| Rating | Foam |
|---|---|
| 4 | Non-stabilised |
| 5-6 | Stabilised |
| 7(i.e. no visible change) | Stabilised plus purer isocyanate |

## AIR FILTER END CAPS

Air filters require to have good resilient and caps which provide a good seal between the the filter and its casing to prevent unfiltered air reaching the engine. The conventional material used for this application is PVC plastisol, with the PVC being poured onto the end of the paper filter in an open mould. The PVC requires curing in an oven. Polyurethanes are replacing this material on the basis of their superior mechanical properties and processing characteristics, as exemplified by:

1. High speed of cure at ambient temperatures.
2. PU has a lower compression set/stress relaxation and therefore gives a more permanent seal.
3. Better oil and petrol resistance, as there is no plasticiser migration.
4. Lower density.
5. Process flexibility (can mould large or small parts of many different shapes).
6. Lower tooling costs.

Good foam flow and good adhesive qualities are required in the rising foam. These are very similar to the requirements of the steering wheel, but here we do not need integral skins, and the foam must be very soft (less than 30 shore A). A speciality isocyanate is now available which combines the low iron content for flow and surface cure with the low funtionality needed for the good tear properties in the final foam. Good tear strength at demould is obviously very important, particularly with the low thickness of polyurethane used in this application.

## COLD CURE MDI BASED FLEXIBLE FOAM

Foam for automotive seating, head rests et is traditionally based on mixtures of toluene di-isocyanate (TDI) and polymeric diphenylmethane di-isocyanate (MDI). Foams based on this blend typically have demould times in the range 6-8 minutes. By switching to MDI (variants of which are used in all the other applications described here) it is possible to reduce the demould time to as little as 2 mins. This increase in reactivity is related to the molecular structure, with the reactive groups on MDI being less sterically hindered than with TDI. In addition to the increased production rates offered with MDI, it also offers the benefit of having a much lower vapour pressure than TDI. The foam itself has a very pleasant feel, being rather more like rubber latex than a TDI based foam.

A range of MDI variants is available to fulfil the various processing and end performance criteria. The highest level of physical properties, for automotive seating, is produced with an MDI varient that requires warmed (50°C) and well maintained high quality moulds. These conditions also produce the minimum demould times (2 minutes), although very few existing production lines can take advantage of such short cycle times.

For application where high levels of mechanical properties are less important (arm rests, head rests etc) and where no mould heating facilities are available slightly different MDI variants are used, with consequentially longer (but still much shorter than with TDI) demould times. The properties of the resultant foams are given in Tables 2a and b.

(a) Standard System (for arm rests, furniture etc).

Typical properties* of cushions made with this system, on Low Pressure equipment, are compared below with foam made from a mixed isocyanate (TDI/MDI) based system.

| | Units | MDI System | MDI/TDI System |
|---|---|---|---|
| Core Density | kg/m$^3$ | 39 | 37 |
| Compression set (@ 50% for 22 hrs at 70°C) | % | 3 | 4 |
| Tensile strength | kN/m$^2$ | 75 | 65 |
| Elongation at break | % | 105 | 125 |
| Tear strength | N/m | 115 | 130 |
| Identation hardness at 40% | N | 165 | 140 |
| Sag factor | | 3.1 | 4.0 |
| Isocyanate Index | | 88 | 90 |
| Jig Dwell Time | mins | 4 | 6-7 |

*Tested according to the appropriate part of BS.4443.

The feel and fingermarking characteristics of the MDI based systems are extremely good.

The hardness and density can be varied over a wide range by altering the amount of Refrigerant 11 and the isocyanate index.

(b) Automotive type systems

Systems have been specifically formulated to meet car manufacturers specifications, and typical properties* are given below:

| | Units | Fisher Body Spec. (Opel) | Ford Spec. | Typical MDI System |
|---|---|---|---|---|
| Core Density | kg/m$^3$ | 50(min) | 45 | 49 |
| Compression set 50% | | 10(Max) | 10(Max) | 6 |
| Tensile strength | kN/m$^2$ | 82(Min) | 120(Min) | 135 |
| Elongation at break | % | 150(Min) | 130(Min) | 140-150** |
| Tear strength | N/m | 260(Min) | - | 270 |
| Indentation hardness 40% | | - | 210+20 | 205 |
| Sag factor | | 2.9(Min) | 2.8(Min) | 3.5 |
| Flammability MBSS 302 | | Pass | Pass | Pass |
| ISO Fatigue Test (% hardness loss) | | | 25(Max) | 16 |

*Tested according to the appropriate part of BS.4443.

**alternative formulations are available producing foam with elongation at break in the range 160 - 170%

Density and hardness can be varied in the usual ways. Again the foam has excellent feel and fingermarking characteristics.

MDI based flexible foams also find application in sound insulation and, of course, in domestic furniture.

RRIM

The benefits of using the polyurethane liquid moulding system together with glass reinforcement (the so-called RRIM process) offers automotive manufacturers the maximum design freedom economically. The advantages of easily being able to process three dimensional structures with low moulding costs, because of the low pressures, to produce products with low weight, good recovery from deflection, low high temperature sag, excellent abrasion and corrosion resistance, have been mentioned in a previous paper. The use of chopped fibres of significant length (e.g. 1.5 mm) as opposed to hammer milled glass offers a number of advantages. Because of the greater length, the reinforcing effect is much greater. Indeed, chopped 1.5 mm fibres are between $2\frac{1}{2}$ and 3 times as effective at reinforcing polyurethanes as is hammer milled glass (see Table 3). Thus, 8% of chopped fibres gives a similar effect to 25% of hammer milled glass. The cost of the system reinforced with glass fibres can, therefore, be reduced by the further incorporation of cheap fillers. Such cost savings can be quite significant in practice.

Table 3    Measured RRIM physical properties

| Nominal Glass Content | Measured Glass Content (%) | Mean Thickness (mm) | Mean Density (gcm$^{-3}$) | Mean Secant Modulus at 0.5% Strain (MPa) | |
|---|---|---|---|---|---|
| | | | | Parallel to flow | Perpendicular to flow |
| Unfilled | - | 4.05 | 1.08 | 320(15) | 296(22) |
| 8% milled | 8.7 | 3.96 | 1.10 | 388(15) | 290(10) |
| 15% milled | 14.9 | 3.97 | 1.22 | 566(11) | 332(8) |
| 20% milled | 19.8 | 4.08 | 1.21 | 753(5) | 376(9) |
| 25% milled | 24.4 | 3.91 | 1.16 | 1085(73) | 493(55) |
| 30% milled | 28.1 | 3.92 | 1.28 | 1260(26) | 702(18) |
| 1% chopped | 1.6 | 3.72 | 1.18 | 248(24) | 222(28) |
| 3% chopped | 3.1 | 3.77 | 1.17 | 350(46) | 267(30) |
| 5% chopped | 5.2 | 3.80 | 1.17 | 463(25) | 250(10) |
| 7% chopped | 7.7 | 3.98 | 1.10 | 1007(16) | 565(25) |

N.B. Standard deviations are given in brackets

# C291/81

# Amborite for the machining of grey cast iron, in the automotive industry, and hard ferrous materials

P J HEATH. PhD, CEng, MIM
De Beers Industrial Diamond Division (Pty) Limited, Ascot, Berkshire
K STEINMETZ,
De Beers Industrie-Diamanten (Deutschland) GmbH, Germany

## Synopsis

AMBORITE* is a tough cutting tool material which is composed of a polycrystalline mass of cubic boron nitride. It was initially introduced into industry for the machining of ferrous workpieces with hardnesses in the range 45-65 HRC. Its physical properties permit high stock removal rates to be achieved. The milling, both of fully hardened irons and steels and of grey cast iron components, is a growing application in many areas of industry. Its extreme wear resistance on grey cast iron enables tolerances to be maintained for much longer periods than can be achieved with conventional tooling.

## Introduction

Machining is an expensive process and the decision to use one particular tool material in preference to another should be based not only on technical but also on economic considerations. In many situations it is obvious that cutting tool material "A" is, or will be, more suitable than tool material "B". For example, the machining of a 58 HRC white cast iron using high speed steel cutting tools is both technically and economically impracticable. As a result, this type of hard ferrous material has, until recently, either been ground with conventional abrasives or machined with ceramic or tungsten carbide cutting tools. Although, with these techniques, tool costs are relatively low, overall machining costs are very high because of the slow cutting speeds and long machining times necessary. For these types of material the use of superior and apparently expensive cubic boron nitride (CBN) cutting tools is not only technically warranted but also economically justifiable. Tool costs may be higher, but machining times are reduced so dramatically that considerable overall cost savings can be achieved[1]

At the opposite end of the hardness and machinability scale, grey cast iron can easily be machined with high speed steel, tungsten carbide or ceramic cutting tools, and the decision as to which one to use will be based mainly on economic arguments. In low volume production situations the use of high cost CBN tooling cannot be justified, but in high volume situations, automotive transfer lines for example, tool costs often become irrelevant and tools which give even a modest increase in, say, tool life are justifiable simply because very expensive downtime can be reduced or tool changes can be carried out when most convenient.

## Polycrystalline diamond and cubic boron nitride cutting tools

Diamond is the hardest material known and polycrystalline diamond cutting tools have been in use for a number of years for the machining of non-ferrous materials such as plastics, wood, glass-fibre reinforced plastics (GRP), copper, aluminium/silicon alloys, etc. For these materials the high initial tool cost is more than compensated for by the extremely long tool lives achieved in comparison with traditional tool materials. The polycrystalline diamond material manufactured by De Beers is called SYNDITE*, however, while diamond and diamond cutting tools have been and are being used for the machining and grinding of ferrous materials, in many cases diamond is not suitable as it can react chemically with iron at the cutting temperatures generated during machining and very high wear rates result. However, the second hardest material known to man - cubic boron nitride (Fig 1) - does not have this unfortunate property and polycrystalline cubic boron nitride tools - AMBORITE (Fig 2) - have now been developed which are technically and economically superior for machining both hard ferrous materials in excess of 45 HRC and also grey cast irons, in high volume production situations in particular.

## AMBORITE

AMBORITE is manufactured by subjecting randomly orientated, carefully graded AMBER BORON NITRIDE* grit to high temperature and pressure in the presence of a metal. This metal subsequently reacts to form a ceramic binder phase and the result is a tough polycrystalline cutting tool material which is significantly harder than either tungsten carbide or ceramics, and which, although not as tough as carbide, is much tougher than conventional ceramic tool materials. The physical properties of AMBORITE have been discussed in detail elsewhere[2]. The hardness and transverse rupture strength of AMBORITE in comparison with various other tool materials is shown in Table 1 overleaf.

AMBORITE also has a much higher thermal conductivity than conventional ceramics, which makes it insensitive to thermal shock and able to cope well with interrupted cutting even on hard ferrous workpieces.

---

\* Registered Trade Mark

| Material | Hardness Knoop (GPa) | Transverse Rupture Strength (GPa) |
|---|---|---|
| Diamond | 56-102 | - |
| CBN | 43-46 | - |
| SYNDITE (025) | 49.8 | 1.10 |
| AMBORITE | 40.5 | 0.57 |
| Tungsten Carbide K10 | 17.9 | 1.70 |
| Alumina | 17.1 | 0.26 |

Table 1    The relative hardness and transverse rupture strength of various materials

## Dimensions and tolerances

AMBORITE is available in ISO Standard 'M' tolerance, square and round inserts (Fig 3), with either 12.7 or 9.52 mm side length or diameter. The cutting edge may be either chamfered, type "T" (0.2 mm x 20° negative), or unchamfered, type "F", as shown in Fig 4. Chamfering increases the life of the tool and this edge condition is generally recommended for roughing cuts on hard workpieces. In situations where fine cuts or low cutting forces are required, the unchamfered edge may prove more suitable. The inserts are all 3.18 mm thick and composed of solid AMBORITE. Unlike other CBN polycrystalline materials, AMBORITE is not backed with tungsten carbide. This solid format not only improves the performance of AMBORITE but also doubles the number of available cutting edges.

## AMBORITE machining hard ferrous materials

Previous work has shown that AMBORITE can be used at high stock removal rates on hard ferrous workpieces such as fully hardened tool steels and chill or white cast irons[3,4]. When considering the harder end of the ferrous workpiece spectrum, the typical hardness range over which AMBORITE should prove economical is approximately 45-65+ HRC.

Figs 5 and 6 show time-cutting speed-maximum chip thickness ($T$-$v$-$h_{max}$) diagrams for AMBORITE and ceramic tools when machining D3 cold work tool steel (58 HRC) and chill cast iron (55 HRC) respectively. The technique of graphically showing the relationship between tool life, cutting speed and chip cross section has been described elsewhere[5]. The data shown in Figs 5 and 6 was obtained under laboratory conditions and demonstrates the superior performance of AMBORITE in comparison with the $Al_2O_3$ + TiC ceramic tools which were used as the control. For example, referring to Fig 6 - the $T$-$v$-$h_{max}$ diagram for chill cast iron - it can be seen that for a 2 mm depth of cut, if a 40 minute tool life is required, a ceramic tool could be used at a cutting speed of 20 m/min and a feed rate of 0.10 mm/rev whereas AMBORITE could be used at 60 m/min and a feed rate of 0.32 mm/rev. This is equivalent to an almost tenfold increase in stock removal rate - from 4 $cm^3$/min for the ceramic tool to 38.4 $cm^3$/min for AMBORITE.

## How AMBORITE works on hard ferrous materials

AMBORITE works by generating heat. A negative cutting geometry and a high cutting speed produce heat which continuously softens the material to be removed in the cutting zone. The use of coolant is unnecessary and generally not recommended. Despite the heat generated, the workpiece remains cool and its hardness is unaffected. The quality of the toolholder used is important and it is desirable that the AMBORITE tool should be snugly supported on a separate, substantial, ground carbide support shim. This gives the necessary mechanical support and also provides a good thermal path for the dissipation of heat.

## Typical hard ferrous applications for AMBORITE

1.  ### Machining of Ni-HARD and high chromium irons

    Ni-HARD, a white, nickel chromium, cast iron (specified in B.S. 4844 Part 2), and the high chromium (18-25%) irons are used extensively for their abrasion resistance qualities in pulverising, crushing and grinding applications in the cement, mining, coal and power industries. Hardness is typically 55-58 HRC and, before the introduction of AMBORITE, these types of material were generally machined by turning slowly with tungsten carbide tools or by grinding. Typical stock removal rates when grinding or turning with carbide are 5 $cm^3$/min. Follsain Wycliffe Ltd[4], for example, found their machining times on a particular Ni-HARD casting (Fig 7) were reduced to one fifth with AMBORITE, despite the component involving a difficult interrupted cut.

2.  ### Machining rolls for the steel and paper industries

    Rolls for the steel and paper industries are, of necessity, large and hard. The physical properties which make them suitable for their purpose also make them difficult to machine. There are inumerable alloy types but, essentially, rolls fall into two groups - chill cast iron or forged steel. High chromium chill cast iron rolls, in particular, pose a special problem since relatively large volumes of stock must be removed from the casting. The first cut is always very difficult because of the hard, often porous skin which develops during casting. AMBORITE cutting tools have proved very successful for the machining of new rolls and re-machining worn or damaged rolls (Fig 8). The use of multiple insert tool holders (Fig 9) enables even higher stock removal rates and further machine/labour cost savings to be achieved.

3.  ### Re-machining of thread rolling dies

    The worn threads on high speed steel thread rolling dies typically take two hours to remove by grinding or by turning with carbide tools. Clarkson International Tools Ltd. found AMBORITE was capable of removing the worn, fully hardened threads in 10-12 minutes in a single pass (Fig 10). It is interesting to note that successful machining required the cutting to be done;

    (i)    in the direction of the threads

(ii) at very high cutting speed and low feed rates

(iii) generally with a deep cut sufficient to remove threads in one pass

## Milling of hard ferrous materials

Milling of hard ferrous materials is generally considered impossible. Carbide tools have the necessary toughness but have insufficient hot hardness to give acceptable tool life on hard workpieces. Ceramic tools, on the other hand, possess reasonable hardness and hot strength but are thermally shock sensitive and their low thermal conductivity and inherent brittleness make them unsuitable for severe interrupted cut situations.

Milling heads have already been developed especially for AMBORITE by Montanwerke Walter GmbH and Richard Lloyd Ltd. The cutter, shown in Fig 11, is fitted with adjustable cassettes holding round (RNMN090300T) inserts. Fig 12 shows the comparative performances of ceramic and AMBORITE tools when milling induction hardened Meehanite (55 HRC), this material is commonly used for machine tool slideways. Despite AMBORITE being used at almost twice the cutting speed used for the ceramic tool, the flank wear rate on the AMBORITE was considerably lower.

## Machining of grey cast iron

With hard ferrous materials, hardness is generally considered a reasonable guide to machinability. In contrast, however, the microstructure of grey iron is a more fundamental indicator of machinability than hardness. Table 2, below, shows the effect of microstructure on tool life when machining grey cast irons having different micro-constituents[6].

| Matrix Microstructure | Brinell Hardness No | Tool Life Index |
|---|---|---|
| Ferrite | 120 | 20 |
| 50% Ferrite 50% Perlite | 150 | 10 |
| Coarse Perlite | 195 | 2 |
| Medium Perlite | 215 | 1.5 |
| Fine Perlite | 218 | 1 |
| Fine Perlite with 5% free carbide | 240 | 0.3 |

Table 2   Showing the relationship between machinability and microstructure

The microstructure of grey iron used for brake discs, for example, is shown in Fig 13. The graphite flakes act as discontinuities for the breaking of chips and also provide lubrication. However, in practice, the machining of grey iron components is often made difficult by the presence of chilled surfaces or thin sections where hard white iron ($Fe_3C$ - cementite) can be produced or by the presence of adhering or embedded sand etc. in the casting skin. Fig 14 shows the microstructure of the skin of a sand-cast brake disc. Embedded sand particles and the large amount of hard cementite are clearly visible. The following are typical examples of grey cast iron machining from the automotive industry where the high hardness and abrasion resistance of cubic boron nitride make AMBORITE economically justifiable.

1. Brake discs

Machining through the hard abrasive skin of grey iron components can give intolerably short tool lives. For example, Fig 15 shows the comparative performances of both conventional ceramic tools and AMBORITE when used to chamfer brake discs under indentical machining conditions. The increased performance in terms of tool life more than justifies the increased cost of AMBORITE and the time saved from a reduced number of tool changes is a further bonus. Fig 16 shows brake discs being machined with AMBORITE on a specially designed double-spindle production machine.

2. Boring of cylinder blocks

Automotive cylinder blocks are generally machined in the "as cast" condition and the normal procedure is to finish the bores before honing, using ceramic tooling. The usual criteria for tool life in this operation are the surface finish of the bores and their deviations from roundness. Typically, a maximum peak-to-valley height ($R_Z$) of less than 20 $\mu$m is required and out of roundness should be less than 30 $\mu$m. The final finishing cut, in particular, makes exacting demands on the tools used, since fine tolerances must be maintained for long periods. The use of AMBORITE tools is beneficial and Fig 17 summarizes the results obtained during vertical boring of cylinder blocks. Fig 18 shows 6-cylinder engine blocks being machined at a three-spindle finish boring station.

It should be noted that, because AMBORITE has a higher edge strength than ceramic, it can be used in the unchamfered edge condition. The final finishing cut is generally smaller than the width of the standard 0.2 mm wide chamfer put on ceramic tools and cutting forces are, therefore, higher with these tools due to the exaggerated negative cutting geometry. The use of an unchamfered edge gives a very clean cut with reduced cutting forces.

Again, the more expensive cubic boron nitride tools are justified, not only from the overall increase in tool life but also from the cost savings which result from a reduced number of tool changes and stoppages for tool adjustment. Further economies can be made by making full use not only of the insert corners, but also of the insert edges. It is common practice, once all eight corners of each AMBORITE insert have been used, for the insert edges then to be used in chamfering operations at another station.

## Conclusions

1. AMBORITE cutting tools have physical and mechanical properties which make them technically and economically superior to conventional cutting tools for certain machining applications.

2. AMBORITE cutting tools are not backed with carbide and consist of solid cubic boron nitride. This format makes them capable of

high stock removal rates on hard ferrous materials. For this type of material the higher cost of the tool is offset by the time saved.

3. In high volume, production line situations on grey cast irons, the use of AMBORITE can give considerable cost benefits. Tool life is increased and non-productive tool changing and tool adjustment times are reduced.

## References

(1) HEATH, P.J. 'Comparison of the economics of machining with AMBORITE and conventional cutting tool materials', De Beers Industrial Diamond Division (Pty) Ltd., to be published

(2) PIPKIN, N.J., ROBERTS, D.C. and WILSON, W.I. 'AMBORITE - a remarkable new cutting material', De Beers Industrial Diamond Division (Pty) Ltd., Diamond Information/ Metalworking Report No. L44

(3) NOTTER, A.T. and HEATH, P.J., 'Machining of hard ferrous materials with AMBORITE', Industrial Diamond Revue, Volume 40, July 1980, 244-251

(4) HERBERT, S.A. and HEATH, P.J. 'AMBORITE - an answer to the Ni-HARD machining problem', Industrial Diamond Revue 2/81, Volume 41, Number 433, 53-56

(5) 'AMBORITE - the analysis and prediction of tool life', De Beers Industrial Diamond Division (Pty) Ltd., Technical Information Leaflet No. T5.1

(6) 'Machining of cast iron', American Society for Metals, Metals Handbook, Volume 3 - Machining, 8th Edition, 333-352

Fig 1    ABN — Amber Boron Nitride — the second hardest material known to man

Fig 2    Amborite is manufactured from cubic boron nitride grit using advanced ultrahigh pressure, high temperature technology

### SQUARE SNMN

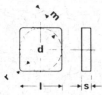

| REFERENCE NUMBER* | l mm | s mm | r mm | m mm | M-TOLERANCE (±) | | | |
|---|---|---|---|---|---|---|---|---|
| | | | | | l, d | s | r | m |
| SNMN 120312 (F or T) | 12·7 | 3·18 | 1·2 | 2·137 | 0·08 | 0·13 | 0·10 | 0·13 |
| SNMN 120316 (F or T) | 12·7 | 3·18 | 1·6 | 1·973 | 0·08 | 0·13 | 0·10 | 0·13 |
| SNMN 090312 (F or T) | 9·52 | 3·18 | 1·2 | 1·480 | 0·05 | 0·13 | 0·10 | 0·08 |
| SNMN 090316 (F or T) | 9·52 | 3·18 | 1·6 | 1·310 | 0·05 | 0·13 | 0·10 | 0·08 |

### ROUND RNMN

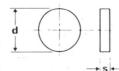

| REFERENCE NUMBER* | d mm | s mm | M-TOLERANCE (±) | |
|---|---|---|---|---|
| | | | d | s |
| RNMN 090300 (F or T) | 9·52 | 3·18 | 0·05 | 0·13 |
| RNMN 120300 (F or T) | 12·7 | 3·18 | 0·08 | 0·13 |

*The final letter, F or T, refers to the presence (T) or lack of chamfer (F). Please refer to *Chamfer* section for details.

Fig 3    Amborite dimensions and tolerances

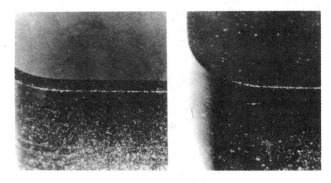

Fig 4 Chamfered (T) and unchamfered (F) edges on Amborite. Chamfer $20°$ x 0.2 mm wide

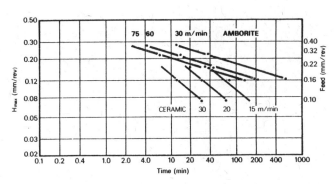

Fig 5 T-v-$h_{max}$ diagram for round, chamfered Amborite (RNMN120300T) and ceramic tools on D3 (58 HRC). Depth of cut 2 mm

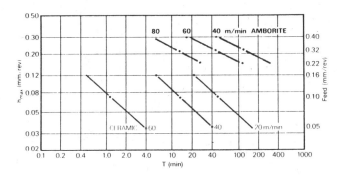

Fig 6 Round chamfered Amborite (RNMN120300T) and ceramic tools on chill cast iron (55 HRC). Depth of cut 2 mm

Fig 7 Amborite cutting tools used to machine a Ni-HARD (55-58 HRC) component

Fig 8 Machining and re-machining of rolls used in the steel and paper industries

Fig 9 Multiple insert toolholders enable even higher stock removal rates to be achieved

Fig 10  Damaged threads on high speed steel thread rolling dies removed in a single pass

Fig 11  Montanwerke Walter milling head developed for the machining of hard ferrous materials using RNMN090300T Amborite inserts

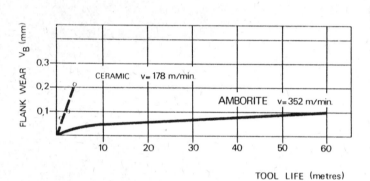

Fig 12  Life comparison between Amborite and ceramic tools in the milling of hardened Meehanite cast iron (55 HRC)

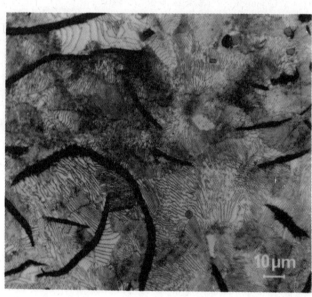

Fig 13  Microstructure of grey cast iron used for brake discs (magnification x 630)

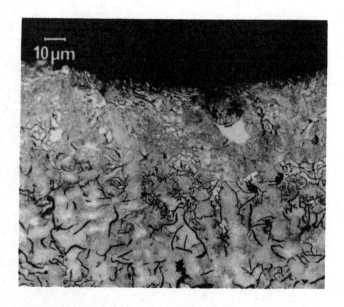

Fig 14  Microstructure of the chilled skin of grey iron, brake disc casting (magnification x 200)

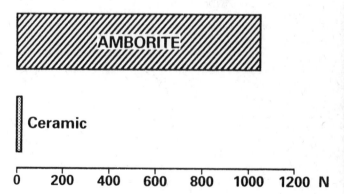

Fig 15  Comparison of Amborite and ceramic inserts in brake disc machining, N = Number of discs machined

Fig 16 Brake discs being machined with Amborite on a specially designed double-spindle production machine

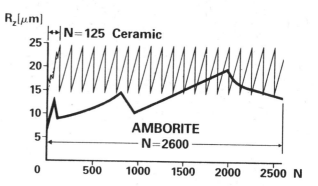

Fig 17 Surface roughness $R_Z$ against number of machined workpieces N for Amborite and ceramic inserts in fine boring of cylinder blocks, N = components per cutting edge

Fig 18 Finish boring of 6-cylinder engine blocks using Amborite

# C292/81

# Manufacturing and supply strategy in the automotive industry

B A KNIBB, CEng, MIMechE
A T Kearney Limited, London

SYNOPSIS     The recognition of the true missions of the manufacturing business together with clear responses are crucial to success.  Too often, companies realise after the event that their plants, processes and systems are just not designed to take the task being thrown at them.  This paper, based on recent assignments in U.S. and European automotive companies, examines the forces acting on manufacturing and seeks to demonstrate how success can be achieved.

## INTRODUCTION

Long-term economic survival of automotive manufacturing companies can only be ensured by striving for and maintaining the position of lowest cost producer on an international scale. The hectic development and application of new technologies is all very well provided they match that principle. There is abundant evidence to suggest that this is not always the case.

It is also worth stating the obvious: the post recession world will be very different to all previous periods. Most companies involved in the motor industry have experienced major shifts in their business over the last 5 years. The current recession has accelerated the changes. There is no way that much of what went before can ever be recovered.

Most companies are determined not to allow – and cannot afford – the serious over-manning that has been a feature of the past. But in many companies the information systems and management tools are not capable of properly merging this intention with all the influencing factors.

### A World Automotive Industry Perspective

One of those factors in automotive manufacturing is the world market which impacts upon it.

During the 80's most markets in the world – and certainly the most important ones – will be near to maturity. Figure 1 (ref.1) shows the projected situation for car sales and production over the 1979/1990 period.

The centre markets – those of North America, Europe and Japan – will level off over the period.  The new markets of Latin America and Comecon will continue to expand but most are closed to Western manufacturers unless they are prepared to put in manufacturing facilities. The fringe markets – the rest – will not represent a sufficiently large proportion of the total to have a great deal of economic significance.

Mature markets have to be treated quite differently to growth markets.  In growth markets new technologies, increased capacity and cost reduction go hand in hand, almost as a matter of course.  Products and processes tend to ride down the cost/experience curve with relatively little effort.  Cyclical fluctuations do not interfere with the equation too much because more growth is always round the corner.

By contrast, in mature markets, it us necessary to consolidate and reduce costs.  That has to be done by forcing a route down the cost curve and, above all, looking for the opportunity to reach a least-cost mode before the competition.

But maturity is not the only market factor that the auto industry has to cope with.  There are four other significant events, or races, occurring.

1.     The geographic race – which manufacturing nations are going to achieve and maintain dominance?   Europe's import/export ratio has already moved unfavourably, and the Continent as a whole will be a net importer in 1982/83.

2.     The OE race – which vehicle builders are going to survive?   Estimates have been made about the critical mass of two million vehicles a year for survival in 1990.  Government and other influences will obviously play a big part in that equation but the race is none-the-less on.

3. The models race - which models within the OE range will be continued and which will be dispensed with? We have already seen the moves toward down-sized cars, but model rationalisation has to occur as well, even at the lower end of the size scales. In 1978 there were 89 cars of European origin sold on the UK market (Figure 2). By 1990 there will probably be well under half of that and what's more, a large proportion will be running at very high unit volumes.

4. The technology race - what will the vehicles of the future be like in a technical sense? Quite clearly, the most important part of this race is to do with power plants, but close behind are such aspects as new materials, safety systems and the whole field of electronics applications.

All four of these races will create dramatic change in the manufacturing and sourcing patterns of the OEMs. The results of the cost of technological change, economics of survival and the threat of rapid and substantial import penetration are already in evidence: world cars; world sourcing; and collaborative deals between both OEMs and suppliers are just some examples.

Less obvious is the impact of these changes on component suppliers. Let us not forget that something like two-thirds of the cost of the average vehicle in Europe goes in outside supply items. Figure 3 shows an A.T. Kearney estimate of the automotive supply industry in 1990 compared to 1979. Significant points to note are that:

(a) Despite a 10% increase in car production the value of supply business will stay about the same in real terms. The combined effects of downsizing and intra-OE deals foster this relative decline of the supply business, although these are compensated to some extent by the fact that some outsourced parts will be technically more sophisticated.

(b) International sourcing within Europe will increase from about 10 to 25%.

(c) There will be a reduction of one-third in the number of suppliers serving the European industry.

## Business Strategy

Whether a company is an OEM, a supplier of highly complex parts or raw material supplier the impact will be very significant. Only by being able to assess the most appropriate course successfully can survival be ensured.

A properly defined business, product and the market strategy is a critical step in defining that appropriate course. And the key questions that must be answered in the strategy are those concerned with what products to what markets and at what price and volume.

Whilst this paper does not attempt to cover business strategy in detail it is nonetheless fundamental to building up a manufacturing and supply strategy.

## MANUFACTURING AND SUPPLY STRATEGY

Manufacturing and supply strategy is driven by the business strategy. It is:

> "A framework within which manufacturing investment and restructuring plans can be developed which is not only consistent with the business strategy but enables it to be achieved."

First, it is concerned with the scope of resources - what to make and what to buy, and if an item is to be made, what technologies should be used. Secondly, it addresses the question of deployment of those resources, where to manufacture, how to organise the function and what systems should bind it together.

Thirdly, it has to be dynamic in concept, capable of meeting change without exorbitant cost.

The complexity of these planning decisions in the automotive industry is frequently not appreciated. If we take just one of those stages - make/buy - and look at the effects of some of the likely market and product changes then some measure of the task can be assessed. Figure 4, based on the passenger car market, suggests a vertical segmentation based on four categories of component: primary and raw material, core, systems and outer.

If we take the raw materials area for a start; traditionally a large proportion of the parts are out-sourced (O-S) at present. It is almost certain they will continue to be so, as smaller numbers of high unit volume cars are generated. In some areas, however, if advancements in technology occur - carbon fibre, ceramics, etc., - where the OEMs do not have the resources or technology to "go it alone", but nonetheless want to maintain a level of control, there is likely to be a trend towards the development of OEM/supplier deals.

Similarly, going up a level to core components, if unit volumes increase there will be a much more pronounced move towards in-house manufacture or joint OEM production, providing technology remains roughly as it is today. If technology advances, as it will do in certain cases, such as transmission systems, there is likely to be a move towards supplier and OEM joint venture deals of the type mentioned on the raw material sides.

With systems, providing technology stays at a moderate level and unit volumes are high, the original equipment manufacturers are likely to favour continued out-sourcing. (These products tend to include a large number of proprietary items with a fairly large worldwide sourcing potential). On the other hand, if technology is high or advancing rapidly, then it is much more likely to produce, with the encouragement of the original equipment manufacturers, a supplier/supplier joint venture situation. We have already begun to see this of course with deals like Lucas CAV and TRW and Weber and Carter.

The really crucial message from Figure 4 is that as a result of the trends towards higher unit volume and advances in technology some of those boxes or segments will exhibit higher growth rates than others. Figure 4 shows the growth areas for cars. A different pattern will be relevant for trucks or other vehicles.

So far, therefore, we have a connection between market development and make/buy decisions. But in practice, the situation for individual companies is inevitably more complex than that. Knowing the trend of market forces is one thing but placing one's self in position in relation to them as well as to specific customers and the competition requires some more detailed appraisal techniques.

Similar degrees of complexity and uncertainty are relevant to the other areas of the manufacturing strategy: plant location, flexible or transfer line production, planning and scheduling systems will all interact with each other and the make/buy decision. The process, thus, becomes one of unravelling the strings of interconnection and creating an integrated approach to the future.

The situation cries out for a coordinated approach to all aspects of manufacturing and supply strategy.

## The Approach Methodology

There are three primary analyses required. Together they produce optional solutions or programmes for evaluation and implementation. The three analyses approach the subject from somewhat different directions, but running throughout them is the notion that within the market environment that we choose to be in, our aim is to drive our costs down to something lower than our competitors'. The three are:

(a) Us relative to where we want to be – what manufacturing businesses we are required to be in as a result of our product and market objectives, and what are the resultant manufacturing missions?

(b) What makes the factory tick? What is the current status of our existing resources? What are our core strengths, weaknesses and the extent of shared resources? This analysis has to assess the projected situation as well as the present one.

(c) Us relative to the outside environment – how do the activities that we perform compare with the way they are done outside, either by our competitors or by non-competitors? The crucial point here is that anyone, competitor or otherwise, who is in a position to go down the cost experience curve faster than we are is worthy of consideration.

If he is a direct competitor then we may have to change more than our manufacturing strategy to beat him. If he is not a competitor we might be able to jump on his experience curve by out-sourcing from him rather than doing the activity in-house.

All three analyses should be conducted in parallel. They are dealt with in detail below.

## A. MANUFACTURING MISSIONS ANALYSIS

Most companies in the automotive world are in a variety of different manufacturing businesses. This can be most easily seen in the volume/variety aspects of the car market – manufacturing a Ford Escort in high volume/low variety requires a different manufacturing process than a Jaguar XJ-12 produced in low volume/low variety, and both demand a different approach than does a diesel engine for third party use being produced in low volume and high variety.

## Categorising the Manufacturing Task

The first stage in the process demands that we look at the products and markets in a way that focusses on "manufacturing sensitive" parameters. These will include such things as volume, rate of product change, bill of materials complexity, responsiveness to customer lead time demand, dimensional tolerances, etc.

By assessing each product/market class in this way, putting a measure on each parameter and then comparing affinities between the products, a foot print of manufacturing businesses can be obtained. Figure 5 shows this for a family of diesel engines. The resulting manufacturing business categories were:

I  Low unit volumes, high variety, stable product designs.

II  Medium/high unit volumes, high variety stable product designs.

III  High unit volumes, low variety, erratic demand and rapidly developing product designs.

Questions of what constitutes "high" or low volume, or levels of variety, are obviously important in this categorisation – but only in relative, rather than absolute, terms.

The segregation of the manufacturing businesses in this way, together with the relevant volume projections for each business provides the discipline for determining how we should structure and organise ourselves to exploit our advantages and eliminate our weaknesses.

## Manufacturing Missions

Each business or manufacturing category is likely to have certain "success factors" associated with it. These might be:

Cost            cost/price sensitivity.

Performance      product superiority.

Adaptability     reaction to changing product requirements.

Reliability      product dependability.

Responsiveness   achievement of changing customer service time requirements.

Flexibility      reaction to changing demand level requirements.

From a management point of view it is necessary to focus effort on two or at most three of these. One cannot do all things equally well and many of the above factors are not mutually compatible.

The combination of factors for a manufacturing business is called its mission. Each manufacturing category, by definition, has its own unique mission, otherwise it would not be a separate category. For our high volume/low variety and stable business the mission might be cost and responsiveness in that order. For the high volume business with a high degree of product change it could be adaptability and cost in that order. (It should be noted here that the apparent relegation of cost to second place is not a contradiction of earlier comments. All it means is that in a given market situation the customer may be less concerned about absolute price than in adaptability. One's price relative to the competition is as important as ever).

## Manufacturing Responses

The main manufacturing mission for each category of the business dictates the response in terms of scope and deployment of resources. Below, I have divided the response options into four key questions:

### Scope of Activities

| Level of Vertical Integration | Process Technology |
|---|---|
| "What degree of make/buy is most appropriate?" | "What process is most appropriate for make parts?" |

### Resource Deployment

| | |
|---|---|
| "How should physical resources be allocated/focussed?" | "How should the resulting environment be controlled and managed?" |

Taking just the scope of activities question and applying it to two of our diesel engine categories we get the result shown in Figure 6.

A similar matrix can be drawn for the deployment of resources, wherein questions such as the type of layout (group, line, product or function) and the type of systems for planning and scheduling or stock control can be answered.

## Development of a Manufacturing Response Plan

For each manufacturing category we now have a mission and an ideal response. The next step is to compare that with what exists, determine the mismatch and then identify the action required to remove it. That process can only be superficial until the other major analyses are completed but nonetheless will provide a useful indicator of direction.

## B. ANALYSIS OF PRESENT RESOURCES

The previous analysis looked at the direction we should be taking. This one looks at all the activities we already perform and compares them in added value terms to each other and the products that they produce.

For the purposes of this exercise an activity is defined as "a process or group of processes which can be considered homogenous enough to have a unique learning curve or cost behaviour pattern." It might be a group of multi-spindle auto lathes or a complete assembly line. It may even be a single specialised operation. Part of an analysis matrix - for a car electrical product - is shown in Figure 7.

The identification of activities and degree of dependence each activity has on the others around it, as well as the amount of support it provides to which products, produces some key guidelines for decisions.

(a) It focusses attention on those activities which have the greatest leverage in terms of long-term cost reduction potential. These "cost driving factors" can be related to the straight learning curve effect, economies of scale, level of utilisation, technology steps or any combination of all of them. In the example of Figure 7 the cost factors most pertinent to the assembly areas were high materials and labour utilisation plus a degree of experience curve effect, particularly as frequent new products were introduced. In the case of the high precision automated machining sections utilisation of equipment and being in the right technology bracket had the most influence, closely followed b· a low rate of changeover.

(b) It identifies and demonstrates the areas where we are likely to see different cost curves over time.

(c) It shows which are the true core activities of the business and which are the peripheral activities.

(d) It makes it possible to understand the balance of resources devoted to each product. In the case of Figure 7 the two products concerned had relatively similar shares of each activity because both had to go through all processes. But in practice, product B was on a fast and erratic growth path. This had significant ramifications for the management of each of the activities and their organisation.

(e) It enables a comparison through time of the impacts of product life cycle differences, including that of specific decisions to "kill-off" products or move to other forms of manufacture.

(f) It feeds into the manufacturing missions analysis to aid the matching process.

## C. ANALYSIS RELATIVE TO THE ENVIRONMENT (RESOURCE PORTFOLIO ANALYSIS)

Each activity that is performed has some similarity with similar activities performed outside the company. The cumulative effect of production going through the activity is a cost/experience curve. In manufacturing industries, such as automotive, this can be shown to be between 15 and 25%. That is, for each doubling of cumulative experience the cost should go down by between 15 and 20%. Absolute economies of scale are also another clear and well recognised means of reducing costs. Therefore, from both points of view the size of an activity has an important influence on costs.

I mentioned earlier that a mature market demands concentrated action to force cost down a relevant experience curve if competitiveness is to be maintained. This might be done by combining activities to give the required economies of scale, or it might be by specific cost improvement action plans. It is also highly relevant to look outside. There may well be activities that under the business mission analysis should be done in-house, and where the products/activity analysis demonstrates a case for keeping them inside but nonetheless can never reach the "lowest cost" position because a direct competitor is carrying out the same activity at a much higher volume. Alternatively, there may well be an outside source of supply who is shooting down the learning curve faster.

A well known example in the automotive industry is the micro computer control module for engine management. To the manufacturer of fuel injection equipment, looking at the situation in isolation, the manufacture of these modules might well appear attractive - they are an important part of present business, they will be even more important in the future and they will represent a high proportion of total end costs. Therefore, from an initial cost and control-over-supply point of view, in-house manufacture might appear to be the right thing. However, when looked at against the high volumes achieved by outside suppliers, feeding the same or similar products to a wide variety of industries, the picture can be quite different. Specialist producers can be two or three generations of technology and several orders of magnitude in production experience down the road before we are past the start gate.

To a greater or lesser extent each activity we perform exhibits these features and is therefore subject to the same analysis. Indeed, we may find some where we are now the leaders and can consolidate and maintain that leadership by selling some of our capacity, or by setting up a separate activity-centered business feeding both us and external customers.

The detailed approach used in this analysis will depend very much on the nature of the activities being performed. Such issues as "how wide one spreads the net" when comparing market share and growth rates and "which companies in practice are candidates for the title of competitor" can only be decided by reference to specific cases. However, the fundamental approach is the same for all activities. Looked at in the simplistic form shown in Figure 8, some key messages can be obtained for each activity:

### High Growth High Relative Size

(Quadrant A): Activities in this box are almost certainly true core activities where in-house manufacture is virtually essential. They should therefore be driven towards the lowest cost most efficient mode.

### Low Growth High Relative Size

(Quadrant B): These activities are likely to be areas which were in quadrant A at one time but where more widespread use of the technology is bringing other competitors into the field. The message here is to drive them as hard as possible but be mindful of a future situation which might make outsourcing more economic.

## High Growth Low Relative Size

(Quadrant C): Anything here could be a future core activity to be nurtured and developed. But an element of uncertainty is an intrinsic feature of this area: a sufficiently sustained high rate of growth is necessary to move to a dominant size position. If the uncertainty is great outsourcing might be the best short-term solution.

## Low Growth Rate Low Relative Size

(Quadrant D): Activities here are almost certain to be peripheral and frequently uneconomic. They are obvious candidates for outsourcing, subject to there being no product/market developments on the horizon which could change the position.

Frequently, our studies have shown that activities in quadrant C have been brought in-house on the basis of an economic evaluation which shows a good potential return on investment. In such cases we have invariably found that there are fundamental flaws in the costing system or evaluation process. Usually, insufficient allowance has been made for the impact on overheads, management time, materials systems or inventory. Therefore, this analysis can serve the useful dual purpose of taking a look, from a somewhat different direction than normal, at the investment decision making process.

## COMBINATION OF ANALYSES

Drawing together the results of the three parallel analyses to produce an effective result is perhaps the most critical step of all. However, it is relatively straight-forward. Our experience in the automotive industry shows that:

1. It is highly improbable that more than three, or at most four, different business missions exist within any manufacturing activity.

2. The focussed approach to resources in analysis B is likely to be forced towards an 80:20 picture; concentration of efforts on the top twenty percent of the activities influencing eighty percent of the cost.

3. The Resource Portfolio analysis will also be guided by the 80:20 rule. In addition, the open and well defined nature of the automotive business makes it relatively more easy to identify competitors and sources of supply than in some more diverse industries.

The logic path for combining the analyses is shown in the example of Figure 9 which concerns off-the-road vehicles. Each of the options produced underwent rigorous tests prior to choosing the right one to implement.

In summary, focussing assembly operations on two manufacturing missions and machining into one location, the company was able to increase pre-tax earnings by more than 50%.

## CONCLUSION

A.T. Kearney's work in the automotive industry over recent years has led to the development of an effective manufacturing strategy methodology. It greatly facilitates the up-front task of providing the interface between product/market objectives and manufacturing responses. It also clearly identifies and evaluates the opportunities and pitfalls which present themselves in relation to a particular company's endeavours.

Above all, the process has to be seen as something which is adaptable to a dynamic situation. Also, the strategy can only really provide the framework for the decision-making process - managers still have to make the decisions. And that may mean scrapping the strategy and starting again if world events dictate it. However, with a well constructed manufacturing and supply strategy, catastrophic change should not be necessary; future development being achieved more by tuning and refinement than wholesale surgery.

## REFERENCES

(1) M. Hinks-Edwards, Director Euroeconomics. From a paper presented at the SMMT/A.T. Kearney conference on the Vehicle of the Future, October 1980.

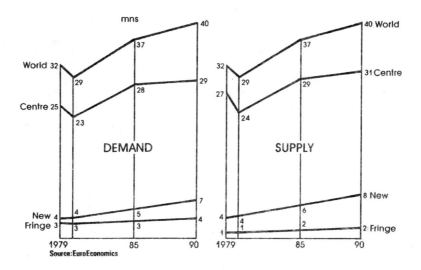

Fig 1    World car industry — 1980s

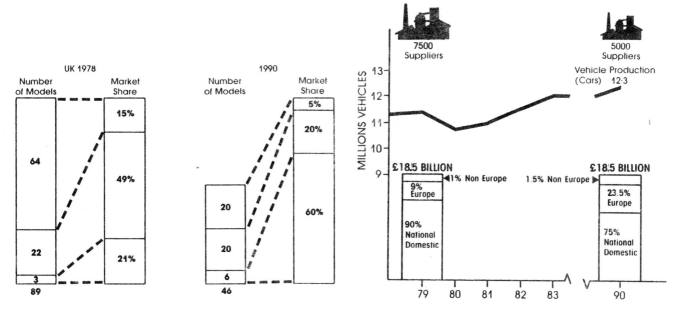

Fig 2    Models and market share — Western European produced
models

Fig 3    Supply industry impacts — original equipment business

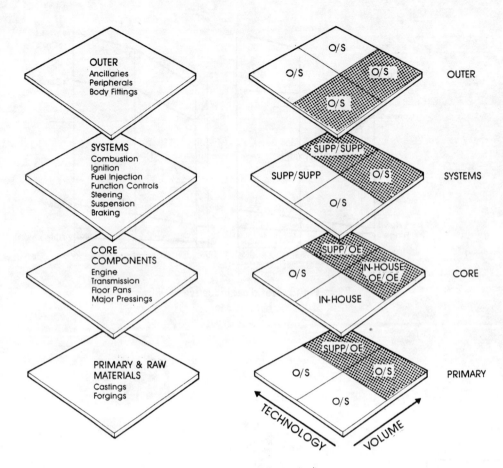

Fig 4    The impact of market forces on the make/buy process

**Fig 4 left pyramid labels:**

OUTER
Ancillaries
Peripherals
Body Fittings

SYSTEMS
Combustion
Ignition
Fuel Injection
Function Controls
Steering
Suspension
Braking

CORE
COMPONENTS
Engine
Transmission
Floor Pans
Major Pressings

PRIMARY & RAW
MATERIALS
Castings
Forgings

**Fig 4 right labels:** OUTER, SYSTEMS, CORE, PRIMARY; O/S, SUPP/SUPP, SUPP/OE, IN-HOUSE, IN-HOUSE OE/OE; TECHNOLOGY; VOLUME

| APPLICATIONS SECTORS / PRODUCTS | AGRIC. | MARINE | TRUCK | VAN | PASS. CAR |
|---|---|---|---|---|---|
| 1 | | | III | | |
| 2 | I | | | | |
| 3 | | | | | |
| 4 | II | | | | |
| 5 | | | | | |

Fig 5    Manufacturing business footprint — diesel engines:
   Category 1,   Low unit volumes, high variety, stable product
                 designs;
   Category 2,   medium/high unit volumes, high variety stable
                 product designs;
   Category 3,   high unit volumes, low variety, erratic demand
                 and rapidly developing product designs

|  | CATEGORY II | CATEGORY III |
|---|---|---|
| MARKET CHARACTERISTICS | HIGH VOLUME, LOW VARIETY, STABLE PRODUCT | HIGH VOLUME, UNCERTAIN DEMAND, HIGH RATE OF PRODUCT CHANGE |
| MISSION | COST & RESPONSIVE-NESS | ADAPTABILITY & COST |
| LEVEL OF VERTICAL INTEGRATION | HIGH – TO GAIN MAXIMUM ADVANTAGE FROM ECONOMIES OF SCALE | LOW – AVOIDING IN-HOUSE ACTIVITIES EXCEPT FOR CORE ITEMS |
| PROCESS TECHNOLOGY | SPECIAL PURPOSE AUTOMATED EQUIPMENT | FLEXIBLE MACHINING CENTRES, PRODUCT DEDICATED BUT CAPABLE OF EASY CHANGEOVER |

Fig 6    Scope of activities — diesel engines

164

| ACT NO. | ACTIVITY DESCRIPTION | TOTAL VALUE ADDED | PRODUCT A VALUE ADDED | PRODUCT B VALUE ADDED | PRODUCT C VALUE ADDED |
|---|---|---|---|---|---|
| 1 | HOUSING MACHINING | 2.0 | 0.8 | 0.4 | |
| 2 | BARRELL MACHINING | 2.0 | 0.8 | 0.4 | |
| 3 | TUBE MACHINING | 1.5 | 0.6 | 0.3 | |
| 4 | MASTER RING MACHINING | 2.5 | 0.8 | 0.5 | |
| 5 | ROTOR MACHINING | 3.0 | 1.0 | 0.6 | |
| 6 | DRIVE SHAFT MACHINING | 1.8 | 0.7 | 0.4 | |
| 7 | CONTROL UNIT ROTOR | 2.0 | 0.8 | 0.4 | |
| 8 | CONTROL UNIT HOUSING | 0.5 | 0.2 | 0.1 | |
| 9 | ROLLER SHOES | 0.5 | 0.2 | 0.1 | |
| 10 | SECONDARY HOUSING ITEMS | 0.8 | 0.3 | 0.3 | |
| 11 | MISC. COMPT. MACHINING | 7.0 | 3.0 | 2.0 | |
| 12 | PRESS OPERATIONS | 1.5 | 0.6 | 0.3 | |
| 13 | BARRELL & TUBE ASSY. | 0.8 | 0.2 | 0.2 | |
| 14 | ROLLER & BARRELL ASSY. | 1.0 | 0.4 | 0.2 | |
| 15 | FINAL ASSY. | 1.8 | 0.7 | | |
| 16 | TEST | 3.3 | 1.0 | | |
| TOTAL | | 32.0 | 7.4 | | |

Activity groupings:
- AUTOMATED TRANSFER MACHINERY: 1–2 (and 3)
- AUTOMATED HIGH PRECISION UNIT MACHINERY: 3–9
- GENERAL MACHINERY: 10–12
- MANUAL ASSEMBLY & TEST: 13–16

| ACTIVITY GROUP | FACTORS GIVING LOWEST COST MODE |
|---|---|
| AUTOMATED TRANSFER MACHINERY | EQUIPMENT UTILISATION |
| AUTOMATED HIGH PRECISION UNIT MACHINERY | PROCESS TECHNOLOGY & MACHINE UTILISATION |
| GENERAL MACHINING | LABOUR UTILISATION, BATCH CONTROL |
| ASSEMBLY | LABOUR UTILISATION, MATERIAL FLOW |

Fig 7    Resource analysis — activity/product value added chains: car electrical products (figures in £millions)

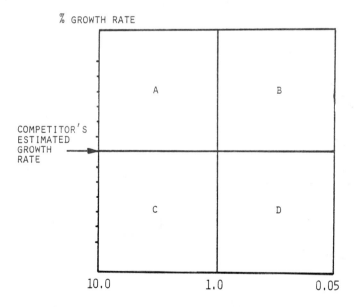

Fig 8    Resource portfolio analysis — relative size of activity (to activity competitor)

1. CURRENT SITUATION

3 SEMI-AUTONAMOUS PLANTS

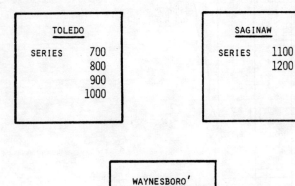

| TOLEDO | |
|---|---|
| SERIES | 700 |
| | 800 |
| | 900 |
| | 1000 |

| SAGINAW | |
|---|---|
| SERIES | 1100 |
| | 1200 |

| WAYNESBORO' | |
|---|---|
| SERIES | 400 |
| | 500 |

2. ANALYSES

MISSIONS ANALYSIS FOUND:-

2 MISSIONS WITH UNIQUE SUCCESS FACTORS

    A.   LOW COST/STABLE VOLUME

    B.   INNOVATIVE ENGINEERING,
        HIGHLY FLEXIBLE OPERATION,
        INCREASING VOLUME

RESOURCE ANALYSIS SUGGESTED:-

COMPONENT FOCUS IN MACHINING & PRODUCT
FOCUS IN ASSEMBLY WOULD GIVE GREATEST COST
DRIVING POTENTIAL

RESOURCE PORTFOLIO CONCLUDED:-

MAKE/BUY BALANCE O.K. BUT GREATER
PROCUREMENT COORDINATION REQUIRED

3. OPTIONS

4. RECOMMENDED ACTION

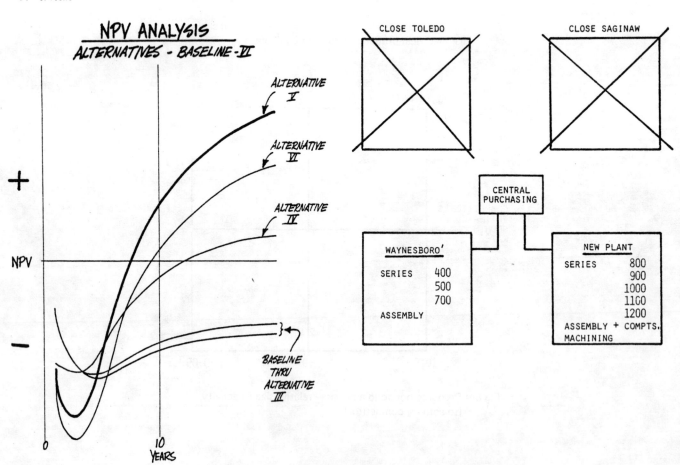

Fig 9    Off-the-road vehicles manufacturing strategy — US company

# C293/81

# See-why: interactive simulation on the screen

E FIDDY, MSc, PhD and J G BRIGHT, BA
BL Systems, Oxford
R D HURRION, PhD
University of Warwick

SYNOPSIS . This paper describes a technique called Simulation and its use in aiding the design and control of industrial processes. The technique, to date, has suffered from limitations which have prevented the wide acceptance which it should enjoy. The writers believe that these weaknesses have largely been eradicated by the concepts of 'Visual Interactive Simulation' and their implementation in a computer package called SEE-WHY. After briefly outlining the history of simulation, its inherent weaknesses are discussed. The paper then deals with how these limitations have been overcome, and gives practical examples of the use of SEE-WHY in tackling problems of plant layout and control in the Automotive Industry. Special stress is given to the natural barrier between human and computer, and the paper shows how this barrier has been successfully breached, allowing each to do what it is best at.

## 1 What is Simulation?

### Introduction

The verb 'to simulate' is used fairly widely in the English language. 'He simulated a fit of rage'...' 'This white sheet will simulate a table cloth...' 'We can use PVC to simulate leather...' All these examples imply the idea of 'copying' or 'mimicking' some real condition but using an alternative means.

In the Management Science field, a much stricter definition is applied. 'Simulation' to the Management Scientist means the creation of a model-an abstraction and simplification of a real life process. This simulation model mimics the real process in a sufficiently accurate manner to allow tests and experiments to be carried out on the model, and not on the 'real process', thus avoiding the possibility of 'trial and catastrophe'. Novel ideas can be tried out, and firm conclusions reached, which may then be confidently applied to the real process.

Note the general nature of a 'real life process'. Although this broad generality will be somewhat constrained later, it is true to say that a simulation model can be created of almost any process. Customers at service counters, products on an assembly line, automated stores, chemical processes, transport systems, traffic on road networks, tidal flows, telecommunications systems -all these areas and many others have been tacked by simulation.

### Physical models - pros and cons

Simulation models can take many forms. The type which will be recognised by most people is a 'Physical Model' (chess is a well-known example of simulating a war, although the rules ritualise the players' actions to a high degree). The 'Flight Simulator' used in training pilots is another example (no room for trial and error in a real aircraft). Monopoly avoids the risk of actually paying out large sums of money as a property speculator even if its value in learning the property business is limited.

But why bother with the physical appendages of these games? They are all played within the constraints of a 'rule book'; for example, in Bridge, East always bids after North, a trump card always betters a card of another suit etc. So why not write down the rule book and play using pencil and paper only? This approach has the advantage that any new game could be played by writing the rule book. Translating this into an industrial context, there would be no need to build a physical model of a complex plant-possibly a very expensive and time-consuming business.

However, there is more to Bridge, Chess or a Flight Simulator than the rule book. When East must lead a card, how does he decide which card to play? When an unforeseen fault develops during a simulated take-off, what action does the trainee pilot take? In order to differentiate the 'rule book' from decision formulae (or rules, or skills) developed by the human during play, we shall call the latter 'decision rules'.

### Non-physical models

At this point, we narrow the definition of simulation even further and talk about 'Discrete Event Simulation'. In a simulation model an attempt is made to reproduce the movements and flows of 'entities' - products, people, machines - from one state to another as time progresses. The basic structure is as follows: using the 'rule book' and the 'decision rules' as defined above, the model moves forward in time from event to event updating the status of the entitites as each event occurs. Nothing happens between events. For example, in simulating a lift system, at the event 'arrive fourth floor' some passengers would leave the lift and others join it - their status would change. Nothing happens between the events 'leave fourth floor' and 'arrive fifth floor'.

Now, if we can write down the rules - the rule book and the decision rules-there is a handy tool available to speed up the whole business of running a simulation model. Get rid of the pencil and paper, and program the rules into a computer. Indeed, such are the advantages of speed and accuracy which accrue, that there is a proliferation of computer languages and packages available for this very purpose. These all have a common feature; they enforce a structure irrespective of the real process being modelled. In essence, the structure defines each event, and moves forward from one event to another according to whether an event <u>must</u> follow, <u>could</u> follow, or <u>cannot</u> follow another, the rules defining which of these three alternatives is chosen. Within this structure, the analyst's thought processes can concentrate on the rules.

Management Scientists for many years created simulation models by coding the rule book into the computer and then making plausible assumptions about the decision rules which should be used in running the model. The rule book usually presents no problems, but a nagging doubt remains - are the decision rules programmable?

## 2  Is Simulation possible?

Unfortunately, for simulation, real life rarely does proceed with every event being decided by a clear rule. Some would argue that this does not invalidate the fundamental assumption of simulation - and that real life <u>should</u> be run as a mechanism whose rules are discovered by simulation. One has only to note the vast amount of effort put into computer chess to realise that, even with a relatively simple closed system, discovering programmable rules which are more effective than the human brain (or some human brains!) is extremely difficult. A dynamic system like a steel plant or an automotive factory is orders of magnitude more complex than a chess board and its internal structure and environment are in a process of continual change. It is inconceivable even in theory that such a complex changing system could be run most effectively without assistance from the human brain, even though parts of it might be. And the theory is borne out in practice; production controllers and schedulers, making decisions even for quite small parts of the system, have had rules thrust on them by Management Scientists but they revert to a process of ad-hocery as soon as they can!

Plant controllers live in a world of crises. They are therefore more interested in getting help in a crisis than advice on how to deal with normality. Is there, therefore, any validity in trying to discover practical control rules by using an environment of statistical normality when running a simulation? Such rules normally do the wrong thing when crisis events occur - which they do all too commonly: running simulations for longer time periods to gain statistical significance does not overcome the problem.

Computer simulation can easily hide this major philosophical weakness from the 'owner' of the problem. He can be misled by the apparent power of the weapon: even if 'he is aware that it is not done well, he is surprised to see it done at all'. He may be too ready to accept 'the answer' to the problem, and not want to know the assumptions and short cuts taken in the model. It sometimes goes further than this: 'simulate this and prove it will work'! This lack of communication between client and modeller and failure to really gain a mutual understanding of what is in the model and what the model is saying sometimes suits the modeller as well-because, given perfect communication, all the weaknesses of the model would become apparent!

## 3  Simulation in BL

The use of simulation in British Leyland started in earnest when the Metro Plant was being designed. The Operational Research Unit was asked to consider a number of problems on layout, size of buffer stores, routing decisions for different model derivatives and most importantly, how should the whole process be controlled. The models were developed using the IBM simulation package, GPSS. It became apparent that Management wanted answers, and in the hurly-burly of real life, did not have time to absorb the vast amount of assumptions underlying these answers.

For this reason a physical model was built (see Fig 1). This provoked a much greater degree of involvement from Management - they could see it and play with it - and in many cases increased their understanding of what simulation was. It was possible to get mutually agreed and more articulate statements of what the real problems were - but naturally it took a lot longer to get the answers out to them! Handling grubby counters is a slow and unpleasant activity. Could the model be automated gaining speed, removing the sweat, but without losing the hands-on feeling?

At this point the work of Dr R D Hurrion at Warwick University was encountered. The concepts he had formulated seemed directly applicable. These were two: firstly to display on a colour screen a diagram of the plant which the user could relate to and receive a 'moving picture' of the dynamic system under study, and secondly it was possible to interact with the model: this had two major advantages

It was possible to alter, interactively, the layout on the screen, or the control rules embedded in the model, at any point in time. It was possible to develop a simulation model where some of the decision points could be driven by rules programmed into the model, but where others could be input by the model controller who was aided in this by looking at the current status of the plant as shown on the screen. In this respect the two essential concepts were symbiotic.

## 4  Advantages of Visual Interactive Simulation
## Learning from simulation models

In the writers' view, the approaches of Management Science have had a major obstacle to deal with: the activity involves persuading the owner of the problem to change his mind. If the Manager came to his problem 'carte blanche', Management Scientists would have an easier ride. This rarely happens, however. The difficulty lies in 'unmaking' someone's mind when it is already made up. To a large extent Management Science is now recognised as not being an activity where answers are provided, but where processes are supplied to the Manager to help him reach his own answer. This is a psychological point, and of the utmost importance. Managers who are given an answer at the end of a long exercise are usually not psychologically prepared for it. They would be if they went on the voyage of discovery together with the Management Scientist, following all the blind alleys in reaching 'the answer'.

These points apply particularly to simulation. Problems solved by simulation models normally follow a well-defined path.

The modeller attempts to prise out of the Manager his objectives, constraints and alternatives, and the Manager's emotional attachment to some of them cannot be avoided. Then follows a period of cerebration...eventually the answer is handed over. In most cases, the modeller is aware of a deeper understanding he has obtained from doing the work, and also of reservations about the answer. This is compounded by his uneasy feeling that the owner of the problem has not partaken of the most valuable part of the exercise and is (if the exercise is successful?) latching on to the answer but ignoring the assumptions that underlie it.

Contrast this with a situation where the Manager can watch the model perform, can feel confident that the rule book has been correctly written into the model, can try different decision rules and can modify the model accordingly-in short, he can go on the voyage of discovery together with the modeller. He learns simultaneously with the modeller. He knows the branches in thinking which led to the solution. He is thoroughly conscious of the assumptions on which the answer is based.

In this process many hard constraints (we have done it this way for 20 years...) will evaporate, and the overlapping and sometimes conflicting objectives, so difficult to specify at the start of the exercise, will emerge.

Finally, any sort of model is a splendid vehicle for driving the imagination to think of new alternatives. Very often it is the modeller only whose imagination is spurred. This is sad, since the Manager will normally have a more practical bent for knowing which alternatives are acceptable from a wide range of viewpoints. So, if he is a constituent part of the voyage of discovery, his imagination can be driven by the model in a way that is absent from most Management Science projects.

## The human brain and the computer

Earlier we made the point that, in most complex dynamic systems, human controllers make decisions for complex reasons on the basis of complex information. This presents a major problem for normal simulation. For it is necessary to program into the model a 'formula' at each decision point. The impossibility of doing this for many such decision points has already been mentioned. In fact, our work has shown that when a simulation model is seen running on a screen, such programmed rules, however 'clever', make decisions which are inferior to those which a human being would take.

This raises a point of vital importance. When playing a game like Monopoly, one learns to make decisions, generally improving with time. But is it ever possible to specify the decision rules, hand them over to a complete novice, and expect him to perform as well? The significance of a visual interactive simulation model is that it allows the interactive input of decisions reached by looking at complex patterns of information (as in real life), and utilises that versatile machine, the human brain. By 'playing' with such a model, it is possible to discover whether a programmable decision rule exists, and, if so, to get some idea of its limitations. This is better than plumping for a programmable rule and assuming it is reasonable simply because one has not been given the opportunity to see where it falls short.

## 5 SEE-WHY - its use

### Introduction

It is now proposed to give some examples of the use of SEE-WHY simulation models to illustrate the points made in Chapter 4. We stress that a verbal description of these models, with mono-chrome stills of the screen, can give only a poor insight into the value of the tool - this fact is why SEE-WHY was developed.

### Model A

Figure 2 shows the SEE-WHY screen diagram of the whole production process for one of BL Cars' models. Although the resemblance to Figure 1 is perhaps only dim, Management can, in practice relate to it as easily as to the physical model.

Each letter represents a particular derivative of the car. The main processes and stores are shown, some in detail and others in summary form. When the model is running it shows the vehicles passing through and between the production processes and stores. Timings of movements can be checked with the aid of a clock at the top of the picture. The model runs at roughly 20 times real-life speed.

This model was used to tackle problems of the following kinds: required size of buffer stores; how low should contents of stores be before action is required in upstream/downstream processes; can the store control rules meet required sequences of derivative types; effects of dedicating certain products to certain lines, or certain paint colours to each paint shop; what action is required when some derivatives cannot be produced at the assembly stage - should earlier processes be rescheduled and, if so, when.

Management spent a considerable amount of time watching this model of their plant perform, because they were able to relate easily to the model. They were able to satisfy themselves that the model was realistic, and, having gained confidence in its validity, obtain a firm grasp of the assumptions in the model. Once this stage was reached, wholehearted commitment to useful experiments, specified by Managers and modeller, followed.

### Model B

The Model described above is essentially a 'macro' model, its purpose being to look at the whole plant performing. In any such model it is necessary to simplify the control rules operating at each store or process in order to keep the model to a manageable size and to ensure that it runs quickly.

However, there will usually be a requirement to look in more detail at some of the intricacies of an individual store or process. For example, the store between the robot lines and the finish weld lines in Model A is quite a complex mechanism in its own right. Model B looks in detail at just this store, at a level of detail much more complex than that used in Model A. The SEE-WHY screen picture is shown in Figure 3.

This model studies the flow of slings(S) and car bodies(B) through the store. A sling picks up a body at one of the two lift points (top left) corresponding to the end of each robot line, and the body is moved into one of the store lanes.

At the output end of the store, bodies are moved via the conveyor to one of the four drop points (top right) corresponding to the start of each finish weld line.

There are strict rules about the order in which bodies are fed through the store. In essence, the whole store must operate in a first-in-first-out mode so that the sequence of build on the robot lines is carried through precisely to the finish weld lines.

This model is slightly unusual, in that the real-life process which it represents is itself controlled by programmable logic controllers (PLC's) without human intervention. The problem was that the PLC's, supplied and programmed by the manufacturers of the store, caused the whole system to 'jam up' under certain conditions of input if one or more lift/drop points broke down.

The visual representation of the dynamics of the system led fairly rapidly to the specification of a new set of PLC rules, generated jointly by Management and modeller, which completely overcame the problem. It is believed that this successful outcome would have taken much longer to reach using 'orthodox' simulation, if indeed it could be reached at all!

It is also worthy of note that 'normal' operation of the store was not the subject of investigation. The prime purpose of the model was to study the build up of 'crisis' situations, and to generate a new set of rules to handle them.

### Model C

In an automotive plant, there is a major decision point immediately prior to the paint process. Bodies-in-white (unpainted body shells) arrive at the paint plant and a decision has to be made on which colour to paint each body. For various process reasons, it is best to paint batches of bodies in one colour, aiming at a batch size of between 20 and 40. The bodies making up the batch may be of several types.

After painting, the bodies are routed to a painted body store ready for assembly. Each assembly track has strict sequencing rules which control the selection of body types to be launched onto the track.

Thus control of the painted body store is critical if the required sequences are to be met. Further, there is an interaction between paint batch size and the contents of the painted body store, since each colour painted will produce a different 'mix' of body types.

Model C covers this area in one of BL Cars' plants. The screen layout is shown in Figure 4. Unpainted bodies arrive along two conveyors (note that there is no store at this point) and must be fed into the paint shop, with a specification of the colour in which they are to be painted.

At the top of the screen is a matrix showing the number of orders for each body type and each colour. This enables the model 'controller' to choose the colour of each batch when the previous batch ends (either complete or, if the correct body type is not available, short).

A certain percentage of painted bodies will need rectification (left side of screen). Good bodies proceed directly to the 10-lane painted body store, where they will be joined (later) by bodies from the rectification process.

Lane discipline in the painted body store must be such that the required assembly track sequence can be met always by a painted body at the head of one of the lanes.

It is virtually impossible to find a programmable rule to control the selection of the next paint colour. Thus the first line supervision were invited to play the model and a set of robust guidelines created within which this human decision maker could work. Indeed, so successful were they that the sequence onto assembly could be controlled even more accurately, enabling like colours to be batched on the assembly lines. This meant a considerable easing of the material control problems at the assembly line side.

### Conclusion

A large number of plants have been studied using SEE-WHY. The advantages of such an approach may be summarised as follows:

The facility designer and the production controller can be brought together from the outset. This avoids the eternal problem of the designer's lack of attention to the minute-by-minute operation of the plant.

Layout and control decisions are no longer made lightly and without checking. Models are now used to investigate the effects of changes in order mix, volume, paint colour range, etc, in order to validate decisions often made rather arbitrarily.

The performance of control rules in crisis situations is far more important than the 'normal' operation of a plant. SEE-WHY shows up any shortcomings in the rules.

All these advantages are due to SEE-WHY's ability to capture Management's attention and prepare them psychologically for solutions which they help to generate.

SEE-WHY can deal with any dynamic system, and is in no way specific to the automotive industry. It has already been used in the pharmaceutical, heavy engineering, telecommunications and various service industries.

### 6 Facts and Figures about SEE-WHY

### The Display

Very early in the development of SEE-WHY the decision was made to concentrate on the use of a colour display. This decision was taken without any real doubt, since the use of colour enhances several-fold the quantity of information which can be conveyed in a given time and utilises the perceptive capabilities of the viewer to the full.

Colour enables a far more concise method of 'coding' than would be possible in monochrome. Consider the requirement to display, for example, two features of a product (eg. size and urgency) at some point in a manufacturing process. A single character (A-Z) can represent size, and the colour of that character the urgency. In this way, the 'information density' available on a colour screen is vastly superior to monochrome.

As far as the viewer is concerned, the human ability of 'pattern recognition' is brought into play by careful design of the screen picture. Appropriate choice of colours together with the use of 'blinking' and double height, creates meaningful displays which are retained in the viewer's mind for recall and comparison at various stages during the running of the model.

We restrict the use of colour to eight foreground and eight background colours, and utilise even this restricted set with caution, in order to avoid 'overloading' the viewer (possibly to the point of nausea?).

Although the display is essentially a diagrammatic representation of the process being modelled, it is updated dynamically. As each event proceeds, the change of status is shown immediately on the screen. The alternative - displaying 'snapshots' at predetermined intervals - was felt to be undesirable since the viewer may 'lose touch' with the dynamics of the system between one display and the next. Indeed, there is an enormous range of perceptive abilities to cater for! Some client Managers happily follow a very rudimentary display. Others require considerable 'animation' of the picture before they will accept the realism of a simulation model. The Management Scientist must be sensitive to these differing requirements.

The Package

The SEE-WHY package consists of a set of FORTRAN callable subroutines. Originally developed on an IBM 370/3033, and later converted for use on DEC PDP11 series hardware, the system now runs on a Cromemco Z-2H, System 2 or System 3 microcomputer. Bank switching is used to access the 192K Bytes of memory which the system requires. In all cases, the CPU is a Z80A.

The colour display is an Intelligent Systems Corporation 8051 system. This has its own 8080 processor, memory, and manufacturer-supplied software (including BASIC and file control system). The processor is used by the SEE-WHY system to convert messages in ASCII printable characters to a form suitable for driving the screen. This software occupies 8K of RAM in the VDU.

SEE-WHY simulations are written as a FORTRAN IV program, calling the appropriate SEE-WHY routines as required to maintain the simulation data and update the screen. If desired, the 'standard' displays implemented in the package can be replaced or supplemented by user-created pictures.

A wide range of standard interactions is available. Almost any item of data in a SEE-WHY model can be inspected and modified. The facility also exists to write specific interactions for a particular model, making it easy for the non-technical user to play with a SEE-WHY model by creating simple 'plain English' questions and answers.

The power of the interactive facilities is such that a wide range of runs under various conditions can be performed without the need for rewriting and recompiling the model. Further, they are an excellent debugging tool, and analyst utilisation is extremely high compared with non-interactive simulation languages.

As currently configured, the Cromemco microcomputer allows user programs up to 32K bytes in size. However, this storage is for the compiled user code only: overheads such as the FORTRAN run-time library and the SEE-WHY routines are held elsewhere in memory, and the simulation data is also stored elsewhere. As a result, large programs can be accommodated despite the apparently small user area available.

Indeed, FORTRAN programs as large as 100K in source form have been compiled into the available space without needing any special treatment.

SEE-WHY as originally developed was run on a remote IBM Mainframe under TSO, over a 300-baud telephone line. While there was no shortage of processing power, the line speed meant a relatively slow running display. Conversion to the DEC hardware largely overcame this problem, but the system lost its portability since fast dial-up lines are not generally available. The Cromemco version offers the best of both worlds: portability with ample speed, despite the smaller processing power compared with the mainframe/mini hardware.

7   The Future

Apart from developments in Visual Modelling generally, there are two areas in which SEE-WHY could progress.

One line of advance is the provision of a 'front-end'. This is a pre-processor which can be used to create the FORTRAN source text, using as input simple data on numbers of entities, sets, time-series etc, required by the model under construction. Such a facility increases the speed of model-building by accelerating the 'routine' parts of simulating coding. However, the complex logic associated with some events does not lend itself to such treatment, and the development of a 'front-end processor' has been deferred for the present.

A second development under serious consideration is really an extension of the interactive capabilities of SEE-WHY. Not even an experienced SEE-WHY simulation writer can predict all the questions likely to be asked of his model, or suggestions for changes and improvements to it. Therefore, there are occasions when it is necessary to 'go away' and rewrite parts of a model. The idea of creating and running simulations 'while-u-wait' is believed to be a possible way of getting round this problem. However, a considerable amount of development work is needed if we are to provide the facility to create genuine 'while-u-wait' models of a truly general nature.

Fig 1

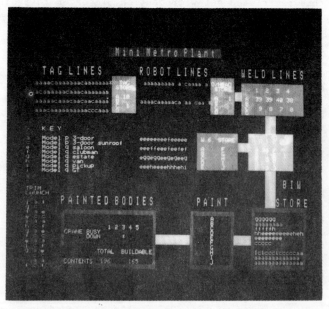

Fig 2

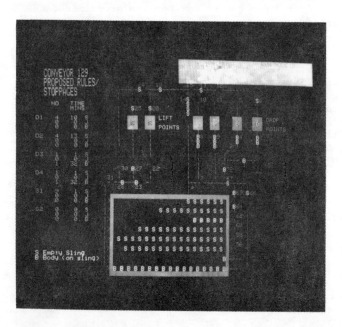

Fig 3

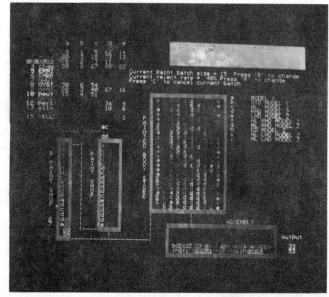

Fig 4

# Advances in SMC and DMC materials and manufacture

B D ELLIS, BTech
BTR Permali RP Limited, Gloucester

SYNOPSIS  The paper covers advances in the formulation and manufacture of components moulded in Polyester Dough moulding and Sheet moulding compounds with particular reference to newer moulding techniques and the development of tough materials and high temperature resistance grades for Under Bonnet applications.

INTRODUCTION

One of the most important growth areas of glass fibre reinforced plastics has been that of sheet moulding compound (SMC) and dough moulding compound (DMC).  It has enabled moulders to effectively compete in major volume markets such as transportation, electrical and business machines.

Sheet and dough moulding compounds are composites of speciality polyester resins, inorganic fillers, high temperature catalysts, thermoplastic polymers, mould release agents, pigments, chemical thickeners, and glass fibre reinforcement.   DMC has a shorter fibre length (3-12 mm) than SMC (12-50 mm) and consequently has lower physical properties than SMC.

SMC is a composite material, as indicated by its name, which is in an easily handleable sheet form, assisting manufacturing efficiency and scrap reduction.   SMC provides greater versatility in moulding high strength composites, with a variety of complex shapes including intricate rib and boss design.

The growth of the industry has been due to the unique characteristics of polyester SMC and DMC.

1.   Design Flexibility

SMC and DMC can be moulded into an almost infinite variety of sizes and shapes.  Parts can be designed with ribs, bosses, inserts and varying wall thicknesses.

2.   Parts Consolidation

Consolidation of parts has made it possible to combine up to 20 separate assemblies into one polyester moulding.   With the cost of individual manufacture of the parts and subsequent assemblies, major economies are obvious.

3.   Dimensional Stability

SMC and DMC hold their contour and dimensions over wide ranges of temperature and stresses.

4.   Tooling Costs

Tooling costs of SMC and DMC mouldings are extremely competitive in comparison with other material and processing techniques.   Proper design will require fewer moulds and processing steps to produce a finished part.

5.   Corrosion Resistance

Corrosion resistance is an inherent property of polyesters, making them ideal for many critical environments.

6.   High Strength

Glass fibres reinforce SMC polyester resin systems to give performance equal to or better than metals.

7.   Light Weight

On an equal volume basis, SMC is considerably lighter than metals (for instance it can be 35-40% lighter in weight than aluminium).  This light weight, along with high strength, provides a strength to weight ratio competitive with metals and other materials.

8.   Moderate Finishing Costs

Some SMC and DMC's are produced in moulded colours and others with tooling techniques, textured surfaces.   While painting is required for the automotive grade SMC's, their surface smoothness does not require the need for sanding and other post mould operations.

Unquestionably the realisation of many SMC and DMC parts has been significant, and many new advances will continue the progress of SMC and DMC.   Large steps are being made, not only in Compound formulation, to existing grades of SMC and DMC, but new families of compound are emerging along the new manufacturing techniques as technology moves forward.

Developments to Standard Moulding Compounds

1.   Low Profile SMC and DMC

The best surface finish obtainable is termed low-profile.   This carries with it implication other than that of extremely low shrinkage (less than 0.0005in/1in).   These materials show no long or short term waviness.   These materials exhibit minimal shrink over ribs and bosses and can be painted to meet automotive acceptance standards.

Improved control to molecular weight distribution of the polymers used in conjunction with the polyester resins has provided more uniform shrinkage control, in dimensionally critical applications.

The most widely used low-profile additives today are polymethylmethacrylate, impact modified polystyrene, polyvinyl acetate, polyvinyl chloride, polyethylene, styrenebutadiene block polymers, etc.

The resins used alongside these additives to achieve low profile compounds are high reactive resins, having a high cross-link density to achieve low-profile systems.

## 2.   Energy Absorbing Grades

Initial resin systems in moulding compounds were extremely brittle in nature. Today polyester resin producers, with better understanding of the cross-linking mechanism of polyesters with the low-profile additives, have produced tougher resin systems. Energy absorbing systems are now available exhibiting low-profile properties.

Polymer technology has evolved in which polyester resin backbone has been modified to produce cured resins with much tougher characteristics and greater tensile elongation.

Improved toughness characteristics in automotive applications have resulted in reductions in scrap due to handling damage, reduced shipping damage, fewer painting problems due to surface cracking and less part work due to edge chipping, cracking, and deflashing operations.

These advantages are attained with no sacrifice to cure cycle, surface quality, paintability, stud or insert retention or mouldability.

Principal physical property differences are in the flexural modulus which is reduced, greater areas under stress-strain curves, and a drastic reduction in reverse impact damage.

Reverse Impact tools are means of examining laminates by a loaded falling dart or ball. Comparative data is attained by examination of the initiation of surface crazing on the side opposite to impact on the laminate or moulding.

## 3.   Low Density SMC and DMC's

Conservation of energy through weight savings has meant the need for compound technology to produce light weight materials. Compounds with densities in the range 1.1 - 1.4 $gm/cm^3$ have been produced, compared with standard grade compounds 1.7 - 1.9 $gm/cm^3$.

This density reduction permits the moulding of parts with weight savings of up to 40%, while retaining the excellent physical, electrical and flame retardant properties of polyester moulding compounds along with the processability of conventional materials (Table 1).

The reduction in density has been achieved by the introduction of hollow glass microspheres as a filler material. This enables the compounder to tailor the material density to meet individual part requirements for weight. Limitations exist creating problems in the compounds processing, and reductions in physical properties.

The Table shown illustrates how, with controlled selection of additives, glass fibres, and glass spheres, the strength of low density components can approach the physical strengths of standard density compounds.

Low density compounds offer low pressure moulding capability, with moulding pressures as low as 300-500 psi with no crushing of microspheres unless moulding pressures in excess of 1000 psi are used. Low density compounds show improvements in 'sink' resistance, surface profile and shrinkage control due to their lower resin volume content.

Low density grades are possible in all possible grades of compound e.g. fire retardent, chemical resistant, electrical, low profile and energy absorbing.

## 4.   Chemical Resistant Grades

Improved chemical resistant grades are now available which will match the best corrosion resistant metal finishes. Conventional corrosion resistance has been based upon the bisphenol A type resin, but these are being replaced by vinyl ester resin which has greatly improved chemical and heat resistance.

## 5.   Electrical Grades

Electrical grades have been established for many years because of many inherent features, arc resistance, dielectric strength, non tracking, impact strength, heat distortion, creep resistance, flammability and pigmentability (Table 2).

New areas are being established. These areas largely dominated by phenolics are being created by uprating voltages. Under these circumstances, the high tracking resistance of DMC's becomes advantageous. Phenolics under high voltage have a low tracking resistance, the surface breaks down forming a conductive carbon layer and so lowering the arc resistance. Here the superior mechanical and electrical properties of polyesters outweigh the higher cost:

(i)    toughness - the impact strength of polyester is 10 x that of g.p. phenolic;

(ii)   arc and track resistance - polyesters have far superior arc and track resistance;

(iii)  asbestos free - unlike many phenolics, polyesters are asbestos free;

(iv)   cure cycles - polyesters are faster curing than phenolics;

(v)    colour - polyesters are available in a wide range of colours.

## 6.   Injection Moulding Grades (DMC)

DMC's may now, in addition to compression and transfer moulding, produce mouldings by the process of injection moulding. DMC injection moulding will give higher production rates due to the highly automated presses, plus excellent surface appearances and reduced finishing times. The high gloss achievable by using DMC's has opened up new fields in the domestic markets, coffee pot bases, toasters, irons, deep fat fryers, in addition to the numerous applications previously compression moulded, which can be produced more economically by injection moulding.

Numerous electrical components are being produced by this process, plus encapsulation of solenoids, load cells, etc.

Reductions occur in physical properties due to the breakage of fibres during processing by injection moulding, but these are being reduced as understanding increases with regard to sprue, runner and gate sizes in relation to these unique materials (Table 3).

The latest family of polyester compounds is the granulated polyester moulding compound. Automatic or semi-automatic moulding of reinforced thermosetting polyester is possible by using dry free-flowing granules. These grades will continue polyesters growth into injection moulding. Conventional injection moulders will be able to use these materials with no alteration to the process or with handling problems which exist with conventional DMC's. Granular polyester moulding compounds generally exhibit excellent electrical properties, good dimensional stability, high heat and flame resistance, higher impact properties and faster moulding cycles than phenolics.

## 7. EMI/RFI Shielding Grades

With the increase in use of SMC and DMC in electronic and electrical devices, two problems have become apparent, electrostatic discharge (ESD) capabilities and Radio Frequency/Electromagnetic Interference (RFI/EMI) shielding. The solution to these problems is to alter the insulation properties to impart electrical conductivity either internally or as a secondary operation. To achieve the ESD capabilities conductive pigments, metallized glass fibres, metallic flakes or carbon fibres, can be incorporated within the SMC reducing the resistivity from $10^{14} - 10^{16}$ ohms/sq m to $10^3 - 10^5$ ohms/sq metres.

The problem of RFI/EMI shielding is greater. Shielding is a process by which undesirable energy in the form of radio noise, electrical noise, and radio frequency interference is isolated by incorporating an electrically conductive barrier between source and the equipment requiring protection. Approaches like those used in ESD seem promising but major advances have been in deposition of metallic film barriers. These include methods such as vacuum metallization, flame spray, conductive paints and electric arc metallization techniques. These techniques will be required if developments along the lines of SMC bonnets are to become realities.

## Structural SMC's

### 1. R-SMC (Random Glass Orientation)

The uses of glass reinforced polyesters is extended from one where appearance is a prime target to 'structural' applications, where parts are required to be load bearing. To achieve this aim, new classifications of SMC's are being produced with greatly increased glass contents, up to 70% compared with the normal maximum of 35-40%. These high glass contents do not allow for the composite to be low-profile and are therefore for non-appearance parts only.

R-SMC is produced from fibre chopped to a length of three inches or less in a random pattern. With R-SMC the only modifications needed to the machinery are in the compaction rollers, where a chain belt mechanism is added to aid fibre wet out (Fig. 1). As glass contents increase, the mouldability decreases with R-SMC. Ribs and bosses are possible but with increasing difficulty, as glass contents increase, of obtaining good glass flow and consistency, and therefore some short fibres may be necessary.

R-SMC is isotropic but becomes anisotropic on flowing in the mould. Therefore, to achieve maximum strength a charge, with maximum mould coverage, should be used to minimise flow lines. Typical properties are shown on Table 4., R30 denoting 30% glass, R50 glass, etc.

### 2. C-SMC and C/R-SMC (Continuous and Continuous/Random SMC)

C-SMC is a sheet moulding compound containing unchopped glass fibre deposited unidirectional with the machine direction. These can be deposited with a percentage of random chopped roving (C/R-SMC), glass contents of each type following the appropriate letter. Modifications to the SMC machine now require a second feed of unchopped rovings to the resin matrix on the horizontal bed of the machine (Fig. 2).

Flow limitations with this type of SMC would require 100% charge coverage although some degree of flow is possible perpendicular to the continuous rovings.

Incorporation of any bosses, ribs, or other features would not be possible.

The system will have maximum physical properties parallel to the direction of fibres, but low values when tested perpendicular to the fibres (Table 4). This feature limits the applications to such specialities as leaf springs, door beams, bumper supports, etc. The transverse properties will increase as the proportion of random chopped rovings increases and this will also allow a small degree of flow and shallow bosses.

### 3. O-SMC and O/R SMC (Oriented and Oriented/Random SMC)

O-SMC is made from a combination of long and short fibres, the long fibres being in excess of three inches and oriented in the machine direction. This combination of fibre lengths results in a compromise material between the good flow properties of R-SMC and the superior mechanical properties of C-SMC.

A secondary cutter is required on the SMC machine to produce the longer oriented glass fibres (Fig. 3). O-SMC and O/R SMC has a compromise of all properties of R and C-SMC in respect of physical properties, flow and degree of complexity of the mouldings (Table 4).

Major interest in these series of compounds must result from the significant weight and cost savings which can be achieved when compared with either steel or aluminium. Flexural strengths are greater than steel or aluminium, stiffness falls between steel and aluminium, and with higher glass contents the tensile strengths are increased (Table 5).

## Thick Moulding Compound

Thick Moulding Compound (TMC(R)) has been emerging in the U.S.A. after introduction from Japan but this development has not yet followed into Europe. TMC (R) is a form of hybrid between standard SMC and DMC but with a greater formulating range.

TMC(R) is capable of being compression, transfer or injection moulded and in the latter case producing improved physical properties over DMC or SMC.

TMC(R) is a three dimensional tabular structure with a thickness of up to 2". it has superior physical properties to SMC, which has only a two dimensional structure, and does not suffer from the fibre degradation which occurs during the mixing of DMC by the Z-blade mixer.

TMC has very good glass distribution, even in areas of high flow. This arises from the three dimensional glass network found in the slabs of this unique compound.

Comparison of physical properties is shown in Table 3.

## Case Histories and Examples

With particular reference to these advances in Materials and Manufacturing technology, a review of several components will be made.

### a) Ford Inlet Manifold

This development highlights the potential of plastic components in the higher stressed and more aggressive environments under bonnet.

The inlet manifold was an aluminium die-cast moulding with areas of severe undercuts, eliminating the possibility of retractable cores when compression moulded. The plastic selected had to meet the demanding under bonnet environment of hot oil, hot coolant, and fuel individually or together. The mouldings must be made to machining tolerances to eliminate secondary operations and maximise the cost savings.

The coolant involved was varying from water to 50% ethylene glycol, at a pressure of 105 kN/m$^2$ up to 100°C, and with a fuel/air mixture at 0.68 - 1 bar and temperatures up to reflux.

The manifold during its operation would be subjected to the following stresses:

compression derived from bolt torque when fixed to the engine head;

constant load weight of carburettor and air cleaner;

creep derived from constant load at high temperatures;

fatigue due to engine movement during running;

thermal stresses due to changes in temperature conditions under load and in particular the changes occurring within the component;

impact strength such that during service the component would be undamaged if a wrench was dropped on it.

The choice of material was quickly selected as a thermoset material; epoxies were too high in price and subject to aqueous attack. The choice was between polyesters and phenolics, and a polyester was chosen because of its low/non shrink characteristics.

Isophthalic polyesters are resistant to hydro-carbons whereas a bisphenol A resin is resistant to aqueous attack and therefore some com-promise was essential.

The acceptance level was set at 70% strength retention after water/anti freeze 50:50 immersion for 500 hours at reflux, and petrol at 500 hours at reflux, with flatness tolerances 0.075 mm.

A one-piece moulding was specified due to the additional cost which would be necessary for adhesive application and curing. A fusible metal core with a melting point above that of the polyester moulding compound was consequently used. Minimum ribs and wall thickness mod-ifications were allowable and a moulded-in aluminium hot spot was necessary to form the top surface of the water jacket to evaporate fuel droplets.

Many compounds were moulded but when examined showed internal cracking, failing on the water jacket pressure test with the exception of one isophthalic formulation. A compromise material was examined by substituting a bisphenol A resin in place of the isophthalic in the formulation, but although meeting the water jacket tests, failed on the dimensional tolerances. A low-profile agent could not be found for the bis-phenol A system so a material based upon an SMC formulation, using a polypropylene mateante resin with an acrylic thermoplastic as low-profile agent, was produced which gave mouldings of acceptable standard with improved dimensional tolerances. Strength retention properties were also increased to meet the acceptance level of 70% (Fig. 4 & 5).

Rig testing and thermal cycling on engine test beds were the next series of development tests which were overcome before final vehicle testing. Final vehicle testing produced a leakage problem at 20 000 km. Expansion due to temperature, caused compressive creep which, when reversed, created a residual tension, warping the bolting face from the cylinder head. This last material problem was overcome by lowering the linear expansion rate resulting in the final compound (X52).

Final driveability and performance testing showed that the impossible had been achieved, 'The Plastic Intake Manifold'.

### b) 1980 Ford Light Truck Tailgate

A two-part prototype tailgate was produced for the 1980 Ford Light Truck (U.S.A.) using two different SMC constructions, which in combin-ation gave a 27% weight saving over the produc-tion steel assembly.

A vinyl ester 50% R-SMC was used for the inner panel of the assembly and a random 30% standard low-profile automotive grade SMC was used for the outer panel.

The high strength of the R-50 SMC was utilised in a 'drum drop' and 'top edge impact' test which the tailgate came through successfully. Vehicles fitted with these tailgates were put through the full proving tests and significant superior performance was achieved by the composite tailgate.

### c) 1981 Corvette Leaf Spring

C-SMC has made this project possible and is in production on the current 1981 Corvette. The 7.5 lb monoleaf composite spring has replaced a 43 lb ten leaf steel spring. This has utilised the high strength of the SMC in the direction of the continuous fibre orientation, and the increased stiffness from the glass orientation, and the high glass content.

## d) Prototype Peugeot 305 Model Front and Rear Doors

A joint project by Automobiles Peugeot and Owens Corning Fibreglass produced a prototype two piece SMC door for the Peugeot 305 Saloon Car. The outer panels were produced from standard low-profile SMC and the inner panels were moulded from an SMC containing continuous strands of glass fibre in conjunction with chopped strands.

The outer panel was a 30% SMC and the inner panels a combination of the 30% SMC (standard) and C30/R20 SMC to provide the strength and stiffness necessary.

Weight savings were achieved on front and rear doors of 37% on each, a saving of 16 kgs per car.

## e) B.L. Rover SD1 Rear Parcel Trays

The product was specified in low density SMC with an s.g. of 1.4, with a heat deflection test. This was achieved by producing a high glass content SMC based upon a high reactivity rigid resin, incorporating glass microspheres to reduce the density from 1.8 $gm/m^2$ to 1.4 $gm/m^2$. The deflection test at 100°C required a high heat distortion resin and an increase in glass content to achieve the acceptance level.

## f) Prototype Rocker Box Covers

Various rocker box covers have been produced from DMC and SMC's. Low-profile energy absorbing grades are preferred because of their inherent flatness and ability to withstand constant vibrational forces. Prototypes have been running on cars in excess of 20 000 miles with no problems. One added bonus with these composite materials is their sound deadening properties, which can be further enhanced by the introduction of glass microspheres, as in the low density grades of compound.

The demand for these types of materials will continue to increase as fuel prices rise; the need for improved petrol consumption will mean the automotive engineers will be seeking weight reduction in all areas of automobile construction.

There are simple straightforward light-weight compounds that are available for general purpose usage from components such as parcel trays, interior trims, glove compartments, to external body panels.

Underbonnet applications using materials such as X52, used on the inlet manifold, could be used on rocker box covers, water pump, thermostat housings, timing chain covers, pulley wheels and numerous other mouldings.

The new generations of structural plastics are being examined for seat shells, major door panels, miscellaneous cross members, impact absorbers for bumpers, bumpers, and floor components. The improved energy-absorbing low-profile SMC's, as technology progresses, could be used as door and exterior body panels on cars, as they are on vans and commercial vehicles today.

In addition to the energy saved by petrol consumption, the polyester moulding compounds are total energy savers with a significantly lower energy content in the final moulding than their steel or aluminium counterparts. The energy content of aluminium being 7.8 M.Btu's/$in^3$, steel 4.1 M.Btu's/$in^3$ with polyester SMC/DMC 1.1 M.Btu's/$in^3$.

Without doubt, the reality of large moulded SMC and DMC parts has arrived, with future opportunities available through the advances in compounds and manufacturing processes described. These will only serve to promote the growth of GRP industry within the automotive sector for the 1980s.

## REFERENCES

(1)  ROWBOTHAM E.M. and SUTHURST G.D.  Achieving the Impossible 'The Plastic Intake Manifold' B.P.F. Reinforced Plastics Congress 1980.

(2)  TRUDEAU G.G. and LINDSAY M.W.M.  SMC The Second Challenge.  36th Annual Conference Reinforced Plastics/Composites Inst.  The Society of the Plastics Industry Inc. 1981.

(3)  WARNER C.C.  Design Considerations for Composite Leaf Springs.  35th Annual Conference Reinforced Plastics/Composites Inst.  The Society of the Plastics Industry Inc. 1980.

(4)  GERARD J., KEOWN J., and LOYAT B. Designing and Prototyping in European Automotive SMC Door.  36th Annual Conference Reinforced Plastics/Composites Inst.  The Society of the Plastics Industry Inc. 1981.

( 5)  TALLBACKA D.W.  TMC Uses and Applications. 35th Annual Technical Conference 1980.  Reinforced Plastics/Composites Inst.  The Society of the Plastics Industry Inc.

(6)  JUTTE R.B.  Structural SMC, Material Process and Performance Review.  33rd Annual Technical Conference 1978.  Reinforced Plastics/ Composites Inst.  The Society of the Plastics Industry Inc.

(7)  BRADISH F.W.  Conductive SMC/BMC Composites for RFI/EMI Shielding.  33rd Annual Technical Conference 1978.  Reinforced Plastics/Composites Inst.  The Society of the Plastics Industry Inc.

(8)  SUNDSTROM G.  Polyesters and Phenolics for Electrical Applications.  Society of Plastics Engineers, Milwaukee 1980.

TMC is a registered trademark of U.S.S.Chemicals.

Table 1 Typical physical properties of low density v standard density SMC and DMC

| Compound | Density gm/cc | Izod Impact at ft/lbs/inch. | Flexural Strength p.s.i. | Tensile Strength p.s.i. | Compressive Strength p.s.i. |
|---|---|---|---|---|---|
| Electrical DMC 15% | 1.80 | 4.5 | 12,700 | 4,600 | 18,400 |
| Electrical DMC Low Density 15% | 1.19 | 3.0 | 9,000 | 4,000 | 14,600 |
| Standard SMC 22% | 1.78 | 10.6 | 17,300 | 6,400 | 18,000 |
| Low Density SMC 22% | 1.24 | 11.5 | 16,000 | 5,500 | 14,100 |

Table 2 Typical properties of DMC and wood flour filled phenolic

| Properties | DMC (10% Glass) | Phenolic |
|---|---|---|
| S.G. | 1.89 | 1.36 - 1.45 |
| Impact Izod Notched ft/lbs/inch. | 2 - 3.0 | 0.26 - 0.30 |
| Tensile Strength p.s.i. | 4,000 | 6,000 |
| Flexural Strength p.s.i. | 10,000 | 10,000 |
| Flexural Modulus $\times 10^6$ p.s.i. | 1.5 - 2.0 | 1.0 - 1.2 |
| Compression Strength | 15,000 | 22,000 |
| Heat Deflection Temperature $^\circ$F at 264 p.s.i. | 400 - 500 | 340 - 360 |
| Track Resistance min. | 1200 + | Tracks |
| Arc Resistance Sec. | 200 - 240 | Tracks |
| Dielectric Strength VPM | 350 - 400 | 260 - 400 |

Table 3 Comparison of physical properties of injection moulded samples

| | Tensile Strength | Flexural Strength | Flexural Modulus | Unnotched Izod |
|---|---|---|---|---|
| DMC Injection Moulded | 2,200 | 7,600 | 1.34 | 4.9 |
| SMC Injection Moulded | 2,900 | 9,200 | 1.17 | 5.0 |
| TMC Injection Moulded | 3,500 | 14,000 | 1.50 | 6.0 |

Table 4    Properties of structural SMC's

| SMC Type | Flexural Strength p.s.i. | Flexural Modulus $10^6$ p.s.i. | Tensile Strength p.s.i. |
|---|---|---|---|
| R-30 | 23 | 1.9 | 11 |
| R-50 | 37 | 2.2 | 23 |
| R-65 | 48 | 2.3 | 30 |
| C30 R20 | 85 | 3.3 | 55 |
| C60 R5 | 100 | 5.3 | 64 |
| C60 | 130 | 5.4 | 81 |
| Steel HSLA 950 | 50 | 30 | 30 |
| Aluminium 7021-T6 | 50 | 10 | 50 |

Table 5    Weight of equivalent performance of structural SMC's

| Material | Volume | Flexural Strength | Stiffness | Tensile Strength |
|---|---|---|---|---|
| HSLA 950 | 1.00 | 1.00 | 1.00 | 1.00 |
| SMC R30 | 0.24 | 0.45 | 0.61 | 1.11 |
| SMC R50 | 0.24 | 0.28 | 0.59 | 0.52 |
| SMC R65 | 0.24 | 0.25 | 0.58 | 0.40 |
| SMC C30/R20 | 0.29 | 0.18 | 0.51 | 0.22 |
| SMC C60/R5 | 0.24 | 0.17 | 0.44 | 0.20 |
| AL 7021-T6 | 0.33 | 0.33 | 0.48 | 0.33 |

## SMC-R Machine

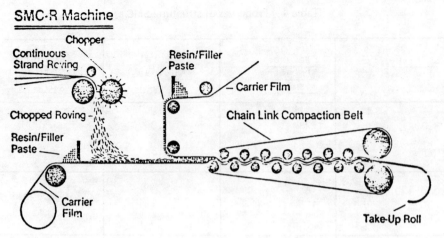

Fig 1

## SMC-C/R Machine

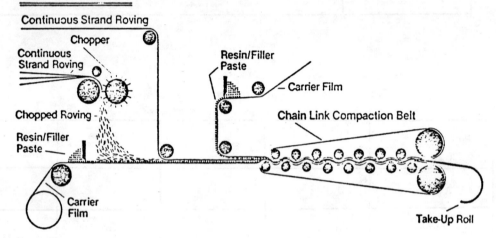

Fig 2

## SMC-D/R Machine

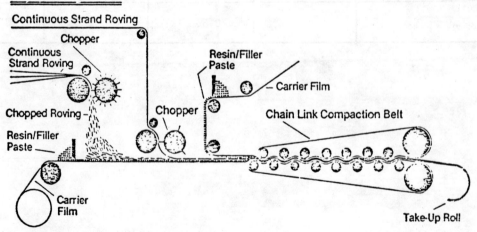

Fig 3

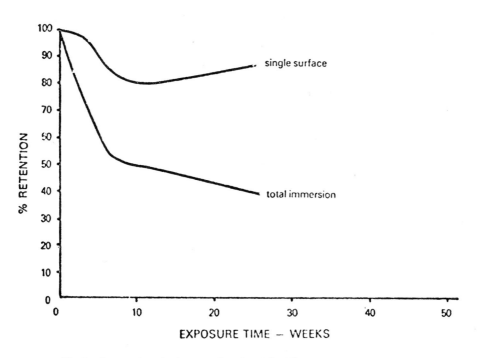

Fig 4   Properties of inlet manifold DMC (X52); percent tensile
strength retention in water and antifreeze (50:50) at 100° C

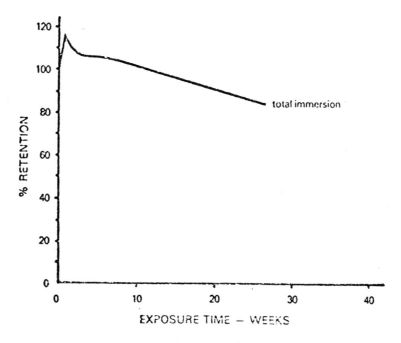

Fig 5   Properties of inlet manifold DMC (X52); percent tensile
strength retention on petrol at reflux temperature

# C295/81

# Undersealing on a high volume production line

D J CARTWRIGHT and D J BRAY, BSc, CEng, MIMechE
BL Technology Limited, Birmingham

SYNOPSIS  Applications of robots to a particular function within a total system must be given full consideration at the planning stage of a project. Systems must be conceived around the robot such that full potential can be made of the robot attributes and account for any short-fall of robot or associated equipment before installation.

To appreciate the above statement a case study will be reviewed in this paper comprising; the original planning and short-comings of an underseal spraying operation within a production environment, and the introduction of a programmable system control to interface robots and ancillary equipment together with added equipment and features. Also the incorporation of preventive maintenance schedules will be discussed and their effect analysed.

The commissioning and the suppliers' support in this project will be shown as being of a fairly typical pattern and again demonstrate the need for total system concept and a high quality of project engineering and technical expertise.  The latter points to the need for a multi-disciplinary engineer/team with a sound knowledge of production, mechanical, electrical, electronic and computing aspects.

Flexibility within a programmable system offers immense scope for development leading to improvements within the state-of-the-art.  Examples of such possibilities are presented for future debate.

## INTRODUCTION

Robot applications fall into comparatively easily definable categories:

1. Spray painting, spot welding.
2. Loading and unloading various machines such as: Injection moulders, Investment casting, Metal presses, etc.
3. Precise handling operations between machines, fettling, arc welding, etc.
4. Assembly techniques.

It is interesting to note from a recent publication that an analysis of 600 typical robot applications throughout industry that activities in the various categories are: (ref 1)

1. 45% installations,
2. 42% installations,
3. 12.5% installations.
4. 0.5% installations.

(This provides a good indication of where industrial robots of the present generation are easiest and most profitable to apply).

Each of the above categories will require different robotic characteristics to fulfill its various tasks within the production environment, and will incorporate considerations relating to:

a) Specific site and task parameters (requirements into which selected robots fall).
b) Reach and weight carrying characteristics of specific robots.
c) Quality objectives and degree of achievement for the robot.
d) Degree of accuracy required.
e) Sophistication of robot control. The degree of complexity required of the robot with regard to electronic control and memory capacity.
f  Ease of programming and future reprogramming with actual site conditions.

The above forms only a small part of the rudimentary requirements one must apply to  robot selection and indeed if a robot is to be the right tool.

Once decided on the robot, the next step is the total integration within the production environment and production system. It is unfortunately true that many of the robots' suppliers are reluctant, or unable, to cope with the total system supply. For the eventual user, a robot can be more troublesome than a 'gang' of men, if it lacks correct integration and interfaces with the working environment.

### Principle Criteria

This application is for the total undersealing of vehicles by robots on a high volume line. The concept of unmanned spray booths is no more a myth. America is already planning legislation for totally un-manned spray boothes in 1985, inevitably Europe and the U.K. will follow suit. Underseal spraying, by nature of its constituent materials, creates an unpleasant, unhealthy atmosphere in which to subject men for eight hour long shifts. The principle of robot engineering is therefore valid. Furthermore, there is a quality aspect to maintain both appearance and life of the finished vehicle.

An investment of the nature envisaged must at this stage, be seen as having justifiable returns, both in line with the flexibility inherent with robots, as well as meeting process criteria. The enemy is to reduce capital outlay by reverting to increased manning; but although quality will evolve through a normal learning curve, it will only be maintained through the diligence of the operators and a consistent labour force.

It is important to gain practical experience of the proposed equipment at the early planning stage. In this way a total system can be evolved, developing along specific themes beneficial to the robot flexibility but always accounting for production requirements within that flexibility. The optimum achievement being a fully automatic system.

## Hindsight Of Project Outset

Unmanned underseal application was the original concept set by Advanced Planning. Its reality at plant level basis was obstructed by lack of understanding for a fully integrated installation in line with production requirements, and with regard to the robot suppliers lack of process knowledge. The effect resulted in what one would consider to be a normal paint shop installation, into which a robot was installed with little more thought than a robot in place of a man. The situation is therefore the right choice of equipment, but an unsuccessful installation due to insufficient attention with regard to total integration.

Of the ensuing problems, some required little effort to remedy, but if we analyse these problems we develop a blue-print for future installations of a similar nature, and at the same time compose sound ground rules upon which to base any robotic operation.

## System Analysis

1       Material Specification and Spraying.

Historically underseal material has been bitumen based. This gives rise to problems with automatic spraying.

a)  Size of constituent particles cause numerous tip blockages.
b)  The air drying nature of the material is not suitable for automatic systems.

Consequently new materials specifications had to be examined. In conjunction with a suitable manufacturer, a Polyvinylchloride (PVC) base material was refined to meet our criteria. The new material significantly relieved technically related problems, requiring precautions only of a general nature.

1.1     To avoid "dead-leg" sections in underseal manifold piping.

1.2     To provide on-line filtration, as close to the spray gun as possible.

1.3     To de-pressurise the system between shifts (pressure sensitive material).

1.4     To monitor fan pattern.

1.5     To provide an automatic tip clearance mechanism.

1.6     To monitor pump pressure, and automatic barrel changeover.

2       Maintenance Facilities.

The system had to be easily maintained and where possible allowances incorporated for introduction of preventive maintenance. Allied to this was a facility to minimise problems of major overhauls or breakdown. Actions incorporated the following:

2.1     Identification of suitable maintenance allocated area for major robot rectification, incorporating ring-main connections to common hydraulic, pneumatic and electrical units.

2.2     Filter blockage identification.

2.3     Gun alignment to fixed datums.

2.4     Establish and initiate preventative maintenance schedules.

2.5     Organisation of training procedures for maintenance and electrical personnel.

3       Programming.

No robot installation will achieve its aim without effective programming. Lack of prior consideration in this case has led to the construction of the following list of points to help identify potential problems.

3.1     Is the type of programming system applicable to the job? (i.e. point to point or continuous path).

3.2     Can the robot be manoeuvred with the degree of dexterity necessary to complete the required programme?

3.3     Is the operator free to concentrate on the aspect of material application only?

3.4     Can a programme be edited easily?

3.5     Has programming to be synchronised with a moving conveyor, if so will this be at production related speeds.

3.6 Has programming to take account of normal production run-up programmes?

3.7 Can programmes be stored, copied and substituted easily; is there ample programme storage capacity to cater for user requirements?

3.8 Is it possible to programme away from the production area using simulated conditions? In this way a planned approach to programming can be developed.

4    Safety

It is important to identify safety requirements at the concept stage. In this way safety systems become an integral part of the system and not problematic to it.

Without a great deal of extra control little could be achieved at the early stage other than prevention of accidental harm to personnel in the area. This was not acceptable for production. Later in this paper the final approach is discussed, allied to overall control and integration of systems.

The aforementioned points represent only fundamental considerations of a totally automatic installation. The original control facility did not cater totally for these. Now we shall identify complete facility requirements and control in line with the original concept.

## Programming, Control and Interfacing

To understand the need for control the facility, the robot and every eventuality need to be studied.

1.    Geometric constraints:
    (a) area of body to be undersealed,
    (b) reach of robot,
    (c) dexterity of robot wrist,
    (d) booth size,
    (e) booth safety,
    (f) underbody conveyor layout.

With the objectives of total underbody coverage and a track speed of 45 vehicles per hour, it is necessary to use two robots. The reach and dexterity of the Trallfa necessitates one robot being placed each side of the track in such a way that it can spray both a sill and into all four wheel arches (Figure 1).

The positioning of the robots along the booth was determined by:
    (a) Non-intersecting trajectories,
    (b) Safety in teaching,
    (c) Safety when one robot location is inoperative and manual spraying substituted.
    (d) System control constraints when conveyor power stops are used and consideration was given to body accumulation problems.

2. Computer Simulation

On establishing the complexity of the task it was decided both as an aid to understanding and communications that an attempt would be made to graphically simulate the sequencing with a computer. This was simply done on a Commodore PET computer using BASIC as the language.

The exercise proved very useful in highlighting problems and as an aid in selling the system.

## Trallfa Programming

1    Manipulator Lead-Through Teaching

The simple matter of selecting teach mode on the console and a man on the trigger to do the necessary recording became an art using four people.

1.1 A conventional spray gun operator could not simply pick-up and go. It was necessary to gain much practice in manipulating the robot through complex and strenuous routines.

1.2 To obtain coverage of both the underbody and the sills within the cycle time, two operators were needed and a hand-over and hand-back sequence was required.

1.3 The fatigue in manoeuvring the robot through its teaching sequence, required a third man on the robots elbow to assist in rotation, thrust, retraction and counterbalancing. The fatigue was due to the repeated re-programming necessary to obtain production useable programs.

This may be a point in favour of a light-weight teaching facsimile, but in this case, with hindsight, it is felt that this would have introduced more problems than it solved.

1.4 To operate the console and pace the spray team, a fourth man was needed responsible for making and keeping recordings, logging events and preparing the team for starts and finishes of cycles.

2    Programming Limitations

The robot, although using some of the latest electronic systems, is still little more than a machine with a memory.

2.1 The start and finish of a program needs to be within 150mm of coincidence.

2.2 The identification system ideally needs to operate without using a shift register, that memorises the body type between the identification point and the robot start signal point.

This will not only reduce the monitoring required during teaching but significantly reduce the 'Start-Up' procedure for the robots.

2.3 The editing of a program was deemed too difficult. This means that an acceptable program has to be complete and consistent in its coverage and without any over-spray. This was not easy.

Editing is technically possible with the Trallfa robot by using a cascade of small programs, any one of which may be re-recorded. This represents little problem on a stationary target as the position does not vary with time or length of program. In synchronous recordings it would be essential to start all re-recorded sub-programs on their original position counts, (derived from the conveyor pulse generator after the primary start signal), and physically start and finish the manipulator very close to its original start and finish points.

2.4 The conveyor must keep moving at the constant speed throughout the recording cycle. A track stoppage prematurely terminates the recording and a speed change will give fluctuations in quality of coat thickness. The latter is due to the airless spray techniques which depends on a constant flow rate.

## System Factors Needing Control

The following notes may act as a check list for items needing monitoring and control.

1. Safety

This is a complex system designed to overcome lack of space and reduce the number of times a robot is stopped.

Is there a local emergency? - stop robots and conveyor.
Is the robot in collision?
Is the emergency remote? -stop conveyor.
Is the system being programmed?
Is an operator in the booth? - interlocks for one operator.
Are robots operating correctly?
Are conveyor power stops operating correctly?

2. Underseal Supply

This is an airless spraying system utilising two pumps, only one of which operates at a time.

Is pump on?

Is drum nearing empty?
Is changeover drum ready?
Is spray pattern correct?
Is underseal supply line pressurised?
Are filters needing replacement?
Are filters blocked?

3. Robots

The two robots are continuously monitored for operating characteristics: e.g. hydraulics, temperatures, computer functions, datum checking.

4. Identification

The system is capable of identifying up to 63 body types and is self-checking between each body.

5. Conveyor Synchronisation

A pulse generator synhcronises the robots with the actual conveyor speed. This is continuously monitored for functioning.

6. Underseal Processing Line

Both masking and demasking areas need monitoring for process problems, emergencies and bodies on conveyor.

7. Rectification

Any factor which causes discontinuity in the application routine directly identifies a body in need of touch-up. i.e. spray blockage or partial blockage, conveyor stoppage.

It is then important to ensure rectification by calling for a touch-up and scheduling a conveyor stop, if not completed in time.

## Control and Interfacing

Early in the installation of the system it became very evident that the robots and the planned box of relays would be inadequate to control this system. Therefore to meet the launch commitments, a simple 'Phase 1' with just robot control was implemented. Phases 2 and 3 to give a de-manned facility were planned using a Programmable Controller (PC) to run the system and modifications to the conveyor to implement control.

1. Phase 1, Rudimentary Control by Robots.

System inputs: Identity logic, Synchronising Pulse Generator, Robot Collision Strips.
Robot Output: Spray Solenoid.

The control and interfacing was directly with the robots own modules with the addition of one relay to source the power supply to the identity and pulse generator equipment from a functioning robot.

This means of operation relies on two operators, one to watch the robots and one to touch-up as required.

2  Phase 2, P.C. Control.

The objectives in using a programmable controller (PC) are:
To run the system in all eventualities.
To provide monitoring and some diagnostics.
To communicate with the conveyor P.C.,
To indicate operator or maintenance attention.
To reduce touch-up and rectification to a minimum.
To assist in system safety.
To reduce manning by at least one man/shift.

2.1  Running of the system.

This involves tracking each body from its identification until its clearance from the rectification area. If any abnormalities are monitored, the P.C. responds by calling the appropriate assistance and scheduling the stopping of bodies and the conveyor. After clearance the P.C. will control the re-start-up situation. This involves the Phase 3 modifications to the conveyor.

2.2  Monitoring and Diagnostics

Although not all the monitoring and diagnostics are performed by the P.C., it is packaged with the P.C. cabinet as an indicator panel.

Alarms and information identify the problem area and signal the attention of either Maintenance or a Process Operator.

3  Phase 3 Conveyor Modifications

At the time of writing, this phase is not completed.

It is necessary to introduce three power stops (see fig. 2 ) and a series of limit switches onto the conveyor to obtain full P.C. control and scheduling of bodies through booth, together with the final stage of de-manning.

3.1  Function of Power Stops

(a)  Power Stop at Booth Entrance is to inhibit further bodies entering the spray area as a result of a system problem, but still allowing the conveyor to continue running. Or, if there is a mask or demask problem

it will allow the spray area to clear before stopping the conveyor, hence avoiding a touch-up.

(b)  Power Stop at End of Booth is to inhibit incomplete bodies exiting the rectification area. This stop is scheduled by the P.C. and cancelled or released by the rectifier on completion of his task.

(c)  Power Stop in Booth is sequenced to operate in conjunction with the stop at the end of the booth in order to maintain body pitch on the conveyor.

3.2  Function of Limit Switches

(a)  Switches before booth test for correct body separation and chain dogging before spraying commences.

(b)  Switches up-stream of booth measure accumulation and enables the conveyor stop circuit.

(c)  Switches for dog positioning, enabled by conveyor stop circuit, determine the optimum positions for the dogs to be stopped awaiting restart.

CONCLUSIONS

Installations of this nature present many problems covering a wide field of engineering. It is important, therefore, to bring together a team of engineers whose experience and expertise will embrace all aspects of the proposed project. It will be the team's responsibility to:

(a)  assess the project viability,
(b)  to identify and specify total system requirements,
(c)  ensure effective production through associated development work,
(d)  to communicate to all relevant parties, i.e. Production Management, Maintenance, Safety, Facilities Engineering, Finance, Process Engineering and Equipment Suppliers,
(e)  to control installation and commissioning,
(f)  ensure adequate training of both Production and Maintenance personnel.

Total system cost, at the very least will be twice the robot cost.

Flexibility within the control system will take account of any changes during installation and commissioning, as well as allowing for further expansion.

Computer simulation can offer many benefits to the development of robot systems and should be made use of. Several aspects of this project were influenced by such simulation programmes.

It will normally only be under true production conditions that effective programming can be conducted, and it is inevitable that some minor disturbance to production will occur.

Benefits have manifested themselves, through acceptance by Production and Maintenance personnel, efficiency, reliability and consistent outstanding high quality.

The expertise gained in this project has already been applied in the planning and operation of further installations.

## Appendix 1

### Robot Selection

Robot selection was based on the following considerations:

1. Adaptability to the task - dexterity of the flexi-arm movement.
2. Experience in production situations of similar nature.
3. Delivery date allied to project dates.
4. Package terms.
5. Back up facilities in the U.K.
6. Price
7. Control - power and programming
8. Programmability in the production environment.
9. Ease of maintenance.
10. Compatibility with a moving track.

Trallfa were considered better in the majority of the above criteria.

### References

(1) Heginbotham W.B.   Robots and Automatic Factories, Engineers Digest.   p.19-22, December 1980

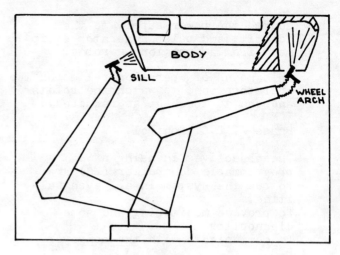

Fig 1   Extremes of robot spray

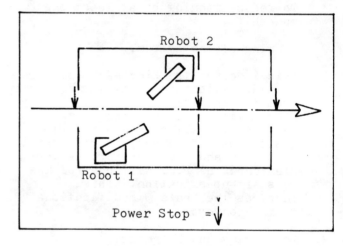

Fig 2   Conveyor power stops

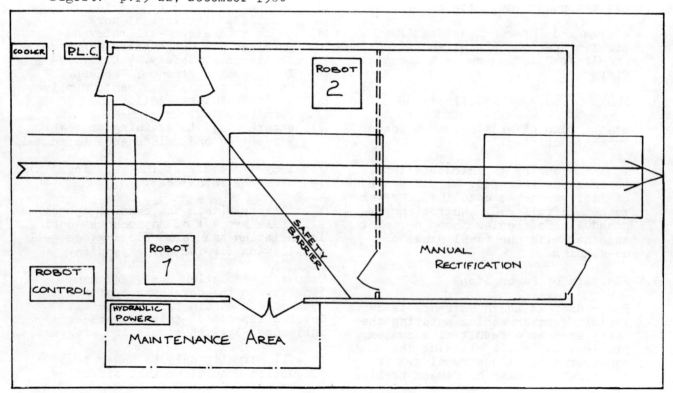

Fig 3   Layout of undersealing facility

# C296/81

# Automation of a new engine assembly facility using multiple computer systems

M W GRANT, BL Systems Limited, Redditch, Worcestershire
R HOWES, BSc, BL Systems Limited, Coventry

SYNOPSIS  During 1980, a completely new engine factory was built in Solihull U.K. to support increased production of 4x4 vehicles.  It has been equipped with some of the latest technology and automation available covering facilities such as Automated Stores, Engine Handling, Engine Testing and Production Planning.  Seven mini computers and sixty-three microprocessors control the facilities and operation aspects of the plant.  They also are part of a fully integrated information management system made up of individual, self contained modules.  Fall back capability is mandatory for all systems, so that any loss of computer control has minimal effect.

## PURPOSE

The planning objectives for the new engine assembly facility were:

to introduce produce improvements to meet future legislation and remain technically ahead of the competition

to expand capacity to maintain market position and to create the flexibility to make advantage of market changes

to introduce improved manufacturing methods and facilities to increase efficiency and enhance the manufacturing environment.

Various facility considerations were taken into account at the planning stage.  These included:

the ability to cater for different production capacities

best use of the site

maximising continuity of production

alternative investment levels.

As a result, it was decided that a high level of automation would form an essential part of achieving the planning objectives.  This paper will describe the design aims, the actual system and the overall system framework that have been employed in applying this number of computers as an integral part of the manufacturing facility.

## DESIGN OBJECTIVES

The application of computer technology at the new engine assembly facility has raised several problem areas that have had to be addressed to meet the planning objectives.

The overriding design philosophy has been that:

Failure of computers must not lead to lost production of engines in spite of the integrated nature of the computers with the plant operation.

As a result of the design incorporating various levels of control of all major facilities.  In addition, owing to the condensed timescales, the computer systems have had to be implemented at the same time as production engines are being built.

The diversity of applications has generated not only technical problems, as would be expected, but also has required a very broad approach to be taken in the question of overall project management and project control.  As a result great emphasis has been placed on these areas throughout the project.

The approach taken was to operate a joint project team consisting of senior represenatives from all the disciplines involved i.e.:

in-house production engineering

engineering consultants to complement and expand in-house production engineering

plant production personnel

systems management.

As a result, all strategic decisions were made in the knowledge of all concerned with actual implementation being devolved to formally managed project teams.  In addition to strategic decision making, the actual progress of the various projects was closely monitored at regular intervals.  This has been found to be vitally important as a result of the inter-related nature of the computer systems.

## MODERN MACHINE SHOP

Covering over 200 000 sq. ft., the layout of the new machine shop is impressive as is its environment, with high pressure sodium lighting and a heating and ventilating system which provides six air changes every hour.

New machinery embraces the latest in technology. In-line transfer machines and sophisticated mechanical handling are used to machine cylinder blocks, bearing caps, cylinder heads, crankshafts and conrods - some of which are common to both petrol and diesel engines.

## AUTOMATED STORES

The flow of materials and components, when and where they are needed is of critical importance to any production operation.

Despite original construction problems, the new engine component store is now complete. It has been designed as a fully computerised facility capable of handling both rough castings and forgings and also finished components ranging from paper gaskets to cylinder blocks.

With a capacity of 3960 pallets and designed to accommodate ten days component stock at the rate of 2000 items daily, the new store has six aisles for pallet storage and one single aisle for small parts. The six aisles are operated by computer controlled stacker cranes.

The store has been designed to give speedy access for the intake (up to 50 deliveries a day) and issue of materials, while at the same time maintaining accurate stock records. The ability to identify the parts in stock and their quantity ensures that engines can be assembled on a planned production schedule.

A 'can build' programme is run daily to identify the build requirements for the following 24 hours. The daily programmes multiplied by a list of parts for each type of engine ensures that all components for manufacture are available and reserved for committed build. The main aim of the store is to give a maximum secure storage area and provide instant and accurate stock records.

## THREE TRACK ASSEMBLY

Within the Assembly Hall there are three new assembly tracks. The first is a 460 ft. Slat Pedestal type which was chosen by assembly operators to allow greater all round accessibility. The engine is built on this track to a closed condition. The second and third tracks, (one dedicated to petrol and one to diesel but retaining the ability to alternate if required) are both 100 ft. long and carry the engines on an overhead monorail conveyor which eventually transports the engines through to the test facility.

## TEST FACILITIES

Every engine is taken automatically through a full test sequence. Automated controls monitor to ensure that engines perform consistently and repeatedly and that the whole of the test operation takes place in a controlled environment.

By comparison with traditional open engine test facilities such as those at nearly every factory for the past 30 years, the test facility at the new North Works is fully computerised and represents the most modern technology available for testing engines.

From the comfort of a sound-proofed, air conditioned corridor, testers are provided with the facts of the engine's performance through a computer terminal. These facts are interpreted and adjustments are undertaken until the engine reaches its required specification before it is transported for final dress and despatch.

## COMPUTER SYSTEM OUTLINE

The principal areas where the computer systems are employed are:

1. An on-line Time and Attendance Recording System (TARDIS).

2. The automated parts store, where the stocking/supply of all parts are controlled (AUTO-STORE).

3. An interactive system that produces engine build schedules (CAN BUILD).

4. A system that controls and routes engines slung on a monorail system around the build and test areas (ENGINE HANDLING).

5. An engine test system where individual engines are tested under computer control (ENGINE TEST).

6. A dedicated network control system (NETWORK).

1. TIME AND ATTENDANCE RECORDING DIRECT INPUT SYSTEM (TARDIS)

TARDIS is a system for the collection of employee attendance and payroll information. The system produces information suitable for the payroll and personnel systems and also provides local plant management with up-to-the minute information on attendance, absenteeism and lateness.

Attendance is recorded by means of an ITR attendance terminal as shown below in Fig 1.

Fig 1    Microprocessor controlled clock

The terminal is controlled by a microprocessor and can record and process details of a person's clocking and the time that they have worked.

As is common practice with manual clocks, a clock card is used, in conjunction with the terminal to record clocking times on all occasions when people enter or leave the plant.

The cards are placed in card racks from where the employees insert them into the terminals. When the cards are inserted the time is recorded within the terminal and the totals for time worked is printed out for the employee. An example of the clock card is shown in Fig 2.

LOUGHLIN
K.
AB200                    001004    ITR
001004        07/05/81

| XX | ⊟ | ⊡ | + + + + + |
|---|---|---|---|
|  |  |  | N    :00 |
|  |  |  | P    :00 |
|  |  |  | 30/04 |
| A | 0731 |  | N  8:00 |
| A | 1300 |  | P    :00 |
| B | 0737 |  | 01/05 |

1
03
40

TIMELORD

ITR INT'L TIME LTD  © 1980

PATENTS PENDING

1000-883-1604B

Fig 2    Clock card

Periodicaly these times are transferred to a
PDP 11/70 mini computer. Also attached to the
same system are VDU's that are used by both the
timekeeper to enter other payroll information
and by the local plant management to inquire on
the latest attendance information.

At the end of a week, all the information is
available within the system to prepare the payroll. Also available is the personnel
information on absence, lateness etc, and the
"hours worked" information for the calculation
of plant performance.

The significant advantages in using this method
are:

It is an effective on-line computerised
attendance recording system. The retention
of the clock card has been readily accepted
by the labour force.

It requires only 25% of the labour to run the
system compared with the previous manual
system.

If the mini computer system fails then the
attendance terminals, being controlled by
their own microprocessors can continue to
operate. This is not true of many badge
readers.

The terminals will operate for a minimum of
24 hrs without power or communications with
the mini computer.

The personnel details, payroll information
and plant performance are available at the
end of a week. This is three days ahead
of manual methods.

2    AUTO STORE

The hardware control of 'plant' processes is
effected by:

7 microprocessors for crane control

2 microprocessors to control the weigh
scales

2 programmable controllers for control of
conveyors.

In turn these are controlled by 2 PDP 11/34
mini computers.

The stores management system functions are
described below:

Goods receiving dialogue is via VDU's for
external deliveries using supplier advice notes
and for internal deliveries (e.g. machined
components) and pallets returned to store using
internally raised documentation.

The pallet documentation is then printed by
computer for each pallet, showing a unique
pallet identification number and its bar code
equivalent plus other relevant details.

The pallet is then directed along the conveyors
and into the store by the management computers
communicating to programmable controllers which
control the conveyors through limit switches,
motors etc.

En route each pallet is halted at the weigh
station to count the contents of each pallet.
The operator identifies the pallet load by
wiping a light pen over the bar code on the
pallet documentation and then he performs a
quantity calculation through prompts from the
VDU.

The choice of aisle is determined by taking into
account:

even distribution of the same parts across
the store

distribution of weight across the store

loading of work on conveyors and cranes

double depth racking considerations.

When pallets have been directed to an aisle and
are in position to be deposited using a crane,
the mini computers instruct the crane microprocessor accordingly.

When pallets are required for issue from the
store the mini computers direct the appropriate
crane microprocessor to perform the required
operations, and whenever possible, deposits and
retrievals are 'paired' to optimise crane journey
times.

The mini computers maintain a 'stock record'
showing quantity of stock held in main and small
parts stores for every part, and also a 'map'
showing where pallets of parts are held in the
two stores. Pallets are held on the store map
as either 'available for production, or 'bonded'.
As a result only pallets available for production
can be issued to production areas.

There are several ways the user can place demands for parts on the store.

'Specific' issues for a particular pallet or batch of pallets.

'Scheduled' issues for a quantity of parts to be issued at a scheduled time.

'Scheduled recurring' issues for a pallet of parts to be issued at regular time intervals.

'Standard' issues as input to the system by wiping a light pen across the bar code of the pallet documentation taken from an empty pallet.

Pallets of parts are 'reserved' for production use by accepting reservations direct from the Can Build system.

The interface to the Can Build system is in two parts:

Pallets of parts are 'reserved' for production use by accepting reservations direct from the Can Build system.

Details of store stock are sent regularly to the Can Build system, when initiated by an operator using a VDU, to allow Can Build to calculate reservations.

The whole Auto Store system has been designed for resilience to various failures:

If an output conveyor break down occurs and a production stoppage is imminent, it is possible to operate a crane manually and operate the conveyor using a maintenance mode of operation.

If a crane breakdown occurs it is possible to continue using the store with the remaining cranes.

If the small parts store crane breakdown occurs, it is possible to access the storage racking manually and remove a container of parts.

If a programmable controller breakdown occurs, a spare programmable controller is available to replace the failed unit.

Both mini computers are working together such that if one computer breaks down, the other computer continues on its own. This change-over is an automatic process, and the user loses certain non-essential functions of the system e.g. some enquiries. When the failed computer is repaired, at the instigation of the user, it can automatically be brought back into line with the single processor, and dual processing can continue.

If both mini computers break down, the store can be operated in a manual mode of operation using the programmable controllers. When either a single or both computers are again available, all transactions which took place during the breakdown period have to be input to the system.

If a VDU, printer, or light pen breakdown occurs, spare units are available to replace the failed unit. VDU transactions are compatible with entry via a keyboard printer. Also, reports or tickets can be re-routed to one of the remaining printers.

3.  CAN BUILD SYSTEM

This system runs on a PDP 11/70 system with terminals in the offices at Solihull and an office some miles off site.

The system performs the following actions:

Confirms that adequate unreserved stocks are held in the auto store to enable a proposed engine build programme to be completed, and reserves that stock when the Major Unit Controller commits to that programme.

Forecasts the requirements for store items over a user-defined period, and predicts stock-out dates based on current stock holdings.

Creates a daily Work-in-Progress (WIP) count for each stored part number.

Prints an engine build card for each major unit (engine) included in a daily build programme.

In addition a Bill of Materials (BOM) system is constantly available to the analysts so that changes to engine specifications may be applied to the computer structures as soon as the details are received from the engineering department.

Major Unit Controllers (MUC's) will compile a build programme covering 1 days production 1 or 2 days before that build is due to commence. Prior to entering the programme to the computer system the current stock information will have been transferred from the Auto Store system via the Network system. The programme is then exploded from major unit to store item level, and requirements at this level are checked against the unreserved stock, and shortages highlighted. After possibly several amendments the MUC will commit to a particular programme, and the stock quantities that must be reserved to meet that programme are sent to the Auto Store system via the Network system.

In addition the MUC may at any time forecast requirements for store items in the long, medium or short-term future. This forecast enables material controllers to change deliveries and enables machine shop management to plan future work loading.

The Can Build system receives, via the Network system, issue data from the Auto Store system and build data from the Engine Handling system. It also receives manually entered transactions in respect of miscellaneous stock movements. The Can Build system then creates a current WIP value for each part number at store item level.

An Engine Build Card is attached to each cylinder block as it is loaded to the assembly line. The card bears a part number, specification reference, build programme reference and serial number and some less important data. This information is shown on the card in normal printed form and in bar coded format. The bar codes are read by light pens on-line to the Engine Handling system and are used to track the engine.

The system provides a full set of enquiry transactions based on the BOM. Details of the current daily build programme and five other programmes may also be displayed.

Being essentially a batch system the security aspects are concentrated on data security and data integrity, rather than on optimised up-time. The high level of data security is achieved through the use of a proprietary database management system, TOTAL.

4. ENGINE HANDLING SYSTEM

The Engine Handling system uses two PDP 11/34 mini computers with one of the systems operating as a 'warm stand-by' to the operational system. The system controls and monitors the routing of trolleys (and hence engines) on the overhead monorail and is designed to automate fully the handling of engines off the assembly line, through the engine test cells until satisfactory and to the despatch area.

The main facility feature are:

    1500 metres of overhead monorail
    200 trolleys (and hoist units)
    Pre-test buffer store (75 units)
    24 test cells
    Despatch storage (1200 units)

There is close co-operation between the Engine Handling system and the Engine Test system. As a result of this, a fuller description of the functions of the Engine Handling system can be found in the next section.

As in other areas, there are several modes of operation:

    In automatic mode, the computer controls, by one of the two systems, the routing of trolleys, together with a full management control system.

    In the event of a single computer failure, all the peripherals are manually switched to the standby system.

    In maintenance mode, each unit (e.g. switch, side transfer) is capable of individual manual operation using a pendant control. This facility is required for maintenance/repair/check-out operations.

    In manual mode, neither computer is in control of routing of trolleys, and is only able to monitor and log operations.

5. ENGINE TEST SYSTEM

The control of the engine test cells is split between several different computers:

    Each of the 24 engine test cells has a microprocessor to control the signal conversion and conditioning of input and output from the test cell/engine to the Test Cell Computer system.

    Of a total of 24 engine test cells 6 are for audit testing and 18 for production testing of engines.

    Each audit cell and each pair of production cells are controlled by a microprocessor based Test Cell Computer system.

    Each Test Cell Computer system controls the operations of the engine testing process, and provides an interface to each test cell operator via a VDU.

    A PDP 11/34 mini computer based Master system co-ordinates all the activities

of the Test Cell Computer systems, and provides enquiry facilities, hard copy reports and an interface to the Engine Handling system.

The main functions of the Master system are:

    To provide the test rigs with engine build details (as supplied via the Engine Handling system).

    To provide a real-time display of the status of the test system facility.

    To collect remotely the data recorded during the testing of an engine.

    To act as a central point for the production of permanent test specifications, engine mapping, and operator number files.

    To produce on demand, shift and weekly reports.

    To collect the data logged for audit testing, print a hard-copy report and archive it to magtape.

The functions of the production and audit Test Cell system are:

    to acquire and output real time analogue and digital control signals.

    to monitor certain engine parameters for warning or alarm conditions. The engine is shut down if the safe limits are exceeded.

    to service the operator's keyboard and VDU.

    to obtain the engine build details (either from the Master system or from manual entry) and hence determine the test specification to be used for this engine.

    to sequence automatically the engine through the test specification, logging data at the specified data points and to check certain parameters against pre-defined pass/fail limits.

    to control the engine via hardware set-points with outer loop software control to compensate for drift.

    to transmit test bed status and complete test results to the Master system.

    to receive from the Master system new test specifications, modified engine mapping data, and new operator numbers.

    the audit rigs automatically sequence through all defined repeats on the test specification, retaining all logged data, and are capable of editing all entries in the test specification.

When an engine arrives at a test cell, the Engine Handling system automatically informs the Master computer of the engine serial number, power unit number, retest indicator, and the cell number. This information is then forwarded to the appropriate test cell.

On completion of testing at the production test bed, the test results are transmitted up to the Master. On receipt of the test results at the Master system, the Engine Handling system is informed of the engine's serial number, its cell number and PASS/FAIL indication. The engine is routed accordingly.

After assembly, and before testing, the
engine is visually inspected. Should the
engine require any rectification it is
directed to the rectification area. The
Engine Handling system passes with the
appropriate code, the engine number and any
defect codes to the Master computer in order
for them to be printed in the rectification
area.

When the engine arrives at final dress, the
Engine Handling system informs the Master
computer of its arrival and its engine
number. The test results stored for this
engine are then printed at the dispatch area.

In this area there are two modes of operation.

Test Cell Level

Each pair of production test cells (or single
audit test cell) can operate in a stand-alone
mode, via its own Cell Computer system. This
mode is applicable when the Master system is
unavailable.

Test Master Level

The Master system, co-ordinates the activities
of each Test Cell Computer system to provide:

communication between cells and external
systems such as Engine Handling.

consolidation of test cell results for
extensive management reporting.

6   NETWORK SYSTEM

A single PDP 11/34 mini computer system acts
as the central physical link between all
North Works mini computers at Solihull and
the mainframe systems 15 miles away. Data is
stored and forwarded under operator control
to the mainframe systems. It also provides
the link between the applications which
enables any processor to pass data to any
other processor in the North Works system.
In addition to using proprietary networking
software, system level statistics are
maintained for auditing and diagnostic
purposes. At present, there are only PLC's
in the machine shop, but there would be no
difficulty in installing a mini computer
between the Network system and the machine
shop. The diagram in Fig 3 shows the
computer network.

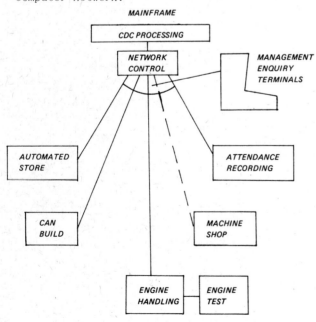

Fig 3   North Works mini computer network

## SYSTEM FRAMEWORK

In an attempt to implement the aforementioned
design several basic concepts have been
followed in the design of all the systems.
These are:

several levels of control in a single
application

single application systems

commonality of equipment and techniques

The control hierarchy can be best explained by
reference to Fig 4.

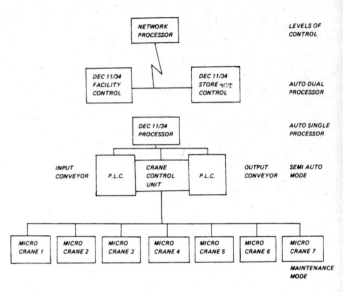

Fig 4   Stores control hierarchy

There are four levels of control possible in
the Auto Store.

Maintenance Mode    each crane and the conveyors
are manually controlled on
an individual module basis.

Semi-auto Mode      in this case, the store
location for input and
output of pallets is manually
'dialled-in' to the crane
control unit. PLC's control
the input and output
conveyors.

Auto Single Processor    in this case, there is
no fallback facility
and a degraded level of
enquiries.

Auto Dual Processor    this is fully automatic
with all facilities; both
process control and
management
information being
provided at all times.

In addition to catering for graceful changes
between modes, the various levels also cater
for unexpected failures.

A similar structure is also applied to the
Engine Handling and Engine Test systems.

The desire to have single application systems has permitted the following aims to be met:

To allow the systems to be developed in parallel.

To achieve a reliable solution by having a controlled degree of redundancy.

By distributing the processing, the effect of failure is contained, hence increasing the overall availability of the system.

By distributing the system amongst different types of equipment e.g. minis, micros, PLC's, the suitability of the equipment to the task can be optimised.

The different response requirements of the different parts of the system can be best met by the use of distributed single application systems.

The commonality of equipment and techniques means that all the mini computers are from the same supplier with similar commonality on the software side to the extent of:

Programming language RTL/2.
Operating System, RSX-11M.
Database Manager, TOTAL.
Communication software, DECnet.
An internally developed teleprocessing monitor.

The distribution of computer equipment is shown in Table 1 and 2.

| PROJECT | MICRO | | MINI | |
|---|---|---|---|---|
| ENGINE HANDLING | | | PDP 11/34 | 2 |
| ENGINE TEST | INTEL 8080 | 24 | PDP 11/34 | 1 |
| | LSI/11 | 15 | | |
| CAN BUILD | | | PDP 11/70 SHARED | 1 |
| NETWORK | | | PDP 11/34 | 1 |
| TIME & ATTENDANCE | | 15 | PDP 11/70 SHARED | 2 |
| AUTO STORE | CRANES | 7 | PDP 11/34 | 2 |
| | TOLEDO WEIGHSCALE | 2 | | |
| | | 63 | | 9 |
| | | | PLC (MODICON) | 2 |

TABLE 1 COMPUTER POPULATION

| TYPE | QUANTITY |
|---|---|
| VDU's | 29 |
| PRINTERS OR K/PRINTERS | 21 |
| LIGHT PENS | 23 |
| TIMELORDS FOR ATTENDANCE CLOCKING | 11 |
| COLOUR GRAPHICS VDU's | 2 |
| 'SPECIALS' | 10 |
| TOTAL | 96 |

TABLE 2 COMPUTER PERIPHERALS

In itself, the interconnection of all these devices presented a significant problem that has been solved by using a Videodata system based on a single core cable.

The communications cable has been installed throughout the machine shop, stores, assembly, test and engine despatching areas. This enables data to be transmitted to and received from the plant, computer terminals and the computers of all types.

This approach has provided a cost effective solution as regards the physical connection of data links, whilst providing the degree of flexibility which will enable an expansion of the communications systems to be achieved in the most effective manner.

The cable schematic is shown in Fig 5.

A further major benefit of using this communication cable has been in the area of management information. As was mentioned previously, great emphasis was made on the availability of information for managers, but at the same time it was desirable to avoid a proliferation of terminals. This has been solved by having management information terminals that can be switched by hardware between systems at the terminal itself rather than by using complex routing software between all the systems.

CONCLUSION

The systems described above are now in the final stages of implementation and acceptance by the plant. All the detailed functional requirements have been met, but it is interesting to dwell on some of the other problems.

The idea of using a large project management forum whilst generating sometimes protracted and often heated discussions did lead to total support once decisions had been made. One important result of the involvement by all disciplines has been very good communications between them.

It was decided that a multi-level hierarchy would represent the application framework best able to meet the business requirements. As a result of applying 'single application systems' to this hierarchy, there has been the flexibility to choose the type of computer most appropriate for each application. The ability to integrate over 70 computers into a sensible, manageable, yet powerful structure has been achieved by careful design based on this hierarchy of single application systems. In turn, these have been supported by our own computer hardware and software standards, particularly in the area of communications.

Compared to many manufacturing control systems, far greater emphasis has been placed on the information handling side, to the extent of employing on mini-computers modern data processing software such as teleprocessing monitors, databases and switchable terminals.

We believe it has been demonstrated, at the request of users for more information, that facility control and management information systems can be designed to cohabit effectively over multiple computers and yet retain the flexibility to extend the system to cater for future enhancements by being part of a sound overall system framework.

ACKNOWLEDGEMENTS

Th authors wish to thank Land Rover Ltd for permission to present this paper describing the North Works facilities at their Solihull factor

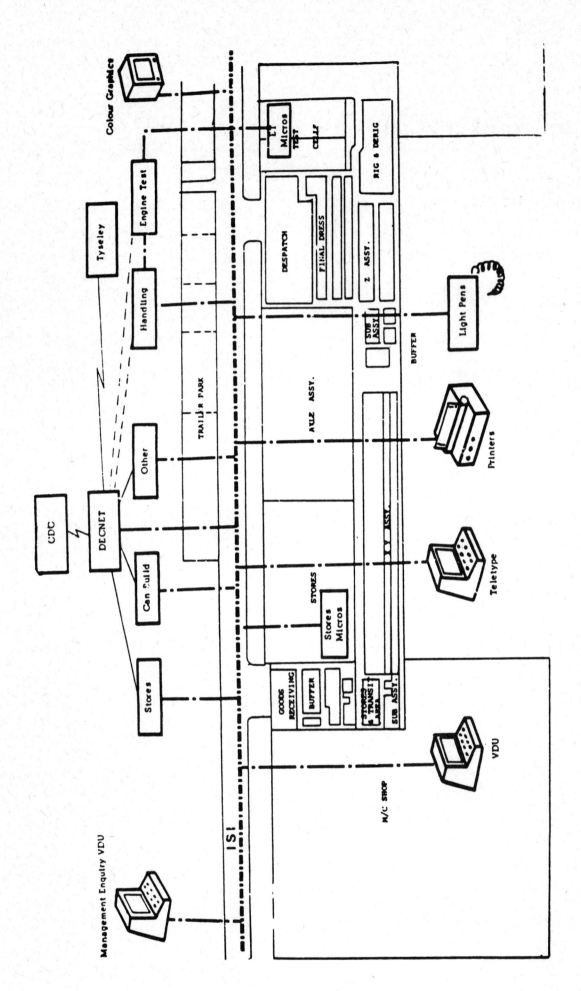

Fig 5    Communications cable schematic

# C297/81

# Reinforced reaction injection moulding

M A POTTER

Since BAYER introduced the RIM polyure-thane process at the Dussledorf Fair in 1967, automotive manufacturers have been steadily incorporating these urethanes in their designs.

In the early days much of the use was interior, as armrests, steering wheels, etc. The exterior applications were primarily restricted to the front and rear bumper area as on the VW Porsche or overriders. The introduction of regulations in 1971 (FMVSS 215) in the US committing car manufacturers to reach specified standards, gave a boost in the exterior application zone,

A profusion of models appeared in the US and Europe, using RIM as a method to meet these laws. They can, almost, be divided into two sections, bumpers, as on MGB/TR7, etc., and facias e.g. Porsche 928.

The former consists of a PU bumper which is then affixed to a metal armature and the assembly then mounted to the car. The latter serves as a cover for the energy management foam, or other systems, and plays little part in fulfilling actual crash test requirements. This is commonly referred to as the "soft face" system.

## BUMPERS

These use the deformation of ribs incorporated in the rear face design to absorb some of the required crash energy over the required temperature range $-30^{\circ}$C $+65^{\circ}$C.

Such bumpers have been fitted to, among others, MGB, TR7, VOLVO 343, Ford Capri (Federal version).

The Ford Capri bumper was finished with a body matching PU paint. Its disadvantage is mainly weight. The armature being the main source of this weight. Energy absorbing foams can be used to fulfil localised impact needs.

In recent times a stiffer type of system has been developed which enabled the use of an armature to be avoided and thus the undesirable weight. Such a system

is fitted to the Peugeot 505 and will provide damage resistance up to 4 km/hr.

Similar PU systems have been developed for use as air dams or skirts providing the necessary stiffness that such an application needs as well as deforming under impact. Such a spoiler can be found on BMW series and Mercedes. Contrast or matching PU paint being used to finish the part.

Typical Properties of a Bumper System are:

| | BAYFLEX 90 | | BAYFLEX 103 |
|---|---|---|---|
| Density | 950 | kg/m$^3$ | 1075 |
| Tensile Strength | 14 | MPa | 32 |
| Elongation | 275 | % | 160 |
| 50% Modulus | 6 | MPa | 25 |
| Shore D | 36 | | 65 |
| Elasticity Modulus | | | |
| at $-30^{\circ}$C | 500 | MPa | 1500 |
| "  $+20^{\circ}$C | 100 | MPa | 750 |
| "  $+65$ | 20 | MPa | 400 |

## "Soft Face"

As its name implies, this is a deformable cover over the energy management system, whether it be an hydraulic system or another method. This unique approach made its first appearance in the U S in the early 70 s, on models such as Chevrolet Corvette, Chevrolet Monza, Buick Skyhawk, Oldsmobile Starfire. In model year 1981 over 50% of all U S cars used this type of approach. The wide range of styling possibilities enables model variation or facelifts to be made at reasonable cost. (Current U S Models.) Such parts are painted to body colours with a polyurethane paint, but this subject will be covered later. Mounting is made by attaching the moulding to light metal strips which then permit bolting to the vehicle body.

As the material has a relatively low modulus, support can be made by use of foam blocks so placed in the part to ensure contour continuation is not impaired. Typical Properties are:

## BAYFLEX$^R$ 101

| | | |
|---|---|---|
| Density | 1000 | kg/M$^3$ |
| Tensile Strength | 20 | MPa |
| Elongation | 180 | % |
| Shore D | 56 | |

Elasticity Modulus

| | | |
|---|---|---|
| – 30°C | 950 | MPa |
| + 20°C | 300 | MPa |
| + 65°C | 120 | MPa |

For the smaller European car such soft fronts can only be of benefit at the expense of probable weight increase. Only two vehicles in Europe were fitted with 'soft faces' - Porsche 928 and Ford Escort RS 2000.

## Other Exterior Uses of RIM

Apart from bumpers and soft faces, side body mouldings, as fitted to the 'S' Class Mercedes, overriders, as on the late Spitfire and mudguard flaps on trucks are showing trends that may widen such application.

## Production of RIM

It is probably opportune to quickly review a typical RIM layout.

There are a range of Manufacturers of plant and of the clamp units used for mould handling. Generally RIM is now moulded horizontally but clamps with variable geometry capability are available.

## Reinforced RIM

The plant design follows the RIM principle of high pressure counter-injection into a mix-chamber of small (5cc) volume at pressures up to 250 bar. Today's machines all have self cleaning mix-heads, thus ensuring low vapour levels and reduced losses.

Two types of equipment design are available. A basic RIM approach using the polyol pump as an hydraulic source for a mono cylinder to metre the filled resin e.g. Cannon, Kraus Maffei or, twin hydraulically driven cylinders e.g. Hennecke, Cincinatti Milacron.

To date, glass is the most favoured additive, either in milled or chopped form. It is also possible to convert existing RIM machines to RRIM operation by using the polyol pump as an hydraulic drive for a mono cylinder unit.
A typical schematic layout for RRIM is shown.

Much has been written (and said) of the advantages of milled against chopped glass and vice-versa. It is not this writer's intention to add to the discussion, but only to comment that the properties desired can be usually achieved by both approaches. Therefore, so long as the specification can be met and maintained, the moulder, with consultation from his machine manufacturer, can choose what he prefers. Typical properties for glass reinforced RIM are shown below. Bayflex$^L$ 110/50 was used as the matrix. This system demoulds in 20-25 seconds, even on complex shapes.

### Bayflex 110/50
#### Chopped fibres, 1.5 mm

| | | |
|---|---|---|
| % Glass | 0 | 6.8 |
| Density | 1.09 | 1.25 |
| Flex Modulus | 325 | 725 |
| Sag 30mins/160°C | 9 | 1.5 |
| Coeff. of Expansion | 180 | 45 |
| Charpy Impact/-30°C | pass | 45 |
| Elongation | 280 | 50 |
| Tensile Strength | 28 | 25 |

### Bayflex 110/50
#### Milled fibres, 0.2-0.4 mm

| | | |
|---|---|---|
| % Glass | 25 – 30 | |
| Density | 1.25 – 1.3 | kg/m3 |
| Flex Modulus | 1500 | MPa |
| Sag 30mins/160°C | 2.0 | mm |
| Coeff of Expansion | 35 | 10$^{-6}$/°C |
| Charpy Impact/-30°C | 40 | KJ/m$^2$ |
| Elongation | 80 | % |
| Tensile Strength | 25 | MPa |

This data was obtained from samples cut in the direction of material flow. Those mechanical properties in the alternative direction (90°) are markedly different. This anisotropy dictates that mould gating must be made with care as to its position.

Recently, developments using glass platelets have shown that the anisotropy can be avoided. This is an area of development to be watched with interest.

Despite much verbosity, few RRIM parts have reached production cars. To the writers knowledge, these, are, the Oldsmobile Omega Sport 1980 (front wings) the Pontiac Sunbird 1978 (rear deck spoiler), Porsche 924 Carrera GT (wings front and rear, front air dam) 1981 and some Fiat 126 replacement bumpers.

No doubt that as confidence and reliability continue we should see many more applications in the future on, for example, the proposed 'P' body car from General Motors which will feature RRIM as bolt-on body panels, among other plastic parts.

Why use RRIM? As the demand for more MPG continues, body weight must be reduced. RRIM is a material which offers low coefficient of linear thermal expansion, good impact strength, good surface finish from a good tool and the ability to be moulded into complex parts in a relatively fast cycle. Demould times of 20 seconds are now achievable. But as is with any material, adding fillers brings some benefits and also some losses. The gain of increased modulus and improved C of E is made at cost of impact strength and elongation. The choice and level of glass fillers can only be made after evaluation of the properties and the part function.

Fibres contained in the raw materials do break on recirculation and injection by the RIM process. The degree of attrition that occurs is influenced by a number of factors including:

> Throughput
> Pressure
> Pipe Diameter
> Injector size
> Time

As more experience is gained in the use of glass as a reinforcement, so the process reliability will increase. Such real experience cannot be reproduced in the laboratory workshop, but only under production conditions in the industry. Therefore RRIM will learn a lot from projects such as G.M.'s 'P' Body car (1 000 000 predicted production)

To reach such a situation, development mouldings must be produced and this is one attractive area for both RIM & RRIM, as low cost tools can be used for development.

TOOLING

RIM develops relatively low pressure in the mould cavity (some 40psi), so sturdy tools of epoxy resin can be utilized, although, with the knowledge that finish is not to the quality to be expected from a steel mould. Epoxy tools can produce 1,10,100 or 1000 parts off. Unfortunately it is not always possible to predict when the last moulding is being made. The 924 Carrera GT body panels were produced from epoxy tools for the series, circa 400, and such parts have a good quality finish. Temperature control is one of the most important factors in successful moulding. RIM is a very exothermic process and tools are normally run at 55-60°C.

Exotherm increases the surface temperature of tools to well over 100°C The choice of epoxy resin must be made with that fact in mind - more tools fail due to thermal cycling than any other cause, except for the human factor, of course.

Production tooling for realistic numbers is still in steel and, so far, the little wear that has occurred due to fillers in the system is restricted to the sprue area which should be made of hardened steel.

With modern fast systems, the filling time for mouldings is about 1.5 seconds. Therefore, to achieve a fill

velocity of 1.5 - 2.5m/sec, gates need to be designed to accommodate this speed. Higher velocities can lead to air entrapment caused by turbulence and therefore rejects.

There is a wide range of machines, designed for RRIM, on the market. The criteria for machine choice are important.

1)  ratio accuracy - variation causes property changes

2)  temperature control - causes ratio and mix quality variation

3)  shot capacity - the machine must be capable of dispensing the material within the starting time of the reaction.

Many machines have been too small for the weight of the part required. This is especially true for very fast systems or where the ratio of the materials to be used falls outside the limits of the pumps fitted to the machine.

PART PRODUCTION

The sequence of production for RIM, or RRIM, is the same.

1. Application of release agent to the clean mould. This is, at the moment, still necessary for each shot. Application is usually by spray gun and can be carried out automatically provided that the cavity of the tool can be coated evenly. (Time allowed 20-30 secs)

2. Close Tool. Sometime RIM parts need to be moulded at an angle to assist venting. Clamp units are available to fulfil this function. (10 secs time allowed).

3. Machine recycle and shot. In production a mixhead is usually attached to the parting line of the tool. Machines can have more than one head, but there are restrictions, especially with RRIM. Recycle can be carried out during Clamp closure. (Shot time 1-4 secs)

4. Cure time. The injected material must react and develop enough "green strength" to permit careful handling. (Time allowed, approx 30 secs for a fast system.

5. Tool opening and part stripping (20 seconds allowed)

6. Tool cleaning. RIM rarely strips clean, flash usually must be cleaned off by hand. (Time, approx. 60 secs)

The total cycle is approx 2 to 4 mins, depending on the part complexity and the PU material selected.

If a moulded past is to be painted, it must be degreased. Release agent is removed by either, vapour degreasing with, e.g. Trichloro-ethane, or, power washing with water. After cleaning, the part should be placed in an oven at over 100°C for 20 mins to either drive off absorbed degreasant or to dry off water.

The part is then ready for painting.

## PAINTING

We strongly recommend the use of a PU paint for all RIM parts. As far as front and rear ends are concerned this is the ONLY choice. The paint must be more flexible than the PU substrate.

On side application (wings, doors) other paints could be used with success as limited deflection on body parts are to be anticipated, unlike front and rear.

From demould, to the end of the finishing cycle, the parts are supported on a jig to prevent distortion before the material develops full strength and, especially, during heating/painting cycles.

## WHAT OF THE FUTURE?

We have mentioned front ends, wings, bumpers and overriders. RIM parts can be fitted almost anywhere on the body provided that it is not load carrying.

RIM offers reduced body weight - Porsche 924 front wing would be 3.5kg in steel. In PU it is only 1.5kg.

It offers resistance to knocks and recovery from minor collision which metals, and some other plastics, cannot.

It will not corrode.

It offers more design freedom and the ability to combine different parts as one.

The Plant investment is both attractive and versatile.

A RRIM machine, with four heads, will cost about £120 000 ex works. Each clamp unit from £80 000 to £120 000 depending on platen size. At two or three minute cycle per clamp this capital investment will compare very favourably with any other process.

Although the USA leads in RIM production there is no reason why Europe cannot follow, as long as vehicle design permits. Many existing restrictions on the use of plastics stem from the industries paint stoving schedules for metal parts. When these temperatures come down to areas where plastics can be run on the same track, then the existing on-costs for finishing will reduce to a level where it will become an advantage to use them.

Vehicle design needs to be altered to permit the use of PU. Many current vehicles cannot easily be redesigned.

In this paper the writer has referred to RIM as a Polyurethane process. It should be appreciated that RIM is not only a PU process and that the future may offer alternative materials with attractive properties.

We feel that RIM in all its guises offers designers and engineers a reliable material to suit their needs.

As energy conservation becomes more acute, the industry must rationalise its thinking and we as an industry are ready to support both on development of design and if necessary special materials to make design possible.